THIRD EDITION

Religions in Practice

An Approach to the Anthropology of Religion

John R. Bowen

Washington University in St. Louis

PEARSON

Boston   New York   San Francisco
Mexico City   Montreal   Toronto   London   Madrid   Munich   Paris
Hong Kong   Singapore   Tokyo   Cape Town   Sydney

Series Editor: Jennifer Jacobson
Editorial Assistant: Emma Christensen
Marketing Manager: Kris Ellis-Levy
Senior Editorial-Production Administrator: Karen Mason
Editorial-Production Service: Denise Botelho
Composition Buyer: Linda Cox
Electronic Composition: Galley Graphics
Manufacturing Buyer: JoAnne Sweeney
Cover Administrator: Joel Gendron

For related titles and support materials, visit our online catalog at www.ablongman.com

Between the time Web site information is gathered and then published, it is not unusual for some sites to have closed. Also, the transcription of URLs can result in typographical errors. The publisher would appreciate notification where these errors occur so that they may be corrected in subsequent editions.

Library of Congress Cataloging-in-Publication Data

Bowen, John Richard.
  Religions in practice : an approach to the anthropology of religion / John R. Bowen.—3rd ed.
   p. cm.
  Includes bibliographical references and index.
  ISBN 0–205–41814-7 (alk. paper)
   1. Religion. 2. Religions. 3. Ethnology—Religious aspects. I. Title.

BL48.B625 2004
200—dc22   2004045068

Printed in the United States of America

10 9 8 7 6 5 4 3 2 1   RRD-VA   09 08 07 06 05 04

*To Vicki,
for love and support*

Contents

7   *Healing through Religion* 89

8   *Sorcery, Witchcraft, and Modernity* 104

Preface

*A*s in the previous editions of this book, I have tried to write about religion from my own perspective for as wide an audience as possible. As an anthropologist, I emphasize the ways in which people engage in religious activities. I take a broad view of "religion," including in its domain those activities that, in one way or another, invoke realities and powers beyond the reach of ordinary senses. Religion thus includes healing through spirit possession, sacrificing to appease gods, uttering spells, reciting scripture, and many more things.

In each chapter, I consider a specific dimension of religion and draw examples from both small-scale religions and large-scale ones. In my discussions of large-scale religious traditions, such as Islam, Hinduism, and Catholicism, I focus on one or more emphases within that tradition rather than attempting to survey all its dimensions and branches. For example, I examine the importance of sacred speech in Navajo, Islamic, and Protestant traditions in Chapter 11, with extended examples drawn from Quaker and Baptist churches as well as from Luther's writings. A study devoted to Protestantism per se would have included material from Lutheran, Presbyterian, Methodist, and other denominations. This book, concerned with comparisons across religions, has to be more selective.

The book is intended to be read on its own by any interested reader. As a course text it can be supplemented in various ways. In an anthropology course it might be combined with ethnographic case studies, either those referred to in the chapters or others. In a course on comparative religions it could be used together with some of the many excellent introductions to Islam, Hinduism, religions of China, and other large-scale religions. Also very effective are video clips and films on pilgrimage, church singing, sacrifice, and other practices. For additional suggestions of teaching materials check the Allyn & Bacon Web site *www.ablongman.com/anthropology,* and my own site: *www.artsci. wustl.edu/~anthro/blurb/b_bowen.html.*

New to the Third Edition

*T*his textbook continues to evolve. Here is a description of the most signifcant revisions in this third edition:

- Chapter 1, "Studying Religion through Practice" brings the entire volume up-to-date by relating the approach taken in the text to post–9/11 concerns. A new section contrasts the approaches taken by anthropologists to those working in the sociology or psychology of religion.

- A new Chapter 2, "Social Theory in the Anthropology of Religion," considers the role of social theory in shaping the study of religion through an examination of the contemporary importance of work by Tylor, Durkheim, Marx, Weber, Freud, and more recent theorists.
- Chapters 3 and 4 from the Second Edition have been combined into a single chapter in this third edition—Chapter 4, "Rituals and the Shaping of Emotions."
- Chapter 6, "Patterns, Powers, and the Self" includes new sections on sports magic and new religions in the United States including Wicca or modern witchcraft. This chapter contains some content from former Chapter 12, "Transmitting Religion" from the previous edition, which is not in the third edition.
- Chapter 7, "Healing through Religion," has been retitled and rewritten, and now contains a section that examines the scientific literature on the healing power of prayer.
- Chapter 8, "Sorcery, Witchcraft, and Modernity" offers a new discussion of sorcery and modernity, emphasizing the way in which people adapt sorcery ideas to modern conditions of unequal distribution of wealth and the presence of powerful states.
- An entirely new Chapter 14, "Religion, Violence, and War," examines the role that religious beliefs and organizations play in promoting violence and war. It begins with a comparative study of the conditions under which sects lead to violence, and then presents an extended discussion of the idea of jihad in Islam, focusing on Afghan and Indonesian contexts.

Acknowledgments

I n preparing this edition of *Religions in Practice* I benefited from the comments of many readers and teachers. These reviewers include Bradley Hertel, Virginia Tech; William Leons, University of Toledo; Diane Levine, Los Angeles, Pierce College; Sean O'Neill, University of Oklahoma; Emily Schultz, St. Cloud State University; Richard L. Warms, Southwest Texas State University; and Kathleen Young, Western Washington University. As always, I owe my perspective on many of these topics in this book to the many men, women, and children with whom I have worked in Indonesia and France. Bri Kneisley gave me valuable research assistance. My wife Vicki Carlson gave encouragement and ideas, as always, and contributed to Chapter 7.

I would appreciate your critical comments and suggestions for additional materials, best sent to me at *jbowen@wustl.edu.*

1

Studying Religion through Practice

*I*n September of 2003 I was on my way to Washington, D.C., to discuss Islam with people engaged in public policy discussions. On the flight I found myself seated next to a congressman. An evangelical Christian about to embark on a fact-finding mission to Iraq, he knew little about Islam but thought I might bring him up to date. Since the entire purpose of my trip was to enlighten Washington people about the complexities of contemporary debates among Muslims, I was eager to oblige.

I began by asking him about his own understandings of Christianity. He related the story of his early days in college and the family business, his search for a more meaningful path, the decision to devote himself to the Lord's work through public service, and then his efforts to understand U.S. history in terms of religion. "The founding fathers thought religion should inform public life and government, but that religion should not itself govern," he explained, contrasting the theocratic Puritans with the Pilgrims, in whose civic religion and politics he saw the model for the United States today. He sought guidance for his own politics in scripture, but thought little of Bible literalists who refused to see that scripture was fitted to its place and time. We must adapt the lessons of scripture to the conditions of today's world, he argued.

Much as I disagreed with the idea that political deliberation ought to draw on religious texts, I saw in his thoughtful approach to scripture a fine way to begin learning about Islam. I explained that many Muslim public intellectuals advocated not a theocracy, but a democratic political structure in which Islamic scripture would provide moral touchstones. Muslims, too, debated among themselves about how best to view scripture. As with Protestant Christians, some Muslims take verses of the Qur'ân to be immediately clear and universal commands, whereas others see some of the verses as historically limited, as the most appropriate way for God to deliver a message to a particular group of people in seventh-century Arabia. What the congressman saw as God's "dispensations" to humans—historical eras marked by divine gifts—Muslims saw as periods of revelation. While I explained that Muslims recognized several distinct schools of jurisprudence as legitimate, as several possible interpretations of God's will that are made by fallible humans, he saw parallels with his own acceptance of differences in religious views among Protestants.

I think we both learned something about religion during our flight. The conversation succeeded because we never floundered among the generalities of what "Islam says" or "Christianity teaches" that produce only confusion or, worse, muddled hostility. Instead we discussed practices, how real Muslims and Christians try to work out what scripture might have to say about their lives, and how they differ among themselves regarding those views. We both understood that neither Islamic nor Christian doctrines explain why people have attacked, killed, or saved one another, but that people have drawn on those doctrines for various reasons, reasons that required sophisticated analyses of struggles for resources and recognition in Palestine, Iraq, Saudi Arabia, and in the United States itself. At arrival we parted, not in agreement about religion and politics, but in at least partial agreement about how to understand other people's religions and politics.

I begin with this story because of a sense of immediacy I have about the importance of correctly understanding the roles religion does and does not play in modern public life, and the contributions the anthropology of religion can make to this understanding. The issue arises most pressingly with regard to contemporary armed conflicts, from those in the Balkans in the 1990s, through the continuing struggles in parts of the former Soviet Union, Kashmir, Indonesia, and Palestine, to the post–9/11 security debates about Islam in the United States and Europe. Are people fighting because of their religion? Does their religion shape how they think and act? Or is it just a way of mobilizing support? How far can religions be stretched to adapt to new ways of life?

These basic questions are less often posed than are the answers to them simply assumed. In less dramatic ways, many people living in Europe and North America continue to search for new forms of religiosity within or alongside established religious organizations. The fast-rising Christian churches in Melanesia, Africa, and Latin America are posing new challenges to indigenous religions. Muslims are engaging in internal deliberations about how to rethink issues of gender, of the public sphere, and of their religion's place in European and North American societies. Practitioners of smaller-scale religions throughout the world find themselves struggling for recognition or survival.

What Is "Religion"?

*D*iscussions of religion are often based on knowledge of only a few familiar religions. Many U.S. politicians and school officials who support a moment of silence for prayer in schools, for example, assume that all religions include the practice of silent individual prayer to a god; and some people find the Islamic practice of five daily prostrations before God disruptive. German officials have declared that Scientology is not a religion. Indonesian officials exclude animist beliefs and practices from the category of religion.

What then is "religion"? I view religious traditions as ever-changing complexes of beliefs (including those authoritative beliefs called "doctrine"), practices (including formalized rituals), and social institutions. But how do we decide which beliefs, practices, and institutions are to be called "religious"?

In most Western traditions one finds two very common definitions. One emphasizes an individual's beliefs; the other, his or her emotions. The first defines religion as a set of shared beliefs in spirits or gods. The second identifies religion in terms of a sentiment of awe and wonder toward the unknown. For me there is no hard and fast definition of religion. This book examines a wide variety of ways in which people in different societies and times have thought about the world beyond the immediate sense-world. Some posit a set of deities; others do not. Some have a distinct sphere of life called "religion"; others do not distinguish religion from the rest of life.

Sufficient for our purposes is that the collection of phenomena we will study—prayer to God, uses of magic, death rituals—all involve the idea that there is something more to the world than meets the eye. This definition is much broader than standard Western usage. What if we said that religion was whatever involves a stated belief in spirits or gods? In those cultures strongly shaped by modern Christianity, people do indeed tend to think of religion in these terms. The idea of a separate religious sphere is recent, even in Western history. In other societies people define the world in different ways, treating as a natural part of everyday life actions and ideas that we would want to include in a cross-cultural category of religion.

Consider the practices of the Azande people of the southern Sudan that ethnographers have labeled "Witchcraft." According to the Azande, some people carry in their bodies a substance called *mangu*. This substance is inherited, and it sends out emanations when the person feels jealousy, anger, or other negative emotions toward another person. The substance causes things to happen, and it fits into everyday ways of explaining misfortune. "I tripped at a place where I never trip; it must be witchcraft that caused me to trip."

When the person causing a particular misfortune is discovered (by using oracles) the person is asked to blow water from his or her mouth and to say: "If I was doing harm, I certainly did not mean to, let it be gone." And that is the end of the matter. The Azande do not concentrate on blame or intentions, but on the particular problem at hand and how to solve it. Indeed, they believe the substance sometimes acts on its own without the person's knowledge.

What do we make of these practices? From a Western point of view they refer to a reality beyond the immediately verifiable, and thus we legitimately may include them in a comparative study of religions. The Azande, on the other hand, see mangu and oracles as everyday, ordinary aspects of reality. Some of the Azande who have converted to Christianity continue their use of oracles and accusations of mangu precisely because they do not see those activities as part of a separate religion, but more as an American Baptist or Catholic might regard the use of an astrological chart.

The diversity of ideas about what constitutes a particular religion places any student of religion in a difficult position. If I write about a particular religion as the symbols, statements, and practices of a particular group of people, I will almost inevitably differ with some of them as to what their religion is. The perspective of an outside observer, who wishes to include a wide array of opinions and activities, may be much broader than that of a practitioner, who may insist on his or her own view of what properly lies within the boundaries of the religion in question.

I have frequently met with objections to the way I define "Islam" when describing certain Sumatran village practices to students in Indonesian Islamic colleges. For example, many villagers gather at ritual meals to ask ancestral spirits for help in healing the sick or in ensuring a good rice crop. These practices may have their origins in pre-Islamic times, but villagers view them as consistent with their understandings of Islam, and they explain them in terms of prophets and angels. For this reason I include them in my own writings about Sumatran Islam. But for the Islamic college students these practices conflict with proper understandings of Islam. "Those practices are what we try to teach them to throw aside," the students say. For some of them, my own writing could become part of the very problem they are trying to solve, that is, an overly broad idea of Islam.

How do we respond to these challenges? My own response has been to realize that definitions of religion are not just academic matters, but part of the very social reality we are studying. I thus refrain from giving too precise a definition for religion or Islam, and instead look at issues and debates among practitioners over the boundaries of religion, recording what they say and what is at stake for them.

People in the United States have not worked out definitive answers to these questions either. Some people would consider modern forms of witchcraft practiced in the United States to be a religion; indeed, the Rhode Island state legislature passed a law making it so in 1989. What limits the state should place on religious freedom is also a matter of continued debate, no more so than in cases of Christian Scientists denying medical treatment to their children. (Until August 1996, treatment given by Christian Science practitioners was considered "medical" for purposes of Medicare and Medicaid reimbursements, on grounds that to deny them that category would be to violate their religious freedom.)

I propose to define religion in two stages. First, we can use an extremely broad definition, such as "ideas and practices that postulate reality beyond that which is immediately available to the senses." This broad definition allows us to look at a very wide range of things. Second, for each society we study, we ask how *these* people construct their world. They may have a shared set of beliefs in spirits and deities and thus fit squarely into Western definitions of religion. Or they may speak about impersonal forces, such as the East Asian idea of a life force or *chi* that permeates the natural and social world. Or, they may not focus on describing beliefs at all, but rather, concentrate on carrying out rituals correctly, with a general understanding that the rituals are important. (This description fits the practitioners of Jain religion in India [Humphrey and Laidlaw 1994].)

What we call *religion* may look quite different from one society to another—in the relative importance of a shared belief system, in the degree to which religious practice involves strong emotions, and in the social functions and contexts associated with religious practices.

An Anthropological Approach to Religion

What is the peculiarly anthropological approach to the study of religion? These days, most of us reach across disciplinary boundaries to engage with colleagues in other disciplines. As I work on my own current questions, which in 2004 revolve around debates in Europe about religion and politics, I consult the work of specialists from sociology, history, politics, law, and so forth. And yet I find that multidisciplinary research highlights rather than hides the distinctive contributions made by anthropologists. Three closely connected features guide an anthropologist's study of any topic.

First, anthropology is based on a *long-term relationship with people* through fieldwork. We live for a fairly long time, more than one year and sometimes many years, in a particular place. During that time we develop close friendships with some people and gain, we hope, the trust and respect of many more. I spent about six years in Indonesia, about four of them with Gayo people in Sumatra. My experience is not unusual. I developed a very close and continuing friendship with a Gayo family. The eldest daughter now lives in the United States. She began a career with Procter & Gamble in Jakarta, moved to Cincinnati, and then changed her career to pursue interests in consulting and Islamic fashion design. My children call her "Cousin Evi."

Close relationships help us to interpret social life. We trust certain people to report what they think truthfully, and we know enough such people to be able to check our interpretations with people who might be expected to disagree in their views on things. For example, I know people who have very different perspectives on religious rituals, and I can depend on them to disagree with whatever I see. One can compare this source of reliability to that which psychologists obtain by repeating experiments.

Second, anthropologists pursue their study initially through the *local perspectives*. Rather than studying the economy by creating a model of what people might do and then seeing whether they do it, or studying religion by reading scripture and then seeing what they believe, we begin with the ideas and practices we learn about in the field. Then we follow the connections to larger institutions like government agencies, religious schools, or national banks—but we always start from local views of those institutions.

When I studied Islamic law in Indonesia, for example, I began with how Gayo village and townspeople talk about law, how and whether they refer to it when resolving conflicts, and to what extent they make use of courts or religious authorities. Then I study the courts, the universities that educate the authorities, and the national institutions that seek to shape what happens locally, including the Supreme Court and the National Council of Islamic scholars. I learn about colonial law, contemporary civil law, and Islamic codes, but only after studying everyday social life, in order to anchor these codes and institutions in local practices. This feature distinguishes anthropology from disciplines that usually begin with historical, religious, or legal texts, or with national political institutions.

Finally, anthropologists study *connections across social domains*. Rarely do we look only at the economy, or at literature, or at religion. We might wish to focus on one of these domains (indeed it is required when writing a doctoral dissertation), but when we do, we usually discover that our chosen domain is connected to other domains. Suppose I want to learn about rice cultivation and discover that the planting and harvesting is tied to the performance of elaborate religious rituals and that work on the irrigation system depends on local political structures. I have to investigate religion and politics, then, in order to understand how rice is cultivated.

Conversely, my study of Islam in Gayo society involved learning about how rice is grown, how the major rice-growing regions were allocated among villages, how healing takes place, the origins of political parties, and the short history of a poetic genre written in Arabic script—all because they were part of local practices that people explained by referring to Islam. Indeed, I focused on Islam only as a third project; I was brought to it because the topics I came to study—social structure and oral literature—were interwoven with Islamic ideas about society and history. Even when we work in new kinds of sites we retain these features in our work. My current research on Islam in France finds me sitting in religious schools along with Muslim students, interviewing French political actors, and analyzing newspaper stories and law review articles. I don't work in a village, or even in a single neighborhood. (Other anthropologists are carrying out that sort of work alongside of mine.) How is what I am doing different from the work of a political scientist? Well, it comes close to the approach of some of my French colleagues in political science—the French version of that discipline having developed more attention to everyday life than has its more behaviorist American cousin—but it retains a critical difference. I focus on how a wide range of Muslims and non-Muslims talk about matters of importance to them—schools, mosques, political coalitions—in private and public contexts. The "local" setting in which I work is multiple: a set of institutions and events across France in which people deliberate and debate. Starting from these deliberations and debates leads me to look at law, politics, jurisprudence, ethics, the history of immigration, and the perspectives of French social scientists on their own society—in other words, the connections across domains. As one political science friend said to me recently, her eyebrows slightly raised, "you're studying us, too, aren't you?" That it was so more intrigued than troubled her; it was a way of marking our disciplinary differences, and transoceanic differences in perspective, alongside our shared interests in French Islam.

Differences across Disciplines

Consider how scholars in different disciplines approach a question about why people believe the (religious) things they do. As I said before, most anthropologists approach the question through fieldwork. Susan Harding (2000), for example, set out to understand how it is that people become "convicted" (that is, convinced) followers of the Reverend Jerry Falwell's Fundamental Baptist community. Her ethnographic approach was to spend a lot of time in the community, listening to what people said and how they said it. She worked to counteract her basic skepticism toward Falwell by "bracketing," as the phenomenologist Husserl put it, her preconceptions, and trying to accept his statements as true. This approach allowed her to perceive the complexity and the force of the arguments made by the Baptists. It also gave her a strong, personal sense of what it meant to have a soul and to know that Satan is real. She did not convert but she gained a felt sense of conviction.

Harding's work fits the overall account of the anthropological approach that I offered earlier. She got to know people well enough to be able to discuss a wide range of topics with them and to grasp how they saw the world. She tried to start with their concerns, rather than bringing her own categories and ideas to the field. And she did not limit her study to one specific domain, but investigated ritual, schooling, gender issues, and politics.

Most anthropologists of religion teaching in North America or Europe carry out at least their initial fieldwork outside those areas, reflecting the general anthropological emphasis on grasping the widest possible range of human experiences, practices, and ideas. This centrifugal tendency also means that they must study and explain to their readers the social and cultural context within which one finds religion: kinship and marriage systems, local and national political structures, and broad cosmologies and ideologies. One could limit one's reading to the subfield of the anthropology of religion and nevertheless gain a good understanding of anthropology.

Even though many sociologists carry out fieldwork, the fundamental orientation of their discipline is different from that of anthropology, with a greater interest in developing general propositions about social life, but (one might say ironically) less of a concern with broad-based comparative studies. Most sociologists of religion teaching in the United States study the organization of religions, changes in religious attitudes and beliefs, or new religious movements, usually focusing on people and institutions found in the United States. This focus means that they can assume general knowledge of institutions and ideas on the part of their readers, and that they often pitch their writings to generally held concerns, such as the decline in attendance at mainstream churches or the rise in New Age religions.

Penny Edgell Becker's (1999) study of congregations illustrates one sociological approach. She asked how congregations in the United States manage internal conflict. Her concern thus was primarily organizational. She selected a sample of churches in Chicago, choosing her sample to have variation in size, organizational structure, and liberal–conservative orientation. Her concerns were primarily to develop a general model consisting of types of church organizations and concomitant types of conflict resolution. These goals were motivated by a broader theoretical literature in sociology concerning institutions and their cultures in the United States. Along the way she discovered interesting histories of each church and ways of preaching and worshipping, but each of these mini-ethnographies was inevitably partial, useful only to the extent that it contributed to her particular question.

Psychologists more rarely study religion, but a few anthropologists have taken up the methods of experimental psychology to pursue research into why people believe certain religious propositions. Pascal Boyer (2000, 2001), for example, observed that people around the world have a strikingly small number of basic ideas about supernatural beings: that they behave much as ordinary beings or objects do except for a slight variation in their properties. Thus one has supernatural agents who are very much like people except that they can go through walls, be invisible, hear everything, or live forever. We do not find gods who exist only every other day, or who exist in six dimensions, or who think about everything in the world at once, including the contents of all our refrigerators. Why is this? Boyer and others hypothesized that the more limited set of limited god-concepts were conceptually easier to work with for humans. They then tested this idea through experiments with children and adults, and found that it held across a number of different cultures. This work resembles that of other psychologists in that it is carried out through controlled experiments and tests some universal propositions about human minds.

Practices, Contexts, Diversity

*I*n the chapters that follow I examine religious life from different perspectives: the relations of doctrines to rituals; the role of religions in explaining misfortune, overcoming grief, and extending human powers; the ways that rituals of pilgrimage, preaching, and sacrificing shapes religious belief and experience; the ways that images and taboos can be used to organize religious life or change it; and the role of religions in public life.

The emphasis on practice includes the study of doctrines, but focuses on how doctrines are embodied in texts or other forms and how they are understood; this relation of doctrine to practice is examined in greater detail in Chapter 3. Religious practices often invoke texts: someone reads, chants, recites, or sings a text. These textual practices are critical in linking local practices to broader religious traditions.

Certain practices are especially characteristic of one or more religious traditions, and in some chapters I analyze at length those traditions. For example, images are particularly central to Catholicism, and that religion provides the main example for the discussion of imagery and worship in Chapter 9 (but images in Africa, Buddhist Sri Lanka, and Brazil are also discussed).

The particular contribution of ethnographic and social historical studies to knowledge of religion lies in the attention to interconnections among domains of social life, among religion, economy, marriage, politics, and so forth, to the ways that cultural ideas and social institutions shape activities in many of these domains. The importance of such cross-domain connections was underscored by Durkheim and Marx, who continue to have a strong influence on many anthropologists (see Chapter 2). A particular religious practice such as worship may structure communities in particular ways, or lend a religious interpretation to existing social divisions, as when a Hindu priest distributes consecrated foods according to caste standing, or when men and women worship separately in a Muslim mosque, or when church pews are reserved for those who have contributed to the church.

The interpretation of texts and doctrines is strongly shaped by local factors, as Clifford Geertz (1968) showed in contrasting Islam in Morocco to Islam in Java, a contrast I revisit in Chapter 10. Comparing two or more cases of a practice can help to highlight these shaping processes, and in each of the following chapters I engage in such comparisons. In Chapter 4, for example, I contrast treatments of death in Japan, New Guinea, and Sumatra; in Chapter 8, patterns of sorcery in different societies of Africa;

in Chapter 12, pilgrimage in Mecca and around the Japanese island of Shikoku; in Chapter 15, the relationship of religion and state in Germany, France, Britain, and the United States.

Finally, I consider the diversity of religious understandings and practices even in small-scale societies. Diversity includes both questions of how knowledge and ideas are distributed in the society—between men and women, or adults and children, or across other social groupings—and the debates among people about how best to understand the norms and forms of religious culture. Anthropology has often been insufficiently attentive to diversity. This insufficiency has been due in part to the idea that a "culture" is an integrated whole, an idea inherited from German nineteenth-century cultural studies, and in part due to ways of carrying out research by concentrating on a small number of "key informants"—or even, in some cases, one such informant.

We know that the same practice may be interpreted in myriad and diverse ways. Beginning from particular religious practices and then examining diverse interpretations allows us to capture these diversities, and in some cases explain them in terms of accompanying social differences and changes. Certain religious traditions allow a particularly broad diversity of practices to flourish—the case of Japan is explored in Chapter 3. Debates within Islam are explored at several points in this book. I draw on my own fieldwork with the Muslim Gayo of Sumatra and on Islam in France in some of these chapters. I also examine debates within Christianity: concerning the role of the Virgin Mary in Chapter 9, and the nature of divine election in Chapter 11.

The final chapter returns us to the broad debates concerning the place of religion in public life with which I began this chapter. It is with an eye to these debates that I write this book. A great deal of misunderstanding and, to my mind, wrong-headed public policy in many countries, but certainly in the United States, has been based on ideas about religion that ignore diversities, debates, and possibilities. For example, particular features of certain strata of Middle Eastern societies (the role of women, views on Islam law) are frequently confused with Islam in general. Religious beliefs are all open to debate and transformation; attending to those debates reminds us of a sense of the open-ended nature of religious ideas.

2 Social Theory in the Anthropology of Religion

*A*nthropology is not only a general approach and a set of fieldwork methods; anthropologists studying religion also draw from one or more bodies of social theory. Rarely in anthropology does theory become a set of propositions to prove or disprove. Instead, theory serves to suggest questions and guide research. Theoretical choices also predispose researchers to follow certain initial questions, study certain dimensions of religion, and engage in certain kinds of scholarly activities rather than others.

In what follows I make distinctions among several general sets of questions and approaches to studying religion anthropologically, all which have continued to provide guidance for research. We continue to read major works in social theory because they set out those questions and approaches for us. E. B. Tylor asked why people hold certain religious ideas and not others, and this question has retained its importance. Émile Durkheim asked how it is that social norms have such a hold on us, and we continue to pose this question, albeit in new ways. Karl Marx and Max Weber asked how modern capitalism came to dominate the world, and gave very different answers; their work continues to provide starting points for contemporary social scientists. I prefer to distinguish in this way "social theory" as a body of work from which social scientists draw questions and guidance, from specific "theories of society," which may prove more or less perceptive and appealing.

Religion as Intellectual Activity

*O*ne dimension of religion is the intellectual: what do people think exists, and why do they think those things? These questions can survive the rise and fall of specific answers to the question.

In the mid-nineteenth century, the early years of anthropology as a formal discipline, scholars in most disciplines tried to explain the diversity and complexity of today's religions by postulating a process of religious evolution. They were strongly influenced by German idealist philosophers, who saw human history as the development of a set of human essences. These philosophers understood religion as a unity of thought and feeling, intellect and emotion that had developed historically from initial germs. The philosopher Hegel postulated a universal idea of religion that preceded its particular historical manifestations. As it developed over time from an initial germ, it became increasingly complex. This idea of development or evolution did not concern the history of a particular religion or a particular people, but the evolution across time and space of an idea, independent of particular cultures.

This theory of general human cultural evolution provided the intellectual framework for the early anthropology of religion, as well as for social anthropology generally. The comparative study of religion in the late nineteenth century was based on two assumptions: that religion progressed from the simple to the complex, and that one could reconstruct the origins of religion by studying "primitive peoples" in the world today. Many students of the origins of religion did not subscribe to the universal truths offered by their churches, and their accounts were more or less subtle ways of discrediting the absolute truth of Christianity. If Catholic or Anglican beliefs evolved from something very simple then they looked much less absolute than if they had been delivered through divine revelation.

E. B. Tylor and the Origins of Religious Ideas

The most famous study along these lines was *Primitive Culture* (1970 [1871]) by Edward B. Tylor (1832–1917). Tylor was the first person to be appointed to a university position in anthropology in England, in 1884 at Oxford. Tylor argued that primitive people acted as proto-scientists when they created religion, constructing concepts to explain what they perceived through their senses. Tylor (1970, vol. 2) asked: "What is true of all religions?" He looked around him and saw that all religions employed a belief in spiritual beings. The higher ones had souls, gods, angels, and so on, while the more primitive ones had spirits and ghosts. The primitive form of this belief he called animism. He saw this belief as basic to religious development.

"Why do people come to hold such a belief?" he then asked. Well, he answered, they perceive things that lead them to suppose these spiritual entities. They perceive different states of consciousness (wakefulness, sleep, death), dreams (and the appearance in them of places and persons), and shadows. Then they think up things to explain these appearances. "Soul" explains the different states of consciousness, because as soul sleeps, or leaves the body, we lose consciousness or life. "Ghost" explains the phenomenon of dreams, because as we sleep, our ghost or spirit leaves the body and travels to other places, and we vaguely remember these wandering perceptions when we wake. Finally, shadows are one form taken by souls and ghosts. Tylor was able to amass a large body of evidence to support his claims. (Indeed, the ways many people today speak about sleep, dreams, death, and shadows do sound very much like Tylor's account.)

Religion is therefore due to "the plain evidence of men's senses" for Tylor. As it develops it continues to build on perceptions and logic. People reasoned that because animals, too, have life, then they must have souls. If they are killed, then their souls can follow those of their masters to the world of the beyond, and there do work for them. Burial practices from such diverse civilizations as Egypt and China attest to this belief. Furthermore, because plants also live and die, they must have souls as well. All living things, concludes Tylor's primitive thinker, thus have souls; such is the origin of "animism," the belief that all living things are "animated" by souls.

But how is it, asks Tylor, that such ideas have survived until today? One way is through psychological development. As children, we have the very same experiences, and make the very same inferences, as did primitive people: we have dreams and we attribute life to things and play with them as if they were alive. When we grow up we are thus prepared to accept as true, because in some sense natural, the claims of the religions we are taught. We do so because—and here is the second way the early ideas survived—the ideas of advanced religions are merely further elaborations of the primitive ideas. Tylor offers the example of the Eucharist, the Christian ritual wherein bread and wine become, or symbolize, Christ's body and blood. This ritual might appear to be far from primitive religion. But, he argues, it is a development of the idea of sacrifice, which itself was based on the notion that the soul of the sacrificed animal or person would travel to the world beyond.

Tylor's account of religion captures elements that one does, indeed, find throughout the world. The ideas of soul, spirit, dreams that he described as basic or primitive do indeed animate many religious systems. Tylor's weakness, from our contemporary perspective, is that he emphasized an essential commonality to all religious beliefs and thus played down what most anthropologists emphasize today, namely, the diversity of ways in which humans have constructed their religious beliefs and practices. But by analyzing the logic of a set of beliefs, Tylor did inspire his successors to analyze the different ways people have constructed their understandings of the cosmos, their "world views."

An eminent successor to Tylor in this enterprise was James Frazer (1854–1951), whose massive compendium of religion and myth, *The Golden Bough* (1981 [1890]), first issued in two volumes and later expanded to twelve, brought together in a readable style much of the knowledge of the day about comparative religion. Frazer followed Tylor in sharply distinguishing among science, magic, and religion as distinct modes of thought. Religion, in their view, involves acts intended to appease deities; magic, like science, assumes impersonal relationships between certain actions and their outcomes. Magic rests on two basic, albeit mistaken, ideas. The first is the idea of similarity, that like causes like (a green stone will cure jaundice). The second is that of contagion, that contact between two objects allows someone to control one through manipulating the other (a person's hair-clippings can be burned, thereby harming the person). Magic is thus pseudoscience; religion proper involves a qualitatively different kind of activity.

Tylor and Frazer's intellectualist legacy has been to focus anthropological energies on understanding how particular people view the world, taking their world view seriously as an intellectual or philosophical enterprise. Most anthropologists continued to pose these questions thereafter.

In the United States, Franz Boas and his students developed cultural anthropology around a twofold approach to studying small-scale societies. On the one hand, they sought to discern the patterns of each culture as they were reflected in art, myth, kinship, and everyday ways of speaking. On the other hand, they traced the historical processes through which people transmit cultural ideas across societies and also change them. This dual focus on both ideas and empirical processes reflects Boas's own German training in both empirical sciences and idealist philosophy.

Claude Lévi-Strauss and the Structure of Mythic Thinking

Boas's complex approach to myths probably was best continued by the French anthropologist Claude Lévi-Strauss. Lévi-Strauss drew from Tylor's analysis of the intellectual operations detectable in myth-making, but he also, following Boas, sought to trace transformations of myths as they have passed from one society to another. Myths, in his analysis, are composed according to intricate codes, each of which concerns a distinct level of local life and awareness: a code of flora and fauna, one of geography, one of social institutions. These codes are structured as oppositions among categories: cold versus hot, high versus low, mother's versus father's relatives, and so forth. Moreover, neighboring peoples often tell contrasting versions of these myths, and these contrasts across societies indicate that myths reflect differences in local social life, and that they may function to underscore the boundaries between peoples.

In one of his best-known analyses, Lévi-Strauss dissects a myth told among several peoples of the Northwest Coast of North America, the "Story of Asdiwal" (1976). The myth is structured around four distinct codes of geography, economy, society, and cosmology. Events often concern all four codes at once: for example, a marriage involves geographical movement, fishing, a particular kind of marriage institution, and movements between earth and sky. Lévi-Strauss argues that the myth depicts in especially salient ways the contradictions that are at the basis of Tsimshian society. Marriages among families of chiefs, for example, were supposed to create or reaffirm relations of hierarchy among them, but precisely who was superior to whom was debated fiercely at each marriage. The myths depict such chiefly marriages as ending in death and battle, thus representing in heightened form problems inherent in the social structure. The myths also try out alternative realities, such as trying to inherit from one's father and one's mother, "in order to show that they are untenable" (1976, 173).

Differences between two versions of the myth show how myths, as they are transferred from one place to another, are recast in light of local conditions. One version was collected along the coast, from people who make a great seasonal migration from one region to another to catch candlefish in the spring on one river and salmon in the summer on another. In their version of the myth, characters travel great distances and they engage in very different economic pursuits, as do the humans telling the myth. Lévi-Strauss points out that this version of the myth is characterized by strong oppositions between categories along geographical and economic codes. But oppositions are also strong along the social and cosmological codes (for example, featuring people who are distantly related to each other), as if to follow the oppositions generated by the codes of economic life and geographic movement. This priority of some codes, the economic and geographic, over others is mentioned by Lévi-Strauss in referring to himself as a Marxist.

In the versions of the myth that were collected along a river where the residents made fewer movements in the course of the year—they hunted candlefish but not salmon, for example—the oppositions were weaker, again along all four codes. This comparative analysis thus supports Lévi-Strauss's conclusions that codes of a myth are internally integrated, and that they all differ in a systematic way across societies. Others, especially James A. Boon (1990), have used this insight in their own ethnographic analyses of how people structure religious and social life through their use of oppositions and contrasts. In these studies, myths are seen as extended commentaries on the practice of everyday social life.

Religions in Social Life

Although neither Tylor nor Lévi-Strauss conceived of religious ideas and practices as divorced from society, they underscored the intellectual dimension of religious ideas. Boas, too, and especially his students, emphasized the ways in which religious and other ideas cohere in patterns. As we will see, this emphasis on the cultural patterning of religion has retained a central role in anthropology.

At the same time, social theorists stressed that religious ideas, sentiments, and orientations had developed out of specific social conditions. Each of the three major social theorists of modern Europe—Durkheim, Marx, and Weber—crafted some distinctive ways of understanding religion's relationship to broader social processes. All three theorists were primarily concerned with explaining features of modern life—the rise of modern capitalism, challenges to social solidarity, and the peculiar nature of rational and legal authority. In the process of developing their theories they also tried to explain the role of religion in pre-modern societies.

Émile Durkheim on the Social Origins of Religion

Some scholars continued Tylor's quest for the origins of religion, but sought those origins in social life. The sociologist Émile Durkheim (1858–1917), for example, saw the birth of religion in the ideas and emotions generated out of collective social action. "Religious representations are collective representations that express collective realities," he wrote (1995, 9). Durkheim was not entirely the originator of this general idea. Aristotle, after all, had declared that "men create the gods after their own image." The French historian Fustel de Coulanges (1830–1889) and the Scottish scholar of Semitic societies W. Robertson-Smith (1846–1904) linked social organization to religious ideas in ancient societies. Robertson-Smith had argued that the earliest societies had been totemic, that is, they had been organized into clans, each of which had a special relationship to a species of animal—"my clan is a wolf." Sacrificing this animal was a way to communicate and commune with the deities, and at the same time it was a means to strengthen the emotional bonds among clan members.

Durkheim drew from these earlier writers to argue that knowledge in general, and religious knowledge in particular, has a social foundation. His argument was philosophical, against Kant's idea that humans had innate categories of the understanding. But it was also social and moral, and grew out of the concerns of the day (Lukes 1973). Durkheim wrote at a time of great social and moral turmoil in France, when older certainties about God and Church had been excised from public and legal life by the Revolution, but no alternative moral certainties had yet replaced them. The country appeared to be polarized between urban agnostics and rural Catholics. Battles were especially sharp over the future of the school system: should it be secular or Catholic, and if secular, what would be its moral content? No wonder that in his first articles, Durkheim was deeply sensitive to the problem of social cohesion in contemporary society: "A society whose members are not bound to one another by some solid and durable link," he wrote in 1886, "would resemble a loose pile of dust which could at any time be dispersed by the slightest wind to the four corners of the world" (quoted in Alexander 1982, 82). But what are these bonds? And how do they unite people in societies that have not undergone the sort of schisms experienced by France?

As one would expect given the evolutionary way of thinking in vogue at the time, Durkheim sought his answer in a study of *The Elementary Forms of the Religious Life,* the title of his 1912 book. The book posits an early type of social consciousness in those societies where everyone is for all important purposes alike: everyone has the same statuses, duties, and roles. In such societies people's feelings are also alike, and thus strongly reinforce each other whenever people gather together. Moral sentiments, religious beliefs, and other cultural ideas are all very strong, and law, religion, and social norms are strong as well.

Durkheim postulated that religious beliefs and sentiments must correspond to something real, and that they could not be purely illusory or mistaken, as Tylor and Frazer had concluded. They clearly were false if taken at face value. The problem then was to go underneath the symbol to the reality that it represents and that gives it its true meaning. What is "religion"? Rather than defining it as the belief in spirits, as did Tylor and Frazer, Durkheim viewed it as involving a fundamental division of the world into sacred versus profane things. Religion is thus a collective reality that concerns how the members of a particular society divide up the world, rather than an individual reality consisting of what a person believes. But *how* the world is divided into sacred and profane varies greatly from one society to the next; what determines this division?

Here Durkheim accepts Robertson-Smith's thesis that totemism was the earliest basis for social organization and that it was the wellspring of religion. He turns to the religions of Australian aborigines to prove his thesis. In these societies specific groups perform rituals at sacred sites that are associated either with ancestral spirits or with mythical beings that lived during the ancient "dream time" that came before the time we know. Each group also has objects made of wood or stone engraved with symbols of these ancestors or mythical beings, and these *churinga* objects themselves have sacred powers.

Each such social group also has a special ritual relationship toward certain species, such as kangaroo, or certain natural phenomena, such as rain or wind. Members of the group may have special rules regulating their activities with respect to these species, the group's *totem,* and the group can carry out rituals that increase the species' numbers. These rituals sometimes involve eating an item of the species, and Durkheim thought that this practice confirmed the theory that sacrifice and communal eating were the earliest, basic forms of religious ritual.

Durkheim argued that the general idea of spiritual force that underlay totemism existed prior to ideas about spirits or souls, and he cited related ideas from other societies, such as the notion of impersonal force or *mana* in Melanesia. (He also could have cited the Chinese idea of life force, or *chi.*) This same force, at later stages of development, gives rise to ideas of souls, ancestral spirits, and God, stated Durkheim.

Durkheim set out his argument on two different levels. First, he explained the variety of religious ideas by arguing that particular features of societies give rise to particular features of their cultures and religions. Religion thus represents society. So, there are "societies in Australia and North America where space is conceived in the form of an immense circle, because the camp has a circular form." The early division of society into two halves or *moieties* gave rise to ideas of the cosmos as dualistic. In societies such as the Australians just discussed, where people were organized into clans, these people often postulated an animal, or sacred place, or force, as the totem of that clan. These totems were the projections onto a spiritual place of a sense of belonging together in the clan. As the society grew and spread over a wider area, giving rise to a sense of a broad social group with shared interests that spilled over the boundaries of the clan, totemic representations synthesized into the idea of one or more gods, "the god being only a figurative expression of the society," Durkheim summarily stated (1995, 227).

This level of argument presumes that there already is a general religious idea that can be shaped by society. So arguing at a second level, Durkheim tried to explain the emergence of general religious ideas and sentiments in the first place. People sense a moral force that is exterior to them, he argued. This idea is given social content in those moments when people come together in social assemblies, such as dances, meetings, or festivals. These assemblies create a social effervescence out of which religious ideas are confirmed and given stronger emotional meaning. A qualitative change takes place, and people began to feel themselves transported to an altered state.

Religion serves the function of strengthening social solidarity by communicating specific ideas and sentiments, and by regulating and strengthening social relationships. A totem, for instance, reminds you what kind of person you are (a member of a certain clan) and thereby regulates relations among individuals. It also gives you a feeling of strength: speaking of one Australian society, Durkheim wrote: "The Arunta who has properly rubbed himself with his churinga feels stronger; he is stronger" (1995, 229).

This functional perspective on religion gave Durkheim a way of discussing the place of religion in modern society. Religion is no longer a satisfactory *cognitive* solution to the "problem of meaning," in which science is now the master. But religion continues to be *symbolically* important: cult and faith are essential to any society's social solidarity, including our own.

Durkheim emphasized the cognitive, emotional, and social aspects of religious ideas and practices. His *Elementary Forms* focuses on the social origins of religion by way of a theory of collective emotions; but there and in other writings, Durkheim also emphasizes the logical nature of religious classifications. In *Primitive Classification* (1963 [1903]), Durkheim and his nephew Marcel Mauss (1872–1950) compared the symbolic classifications found in Australian, native North American, and Chinese societies. The Zuni Pueblo people of the U.S. Southwest, for example, assign to each of the cardinal directions (plus center, and the zenith and nadir of the sun's apparent motion) a color, a season, and a kind of weather, together with a general force such as creation or destruction, a specific group, and an animal. Durkheim and Mauss claimed that members of these societies have created totalizing religious systems; these systems unite the social, natural, and cosmological realms. Their comparison of logical similarities across these societies inspired later anthropologists to more detailed studies of symbolic classification.

Durkheim's legacy in the field of religious studies was twofold. First, he connected the religious to the social, leading later anthropologists to look for social origins or functions of specific religious practices and ideas. This strain of his legacy was a foundation of British social anthropology, from A. R. Radcliffe-Brown through Edmund Leach and Mary Douglas. For Mary Douglas, for example, the key to understanding food taboos, whether in the Hebrew Bible or in the societies of central Africa she studied in her fieldwork, is to look for the social functions such taboos may have served. She argued that by separating the sacred from the profane, and then by restricting membership in the community to those who observed the rules, food taboos make group membership sacred.

Durkheim also emphasized the ways that participating in collective religious practices confirm faith, and this insight remains compelling. Consider how many European Catholics find visions of Mary to be central events cementing their faith, or perhaps their hope within their faith. In less spectacular ways, the good feelings of participating in something with friends and neighbors may also make the religion particularly "true." Particularly important is the way in which public ritual generates religious commitment. A service, for example, in which many people worship together, can be a wonderfully compelling context, generating a sense of being together and being in the presence of something else. Such feelings, perhaps most startlingly displayed when Christian worshipers speak in tongues, lay behind Durkheim's claim that coming together as a social group gave rise to the earliest ideas of the supernatural. Most people, however, most of the time, experience their activities of carrying out worship, consulting oracles, or avoiding tabooed foods as routine actions. It may indeed be the case that the routine nature of most of religions' demands, the integration of religion into everyday life, provides a social and psychological comfort.

Secondly, Durkheim connected the religious to the intellectual, continuing Tylor's emphasis. "The essential notions of scientific logic are of religious origin," he wrote in *Elementary Forms* (1995, 431). This statement has broadly echoed in cultural anthropology throughout the world, and most notably by Claude Lévi-Strauss, who saw classificatory systems as the product of intense, imaginative intellectual activity. Rather than seeing totems and totemic social organization as a primitive form of identification that then gave rise to higher forms of society and religion, Lévi-Strauss considered them, in his *Totemism* (1963a [1962]), as one among many ways of classifying the world in order to understand it. Particular plants or animals are chosen to be totems not because they have utility or excite awe in themselves, but because they provide a usable symbolic template through which to make distinctions in the natural, social, and cosmological worlds.

Karl Marx on Religion in Capitalist Europe

Durkheim's approach to religion assumed that society, and therefore religion, was an integrated whole. But what if society is not like that, but consists instead of several groups whose interests and ideas are in conflict? How then ought we to understand the social origins and functions of religion?

This question lies behind the work of both Karl Marx and Max Weber. Karl Marx (1818–1883) emphasized the historical process by which different social groups come to dominate social life. The key to this process was the interplay between the material forces of production and the social relations of production: how things were produced and how their production and distribution was organized. Each historical period in European history has thrown up its own distinctive dominant ideology: politics in classical Rome, the Catholic Church in the medieval period, and capitalism as ideology in the modern period. Marx and his collaborator, Friedrich Engels, saw religion as serving ideological functions in all periods, as providing social cement in the face of class divisions, but also as expressing class interests (Marx and Engels 1965 [1946]).

Studies of religion inspired by Marx have looked for the material interests served by movements gathered together under the banner of religion. Engels (1956 [1850]) argued that the religious wars of the fifteenth and sixteenth centuries in Germany, although couched in the language of religious dissent, were motivated by the disparate interests of the nobility, burghers, and peasants. Among these movements were those millenarian Christian movements that prophesied the imminent moment (the "millennium," or thousand years) when the corrupt leaders of the church would face the Day of Judgment. German millenarian prophets combined apocalyptic teachings with calls for the end of the feudal system, supporting Engels's thesis that material interests and religious ideas were intertwined. Engels thus showed the power of religion to subvert as well as to confirm the existing social order. His study launched a distinguished tradition of investigations (for example, Worsley 1968) into the material and religious sources of those radical religious movements whose leaders preach an imminent radical transformation of society, if not the end of the world—"millenarian" in today's general sense of the term.

Max Weber on Religion in Modern Civilizations

Max Weber (1864–1920) also analyzed the relationships between particular interest groups and religious ideas. Weber (1978 [1956]) took the social action of the individual as his unit, distinct from Durkheim's emphasis on social structure and function, and Marx's emphasis on changing modes of production. Weber wrote that one can only come to understand social action by, first, discovering the meaning of the action for the individual and, secondly, explaining it in terms of the social conditions and actions that preceded it. Social science thus involves both interpretation and causal–historical explanation.

Religion provides one major source of ideas and orientations for the actor, and Weber devoted much analysis to the comparative study of religions. His interest was not religious doctrine per se, but the spirit or *ethos* that was produced in individuals by their adherence to one faith versus another, as well as the social conditions that allowed new types of religious orientation to emerge. Weber saw the development of Western society as the progressive *rationalization* of society, a concept that implies both the increasing differentiation of social life into functionally defined domains or spheres—family, economy, religion—and the systematic reorganization of each domain around a single set of values or rules. Economy gradually became reorganized around the maximization of profit; family, around the general solidarity of kin; religion, around the worship of God. In Weber's view of Western world history, religion gradually shed its "magical" character and developed a set of universalistic doctrines about a divine order, and a set of ethical principles that apply to everyone, everywhere.

Weber's theory of religious history is both sociological and universal. Weber carried out separate studies of India, China, Islam, ancient Judaism, and modern Europe. He saw each of these societies as characterized by a distinctive set of religious beliefs, a particular economic ethic, and a specific set of interest groups; his research concerned the interplay of these three elements. In his study of India, for example, Weber argued that the caste system and the doctrine of *karma*—the idea that one's actions in this or a previous life determined the course of one's life—inhibited the development of a rational economic ethic because it led religious energies away from this world and directed them toward the "other world." Only with the development of Calvinist Protestantism in Europe did there arise a religion-driven energy to rationally remold the world; this energy pushed forward modern capitalism.

Weber traced similar developmental processes within each socio-religious system. In the larger-scale societies he studied, prophets arose to challenge an older way of thinking, often in the name of a universal creed and god. But with the demise of the prophet, followers had to "routinize" the movement, creating a religious community or congregation. The eventual development of a rational, differentiated religious system required the parallel development of a bureaucratic state, whether in India, China, or Europe.

Weber's analysis rested on the "ideal types" he created—the other-worldly mystic, the this-worldly prophet. These types give us an initial, clear sense of the contrasts in dominant ideas among large-scale religions. But they are less useful in analyzing the many ways in which people reinterpret and transform those ideas. Weber's ideal types have been questioned by later students of each society. For example, Weber based his claims that the Indian doctrine of karma would retard economic development on the assumption that the doctrine, as contained in religious texts, was also what ordinary people believed. But popular Indian ideas about fate and action in the world are not the same as the textual doctrines (Babb 1983), and they have not prevented people from engaging in modern industrial development (Singer 1964).

Clifford Geertz and the Ethnography of Civilizations

Although a number of anthropologists began to study large-scale societies, or "civiliza-tions," in the 1950s, probably the best-known among them has been Clifford Geertz. In his *Religion of Java* (1960), as well as in other works on Indonesia and Morocco, he analyzes the diversity of religious beliefs in a large Muslim society.

Geertz draws from Weber's emphasis on the answers that large-scale religious doctrines provide for life's key questions, such as: Why is there evil in the world? Who gets to heaven and why? But whereas Weber worked largely from the writings of religious figures and other literate men—those who formed what Robert Redfield (1956) was to call the urban "great traditions"—Geertz relies on the testimonies of ordinary village and townspeople, those people participating in what Redfield called the rural "little tradition." Geertz looks at the diversity of ideas in a single society.

Geertz's method is to define three "streams" of Islam on Java, each situated in a different institutional context: a set of village understandings that focused on spirits and community rituals; a more scripturally oriented Islam of the religious school and the market; and a focus on status and etiquette among noble Javanese. Although criticized for not emphasizing that people in all three streams were Muslims, and that many read works of Islamic doctrine and spirituality, his analysis was able to capture both the variety of ways Javanese men and women talked about religion and society, and the ways that large-scale institutions of politics, economics, and religion shaped their understandings and their actions.

Geertz's approach has been especially influential in the anthropology of religion. Today many anthropologists place even more emphasis than he did on the ways that villagers and religious experts ("culture brokers") interpret and reshape the texts and ideas of religious traditions in their societies. For example, Stanley Tambiah (1970) studied the uses that monks and other villagers make of Buddhist texts in northeastern Thailand. Dale F. Eickelman (1985) traced the career of a rural Moroccan judge. In these and other studies, anthropologists have situated large-scale changes in specific towns and villages and with respect to specific people.

The Psychology of Religion

Cognitive and social approaches to religion sometimes fail to provide a full account of the psychological dimension. The individual as portrayed in Tylor and Durk-heim, for example, is rather one-dimensional: he or she is a would-be scientist, or simply part of a crowd marked by religious euphoria.

Weber and Suffering

Of theorists considered so far, Weber paid the most attention to the psychological dimension of religion. He wished to explain how different religious orientations toward the world would produce different economic ethics, leading to different kinds of economic organization. In particular, he sought to explain how Protestant ideas spurred on modern capitalism in Europe. The key Protestant idea was the doctrine of "unknowable election"—the idea that some people were elected to heaven and others condemned to hell, but that no one could know his or her category nor change what God had preordained. Weber argued that this doctrine, taught by the theologian John Calvin, was so unsettling that people worked hard to succeed in this world, grasping at the idea that the material signs of their success also were signs of God's favor. The "Protestant ethic" was thus the psychological consequence of a specific doctrine, and it, not the doctrine itself, was a key element in the rise of modern capitalism.

Weber thought that the idea of predestination also served to affirm the absolute, transcendent power of God over his creations. The idea explains the presence of evil in the world by stating that God's motives are beyond human understanding. The idea is basic to one of the most powerful and enigmatic of the Bible stories, the story of Job. The story concerns how Job retains his faith in God through a series of terrible tests—he loses his family, health, and wealth. God wagers with Satan, allowing Satan to inflict these sufferings, with Job's faith as the prize. Job has done nothing to deserve his suffering, but suffer he does. Others voice to Job their belief in a rule-bound God: "Does God pervert justice?" asks one. But of course God does do precisely that, or, rather, he stands above human norms of justice. It is human self-righteousness that leads people to challenge God: "Will you condemn me that you may be justified?" answers God out of a whirlwind (40 Job v.8). The point of the story is to show the reader or listener someone who loses everything and yet keeps his faith—and finally understands the total power of God and his demand for total submission to him.

The Book of Job offers to those who read it a sense that their own suffering is not to be argued with but accepted. This acceptance may provide a psychologically powerful, perhaps comforting way to survive suffering. One finds similar narratives in other religions. For many Muslims, the story of the martyrdom of Husain at the Battle of Karbala plays this role. The story concerns how Husain, the grandson of the prophet Muhammad, died through treachery in battle. The story is important to those Muslims who believe that Muhammad's descendants are his rightful successors. Every year, these Muslims, called the *Shi'i,* or "Shiites," celebrate Husain's martyrdom as an enacted narrative of their own suffering, and their position today as a minority within the Muslim world. Processions in which Husain rides his horse through large crowds of celebrants, while some beat themselves bloody with sticks or chains, dramatize and religiously contextualize suffering (Waugh 1977).

Some Christians stage similar reenactments of Christ's suffering on his way to crucifixion. In some societies people volunteer to play the role of the crucified Christ, enduring great suffering as they are hung from crosses. These "Passion plays," public dramatization of suffering and death, remind the faithful of the human drama captured in the phrase, "he died for your sins."

Each of these stories and reenactments represents suffering as part of a broader framework, one that transcends human societies but also adds meaning to human societies. We can see these stories as several responses among many to the general human problem of how to endure suffering. They can enable us to place our own problems "in perspective."

Religion Explained by Emotions

Other social theorists have based their approaches to religion more completely in psychology than did Weber. Although the notion that religion springs from emotions is ancient, an important modern argument along these lines came from David Hume, the philosopher of the Scottish Enlightenment. In his *Natural History of Religion* (1757), Hume argued that religion first came from "the incessant hopes and fears which actuate the human mind." Religion thus offers one way of overcoming anxiety.

This idea was given ethnographic substance by Bronislaw Malinowski (1884–1942), one of the first anthropologists to carry out long-term fieldwork. Malinowski worked in the Trobriand Islands, today part of Papua New Guinea, between 1915 and 1918. He distinguished between the practical, rational knowledge and skills that Trobrianders employ to carry out their everyday tasks and the religion and magic they call on to supplement their knowledge and powers. Ideas about the afterlife help people live despite their knowledge that death awaits them, wrote Malinowski, and funeral rituals add further authority to the idea that something awaits them after death. These rituals and ideas "save man from a surrender to death and destruction" (1954 [1925], 51). Ideas about the powers of spells and prayer to change the world also serve a psychological function; they reduce the anxiety that comes from uncertainty, allowing people to carry on their practical life. Religion and magic are thus not pseudosciences; rather, they arise in response to deep-seated, innate human fears and concerns.

Malinowski was influenced by the psychologist William James (1842–1910) as well as by David Hume. In his *Varieties of Religious Experience* (1972 [1901–1902]), James defined religion in terms of a set of individual human attitudes, as "the feelings, acts, and experiences of individual men in their solitude, so far as they apprehend themselves to stand in relation to whatever they may consider the divine." James advocated *pragmatism* in philosophy and science; in his version of this approach, the experiences one accumulates, whether in the laboratory or in everyday life, are the basis for deciding about truth and falsehood. Since belief in God works toward the general good, it is "true." Religious beliefs are validated when they are shown to have beneficial consequences, such as reducing anxiety and fear.

References today to innate or unconscious psychological impulses usually draw on the writings of Sigmund Freud (1856–1939), the founder of modern psychoanalysis. Freud argued that the psyche was more than the conscious. Powerful drives for self-preservation and pleasure often shape our actions and conscious ideas in ways of which we are only half-aware. These drives in the individual run headlong into societal norms, creating repression and neuroses. Freud's (1930) views on religion were negative. Born of infantile feelings of helplessness and society-caused suffering, religion only keeps us from rationally critiquing and rebuilding our social lives, he wrote. But Freud's ideas about the power of religious symbols have been used by some anthropologists to explain why certain objects—hair, the color white, blood—have the frequent and powerful positions they do in religious ritual.

Other theorists and historians of religion have taken up the issue of how and why certain symbols have widespread power. Among them are theorists who stress the irreducible nature of religious experience. Carl Jung (1875–1961), a student of Freud, saw religion as an experience of awe at the power of the divine, a submission to a superior power that is later codified into doctrines and rituals. Jung followed William James and the theologian Rudolf Otto in finding the truth of religion in these religious experiences. But Jung then postulated a "collective unconscious" of humankind that contains all religious symbols. These symbols stem from "archetypes" that are innate in every human being, and that make possible the translation of religious experiences across persons and cultures. These archetypes—the hero, the earth mother, gods—form the basis of the universal religious experience.

Also viewing religion in terms of archetypes is Mircea Eliade, born in Romania in 1907. Eliade exemplifies the "phenomenological" study of religion, that is, bracketing what we think we know of the external world to focus our study on experience itself as an irreducible phenomenon. For Eliade (1954 [1949]), religious objects, acts, and roles are symbols that have multiple meanings, but that eventually come together in a cosmological unity. This unity is mainly about the primordial creation of the universe. Eliade examines myths and rituals from many societies, interpreting each as fundamentally about the creation of life, order, and the world. The view of religion in terms of universal archetypes has become even more popular through the writings of Joseph Campbell (1949) on myth. As with Tylor's intellectualist approach, however, this approach points to broad patterns but is unable to provide an analytical foundation for understanding specificities: how people have come to create and understand particular religious forms in particular times and places.

Symbols between Society and the Individual

Among anthropologists seeking to integrate sociological and psychological dimensions of religious practices was Victor Turner, whose work has focused on symbols and meanings. Turner is attentive to unconscious meanings and near-universal symbols, but he emphasizes the ways that ritual and social uses of symbolic objects shape their meanings for particular people.

Turner (1967) analyzes the meaning of symbols from three distinct perspectives. He begins by asking how members of the society explain a ritual or unpack the meaning of a statue. He then asks how objects are used in ritual processes and in interpreting their use. Finally, he examines the place of the object in a system of symbols. The meanings he derives from these three perspectives themselves are arrayed between two poles: one around which cluster meanings that relate to general human emotions and desires, especially those of a natural or physiological sort, and a second pole of social norms and values.

Turner's most famous symbolic analysis illustrates this process. His ethnographic work was done among the Ndembu of Zambia, a society organized around matriliny, that is, the continuity between mothers and children. When a girl reaches puberty, the Ndembu hold an initiation ceremony, during which they wrap the girl in a blanket and place her at the foot of a tree, the *mudyi*, known for its white latex. This ritual is thus known as a "white" ritual.

Turner understood the "native symbolic meaning" of the symbols largely from many discussions with one "key informant," a man named Muchona. Based on these discussions, he concluded that the tree stands for human milk, for the ties between the girl and her mother, and for the principle of ties through women more generally. These meanings seem consistent with other Ndembu statements and practices, although discussions with a broader range of Ndembu men and women might have introduced a greater diversity of meanings into the analysis.

These symbolic meanings include both physiological and social poles: aspects of the human body and of social institutions. Turner then considers the way the tree is used in ritual practices, and here he finds several distinct meanings: in one event the tree is the center for all-female activities from which the men are excluded (meaning of women versus men); in other contexts it is associated with the girl undergoing initiation.

Finally, Turner examines the broader system of symbols, and finds this tree to be one among several trees that are used in ritual activities, each associated with white, red, or black. Each color calls forth associations with natural substances: black with putrification and feces, red with blood, white with milk and semen. Although these associations are "natural" in the sense that blood is indeed red, the values placed on these associations are cultural and relatively arbitrary. Is blood good? Powerful? Polluting? The Ndembu highlight certain values and play down others. Red is linked to power and wealth; black is linked to pollution and disease; white is linked to purity and life. They then can interpret the value of various ritual and medicinal objects in terms of this color scheme. Medicines made from the "white" mudyi tree, for example, aid a woman having difficulties breastfeeding.

For the Ndembu, then, the three primary colors provide a template for much of social life, just as do the four cardinal directions for the Zuni. Turner's account of religious ritual situates the ritual in its matrilineal social context, analyzes the Ndembu explanations of rituals and symbols, and considers the emotional power of Ndembu ritual associations. Other anthropologists, for example Gananath Obeyesekere (1981), emphasize the ways that personal, sometimes unconscious meanings of key symbols in a culture shape the lives of individuals. For these and other writers, symbols are studied for their roles in the lives of individuals in particular societies.

3

Ideas and Practices of "Religion" in Europe and Elsewhere

Most people living in Europe or North America are used to thinking about religions as sets of formal beliefs or doctrines. Christian denominational differences, for example, have developed largely from debates about doctrine. A Christian may ask someone who practices another religion: What do you believe?, and not mean, What particular things do you as an individual believe? but, What are the shared beliefs sanctified in your religion? (Many from Muslim and Jewish backgrounds would ask the same question.)

And yet, the relationship between doctrines and religious lives is quite complex in Western as well as in other societies. This chapter considers the genealogy of Western ideas about the nature of religion. Only relatively recently have people in Western societies seen the world as composed of distinct religions, each with its own set of beliefs. The rise of this idea has colored the way Europeans have understood other religions.

We also explore how Japan illustrates very different ideas about religions in practice. People in Japan freely combine elements of more than one religion to resolve problems of everyday life. However, the issue of religion's definition recently has become highly politicized, as people fiercely debate whether Shinto practices form a religion or a state ideology.

Western Ideas of Religion

For most of Western history, religion was regarded as an individual's personal piety or faith. People did not write books about religion, but about faith, on the one hand, and the institutions of the church, on the other.

The word *religion* comes from the Latin word *religio,* whose early meaning appears to have been a power outside the individual, or a feeling relative to such a power. *Religiosus* meant a powerful place and conveyed a sense of mystery. The term also came to refer to the particular pattern of worship, the *religiones,* that was due a certain god (W. C. Smith 1978, 19–31).

The early leaders of the Christian Church adopted these usages from the Romans. Roman authorities forced the early Christians to participate in the traditional Roman cultic ceremonies. If they refused they often were put to death. So, the key issue about religion was how to worship: the Roman way or exclusively the Christian way. This focus on one's own religious rituals as opposed to those of other people gave rise to a new sense of the plural: our way of worship (*nostra religio*) as opposed to the *religiones* of outsiders. In this context the phrase "the Christian religion" was often used to mean the Eucharist, the central ritual performed by people considering themselves Christians.

The concept of religion might then have developed into its current meaning, as a term used to refer to the system of beliefs and practices of each of a number of societies. But it did not develop in this way, and the word religion itself virtually passed out of existence for a thousand years. (An exception is St. Augustine, whose *De Vera Religione* we might translate as "On Proper Piety"; it concerned the bond between an individual and God and not a system of beliefs and practices.)

Despite the general impression, true in many ways, that the European Middle Ages were an age of religion, it appears that no one ever wrote a book using "religion" in the title or as a concept during this period. Not until the fifteenth century, during the Renaissance, was the term taken up again, and then with the sense of a universal capacity for piety and worship common to all human beings. There was to be only one kind of *religio,* but it would exist in different degrees in different people.

The Reformation continued this line of thought; both Martin Luther and John Calvin stressed the importance of individual piety and faith over and against any external religious system, by which they meant the Catholic Church. Luther inveighed against any "false religion," or putting faith in religion rather than in God. Indeed, Luther inaugurated a tradition in the German language of avoiding the term "religion" altogether in favor of *Gottesdienst,* "service to God" (W. C. Smith 1978, 35).

Religion as a Belief System

The idea of religion as a system of beliefs, as opposed to personal piety, did not take hold until the seventeenth century. The change was partly the result of efforts during the Enlightenment to classify and understand the world as a schema, accessible by the intellect. It was also because of a growing diversity of religious claims within Europe and the increased awareness, because of trade and travel, of religious traditions beyond Europe. By the eighteenth century, treatises on religions of the world (introducing religious pluralism) began to appear. The plural "religions" is possible only when we think of religion as a cultural system rather than a person one. There are no plural forms for piety, reverence, or obedience.

As Europeans began to study other religions, they tended to use the religions most familiar to them, namely Judaism and Christianity, as a general model. They assumed all religions would have three central elements: a central text, exclusivity, and separation. The central text was assumed to be a collection of doctrines or beliefs that all adherents shared, ideally, written in a sacred book that had been inspired by a god or gods.

Exclusivity meant that a person was a member of one and only one religion, at least at any one time. Separation indicated that religion constituted an area of social life distinct from politics or economics. The idea of separation developed in modern Western Europe, partly in response to the destructive religious wars of the seventeenth century. John Locke, writing in the late seventeenth century, advocated the separation of state and religion as a way of ensuring toleration and religious freedom. His argument became the basis for the principle of separation of church and state in the United States; nowhere else was it so fully realized.

While this model of religion worked well to describe European practices, it fit poorly with religions of India, China, and Japan. No one book provides a shared creed for practitioners of religion in these societies; instead, each contains a large number of books written on diverse aspects of life and on teachers and organizations of followers. Today we know these collections of texts and teachers under the general rubrics of *Hinduism, Buddhism, Taoism,* or *Shinto,* but these labels are modern inventions.

Nor does the idea of exclusivity fit with norms in these societies. In Japan, for example, people routinely bring offerings to shrines dedicated to local gods (practices associated with the label *Shinto*) and, in the same temple complex, venerate Buddha. The same people may marry in a Christian church. The idea of a separate religious sphere is also alien to many other religious traditions. Muslims, for example, argue that all of life should be conducted in accord with God's commands. Hinduism involves ideas of purity and pollution that permeate all social life.

Other Religions, Other Models

*M*odern attempts to understand these other religions have been based on the European model. By the nineteenth century, books appeared about other religions, introducing for the first time the names that we use today. *Buddhism* was first used in 1801, *Hinduism* in 1829. (Before then writers referred, more accurately, to "the wisdom of the Japanese" or "Hindu teachings.") The term *Islam* also began to be used; previously, Europeans referred to *Muhammadism,* treating Islam not as a religion, but as allegiance to a false prophet (W. C. Smith 1978, 51–79).

The nineteenth-century European notions of what counted as a religion have powerfully shaped how other religions and other countries have viewed religion. For, with few exceptions, the creation of terms for *religion* and for particular religions have been the result of Western, Christian influence.

Take what we often refer to as Hinduism. In India today, religious practice and the precise formulations of doctrine vary from place to place. Indeed, it is a central tenet of religious teaching in India that one should follow the inspiration derived from one's teacher in pursuit of enlightenment. Thus, there is not, nor is there supposed to be, one single formulation of Hindu Religion.

The word *Hindu* itself was not used by ancient Indians to refer to their religion. It is a word meaning "river," and in particular is used as the proper name for the Indus River. Foreigners—Greeks, then Muslim conquerors—came to designate the people living near that river as "Indian" or "Hindu." Under Muslim rule, the term came to be used to refer to all non-Muslims in the country and included Buddhists and Jains. Only recently has *Hindu* been used as a residual term to designate those people, and their beliefs, who are residents of India but who are not Jains, not Sikhs, not Christians, not Muslims, and not animists. But in the 1980s and 1990s some politicians made the creation of a "Hindu India" their party platform, and they succeeded in rallying large numbers of supporters to their cause. Whatever was once the case, today "Hindu" is experienced by many Indians as a unitary social as well as religious category (see Chapter 15).

Consider the Chinese who have traditionally had no word corresponding to the Western idea of religion. They borrowed a word from the Japanese, *Tsung-Chiao*, which the Japanese themselves had created to accommodate the Western concept. Nor did they have words meaning Confucianism, Buddhism, or Taoism in the sense of religions that one joined or left. Instead, people were aware of collections of teachings that could be followed in trying to find a path toward truth; these teachings included the sayings of Confucius, Buddha, and Lao Tse (a possibly mythic figure who urged followers to find the true path, or Tao).

In a rather neat exchange of terms, the Japanese borrowed the word used to refer to indigenous traditions, *shinto,* from the Chinese. In fact the term was first used by foreigners to refer to local practices. The Japanese today use a translation of this term—*kami no michi,* or "the way of the spirits or gods"—to refer to these practices (Reader 1991, 23). The definitions of what is included in "religion" are of much public interest in Japan today. At the end of the nineteenth century, the Japanese government declared that the indigenous, or Shinto, worship at shrines was not a religion. But what came to be called State Shinto, to which the cult of the emperor was central, became an ideological pillar of twentieth-century Japanese efforts to modernize society, and for that reason the cult was abolished under the post–World War II Occupation.

The boundaries of religion were again debated when the new emperor, Akihito, succeeded his father, Hirohito, in January 1989. According to Shinto creed, the emperor is the descendant of the Sun Goddess, and he performs certain rituals at the goddess's shrine when he takes office. Are these rituals to be taken as religious? If so, they imply his claim to be the chief priest of Shinto and the intermediary to the Sun Goddess. But this status was abolished under the occupation, in the Constitution. Are they perhaps just political ritual? There was a fierce debate in Japan over this question, and the matter (which we consider in the next section) remains unsettled.

The names for religions were often provided by outsiders—one can add to the preceding examples that the term *Judaism* is Greek, not Hebrew. The name *Islam,* used from the beginning by the religion's adherents, is the major exception. However, the term means "submission to God," not the set of beliefs and practices themselves. Indeed, the religious scholar Wilfred Cantwell Smith (1978, 114) has argued that if one believes in God as a Jew or Christian, and realizes that from an Islamic perspective Muslims, Christians, and Jews worship the same God, then one cannot truthfully say in Arabic, "I am not a Muslim." One submits to God, after all, in whatever language.

Imposed Definitions of Religion

Even as religions differ in what they include in the definition of "religion," many modern states in Asia, Africa, and Latin America have drawn their ideas of religion from Western, Christian, and, to some extent, Islamic, models. They adhere to a model of religion that does not fit with local beliefs and practices of some peoples within their borders, and may place pressure on them to conform to this model.

Let us turn to Indonesia to consider these problems of state-imposed definitions of religion. Indonesia, the world's fourth largest country, has about 200 million people living on thousands of islands and speaking more than 300 distinct languages. About 85 percent of the people call themselves Muslim, and the remaining 15 percent includes important Christian and Buddhist minorities as well as practitioners of indigenous religions.

The Indonesian government has "belief in one God" as one of the planks of its ideology. The state defines religion as having a sacred book, a monotheistic foundation, exclusive boundaries (such that one person cannot belong to two religions at the same time), and as transcending ethnic boundaries (rather than being essentially an aspect of a hereditary culture).

This model came by way of several large-scale religions. In the early centuries of the present era, rulers adopted the symbols and ideas of Hinduism and Buddhism, sometimes both together. The Indonesian word for religion, *agama,* comes from the Sanskrit, and means "text." The agama of a person was the set of texts from which he or she derived teaching and religious direction: the books of Hinduism, Buddhism, Islam, or others. The idea of a central text does not require that the religion have exclusive boundaries; that idea came later, in the fourteenth through sixteenth centuries, when many rulers began converting to Islam. Islam does insist on absolute exclusivity and on the idea of one and only one true foundational text, the Qur'ân. Christianity, brought to Indonesia at about the same time, shares these ideas.

By the time of Indonesian independence, then, the major religions supported this model of religion. The state decreed that everyone should belong to one of five religions: Catholicism, Protestantism, Islam, Hinduism, or Buddhism. (Confucianism has enjoyed an ambiguous status in these decrees.) One might be surprised to hear that Hinduism, with its many, vividly represented deities, stood for monotheism; the Indonesian resolution of this problem—supported by some Hindus—was to declare that the various Hindu gods were all manifestations of a single absolute deity.

Today, any Indonesians who practice local religions that do not conform to the official model are pressured to join one of the state-recognized religions, although this pressure has begun to ease since the fall of President Suharto in 1998. Those who do not convert may be accused of being atheists and therefore communists, a dangerous label in this strongly anti-communist state. So defining one's religion is a matter of great concern, and for some a matter of sheer survival (Kipp and Rodgers 1987).

What do people who practice other religions do? Some nominally convert but retain some older practices, such as ways of healing that involve calling on spirits to possess a healer and speak through him or her. Other people work to have their indigenous practices counted as a world religion, usually as Hindu. In one such case, a group of people on the island of Sulawesi did manage to become recognized as Hindus, despite the fact that there were few resemblances, other than a few words of Sanskrit, between their religion and anything practiced in India. A problem arose when one member of this group was elected to the local parliament. Members of parliament need to be sworn in on "their book." So what was this fellow's scripture? Well, because the book had to be Hindu, as the group's practices were called that, the parliament wrote to a Hindu association in Jakarta asking for their book. The association sent along a book in Sanskrit (I could not determine what book it was), and the new member was duly sworn in using it. Appearances were saved, and the religion's credentials established: they had a Book.

Wana Practices and Indonesian Definitions

Some people reshape their indigenous ideas in response to state pressures to convert. The 5,000 Wana people of Sulawesi, described by the anthropologist Jane Monnig Atkinson (1987, 1989), practice forms of divination and shamanism, and their ideas about spirits and possession surface in many domains of everyday life. They do not have a distinct domain called "religion."

Central to Wana efforts at dealing with the spiritual domain are the performances called *mabolong*. These rituals of possession and healing are performed by shamans, ritual experts who are possessed by spirits. Shamans are called on to perform mabolong when someone is ill and requires supernatural assistance. Often many people attend these performances. The shaman is invited to feast from a tray of food, and he in turn invites his "spirit familiars" to join him in enjoying the food. He then asks these spirits to discover what is ailing a patient, to rid the patient of foreign objects, and to go with him on a spirit voyage to recover souls or dream spirits that the patient has lost.

Shamans have greater inner powers, and they draw on these powers to keep people healthy and to increase their own social standing. They are heroes in their community. Indeed, they often create new social communities as people seek to live near them. It is in these rituals performed by shamans that ordinary humans engage the spirit world. The Wana have no written texts that prescribe doctrines or beliefs, and their narratives concerning the spirit world are many and varied. What brings their diverse ideas and stories together is collective attendance at shamanic rituals.

But Wana also face intense pressure from Muslim officials and from Christian missionaries to convert to a state-recognized religion, an agama. Wana come into contact with Muslim peoples living on the coast and serving as local state officials, and, more recently, Christian converts living in other upland regions.

As they have come to understand what is meant by agama, some Wana have constructed their own ideas of what their religion must be. These constructions are not about healing and possession, but about what distinguishes Wana from Muslims and Christians: diet, burial practices, and ties to government among them. Most saliently, Wana are people who, unlike Muslims, do eat pig, and, also unlike Muslims, kill chickens by wringing their necks rather than slaughtering them by knife.

Wana have also constructed a set of beliefs along the lines of Muslim and Christian beliefs, but distinct from them. They claim, for example, that they have a single God and

Wana shaman during possession at a healing session, Indonesia. (COURTESY OF JANE ATKINSON.)

that this God is the same as the Muslim and Christian creator. They recently invented a heaven that corresponds to the images of heaven taught them by Muslims and Christians but reverses those groups' teachings about the destiny of the Wana. In the Wana notions, Wana lead poor lives on earth and therefore they will have the best places in heaven. Muslims, by contrast, they believe, will live in pig excrement because they avoid it here. Christians will have only scraps of clouds to eat (an idea probably derived from pictures of Jesus in the clouds in Bible schools).

Most Wana have so far resisted conversion, but even in resisting they have transformed their religion in accord with the dominant, ultimately Western, model of proper religion.

Combining Religious Practices in Japan

*J*apan illustrates an orientation toward religion that contrasts with that which developed in the West. Japanese freely blend elements from indigenous practices, state-inspired Shinto, and the traditions of Buddhism, Confucianism, and Taoism. There has been little or no religious inspiration for "purism." One common saying sums up the division of labor as "born Shinto, die Buddhist," referring to the daily appeals to Shinto spirits during one's lifetime, and the Buddhist priest's responsibility for carrying out funeral rites (Reader 1991). Marriages are increasingly conducted in Christian style, and many Japanese consult practitioners of the New Religions for solutions to recurring illnesses. These sects themselves combine ideas and practices from many sources, including Hinduism, Japanese nativist writings about racial superiority, and indigenous healing practices. To take an extreme example: it seemed not at all unusual or striking to Japanese that the Aum Shinrikyo sect responsible for the 1995 nerve gas attack in Tokyo combined Buddhist and Hindu texts.

Practice and Belief

About 65 percent of Japanese people have told survey-takers in repeated surveys that they have no religious beliefs (compared to fewer than 10 percent in the United States). Only 20 percent to 30 percent say they believe in the existence of spirits (*kami*) or in souls of the dead. But 76 percent of these respondents have in their homes either a Shinto altar devoted to kami, or a Buddhist one devoted to the souls of the dead; 45 percent have both. Eighty-nine percent say they visit the graves of their ancestors to pray for them (Reader 1991, 5–12).

These results are very puzzling to Western readers if we assume that people think of their beliefs as governing their practices. One problem is with the word *religion,* which in Japanese is *shukyo,* a word originally devised to answer pesky missionaries who asked Japanese to state what their religion was. It was taken to refer to a separate set of beliefs, removed from everyday life, and not to some everyday activity like stopping for a moment at a shrine to make an offering. Thus, asking someone in Japan if he or she has a religion or religious beliefs is something like asking a person in the United States if he or she is a member of a religious movement, a question that would elicit denials from many churchgoers.

Many students of Japanese culture have also emphasized that ideas about beliefs and morality are more focused on specific events and situations than is true for European cultures. Anecdotes from World War II relate how Japanese prisoners of war, having just been bent on killing Allied troops, suddenly became model prisoners of war. In their eyes, the situation had changed and so had their responsibilities.

Finally, a pragmatic try-it-and-see attitude underlies the approach taken by many Japanese toward religious ritual. This approach emphasizes the importance of sincerity for the ritual to work, but not a general "belief," and certainly not an exclusive commitment to that religion and no other. It is thus relatively easy, within the Japanese religious world view, to try a new healing religion without abandoning offerings to household spirits and Buddhist deities. This willingness to participate in more than one religion lies behind the common practice of declaring oneself to census takers as both Buddhist and Shinto, marrying in a Protestant church, and attending sessions of a healing sect to seek a cure for an illness. And it is evident in figures about religious membership: about 75 percent of the population are classified as Buddhist by the government, 95 percent as Shinto, and over 10 percent as members of new religious movements (Reader 1991, 6). Japanese do affiliate with religious organizations, and usually more than one.

Perhaps, then, answers to surveys underplay the extent to which Japanese assume that there are spirits at work in the world. It would appear that the practices of keeping an altar at home and reciting prayers for one's ancestors at graveside imply such a set of beliefs. And yet haven't we all engaged in practices for which we are unsure of whether we agree with the associated doctrines? Modern Western religious culture emphasizes the importance of believing in the doctrines behind practices, in the paramount importance of creeds of faith, and this emphasis may make it quite difficult for some people in the United States, for example, to deny belief in God to a survey-taker, whatever his or her doubts might be. Japanese religious culture does not make this same emphasis; consequently, denying the belief while going along with the practice may be easier for the Japanese person than for the American.

This religious–cultural emphasis on practices over doctrines makes it easier for Japanese to combine elements from different religious traditions, as we see in later chapters. First we can explore the roles played by two major traditions—Shintoism and Buddhism—and how people's actions may imply their belief in a proposition about the spiritual world without them directly expressing that belief.

Shinto and Spirits

Basic to the Japanese Shinto tradition are spirits, or *kami* (Earhart 1982), which are located in specific places in the empirical world: in a boulder, or a house, or a shrine. One Japanese estimate is that there are "eight million spirits"—meaning they are innumerable. When foreigners asked Japanese to name their religion, in order to distinguish it from Buddhism, they called it "the way of the *kami*," although it came to be called Shinto in the West (Reader 1991).

The term *kami* refers both to the sense of power felt in things of the world, and to particular spirits. A waterfall is a powerful kami; calling it a kami communicates the sense an observer has of its immense power. Space may also contain kami and may be demarcated by rocks, or by a shrine with boundaries and a gateway. One sees these *torii*, Shinto gateways, with two pillars and one or two crossbeams, throughout Japan and in many U.S. cities. A Japanese rock garden works similarly, demarcating a sparsely filled space rather than, as in European-style ornamental gardens, featuring a dense collection of plants. Although kami can be anywhere, they are not everywhere; these boundaries serve to separate the sacred from the profane.

Perhaps the most important spirits are those in the house. They occupy particular places and protect the members of the household when in those places: the god of the kitchen lives in the kitchen, the latrine god in the latrine, and so forth. There is also a guardian deity of the household as a whole; this spirit is made up of many ancestors who have merged to guard the household as a corporate unit that exists over time. The village has a guardian deity, often a fox god or an ancestor of a founding member. The village, like the household, is a corporate group, with control over irrigation, cooperative use of some land, and religious festivals. Villagers will ask the village god for help in their rice harvest or for success in schooling. Village elites once controlled the shrine festivals for the village gods, but today, with many villagers engaged in urban pursuits, their importance has diminished.

Temple complex near Narita, Japan, with Shinto and Buddhist shrines, and shops selling amulets, books, and other items. (COURTESY OF J. BOWEN.)

Also important to everyday life is the spirit of a rice field. This spirit lives a dual existence, as the figure of Inari, the rice deity, and also as the spirit guarding each particular field. Spirits of the fields and of rice live in the mountains and come down in the spring when the soil is tilled. They guard over the rice, and return to the mountains in the fall after the harvest. They are sometimes represented as fox spirits, probably because foxes, also associated with rice, sexuality, and fertility, were thought to come down from the mountains in spring.

People create new spirits as needed. When the Tennis Players' Association was created in Japan before World War II, someone suggested the creation of a new god, to be named "Heavenly God of Speedy Ball." And in a less individuated way, all equipment, from computer chips to cameras to automobile production machinery, are thought to have a spiritual side. The machines are blessed by a Shinto priest before they are used, and in 1990 engineers met at Tokyo's Chomeiji temple to thank their used-up equipment for the service it had given them. Photographs of the cameras and video recorders were burned as a Buddhist priest chanted verses. Even in the electronics industry Shinto and Buddhism are mixed (Sanger 1990).

Kami can also be the spirits of deceased persons. Sometime famous people will become deified as kami and have shrines built to them, but for a mixture of reasons. One ninth-century court official, for example, had died at the hands of his rivals for power. As a spirit he wreaked havoc with their lives until they built a shrine to him.

Spirits and Social Change

Japanese relationships to spirits developed in a civilization centered on enduring social units: the household, the village, and the Imperial House. Household spirits stood for the continuity of the household over generations. Households in a village were protected by community spirits. And everyone was under the protection of the unbroken imperial line, itself said to come from the Sun Goddess and dating at least back to the seventh century C.E. Although these continuities have been disrupted by massive migrations to cities, older orientations toward spirits of the collectivity—including the emperor and his temples—continue in Japan.

Many kami are venerated in shrines, and some shrines, such as the great shrine at Ise to the Sun Goddess, are the focus of national veneration. The Ise shrine is rebuilt every 20 years as part of a cycle of national renewal of life and fertility; the last rebuilding, in 1993, was widely publicized by banners erected throughout Japan.

Parents routinely take their newborn babies to the local shrine to be placed under the care of the spirit guarding the local community. An offering is placed on the altar, and the shrine priest says prayers requesting these blessings. In the older, agrarian world in which Japanese religions developed, they also would have carried out rites at this

Worship at a shrine, Narita temple complex, Japan. (COURTESY OF J. BOWEN.)

shrine to ensure the fertility of the crops. The shrine also served as the place for community meetings and recreational activities; it was thus the center of social life. Often the community shrine was said to be a branch shrine of a famous national shrine, such as that at Ise. Performing rituals at the shrine thus linked the individual to the community and the nation–state.

Since World War II, Japanese have flooded from country to city and from farming to other occupations. In 1950, 62 percent of all Japanese families lived in rural areas, and fully 50 percent of those rural families were full-time farmers. Just 30 years later, in 1980, only 24 percent of families lived in rural areas, and only 10 percent of these families still engaged in full-time farming. This rapid shift in population has meant that a civilization and a set of religious practices that had developed around stable rural households now had to be modified for urban living. But Shinto shrines have been part of this transformation. People who commute to the city from suburbs or rural areas still visit the shrines to seek blessings for their babies and seek further spirit protection for young children, though now they may dress in Western-style clothes and record the occasions with expensive video cameras.

People living in the cities may return to their ancestral villages for harvest festivals and for the New Year's festival, when they acquire new amulets from the shrines to protect their homes during the coming year. For two years Ian Reader (1991, 61–64) watched proceedings at the Katano shrine midway between the cities of Osaka and Kyoto in what has become a commuter village. He records that on festival days, hundreds of people took trains from both cities to the shrine to seek blessings and purchase amulets. A shrine priest could call on office girls to work as temporary "shrine maidens" on these occasions; at one festival, Reader found himself being blessed by one of his own students who had been engaged to work as such a shrine maiden during the holidays. Businesses sent rice, or sake, to be placed on the altar for blessings (and afterward quickly consumed by visitors). The same priest was called upon to bless a new university building nearby. He had a temporary altar to the shrine spirit constructed inside the new building for the occasion.

Increased ease of transport has meant that Japanese increasingly visit the more famous shrines in larger cities. Several million people visit these shrines each year, while some rural shrines, those not on commuter lines and unable to afford priests, have closed. The social ties affirmed by attending a shrine are less and less local and increasingly national in scope.

Buddhism and Souls

Most of the people frequenting these shrines with their newborns, or at festivals, also participate in rituals drawn from Buddhism (Saunders 1964). The Buddhist religion began in the sixth century B.C.E. in South Asia, when the historical Buddha, Siddhartha of the clan Gautama, found enlightenment after long meditation. The followers of Buddha also seek enlightenment; his teachings provide examples and practices to follow rather than creeds to which followers must adhere.

In South Asia, Buddhism diverged into two major streams. One, called "Theravada" ("the elders") emphasizes the role of the monastic community in mediating between laypersons and Buddha. This stream spread from Sri Lanka to mainland Southeast Asia. The second stream was called "Mahayana," or "Greater Vehicle," for its universalistic approach to salvation. In this stream, individuals are encouraged to engage in practices that lead to their salvation and to enter directly into contact with Buddhas and other deities.

The Mahayana stream of Buddhism spread northward from India through Tibet and China. Japanese scholars learned about Buddhism in China, and for that reason Japanese Buddhism adopts the Mahayana orientation. Mahayana Buddhism emphasizes the illusory character of the world and orients the individual toward a transcendent reality in which he or she might achieve salvation. One sees this emphasis in paintings, where individual Buddhas are depicted floating above the world we live in, transcendent of its specific concreteness. These diverse Buddhas—Fudo, Amida, Maitreya—provide multiple sources of divine aid and multiple paths for individuals to seek salvation.

Each of the several major schools of Buddhism in Japan—Zen, Shingon, Nichiren, and others—combines a set of spiritual disciplines that lead to salvation (Reader 1991). They all evince a special concern for death and treatment of ancestors. Zen Buddhism, the best known in the West of these schools, emphasizes meditation. Indeed, the word *Zen* itself means "meditation." Zen teachers point to the example set by the historical Buddha, Gautama, who achieved enlightenment in this world by sitting and meditating. Zen practitioners may use *koan,* problems that appear unsolvable, as a way of breaking down the barriers that everyday linear thinking places in the path to enlightenment. They practice together in communities of meditators, engaging in strenuous physical labor—scrubbing floors, chopping wood—as additional aids to enlightenment. Laypeople may participate in retreats at Zen temples, and businesses routinely send their employees on special retreats that incorporate some of the austerities of temple life.

Japanese Buddhism's emphasis on individual meditation and enlightenment provides a counterpoint in religious practice to the overall Japanese cultural emphasis on the value and continuity of the group. But Buddhism also adapted itself to those values by assuming responsibility for the care of family ancestors. Even if they have no other contact with Buddhism, and would not state that they believe in Buddha, most Japanese "die Buddhist," that is, their children or other relatives seek out the service of a Buddhist priest to perform a funeral service. The main activity at most temples is in fact not meditation but performing memorial services for the dead. Most Japanese households are affiliated with a particular temple for this purpose.

Before Buddhism, Japanese people considered that each person's soul traveled to a world of the dead, where it continued to watch and intervene in the lives of its relatives. People carried out rituals designed to ease the transition to the other world and to keep the spirits happy. When Buddhism came to Japan, people saw the priests as possessing spiritual powers due to their activities of meditation. They began to call on those priests to perform the funeral ceremonies. Priests added new practices to the rituals, practices designed to guide the spirit toward enlightenment after death. The priest and his associates cremate the body to rid the soul of its impurities, and chant Buddhist texts and prayers to lead the soul toward the state of enlightenment. The word for dead soul, *hotoke,* also means a Buddha.

These ancestors continue to affect the lives of their kin, and both Buddhist priests and practitioners of New Religions are concerned with keeping the ancestors happy and resolving problems that occur when they are not. (See Chapter 7 for an example.)

Buddhism coexists with Shinto in Japan. The temple complex at Nara, which I visited in 1994, contains both Buddhist temples and Shinto shrines, and visitors stop at both. Temples may include images of kami alongside those of a Buddha, although the former are said to no longer contain spirits but only to represent them. The two kinds of entities are represented in clearly contrasting ways. In paintings, for example, kami are depicted in a realistic manner as specific, human-looking personages, sometimes identifiable as historical figures, and always standing near or on the place with which they are associated. Buddhas and bodhisattvas, by contrast, are abstract in their appearance, and not confined to specific spaces. Often they are painted as floating above the ground or on clouds.

Two other religious traditions have also influenced Japanese ideas and practices. Taoism (from *tao*, the "way" in Chinese) developed in China as an approach to understanding the way of the universe. Taoism includes methods of divining good or bad days by consulting calendars. Japanese adopted some of these practices—there was even a bureau of divination in early Japan—but no Japanese would identify himself or herself as a Taoist.

Confucianism, based on the teachings of the Chinese philosopher Confucius (551–479 B.C.E.), has played an important role in shaping Japanese social and moral values (Smith 1983, 37–67). Confucius taught that social order and welfare depended on maintaining the proper hierarchical relationships between persons, particularly those of father to son and ruler to subject. In Japan, these ideas strengthened the notion of the family as a corporate entity, with succession passing from father to eldest son, and that of the nation as a family-like entity headed by the hereditary emperor.

The State and Religion

Japan's rulers have added to their legitimacy by drawing on Shinto and Buddhism. The state has variously promoted one or the other of these two complexes of religious ideas and practices. In its encounter with outside cultures and in particular with Christianity, the Japanese state has created indigenous alternatives—systems of ideas and practices that looked like religion as defined in the West.

State promotion of religions began between the sixth and ninth centuries with the adoption of Chinese ideas that the emperor is both divine and the active ruler of society. Just as village guardians often were thought to be the ancestors of the village elite, the emperor declared himself (or herself) the descendant of the Sun Goddess. (These borrowings were a major source of Confucian influence in Japan.)

Scholars began to teach Buddhism in Japan during the Nara period (710–784 C.E.), named after the capital city of Nara. Emperor Shomu (reigned 724–749) quickly made Buddhism the state religion. Buddhism appealed to the emperor and his advisers because it came from China, along with the writing system and ideas of the divinity of the emperor, and also because it could be made the basis of a state-centered system of religious temples, with scriptures and priests. The preexisting religious practices were

Todai temple, Japan, with statue of the Buddha Nyiori. (COURTESY OF JOHN RENARD.)

decentralized, with local spirits and shrines. Buddhism offered the possibility of constructing a religious hierarchy under imperial control.

In 728, the emperor built the Todai temple in Nara (just south of present-day Kyoto) as the first national temple. The statue of Buddha inside the temple, called "Lochana," still stands as the largest Buddhist statue in the world. Lochana, or Dainichi, is the Sun Buddha. When he was building the statue, the emperor had to seek approval from his ancestress, the Sun Goddess Amaterasu, at her temple in Ise. Reportedly the goddess told the emperor that the Sun Buddha was the same as the Sun Goddess, and approved building the statue.

The emperor then ordered two temples built in each province, one as a monastery and one as a nunnery. Monks and nuns were recruited to these temples to recite Buddhist scriptures and accumulate merit, and then to pass on the merit to the nation as a whole. This form of mediated merit was not part of the Mahayana tradition imported by the state; it was created by the emperor for his own project of state building. By venerating the Sun Buddha, the emperor managed to link Buddha to his own Sun Goddess ancestor. By constructing a national temple system, he linked acts of individual merit-making to the welfare of the nation as a whole, and forged a religious connection between the people and the state. But the temples and their priests, particularly at Todai temple, grew more and more powerful, and the decision to move the Imperial capital to Kyoto in 784 was in part to establish a separate power base away from the temple.

In succeeding centuries the influence of state-sponsored Buddhism waned along with the power of the emperor. But in 1600 the warlord (*shogun*) Tokugawa Ieyasu consolidated power throughout Japan, ending the many centuries of political disorder, and reduced the emperor to a figurehead. Ieyasu once again promoted Buddhism as the state religion, building a new hierarchy of temples. All Japanese were required to register at a temple, proclaim their religion, and use the services of Buddhist priests for funeral services. These state actions were not motivated by religious piety but intended to tighten state control and exclude Christianity, as a disruptive, foreign ideology. Thus, Buddhism was promoted as the best alternative to Christianity, as "not-Christianity."

In 1868 a coalition of warlords and a rising economic elite took power in the name of the Emperor Meiji, and sought to reduce the influence of Buddhism because of its association with the old regime. The Meiji Restoration combined economic restructuring with the creation of a cult of the emperor. A hierarchy of Shinto priests was created, and the result has come to be called State Shinto. Shrines were created to appeal to popular opinion. Foremost among these new shrines were Yasukuni, founded in 1869, where those soldiers who have died for the honor of the state are enshrined and deified, and the Meiji shrine, built in 1920 to honor the deceased emperor. Both produced talismans for people to take home with them, and people were also required to have talismans from Ise in their homes (Hardacre 1989, 79–99).

These efforts were meant to create a religious plane on which individual households would be merged into the state. The Confucian values of filial piety were emphasized as well as the common descent of all Japanese, as in the following section from a teacher's manual used in the 1930s:

> *The connection between the Imperial House and its subjects is thus: one forms the main house and the others form the branch house, so that from ancient times we have worshiped the founder of the Imperial House and the heavenly gods. Our relationship to this house is sincerely founded on repaying our debt of gratitude to our ancestors. (quoted in Smith 1983, 32)*

After World War II, the American forces that occupied Japan insisted that the new Constitution remove the aura of divinity from the emperor. The Constitution states that the emperor is not divine, but only "the symbol of the state and of the unity of the people." The Nobel Prize–winning writer Kenzaburo Oe has written of his and others' astonishment when on August 15, 1945, they heard the emperor speak over the radio. "The Emperor speaking to us in a human voice was beyond imagining in any reverie. The Emperor was a god, the authority of the nation, the organizing principle of reality" (Oe 1995, 103).

The Occupation forces also proclaimed Shinto to be a religion and that because people ought to be able to choose their religion freely it could not be taught in the schools or be supported by state funds. And yet despite this new official ideology, the Sun Goddess Amaterasu continues to be worshiped at the great shrine at Ise. Each time the shrine is rebuilt the ancient mirror that is thought to embody the Sun Goddess's spirit is moved into the new shrine. Six and a half million Japanese visit the shrine each year. Japanese visit Ise the way that Jews visit Israel and Muslims visit Mecca, as a journey to a sacred place.

The precise status of Ise and the nature of the emperor's relationship to the Sun Goddess (if any) became major political issues when Emperor Hirohito died in January 1989. At Hirohito's funeral the following month, the Shinto rites were performed behind curtains, evidently so that visiting dignitaries would not have to acknowledge them. Yet many in Japan criticized these proceedings as tantamount to worship of the emperor and thus a violation of the 1946 Constitution.

Then, in November 1990, Hirohito's son and successor, Akihito, was enthroned. Part of the enthronement procedure is the "great food-offering ritual," in which the new emperor offers special foods to the deities of the heaven and earth and performs a ritual of union of sorts (left ambiguous in official accounts) with the Sun Goddess. The last time this ritual had been performed was in 1928, when the emperor was still considered a god. At Ise he still is thought of as the chief priest of Shinto. There was a great deal of protest from those who considered the ritual to be religious, and thus to violate the Constitution's mandate that state and religion be separated (Weisman 1990).

Similar controversy continues to surround the Yasukuni shrine to the war dead. Prime Ministers regularly visit the shrine, located next to the Imperial Palace in central Tokyo, to venerate the war dead, sometimes in their official capacity. In August 1985, Prime Minister Nakasone with his cabinet made an official visit to the shrine to pay tribute to the war dead. But here Japan's difficulty in facing its wartime history surfaced, because major ("Class A") war criminals executed by judgment of the 1946–1948 Tokyo Trial are among the two and a half million people listed as gods in the shrine's record book. Furthermore, the Rape of Nanking is among the events celebrated, a fact that led China to protest this attendance. Protests by many Japanese led Nakasone to forgo additional state visits to the shrine. In July 1996 a new prime minister, Hashimoto, tried again, but he too had to back down after domestic and international protests.

Veterans' groups continue to enshrine and deify the spirits of Japanese soldiers, however. In 1988, the Japanese Supreme Court backed up one such group over the objections of the widow of a soldier about to be deified. She was Protestant and protested that the deification violated her religious beliefs, but the Court claimed that her religion had no bearing on the group's freedom to carry out the ritual. The idea of religious exclusivity—that one religion excludes others—is not part of the Japanese legal tradition (Haberman 1988).

Death practices, indeed, have all along been important elements in the state–religion nexus. The eighth-century ascendancy of Buddhism was accompanied by a change from burial to cremation for emperors and empresses, following Buddhist practice. During the 1600–1868 Tokugawa period, Shinto nationalists were gradually able to reduce Buddhism's official status—after 1654, although burial rites for the imperial family continued to follow Buddhist practices, the bodies were interred rather than cremated. Only at the funeral of Emperor Meiji's father, Komei, in 1867, were all Buddhist elements eliminated from the funeral, and thus one could say that the funeral ushered in the new Shinto-dominated Meiji era. The government prohibited cremation entirely in 1873, as part of its effort to drive out Buddhism, but it was forced to rescind the order as people pointed out that, already, Japan lacked sufficient space to bury intact bodies (*Far Eastern Economic Review,* March 16, 1989, 66–70).

The place of religion in public life, even the definition of what religion is, continues to be the subject of debate in Japan. What *is* clear in Japan is that lines between religions are fuzzy or, rather, that religions are not defined by the individual's exclusive commitment to one set of doctrines as opposed to others. Japan challenges our idea of what religion means for the individual, for the nation, and for the state.

4 *Rituals and the Shaping of Emotions*

Religious practices include those fixed sequences of actions that we often call rituals. People carrying out a religious ritual try to conform to certain rules to get the ritual right. Sometimes they seek a specific end, such as healing, pleasing a deity, or restoring fertility; they perform other rituals out of a general sense of obligation. We will consider these and many other types of rituals in this book, from pilgrimage to prayer to "rituals of rebellion." In this chapter we consider rituals that mark transitions of various kinds, and explore the way such rituals shape, or are motivated by, emotions.

In most, perhaps all, societies people mark transitions or life stages by carrying out certain transition rituals or rites of passage. These rituals often have a religious dimension, and they tend to cluster around several points in the life cycle: birth, puberty, marriage, and death. Rituals that mark the passage into adulthood may involve changes in name, membership in a new society of initiates, bestowal of new social rights and duties, or, in the category of religiously competent persons, conferral of supernatural powers. Death is also ritually represented as a transition in most societies; death rituals are usually intended to ease the passage of the spirit to another social state and possibly to another world.

Many other kinds of rituals are concerned with transitions. The beginning of an agricultural cycle or the succession to an office may be ritually enacted in ways that resemble life-cycle transition rituals. Anthropologists have long noticed that such rituals are often structured in three parts. Transition rituals shift actors out of their normal social roles, into an intermediate or "liminal" stage, and then reintegrate them into society. The liminal period provides a time for experiencing, sharing, and representing emotions or ideas not usual to social life, as well as a time for accomplishing the tasks of the ritual process.

Transition rituals often emphasize the creation of life: new persons, life after death, or the soil's fertility. Initiation rituals that move people from an immature to a mature state are of course directly concerned with reproduction and biological fertility. But funeral rituals also may tie death to the regeneration of life, refocusing attention and emotions on life and fertility rather than death and loss.

Second, the content and sequence of rituals shape specific emotions in the participants. Feelings of grief are given well-specified forms of expression, sometimes a prescribed period of mourning followed by a break from mourning, sometimes the reverse: stoicism followed by an emotional release. The promise of new life gives hope after loss, and rituals that structure time support the notion that humans can control natural processes of growth, maturation, and death.

Finally, transition rituals represent the social order in a particular way, often an idealized or partial way, and often as if the rituals themselves produce or shape the social order. Relations and differences between men and women, or superiors and inferiors, may be projected onto a cosmic plane, or produced in the ritual itself, especially in initiation rituals that create adolescent or adult males and females. Initiations often reveal secrets, the mere possession of which is the basis for initiates' claims to supremacy over noninitiates. Secrecy creates status and boundaries across a range of social institutions. From members of initiation societies in Africa and New Guinea, to Mormons and Masons, those "in the know" can claim superiority, power, or at least special status. Death rituals often have a different social design, to restore social order after a loss.

Rites of Passage

*T*he sociologist Arnold van Gennep pointed out in 1909 (1960) that transition rituals display a similar sequential structure across cultures. Rites marking birth, puberty, marriage, and death, he remarked, as well as many other rituals of initiation or succession, often are structured temporally as three distinct stages.

The first stage separates the person from the ordinary social environment. It may involve rites to purify the body, seclusion, cutting hair, or simulating death. The separation may be the social recognition of a natural event, such as the onset of menstruation or death, providing a cultural definition for the event. It may create a peer group, such as a group of boys or girls to be initiated. It may define a geographical space, as when Muslims exchange their ordinary identities and clothing for the garb of pilgrims when entering the sacred precincts of Islam in Arabia.

Next comes a stage of marginality, the transitional or *liminal* ("threshold") stage during which the person is outside of normal social life. The liminal person may have to observe certain taboos, or be isolated, or be subjected to beatings and insults, or be elevated to temporary high status. This stage may be as short as a brief baptismal ceremony in a Christian church or as long as certain New Guinea initiation cycles lasting 10 years or more. It is a period of social work, where the liminal person is transformed in bodily or spiritual status.

Finally comes the reaggregation or reincorporation of the individual into society (or into an afterlife society), now possessing a new status. A girl may have become a woman, or a boy a man; a candidate is now a king; the loose soul of a dead man takes up its place in heaven.

The middle or liminal period has key importance to the sequence of events. Consider what happens when a signal event occurs: a girl's menstruation begins; a man dies. The event changes the natural condition of the individual in a way that underscores the limits of society's control over nature. Such events are often thought of as polluting. Ritual removes the person from everyday life and provides time for people to define the event and its consequences; to transform the person in body, mind, and status, and then to define the new state—as a fertile woman, or a soul proceeding to the world of the dead.

Of course, some events that are sequenced as transition rituals are not unplanned acts of nature: the initiation of a group of 10-year-olds, or a baptism, or a pilgrimage. Yet the liminal stage of these rituals, too, provides the setting for a dramatization of the individual's recasting into a new form, a convincing statement that the old has died and the new is born.

Reshaping, Reversing, Communitas

No one kind of process dominates these liminal periods; I mention three here. The first is what Gilbert Herdt (1981, 305) has called the "radical resocialization" of the individual—working the person over until he or she feels and thinks in new ways. Herdt writes of the often violent initiation rituals of Melanesia, which may involve long periods of beatings and abuse of young boys, who emerge shaken, with new psychological and social identities (Poole 1982).

A second process is status reversal, or "ritual of rebellion," when ordinary social relations are turned upside down. An Ndembu chief-to-be is placed in a hut where anyone is free to revile him. "A chief is just like a slave on the night before he succeeds," goes an Ndembu saying (Turner 1969, 101). Such periods may also be part of annual cycles. In fertility rituals held at the beginning of the planting season in some Zulu villages in southern Africa, for example, women reverse their otherwise subordinate roles. Donning men's garments, or singing lewd songs, or milking cows, normally taboo practices. These reversals are thought to increase the chance for a good harvest by appealing to the female spirit associated with the rains and fertility (Gluckman 1963).

Related to these stages are festivals that feature role reversals. In the South Asian festival of Holi, dedicated to the god Krishna, high-caste Brahmans and wealthy people are beaten and chased by low-caste people, such as washermen. Across early modern Europe, rituals held to mark annual feast days frequently featured women (or grotesque female beasts) chasing men, or used floats depicting women dominating their husbands, or had men and women dress in each other's garb. Some of the European rituals, like their African counterparts, were seen as promoting fertility.

Status reversals may have provided an outlet for "unruly" sentiments, as some historians and anthropologists argue, but they also sometimes provided a vehicle for critiques of or even attacks on the ruling order. The historian Natalie Zemon Davis (1965, 121–154) points out that in Europe of the seventeenth and eighteenth centuries, peasants sometimes dressed as women to carry out attacks on government officials, "putting ritual and festive inversion to new uses." Men dressed as women attacked land surveyors and tax collectors, stole the king's deer and tore down his fences. The males were able to distance themselves from their normal roles and responsibilities, but could also exploit the sexual energy dramatized during festival occasions. Ritual thus appears to have fed into politics.

A third, related, characteristic of some middle periods is what Victor Turner (1969, 94–165) called "communitas," a state wherein individuals step outside their normal social roles and experience relative equality and direct sociality with each other, as on pilgrimages or in spontaneous gatherings. (Status reversal may also have this effect.) The Islamic pilgrimage, the hajj, provides an excellent example of equality during the transition stage. The hajj, to be examined more fully in Chapter 12, places all pilgrims in a liminal position once they enter the holy cities of Mecca and Medina. All pilgrims, rich and poor, female and male, wear the same simple white garb as they carry out rituals of submission to God and commemoration of Muhammad's first pilgrimage.

Turner, who wrote prolifically on the subject, argued that communitas was generally associated with liminal stages in transition rituals. (He also saw social life in general as a dialectic of structure and communitas.) But, as the Melanesian initiations mentioned earlier suggest, such an association is not at all a general one. Even some pilgrimages do not support this association, such as that portion of South Asian pilgrimages in which caste distinctions are preserved during the journey. We can best understand the specific form given liminal life in a particular ritual sequence by examining the purpose of the ritual and the cultural context in which it occurs. Liminality does seem to involve the suspension of ordinary sociality, but what replaces that ordinary sociality may vary from a highly regimented, even repressive, order (in Melanesia or in a U.S. Army boot camp) to the spontaneity celebrated by Turner.

Initiation, Secrecy, and Fear

*I*nitiation rites may mark a passage from childhood into adulthood, or celebrate the movement from outside to inside a society or association. In contemporary U.S. society these two kinds of initiation rites seem quite different: joining the Masons is very unlike the celebration of becoming a bar mitzvah, a full male member of the Jewish religious community. One involves joining a volunteer association as an adult; the other is a stage in life for those born into a particular religion.

Yet both processes involve new knowledge and new responsibilities. In many societies, passing from childhood into a condition of full social responsibility also involves entering into a religious association and acquiring new knowledge, sometimes secret knowledge. The rituals that mark this transition often draw out the liminal or middle stage of the transition gradually, and sometimes painfully, revealing knowledge that will forever mark the individual.

Hopi Whipping and Disenchantment

Hopi Pueblo rituals fuse secrets, pain, initiation, and fertility in a way found in many societies. Hopi community rituals designed to make the seasons begin and end, or to ensure a fertile crop, or to guard the welfare of the community, involve dances by men dressed as spirits (Gill 1987, 58–75; Parsons 1939, vol. 2, 467–476). In the public portion of these rituals, men don elaborate, colorful masks, paint their bodies, strap on rattles and bells, and dance in the plaza. They represent *kachinas,* spirit beings, whose power is lodged in the dancers' masks. The dances and singing draw on this power and channel it toward accomplishing the ritual's goal.

Each February a ritual is held to encourage the coming growing season to be plentiful. This festival, called *Powamu,* is the occasion for the kachina spirits to return to the Hopi mesas from their winter homes in the mountains. Every several years the festival includes initiation rites, when boys and girls around the age of 10 are inducted into either the Kachina association or the Powamu association. The children are taken to underground rooms called *kivas,* where the secret portions of rituals are held. There they are whipped by the kachinas. They then assume a fetal position and watch the men with their masks entering the kiva.

The children now realize that the masked figures were only men, not spirits. The shock they experience is fearful and traumatic. One Hopi woman said, "I cried and cried into my sheepskin that night, feeling I had been made a fool of. How could I ever watch the Kachinas dance again?" (Gill 1987, 63).

The whipping communicates both a threat against revealing secrets, and the power of the association into which the child has been initiated. (Full initiation requires a second ritual several years later.) Religious historian Sam Gill argues that the initiation is about the disenchantment of the magical world. Gill points out that initiation rites in other societies also disillusion children of their former beliefs that masked dancers are spirits. The child is torn away from his or her naive belief that what is seen is real and set to participating in the kachina cult activities as an adult. The adult begins his or her religious life as a reflective skeptic. The Hopi woman who recalled her weeping went on to say (ibid.): "I know now it was best and the only way to teach the children, but it took me a long time to know that."

New Guinea Traumas and Homosexuality

Much more severe than the whippings inflicted by the kachinas are the long, painful initiation rituals experienced by young boys in some New Guinea societies. John Fitz Porter Poole (1982) relates that the male initiation cycle in Bimin-Kuskusmin society stretches from 10 to 15 years in a boy's life, usually beginning at seven to 10 years of age. One of its stages takes place in a forest house, where the initiates are secluded, beaten, told they are vile (and that women are vile as well) and tormented. Over succeeding days they are rubbed with stinging nettles, forced to vomit, and beaten. Many actions are taken to firm up their bodies and heighten their masculinity, including rubbing boar blood on their chests. They are also told a series of secret myths and ordered not to reveal them.

The initiators explain that they are making the boys into men. One aspect of that process is teaching them how to control anger, an esteemed quality for a warrior. The boys are furious, reports Poole, but must suppress their anger on pain of further beatings. Throughout the ritual they are deceived by men they had trusted, abused by everyone older than they, and denied maternal support. The trauma is great; some boys go into shock. Some of the initiators express concern, but see the beatings as necessary to make the boys mature. The boys themselves suffer afterward from fearful dreams, in which concern for their body parts is evidenced.

Such processes of "radical resocialization" (Herdt 1981, 305) in this and other societies are intended to wrest the boy from his mother, make his body masculine, his sexuality potent, and his emotional makeup that of a brave warrior. Other New Guinea societies emphasize sexuality more than anger. Gilbert Herdt (1981, 1982) describes the ritualized homosexuality among the Sambia that marks the initiation process. Men are produced from boys in part through the ingestion of semen, which is seen to replace the breast milk they ingested as infants and is intended to wean them from women and make them into men. This form of homosexuality is thus a way of replacing an earlier bodily relation to the mother with a relation to other men and fits with the idea, discussed earlier, that men and women have sharply differentiated but parallel relationships to the social and natural world. Herdt (1982) reports that the boys experience fear, maternal loss, and shame when confronted with the initiated men and when they begin to understand what is expected of them. They share their mothers' fears of male aggression and threats, symbolized by secret (phallic) flutes, which stand for male dominance of women and elder male dominance over the young boys.

Female initiation rituals in New Guinea involve less trauma. Girls are separated from younger girls, but not from women. The rituals described by Nancy Lutkehaus (1995) for Manam Island in Papua New Guinea are directed toward cleansing girls of the pollution brought on by first menstrual blood and turning them into fertile women. As practiced generally in the 1930s, and with some girls today, the rites involve a long series of actions intended to isolate the girl from her normal social state and from her bodily state. She is not allowed to touch herself or her food. Once she has bathed in the sea to begin the seven- to 10-day ritual sequence, the young girls who attend her are also forbidden to touch her. Slits are cut in her back with knives and ash rubbed in to raise scars to mark her as a fertile woman. She jokes with other women throughout the process.

Sadness is introduced with mourning songs sung at the start and close of the ritual, signaling that the girl is renouncing the pleasures of childhood and now expects to bear children and to leave her village of birth to marry.

Pain, fear, demands for secrecy—all are strongly remembered experiences that impress the initiate with the seriousness of the social norms and ideas he or she has learned. Strong emotions and newly acquired secrets further serve to reinforce the separation between elders and juniors and between men and women. Children are indeed radically reshaped into new kinds of humans.

Death Ritual and the Social Order

*I*f initiation rituals underscore conceptions of gender, death rituals make especially visible ideas about the individual and the collectivity. If an individual leaves society, is he or she to remain part of it? In the answer to that question people often highlight their picture, real or ideal, of society and of an individual.

In much of China and Taiwan, villagers conceive of the spiritual world as composed of three beings: ghosts, gods, and ancestors. Each is dealt with differently; for example, offered different kinds of food or money. These three beings are also associated with three kinds of humans. Gods are dressed in the garments of officials and they can punish people and be bribed. They keep records; they are clearly bureaucrats. They are worshipped in temples (Wolf 1974). Ghosts, by contrast, are worshiped outside, with large offerings of food or clothing, and they resemble bandits or beggars—strangers, in other words. Ancestors are, well, ancestors. You owe them a debt for your own life and prosperity, and you feed them as you would feed a human visitor to your home.

This close correspondence between society and supernatural beings suggests that in different Chinese settings people would interpret these beings somewhat differently, and they do: the god who is a police official today may have been an influential country gentleman in the past.

From Spirit to Household God in Japan

In rural Japan, where the individual is thought of as a member of a household and of a community, at death a person becomes a spirit (kami) as well as a Buddha (hotoke). Funerals are performed by Buddhist priests, but death ritual also involves pre-Buddhist ideas of pollution and ritual. A long transition stage allows the spirit to progress from an individual's spirit to one element in the household deity. Death ritual thereby reinforces the notion of spirit collectivity (Plath 1964; Smith 1974).

Death begins a three-stage process of transforming the deceased into a part of the spirit collectivity. At death the body may be cremated or buried; urban Japanese inevitably cremate. In either case, bodily death pollutes the spirit (shirei) as well as the close relatives of the deceased. Death ritual helps to separate the spirit from the pollution. The grave receiving the body is located far away from the residential part of a village and is called the "abandoned grave." In some parts of Japan a second, "ritual grave," consisting of a headstone is built nearer the house. This grave may be tended without encountering the pollution of the dead body. Urban Japanese must rely on funeral parlors. (Today the combined expenses of burial, home altar with tablets, and the services of a Buddhist priest can amount to a middle-class family's one-year pretax income!)

The memory of the deceased individual is preserved for the first 49 days after death. The survivors set up a mortuary tablet on the household altar, together with a photo of the deceased, incense, bells, and other objects. Buddhist memorial services are held for the individual every seven days until the 49 days are completed. The soul also wanders near the house during this period, before leaving on the 49th day.

Sometimes the soul takes some action on its own on the 49th day to settle accounts with the living. In an eighteenth-century puppet play called "The Woman Killer and the Hell of Oil," Yohei murders Okichi, but no one knows that he is the murderer. Yohei arrives on the 49th day of the ritual, just after a rat has run along the rafters of the room, dislodging a scrap of paper with evidence of the murderer's guilt; and the husband of the dead woman exclaims that this was a sign from the dead person. "This I owe to Buddha's mercy," he says.

At the end of this initial period the family holds a series of rituals to transform the spirit of the dead into an ancestral spirit (*sorei*). The photo is put away and the temporary tablet disposed of, replaced by a permanent tablet, usually an upright wooden plaque four to six inches high, lacquered in black or gold, and inscribed with a special posthumous name of the deceased and the date of his or her death. (Buddhist temples provide these after-death names.) This tablet is placed with the other tablets on the altar.

The altar and tablets stands for the house's history (Smith 1974, 1978, 152–165). The household (*ié*) is thought of as a corporate group, the headship of which passes from father to son over the generations. The tablets are the first objects to be saved (standard newspaper accounts of fires say that "flames swept through the building so rapidly that the residents only had time to carry out the altar and tablets"). The tablets are even more important than the Buddha image. As one man put it, the ancestors need help like anyone else, whereas the Buddha can take care of himself.

But the tablet itself is impermanent. After either 33 or 50 years (depending on the region of Japan) the tablet is destroyed and the spirit becomes a god. The spirit is sometimes transferred to the household god in a noteworthy ritual in which the tablet is cast into a river and then a pebble is picked up from the river bed and placed on the household god's altar. This collection of pebbles represents the spirits merged into the guardian god of the household as a collectivity.

Thereafter, services are held for the collective dead, without identifying them singly, both with daily offerings of flowers and on seasonal occasions, in particular: New Year's on January first through third, Obon or the Festival of the Dead or of Lanterns on August 13 through 15, and the equinoxes in late March and September.

The Obon festival, when the ancestors come down from where they live to their villages, has been celebrated at least since the year 606 C.E. One dedicates temples and recites Buddhist verses and makes offering to ancestors. One category of ancestor is especially grateful for these offerings: ancestors who committed misdeeds in past lives may end up on the plane of existence called *gaki-do,* or Plane of the Hungry Ghosts. They suffer from hunger and thirst, and they alone out of all one's ancestors may benefit from offerings one makes to a holy or virtuous person.

But Obon is the time to make offerings to the ancestors generally. The ritual grave near the house is cleared and a path is swept leading back to the house. The household altar is cleaned and a dance (today in decline) is held in the village. People return to their ancestral villages to participate in the festival and end the ritual by taking lanterns and small boats to the graveyard or to a mountain or river to see the spirits off on their return to their abode. Japanese overseas also celebrate Obon. In St. Louis, where I live, it is the time for a Japanese festival at the Botanical Gardens, with the lighting of lanterns around the lake in the Japanese garden.

The long transition stage to Japanese death rituals supports the idea of a gradual melding of the individual into the collectivity and thus also supports the general cultural importance of the collectivity.

Regenerating Life from Death

Death rituals also frequently feature images of journeys to new worlds, enactments of rebirth, or the disinterment and reburial of bones (Bloch and Parry 1982).

Images of journeys are sometimes the material focus of religious innovations. As Sumatran Toba Batak people left their ancestral homeland for big cities, they began to use their new wealth to build elaborate family tombs back home. These tombs were carved in the shapes of boats and other images of soul journeys, and the tombs kept alive a sense of attachment to the homeland and a promise of rejoining the family for the journey to the afterworld. In Ghana, a man named Connie Kway began to carve elaborate, painted coffins in the shapes of boats or birds during the 1970s. These coffins sold for the equivalent of a year's average wage and were snatched up by the rich. They were an innovation; Ghanians had not used fancy coffins before, but because they dramatized the comforting and spirit-raising belief that the dead were going to a resting place where loved ones would see them again, they quickly became popular and spawned imitators. (In 1996 a museum tour of the coffins swept the United States, where they were competed for as treasured folk art objects.)

Death is often linked to life and fertility in the transition stages. This linking may take different forms. Bloch and Parry (1982, 7) argue that death rituals tend to revital-ize "that resource which is *culturally conceived* to be most essential to the reproduction of the social order." The resource may be the land, or human fertility, or some combi-nation of the two. Thus in four African hunter-gatherer societies compared by James Woodburn (1982), social reproduction was thought to depend most importantly on control over nature, and the ritual response to death was to reawaken the productivity of nature.

For the Merina of Madagascar, studied by Maurice Bloch (1982), reproducing the society requires that members of a descent group have their bones buried together in ancestral tombs. Because these related individuals do not live in the same place, they are initially buried where they die. Their bones later are dug up and moved to the ancestral tomb. The initial burial is attended by sadness and mourning, but the subsequent "regrouping" of the body with the ancesters is full of joy and dancing. During this dancing, women repeatedly throw the brittle bones to the ground, smashing them to bits. These actions merge the physical remains of the individual with the ancestral groups as a whole. The ritual also employs the symbolism of birth, entering into and emerging from the tomb as if it were a womb.

Asmat Headhunting and Birth through Death

Consider in more detail the case of the Asmat, a society of about 50,000 people living in the swampy plains of southwest Irian Jaya, the name for the western half of the island of New Guinea that in 1963 became part of Indonesia. The Asmat are best known in the West for the tall *bis* poles, made out of sago palm, examples of which are to be found in many Western museums (Kuruwaip 1974).

The Asmat (Sudarman 1984) call themselves the "tree people." Their environment is wood; stone or metal for tools must be acquired from elsewhere. Canoes, poles, housing are all from wood. Their staple, sago, is also wood. Every four or five days, the men of a clan will spend an entire day finding a large (45-foot-high) sago palm tree in the forest, cutting it down, removing the pith, and then pounding, washing, drying, and roasting the pith into large cakes of sago to be pounded into sago flour. Sago is regarded as a human being. The sago palm resembles a woman: life comes from within it, and the white, milky sago resembles breast milk. When an Asmat man carves a sago palm into a pole he considers his work as very like what he does to help produce a baby. Asmat hold

Drawing of Asmat bis
pole, Irian Jaya.

that the father does not cause conception, but molds the child through frequent inter-course into the shape he or she eventually has at birth (Gerbrands 1967).

Much of the Asmat men's time used to be spent in warfare between clans, fueled partly by their practices and beliefs surrounding death. Asmat believe that deaths are due to malevolent actions by others, that people in other clans kill your own relatives either in an observable way (in a raid, for example) or through sorcery. The spirits of the dead demand retribution or revenge for their deaths (Zegwaard 1959). Asmat once took revenge for a death by taking a head in a raid on another clan, thus continuing the cycle of death and retribution. The relative taking the head would have carved for him a long, 15- to 20-foot *bis* pole. The clan would then drum and dance to entice the spirit into the pole. The relative would dedicate the pole to the deceased, and cry out (for example): "Oh mother, I have killed a man from [place name]." Then the spirit of the dead person, which would have remained in the village until avenged, would begin its journey out of the village and toward a island somewhere off the western coast, later to be reborn as a new human (Kuruwaip 1974).

Today, headhunting is prohibited, and Asmat seem to have abandoned the practice. But they continue to carve images of deceased relatives onto the long poles, to drum the spirit into the pole, and to erect the pole and publicly dedicate it, calling out for the spirit to leave the village.

Through their myths, the Asmat believe the acts of producing sago from palms, carving wood poles, and cutting heads to be situating their lives in the universe. Taking a head reenacts a sacrifice made at the beginning of time. In a widely told story, a being who was both god and man killed his brother and cut off his head, immediately causing the universe to come into existence, and all of culture with it. (In some versions of this story, the god–man cut off the head of a crocodile in order to create non-Asmat people.) Taking a head thus caused life to emerge (Zegwaard 1959).

In practice, the skulls of the dead help to bring about a new birth. In past times the skull used would have come from a headhunting expedition, and thus the same skull would accomplish two important functions: it would allow the spirit to leave the world, and it would bring a new person into it. Today the skull would come from a relative. A young male being initiated into manhood sits for days in the men's house, contemplating a skull between his legs, pressed against his genitals. Then he is carried out toward the setting sun in a canoe, following the journey made by the spirits of the dead. When the canoe has traveled far enough from shore he lies in the bottom of the canoe in imitation of someone who has just died. Then he is thrown into the water, still holding the skull, to resurface as a newly born initiated man.

Cutting the sago is also likened to taking a human head and releasing energy. The palm is thought to have the same spirit as a human. Men attack the palm, throwing spears at it, and butcher the starch. Asmat also draw on these ideas to project human actions onto the animal world. They see an analogy to headhunting in the behavior of the praying mantis. The insect is seen as human in its movements (think of how its stance gave rise to its English name), and the female bites off the head of the male during mating.

Not only is the mantis's cannibalism like taking a head, but it reminds the Asmat observer of the mock, or part-mock aggression enacted by women toward men in everyday life. For when the Asmat men return along the river with the sago palm, women carry out an attack on the canoes from the village shore. The attack is ostensibly to keep malevolent spirits from entering the village along with the palm, but in practice women throw their spears hard and accurately and, not uncommonly, men are injured.

Drumming the spirit of the dead into the *bis* pole also replicates a mythic event. The very first man on earth was called Fumeripits. He drowned in the sea but he was brought back to life by War, the name of the white-tailed eagle, who pressed smoldering bits of wood against his body. Then Fumeripits built a large men's house and carved images of men and women. He began to drum, and they came to life, dancing. The carvers and drummers of today cannot create life, but they can attract spirits through their carving and drumming, thereby reenacting Fumeripits' deed on the spiritual level.

In everyday life, too, Asmat experience the link between heads and the continuity of life. All adults sleep on skulls, usually skulls of close relatives, and report feeling a continued tie to the deceased through this skull-sleeping. Some men will (or did) sleep on the skull of a powerful enemy, claiming that they absorb some of the deceased's power at night. Carving the pole and cutting heads thus not only frees the spirit from the village (and the village from the spirit) but also signifies to the living that the dead will be reborn and life will continue. The ritual also gives the bereaved a concrete way to care for the spirits of their relatives. And since they practice it together as a social group, a single individual's death strengthens the power of their origin myths.

The ritual as it once was carried out allowed the individual to complete a logical and emotional circle: a death, avenged by taking a head, was completed when the skull of the victim was used to release the spirit from the village and then to cause a rebirth. But now the circuit has been shorted at the point of headhunting. The Dutch (when they controlled the territory) had already prohibited headhunting throughout the region, but they had little direct sway over the Asmat. The Indonesian government has been much more direct in its plans to change Asmat lives and religions: it encourages missionaries to promote the adoption of proper religion, with a book, a creed, but no violence. The missionaries offer salvation through communion (which might be interpreted by Asmat as a different kind of cannibalism) and rebirth through baptism (a different path to rebirth through immersion in water).

Secondary Burial

The "regrouping" of bones practiced by the Merina (discussed earlier) is one example of a widespread practice of secondary burial, or the removal and reburial of a corpse. This practice is intended to provide material signs of the transition from life to an afterlife by permitting people to examine the bones of the dead after decomposition has set in. Secondary burial is relatively rare, but it is found in culturally unrelated areas throughout the world—Greece, Africa, Siberia, Indonesia, the Americas, and in early Jewish practice. Medieval Christian burial in Europe often included the display of bones in an ossuary.

Peter Metcalf (1982) provides a detailed description of the practice from the Berawan society in Borneo. In this society, a body is stored in a large jar right after death. After several days the bones are cleaned of flesh and stored in the longhouse or on a platform outside. Months or years later (Metcalf records a range of eight months to five years) the bones of some of the dead, but not others, are removed and placed in a permanent death monument. For the Berawan, the display of bones stands for the passage of the spirit of the dead outside the community. It confirms that the spirit has reached the land of the dead.

Robert Hertz (1960) wrote a comparative essay on the practice in 1907. Hertz used material from Borneo and Indonesia but also made reference to similar practices elsewhere. Based on his reading of available ethnography, Hertz argued that people take the natural fact of bodily decomposition as the basis for thinking about the process of death, the transition from the loss of soul to the passage to another place. Just as the body decomposes, so the spirit gradually leaves the body, transformed to a new state in which the spirit is definitively separated from the body.

The process of decomposition, then, defines three moments in the death process, each of which serves as a sign of the unobservable process through which the spirit leaves the body and the community. At the moment of death the spirit has left the body. During decomposition the spirit is uncertain as to its final home, and during this period it may haunt the living and roam the community. But when the bones are seen to be clean, then the spirit has left for its new home.

Hertz noted that people have a horror of the corpse throughout the world, but that it is not a physical repugnance. The same people fear the corpse but wash it, sit with it, even drink the wash water. The fear is for two reasons. First, the death tears a hole in the community, and the social fabric must be mended and order restored. The more important the person, the more ritual work needs to be done, so only some bones are subjected to secondary burial. Second, the soul remains near the corpse, and until it has left the community it will remain to haunt the living. The rites of secondary burial enact the finality of the passage out of the community.

This analysis explains why Berawan people evinced horror at the practice of embalming when Metcalf described it to them. Embalming for purposes of viewing the body in a "lifelike" state is seen by Berawan as delaying the process of decay and thereby retarding the successful separation of the soul from the community.

Similar concerns are found in the official policy on burial of the Greek Orthodox Church. Bodies must not, commands the church, be buried in airtight caskets lest the natural, and God-ordained, process of decomposition be halted. In rural Greece today, relatives exhume the bones of the deceased five years after the body is buried, and remove the bones to the village ossuary (Danforth 1982). If the bones are clean and white, relatives are assured that the soul has passed to heaven. If decomposition has not been completed, villagers wait an additional two years and then repeat the process. Meanwhile they say prayers for the forgiveness of the person's sins; it is these sins that have retarded the soul's passage and the body's decomposition.

In these and other cases people feel ambivalent about the passage of the soul from the community. People may wish loved ones to remain near them, but they also wish for closure in the process of dying and mourning. Death rituals demonstrate to the living that the dead have left the community, taking danger with them, but also that they remain close by and that they can be called on to help the living. The soul of a Berawan person remains ready to aid the living in times of illness or other need. Asmat send the spirits of the dead away from the community to an island off the coast, but people continue to sleep with the skulls of deceased loved ones and sense that the person continues to remain with them. For people in many societies, death involves desires for both finality and remembrance; death rituals give those desires a material form.

Grief and Ritual Form

*T*ransition rituals marking events such as initiations or death are emotional times. Often the emotions are produced by the rituals themselves. The sociologist Émile Durkheim (1858–1917), stressing the social base for much of religious life, argued that ritual action, especially when in a group, channels and determines emotions. Durkheim maintained that although there might be natural emotional responses to death, they are highly subject to social shaping. Is this view correct? How culturally different are those emotions? What role does ritual play in the interior lives, the feelings, and the grieving of the survivors? Do rituals create emotions or do emotions determine what kind of rituals people create?

Consider the contrast between the way two Muslim peoples mourn the loss of a close relative. In Java, where people typically value the control of their emotions, Clifford Geertz (1960, 73) reports a man he knew well, distancing himself from the loss of his wife, describing how he kept his emotions inside him. A girl who wept softly after her father died was told she could not participate in the funeral events unless she stopped crying. And yet, in Morocco, another Muslim society, the expected behavior is just the opposite. People in mourning tear their clothes and hair and wail loudly and publicly (Westermarck 1968 II, 34–42).

These marked differences in public behavior are between two peoples with the same religion. Ritual forms, linked to dominant cultural values, prescribe sharply contrasting patterns of mourning behavior.

But we cannot assume from such publicly observed contrasts that the emotions and the grieving process experienced by the individual are correspondingly different (Rosaldo 1984). Many Moroccans may feel indifference; many Javanese, great sorrow. Yet men and women in each society are expected to act in certain standardized ways regardless of their feelings. Many people in the United States report feeling quite different from what their public mourning behavior would suggest. Some feel guilty at the gulf between their mixed emotions and the expressions of grief that they are expected to display. Others adhere to religions that urge their followers in a different direction, to maintain a hopeful attitude consistent with a strong belief in the afterlife. Mormon services reflect this attitude, and Christian Scientists argue that bereaved people can and should lift themselves out of sorrow through the sheer force of the will. Yet many adherents to these faiths do grieve, and may find their social networks not offering the support they need (Palgi and Abramovitch 1984).

Is Grief Universal?

Perhaps the most devastating loss to an American adult is the death of a child, and here cross-cultural variation is striking. Psychologists (Bowlby 1980) argue that parents in all societies develop attachments to their children and experience grief at the loss of children. The attachment and the grief seem to have a basis in the evolution of social relationships. Both features are found in nonhuman primates as well as humans. And yet in many societies the deaths of newborns are not accompanied by the same expressions of loss and grief as are the deaths of older children or adults. In many societies children are not named until some number of days have passed after birth, and a death before that time is treated very differently than later deaths. Do these practices indicate that parents feel the loss less? How strongly does such a cultural practice shape emotions?

Two studies in anthropology have addressed this question but reach distinct conclusions. Nancy Scheper-Hughes (1992) argues that some poor Brazilian parents do feel loss less than do most middle-class parents. She emphasizes the cultural malleability of emotions—cultural practices shape emotional response. Unni Wikan (1990), emphasizing the distance between public expressions and inner emotions, finds that Balinese people feel strong grief emotions, but that they follow culturally prescribed practices of working on their grief through laughter and sociability. These and other studies underscore the emotional importance of rituals and other practices during the transition stage after a death—and also the difficulties in generalizing about "private" emotions.

Nancy Scheper-Hughes lived, worked, and studied in a very poor region in northeastern Brazil in the 1960s and then again in the 1980s. Many in the area had little to eat, and infant death was common. Mothers, fathers, and siblings developed an attitude of "letting go" toward those infants who seemed near death, often drawing on an elaborate catalogue of symptoms that pointed to an inevitable death.

Scheper-Hughes tried to make sense of the families' emotionally flat responses by challenging the Western view about attachment and mourning. In that view, attachment is a basic instinct that structures relationships between all human mothers and their children. The death of a child triggers natural responses of mourning, which must be worked through if the survivors are to be able to carry on in a healthy way. But Scheper-Hughes (1992, 400–445) argues that many mothers in fact have an ambivalent attitude toward their newborns. When the mother–infant experience is positive, and when nurturing all one's children is possible, parents invest emotionally in their children and feel great loss at a death. But in poor Brazil and some other places a "lifeboat" ethic leads parents to choose, reluctantly, to nurture only those who have a chance at surviving. Cultural practices reinforce this survival strategy: parents delay naming their infants and hold them much less often than do middle-class mothers.

Death ritual also plays an important part in this survival strategy. In some parts of Brazil, lower-class men and women treat the death of a very young child as a blessing. The child will be taken to heaven, is already a little angel, they say. The wake held for the little child, who is dressed in a white or blue shirt with curled hair and floral wreaths, includes joyous music and samba dancing. Although much more sober in tone in the community where Scheper-Hughes worked, the "angels" were a "transitional object" for these women, she points out (1992, 421), both because the infant is in transition from life to death, and because the dressed-up corpse and coffin allows the woman to let go of her child by giving her an idealized heaven-child to hold onto. Women told Scheper-Hughes: "I feel free" or "I feel unburdened" after the funeral. Grief seemed absent. For some students of Brazilian society the flat emotional response is a mask, a wall against the unbearable. But Scheper-Hughes takes the responses of these women at face value, arguing that culture and ritual succeed in preventing grief responses. The idea that deaths need to be worked through by a process of open mourning, she says, is applicable only in some societies.

Still, it may be difficult to decide between several possible interpretations of Scheper-Hughes's data—are denials of grief a mask, or are denials accurate reports of feelings? Another study of the same area (Nations and Rebhun 1988) reports very different findings. High rates of infant mortality are found in many parts of the world, and yet women mourn these infants. Finally, we should note that arguments for a universal attachment structure are based on cross-cultural research: the major early empirical work (Ainsworth 1967) was not from the West but from Uganda!

Emotions and Their Expressions

Scheper-Hughes's argument was intended to counter universal theories of death, emotions, and ritual. By contrast, anthropologist Unni Wikan draws on her fieldwork in Bali to oppose culturally relativist theories about the malleability of emotions. In Bali, as in neighboring Java, people are expected to preserve a "face" of equanimity at loss or disaster. Anthropologists had long understood the grace and composure of Balinese as a cultural style that focused on beauty and on distancing oneself from emotions. Balinese selves, wrote the anthropologist Clifford Geertz (1966), are quite different from Western ones; they live in a "dramatistic" world composed of masks, roles, and a stage.

Wikan (1990) argues instead that Balinese think and feel their way through the world in ways that are much closer to European ways than earlier anthropologists believed. She describes several months in the life of one woman, who lost her fiance in an accident. Her friends laughed and joked with her, insisting that she laugh too. During the following months she appeared bright-faced and happy, even to her friend Wikan. After several months Wikan did see her cry, and then the woman began to tell of how devastated she had felt through the whole experience. About the same time her friends began to change their ways of being with her, sympathizing out loud with the distress she must have felt. Her emotions, and their understanding of them, were not all that different after all.

But why did she laugh her way through the first few months, and why did her friends insist that she do so? The key lies in a distinctive set of ideas about the relationship between one's "face"—appearances and behavior—and one's "heart"—emotions and thoughts. For the Balinese with whom Wikan spoke, emotions of sadness and sorrow weaken one's life force. A weak life force opens up the body to all sorts of invasions, but most particularly to attacks from sorcerers. These attacks are always near at hand; half of all deaths are attributed to sorcery. Moreover, these sad feelings can spread from one person to another, endangering the community, so one has a social as well as a personal responsibility to keep sorrow at a distance. How does one do that? Whereas we might think of emotions as having a life of their own—grief inevitably following loss—the Balinese think that behavior, including how one forms one's face and the choice to laugh or cry, shapes the heart and channels emotions. Laughing, then, keeps sadness from welling up, and thereby keeps the person strong against murderous sorcery.

Wikan concludes that Balinese appearances of calm and joy are not due to a theater-like detachment from the world, but rather to their strong fears of sorcery and their ideas about how best to combat it. During the transition period after death these dangers are at their highest and thus when the practices of laughing together are most required.

Wikan, then, affirms the distinctiveness of Balinese ideas and practices but sees them as responses to a universal emotion of loss and grief. Scheper-Hughes claims that the emotions of the Brazilians she studied are quite different from those experienced by middle-class families, but she does so by way of a general theory about the responses of mothers (and others) to infants and to risk. Both underscore the critical role of culturally sanctioned practices designed to shape the emotions people feel when a loved one dies. Balinese laughing and Brazilian "angel caskets" bridge the transition period between death and the reintegration of the survivors into the ordinary routines of life.

5 Gender, Religion, and Ethnography

Open any textbook on anthropology, and without difficulty you will find a section where the authors discuss the universality of gender differences. Since the early days of the discipline, anthropologists have written about ways in which male–female relationships are constructed in different societies. But in the 1970s a new feminist anthropology turned to studying gender and sexuality for answers to pressing political and cultural questions about equality and human rights. They asked big questions about gender and inequality. Michelle Rosaldo (1974), Sherry Ortner (1974), and others observed that wherever one finds inequalities in women's and men's access to resources, it is the men who control more than the women. Why, they asked, should there be such consistent inequality?

Rosaldo, Ortner, and their collaborators argued that the answer lay in a political inequality based on biological differences between women and men. Women, taken up with tasks of raising children, were identified more closely with natural processes than were men. Men, considered relatively more "cultural," were able to grab the public podium and control how social matters were represented and how resources were divided. Although this cross-cultural inequality could be (and, they wrote, ought to be) overcome, because humans are not the prisoners of history, it was nonetheless the general human–historical background against which all such overcoming must take place.

Although these authors were careful to note that they were speaking of the public cultural representations in a society and that they did not believe that only men ever exercised power (Ortner 1996, 139–146), their early formulations were followed by criticisms and reformulations, often made by the same authors. For example, Ortner and Whitehead (1981) pointed out that the earlier approaches had downplayed the wide variation in the ways people think about gender and sexuality. In some societies, people assume that biology strongly determines male–female differences. In other societies, however, biology is subordinated when people believe that practices of nurturing, maturing, or being initiated shape a human into a fully male or female person (see also MacCormack and Strathern 1980).

We can probably safely say that people in all cultures recognize differences between men and women, and, furthermore, that in elaborating their ideas about these differences they point to features of physiology and biology and to different roles in procreation. But that is about as far as we take the idea of physiology and gender, because there are widely differing ideas about gender and sexuality. More precisely, and interestingly, people are not unambiguously sorted into the categories "male" and "female" according to a single set of criteria in every society. The Hua in the highlands of Papua New Guinea, for example, classify people both in terms of their external genitalia and in terms of the amount of male or female substance each person is thought to possess. A person accumulates both kinds of substance through physical contact with others, so one's behavior determines one's substantive sexual identity. Some Hua are considered male in terms of genitalia but female in terms of their substance, or vice versa (Meigs 1990).

These feminist critiques were notably as critical of previous methods of ethnography as they were of commonly held notions of gender. Reinforced by renewed studies of well-known anthropological terrains, feminist anthropology explained why an ethnographer's perceptions may be shaped both by his or her prior assumptions and by the limits placed on the field of action in the society being studied.

Creating Gender through Ritual

How does religion come into this picture? Religious representations of people add a degree of cultural force to gender ideas, so that people regard them as universal, or cosmic, or God-commanded, or "natural." Each type of representation has a very different consequence, but they all make what appears to be culturally specific seem inevitable because it is ordered by deities, or because it is simply there, in nature. We can call these the *ideological* consequences of religion, when beliefs are linked in some way to the social and political system. Religious ideas also may be sources of strength for both women and men who wish to challenge how society is put together. Religious ritual also contributes to culturally specific ideas of gender because it casts male and female beings in particular cultural terms.

Producing Men and Women

Let us reconsider the Melanesian initiation rituals we studied in Chapter 4 (pages 47–48), this time as ritual means of producing mature and fertile men and women. These initiation rites are understood as creating sexuality; they highlight the distinctions between men and women (Keesing 1982). Men and women are seen as radically different, and the fluids and powers of one are dangerous to the other. Distinctions, separation, and hostility characterize ritual represenations of gender in many of these societies.

But men and women are also seen as creating biological parallels to each other. Semen and menstrual blood are polluting to the opposite sex in Melanesia (whereas female pollution of males through menstruation is a widespread belief). Female rites are centered on removing menstrual pollution to create fertility; male rites on separating the boys from women.

Male rites sometimes imitate those female rites that are closely linked to physiological events. Thus, men symbolically "give birth" to canoes in the Manam society of Papua New Guinea (Lutkehaus 1995). In some Melanesian societies men "menstruate" by spilling blood from their slashed penises. This act and other blood-lettings on one's own body strengthen sexual powers. In these cases the female body and processes of biological reproduction serve as symbols of social reproduction of men and women.

The parallels and the sexual segregation also support notions that homosexuality is required for male growth (Herdt 1981, 1982; Poole 1982). Men are required to "grow boys into men" in some societies. Older males bleed and multilitate younger males, reveal secret knowledge, and provide them semen to ingest, all in order to strengthen their bodies and their reproductive and aggressive capacities. In some cases men also use semen to fertilize the crops.

Some of these practices have parallels in Amazon societies. In both places one finds an emphasis on male mysteries and solidarity, on the use of such specific objects as sacred flutes and bull-roarers as emblems of male exclusivity and power over females, and threats of gang rape against women who view these male cult objects (Keesing 1982, 9). In central Africa, too, people speak of "growing a girl" and "growing a boy" into an adult through the initiation rituals (Turner 1967, 101–102).

Ritual, Fertility, and Culture

Drawing on these and similar examples, some feminist anthropologists proposed a general theory of gender differentiation (Rosaldo 1974; Chodorow 1974) that turns on the ways in which boys and girls are socialized. They argued that, across cultures, women and men differ in the degree to which they require active socialization into their respective gender roles. Girls are oriented toward the domestic sphere, these authors claimed, and thus can remain within it as they mature. Boys, who are oriented toward the public sphere, must distance and differentiate themselves actively from their mothers. Male initiation rituals bring about and represent this differentiation of males from females.

The Chodorow-Rosaldo theory does explain the role of negative emotions toward women that characterize teachings central to male initiation rituals in some New Guinea societies. Their theory of the *reproduction* of gender differences in the development of each individual human was later expanded by feminist scholars (Collier and Rosaldo 1981) into a theory of the *origins* of gender differences in the early history of humankind; this theory also explained the ideas about fertility underlying many representations of gender.

Contrary to the received wisdom of an earlier era, these scholars argue, in many societies of simpler technology it is men, not women, who are credited with promoting fertility (Whitehead 1987). Many societies based on hunting and either gathering or horticulture in Australia, the Americas, and Africa feature rituals celebrating men's powers to create life without women. Why should this be? Collier and Rosaldo

(1981) argued that ideas of fertility are really ideas about social relationships, and that it is men's power to bring about marriages that these ideas celebrate. And why do men control marriage? Simply put, the story that explains their control starts with their deficiencies: men rely on marriage to eat. Because men do not have automatic access to the foods gathered or cultivated by women, they have a great interest in marriage. Because men must find a spouse, they must secure social ties to potential parents-in-law and brothers-in-law. Men also seek to have their general sociability recognized as both culturally and biologically important, claiming that fertility is the outcome of their social activities. Whitehead (1987) argues that in New Guinea, for instance, male control of intercommunity exchanges of goods and services allows men to claim fertility as their contribution to society and thus justify excluding women from fertility rituals.

This theory uses comparative evidence to suggest origins story similar, in its logical form, to the classic "social contract" theories proposed by John Locke and Thomas Hobbes to account for the origins of society. The feminist theory was proposed at a time when many anthropologists were looking for new origins stories to counter some of the sweeping, male-centered stories such as "man the hunter" (see Conkey 1991). But like all grand narratives the story can account for only some of the social reality it seeks to explain.

For example, women also undergo initiation, and sometimes the initiation process is intended to make them, not the men, more cultural and fertile. Janice Boddy (1989) describes the practice of infibulation found in many areas of the Middle East and northern Africa, when part or all of a girl's clitoris and labia minora is removed as part of a ritual designed to make her into a woman. Reasons given for these operations include the need to protect a family's honor by preserving its daughters' chastity and to curb women's sexual desire.

Boddy points out that the men and women in northern Sudan both subscribe to the general idea that men acquire more reason or rationality (*aqal*) than women do and that women have more emotions and desires (*nafs*). Men say further that women are less able than men to control their desires, viewing infibulation as part of a larger repertoire of social practices (including seclusion and veiling) designed to control those emotions.

Women take a different view. Although they, too, see women and men as differing in their natures, they make concerns about fertility the most important reason for practicing infibulation. Only by undergoing the practice, they say, can women marry and thus have legitimate children.

Women regard carrying out infibulation as continuing the work that God began by creating humans. Only after circumcision and infibulation do girls and boys become fully gendered. It is then that they are expected to behave as women and men, sleeping and eating separately, and no longer playing together (Boddy 1989, 58–59). In a constricted social world where cousins are one's prime marriage partners, turning kin into potential spouses begins early.

Women see themselves as having the central role in structuring the physical and social reproduction of their community by preparing women for marriage and for giving birth. They consider that their activities make them, and not the men, the guarantors of the cultural order. They see men as marginal to the society, mediators between the village world and the outside world. Women's and men's views of gender and culture start from the same position, then diverge widely. Because men dominate public forums of discussion, women's views are less often heard.

Gender Differentiation and Initiation

It has been demonstrated that initiation rituals represent gender relations and are often seen as producing them. And initiation ceremonies generally underscore ideas of gender found throughout the society or carried by a particular religious tradition in that society.

Hopi society is organized around matrilineal clans, and, as in most such societies, Hopi men and women play complementary roles and enjoy status that is more nearly equal than in many other North American societies. As we have seen (in Chapter 4), the initiations of 10-year-olds include both boys and girls. This is in striking contrast to the New Guinea and Amazon cultures, discussed previously, with strong male–female oppositions in social life and strong ritual symbols of gender distinctiveness such as menstrual blood and semen.

Within any one New Guinea society, rituals construct and represent the male and female orders in different fashion. In Manam Island society (Lutkehaus 1995), boys are initiated in cohorts but girls are initiated individually, attended by other girls. The boys become members of secret male societies, whereas the girls become members of women's networks. In classic Durkheimian fashion, the ritual form depicts the most salient form of sociability toward which each gender is headed. Male domination of women within the society is not only actively promoted during the initiation but is supported by the very existence of the men's houses. Women and children are excluded from the houses, and this "very fact of exclusivity serve[s] to create and perpetuate the politically dominant position of men" (Lutkehaus 1995, 200).

Strong themes of male–female difference also run through many African societies, where the major focus is on male initiation and where boys and girls are initiated by strictly segregated paths into different secret associations (La Fontaine 1985). Along the western African coast, for example (in much of Liberia, Sierra Leone, and the Ivory Coast), men are initiated into the Poro association, women into the Sande. Each association has internal grades along which an individual may advance. Most people do not pass beyond the first grade, but at higher grades men or women gain new secret knowledge. Those in the highest grades of the men's Poro wield considerable power in the society; their control of spirits legitimates their overruling the chief. The main theme of initiation and of the associations themselves is hierarchy: between occupants of different grades, and by the Poro over the rest of the society.

Each society has numerous lodges, so called after the example of Freemason lodges. Indeed, Poro members remark on the similarity of their society to that of the Masons. A Liberian man told one European ethnographer: "It is a pity you are not a Mason, for then I could tell you more. The Poro is just like Freemasonry" (quoted in La Fontaine 1985, 94). Creoles in Sierra Leone, ineligible to join a Poro society because they were not tribal members, indeed became attracted to Masonry because it provided them with the equivalent of the Poro. The association, structured around grades and secrets, had become a cultural type, to which Masonry was assimilated.

In Sierra Leone, initiation into the women's society takes girls and women away from villages and into the bush, where they stay for a week or two at a time, dancing, feasting, and acquiring new knowledge. But the girls also undergo infibulation. Although the operation is always painful and often dangerous, and it leads to health problems later in life, many women reject calls for an end to the practice. They point to the value of the camaraderie they enjoy in the women's society. "This is a happy time for us," said one just-initiated 16-year-old girl, pointing to the freedom the women and girls feel among themselves (French 1997). The future of the initiation has become the focus for debate in the country about how religion and custom ought to be understood and changed.

Reanalyses through the Lens of Gender

A principal contribution of feminist anthropology has been to show how the gender of the ethnographer may limit in important ways what he or she learns during fieldwork. One well-known study by Annette Weiner (1976) demonstrated how earlier fieldwork carried out by men missed rituals and knowledge held only by women. When Weiner revisited the site of Bronislaw Malinowski's classic fieldwork, the island of Kiriwina in the Trobriand Islands, she found that women carried out a great number of rituals—most importantly, mortuary rituals—that formed part of the overall system of exchange. Though the ethnography of Trobriand exchange was perhaps Malinowski's greatest contribution to anthropology, Weiner was able to show that he ignored these forms of exchange.

Rituals of Reversal, Reversed

An adequate ethnography of ritual meanings takes account of women's and men's actions and understandings and may lead to the reexamination of older understandings of entire types of ritual. As we saw earlier, the anthropologist Max Gluckman argued that a large class of African rituals could be considered as rituals of reversal or rebellion in which women or powerless people held sway for a short, highly ritualized, period of time. One of his main examples was the "Heavenly Princes Cult" of the southern African Zulu people. Gluckman (1963, 114–115) described the society as "patriarchal," on the grounds that in everyday life women were subordinate to men. And yet in rituals, women were allowed to represent life as if women were dominant. Gluckman argued that these and other rituals reinforced the prevailing social order by providing a symbolic release for potential hostility or resentment.

Gluckman's formulation of "rituals of rebellion" has been influential in anthropology (Turner 1969) and (largely through the work of Victor Turner) in other fields as well (for example, Davis 1965). It has been particularly well accepted in studies of gender and ritual in Africa. But as a recent analysis (Sanders 2000) shows, many of these rituals, at first glance suitable for analysis as rituals of reversal, in fact have a better explanation that depends on understanding the complementary roles of women and men.

Sanders studied with Ihanzu farmers living in the dry areas of northern Tanzania, where attracting sufficient rain is a constant concern. Men predominate in public political affairs and own nearly all property. Men and women will sometimes describe the society as male-dominated or patriarchal. Such a characterization should be taken as part of the social reality to be studied, however, and not the end of analysis. Women control grain and they brew the beer that is the basis for everyday socializing. Furthermore, descent in the society is matrilineal (through women).

Rain is normally encouraged through rituals presided over by two royal leaders, a man and his sister; but in the years when people judge these normal rainmaking rituals to have failed, the leaders will decide to hold a women's rain dance. (Trials of "rain witches" may also be held.) The ritual lasts several days, during which women shove anti-witchcraft medicine into the ground, dance naked into the bush and onto special dancing grounds, and visit ancestral caves, usually while shouting lewd songs. Any man caught in their way is liable to be attacked.

Although the ritual is ripe for study as a ritual of reversal, their performance in these moments of danger is better explained by the local understandings of women's attributes. Women's bodies are thought to be "wet" while men's are "dry," and thus it is women who must work to bring on the rains. Moreover, the women are capable of transforming the dry weather conditions by bringing together gender attributes: their own (wet) bodies with the aggression and violence associated with men. Thus the ritual is not designed— or locally understood—as granting women "power for a day" (or several days). It is not a ritual of reversal, but a transformative uniting of male and female qualities.

Articulating Women's Perspectives through Spirits

We have already seen that in many societies women act and reflect on their actions in ways that are sometimes less public than are the deeds and words of their male counterparts and that their actions have often been ignored by male anthropologists. Certain religious practices seem to be used by women in a number of societies as the means to reflect on and improve their position; for example, possession and mediumship as it is found in eastern African societies, from the *zar* cult in the Sudan (Boddy 1989; Kenyon 1995) to possession by *tromba* in Madagascar (Sharp 1993). These cults and practices are both ways of healing the sick and ways of commenting on social life.

Zar Possession

Most people living in the Northern Sudan are Muslims, and Islam, locally defined, provides the concepts and texts for the prevailing discourse in villages. Men control that discourse and what is considered to be central or peripheral to it. But women produce a different set of messages and ideas, in part through their activities in the zar spirit cult. As Janice Boddy (1989) shows, these activities shape both men's and women's perceptions of themselves and their social and moral norms. Furthermore, the cult and mainstream Islam define each other by contrasts, much as we saw for highland Sumatran ideas about sacrificial ritual.

Zar are spirits prone to possess and cause illness in humans. The word refers to the spirits, the illnesses, and the rituals required to propitiate them. The cult is found throughout northern Africa and Arabia. The spirit world is layered onto the human world and spirits may descend into humans at any time, where they remain. The human must then learn how to let the spirit enter her and how to accommodate her requests so that she will not cause further harm.

Boddy describes a healing ritual that occurred over several days (1989, 125–131). The ritual leader, *shaykha,* speaks to the spirits as the women, one by one, let themselves be possessed. Very much like the Candomblé trance spirits described in Chapter 7 of this book, these spirits represent cultural types and their human vehicles speak and move accordingly. A Western military officer has her human medium shuffle along in a march-like dance, bob formally at the waist, and request a European-style belt and a radio. Two women who are possessed by a Nomad spirit leap at each other brandishing naked swords. An Ethiopian prostitute behaves accordingly (and requests scanty clothing), while another spirit has the possessed woman move after the fashion of a man who is engaged in Islamic repetitive chanting, *dhikr.* As a result of all these possessions, the afflicted woman for whose benefit the session is held is formally considered to have been healed.

In this Sudanese village possession is widespread among married women—40 percent have been possessed—and rare among men. The distinctive perspective that it gives to experience is thus characteristic of women. Like Wiccan associations in the United States, described later, zar provides a set of practices and ideas that can articulate women's perspectives, power, and problems. Like many religious organizations, the cults function more as organized social groups in the cities and more as networks of women in rural areas. They resemble men's Sufi orders and, like them, provide a social matrix for women in village, town, or city.

Boddy meticulously traces the parallels between wedding ceremonies and possession rituals, noting that possession rituals frequently reverse the order of processes that accompany wedding ceremonies. This reversal shows that the wedding symbolism is not inevitable. For example, the loss of blood accompanying sexual intercourse on the wedding night is countered by the ingestion of blood and the use of blood from a sacrificial animal to annoint the afflicted patient at the possession rituals (1989, 332–334). More generally, by providing a parody of weddings, the ritual suggests that there are realities beyond the one experienced by women as they become wives.

As new problems have arisen for Sudanese women and their families, zar cults have expanded and adapted to deal with them. In the present time of great material need, zar specialists may lend needy women money (Kenyon 1995, 240). Zar has also received increasing attention from the Sudanese government, which has promoted and publicized it as part of "Sudanese tradition." Susan Kenyon (1995, 241) reports that in the capital, Khartoum, men have begun to form their own zar cults, and she speculates that they may try to centralize and professionalize the cult, a step that would represent a break with its current psychosocial functions.

Religious Patriarchy and Its Challenges

Some historians and anthropologists see the lineage of Judaism, Christianity, and Islam as sanctioning patriarchy, though others emphasize the cultural roots of patriarchy and point to the way these religions have provided women with resources for liberation.

Abraham and Sacrifice

Some scholars argue that the major narratives underlying the monotheistic religions take on the force of myth, shaping the way followers think about the world. Do these narratives portray the world in a consistently patriarchal way? In a forceful book on patriarchy and religion, Carol Delaney (1998) argues that the biblical story of Abraham has provided a template for thinking about gender within the three related Semitic religions (Judaism, Christianity, Islam) and that this template has had unfortunate consequences for human welfare.

Delaney finds proof that these three religions are thoroughly patriarchal in their founding myths. In Abraham's choosing to sacrifice his child it is implied that the child is his to sacrifice, and that the child's mother, Sarah, does not have to be consulted. Only the father's decision and his son's submission have religious relevance, not the son's or mother's autonomous wills.

In the Torah, the Gospels, and the Qur'ân, the relevant lines of descent are through males, not females. The relationship through the seed of Abraham, thus through serial fatherhood, defines the religious community. Delaney argues that people raised in the traditions of these three monotheisms have internalized the model of faith through sacrifice set out in the Abraham story and enshrined it in laws and institutions such as marriage and the family. The social consequences have included a tendency to abuse children, she writes (1998, 235–241), because the Abraham story has directly or indirectly supported the idea that children are ours to sacrifice.

Delaney (1998, 238) finds connections between certain contemporary Christian child-rearing manuals that urge parents to "break the will" of a child and the Abraham story. And she cites a disturbing account of a 1990 trial of a man who killed his daughter in a manner that replicated Abraham's near-sacrifice of his son—except that in the modern case the deed was carried out. The man was found insane, but Delaney leaves us with the question: If Abraham acted above the law, can someone working from within a Jewish theological framework condemn this man; can he or she be sure that he was truly insane and not another person who had heard God speak?

Fundamentalism and Gender Roles

Another way to approach the question of gender and the monotheistic religions is by looking at speeches, sermons, and writings connected with particular movements. Susan Harding (2000) undertook this kind of research in her study of Protestant Fundamentalism by listening to the preachers and followers of the Reverend Jerry Falwell to understand the force of the way they speak about the world.

The Fundamentalist religious tradition is known for claiming that women and men have separate natures and tasks. Preachers frequently cite St. Paul's exhortation to Christian wives to submit to their husbands "as unto the Lord" (Ephesians 5:22–24). This basic paradigm invests the marital relation with the same sacred hierarchy that characterizes the relationships of all humans to God. In the 1940s and 1950s Fundamentalist preachers described wives as "the weaker vessel" and decried notions of companionate marriage.

Harding observes that one of the norms embraced by Falwell's Moral Majority movement is the wife's submission to the husband's leadership, but goes on to examine the contemporary sermons and speeches through which this norm is communicated and given more complex meanings. She notes, for example, that Falwell distances himself from those norms and that image in his speeches through the use of irony, confession, and self-deprecation.

By the 1970s and 1980s, writes Harding (2000, 161–181), Fundamentalists had come to think of marriage in terms of companionship and complementarity rather than in terms of command and hierarchy. Evangelical feminists had a great deal to do with bringing about changes in the ways preachers spoke about gender relations. (The term *evangelical* places the emphasis on working to convert others, as distinguished from the tendency of some Fundamentalist movements to focus inward on their own communities.) By the 1980s, more evangelical and Fundamentalist women were working outside the home, and their work began to be publicly valued as part of how a Christian life could and should be built (Harding 2000, 172–173). This was a major change but it was made without ever abandoning a reliance on St. Paul's gender-unequal admonition. It was accomplished by affirming the husband's right to make final decisions in family matters while emphasizing the wisdom of his consulting—and sometimes conceding to—his wife. Some preachers, notably Falwell himself, began to adopt an ironic stance toward biblical text even while affirming it in their rhetoric.

A 1986 speech by Falwell illustrates this stance (Harding 2000, 167–168). A strong attack on America's moral decline, with special emphasis on AIDS and single-parent families, changed into a very different style as Falwell made a confession about marriage. Married 28 years, he and his wife had never discussed divorce, even though "we've had some knock-downs and drag-outs [Laughter]. I've lost every one of them [Laughter]. I tell you, men, the best thing you can do is quickly raise your hands and unconditionally surrender because you're gonna lose [Laughter]. Amen? [Amens]" (Harding 2000, 167–168).

Harding points out that the joking reveals the current flux in marital norms but that it, and the entire speech, was addressed to men and not women (176–177). Fundamentalist public speaking, Harding observes, "implicitly privileges men through its rhetorical forms and in its content, which in many and varied ways create a two-tiered audience with men 'up front' and women 'in the back.' " Public Fundamentalist rhetoric remains directed at men and supportive of men even as they no longer can claim a superior role and a monopoly on extra-household activities.

How was this shift possible? At the height of their confrontation with the growing feminist movement during the 1970s, many conservative Christians argued that to stop following Paul's injunction would be to challenge biblical inerrancy. But by the 1990s many Fundamentalists had been able to adopt a more gender-equal style of family life without renouncing their belief in an absolutely true Bible. As Harding points out, this accommodation has been more a matter of selective emphasis than a shift in doctrine. One does not, after all, have to pay equal attention to all verses all the time.

Harding cites another example to point out how interpretation may change without requiring explicit shifts in doctrine. In the 1960s, defenders of racial segregation sometimes cited passages from Genesis to support their position. In 9 Genesis Noah curses the descendants of his son Ham because Ham had seen Noah naked. For those who believe Ham's descendants were the people of Africa the Bible supports continued policies of segregation and discrimination in favor of whites.

Eventually many Fundamentalists agreed to or at least came to tolerate a change in social policy. The passages themselves were not blocks to the eventual demise of segregation; they "simply stopped being cited" (Harding 2000, 181).

As Falwell began to say less and less about how families should be run, activists began to convey new and broader messages. By the late 1980s a new set of evangelical counselors and organizers had taken on the role of reforming family life around scripture. The most successful has been James Dobson, the head of Focus on the Family. From its headquarters in Colorado come a large volume of videotapes, newspaper columns, books, and radio programs illustrating a certain set of norms for family life. The more the message is aimed at a general public, the less religious and the more psychosocial it becomes. Dobson's widely syndicated newspaper columns are virtually devoid of explicit religious content and treat issues of child-raising in a secular psychological idiom. Other social movements, like the Colorado-based Promise Keepers movement, have arisen with parallel programs.

The Fundamentalist and evangelical conservative Christian movements have changed their approach to gender relations in two ways. One is by playing down while never denying the importance of key biblical texts (such as Paul's statements). The other is by expanding the range of media and activities by which "family values" are conveyed far beyond the pulpit to include mass media and new social movements.

Women and Islamic Dress

*I*n recent years, no single religious image has evoked as many conflicting ideas and emotions about gender as that of a Muslim woman wearing a headcovering. The modest dress, headcoverings, and sometimes face coverings worn by some Muslim women have for many onlookers come to symbolize the (hopelessly) patriarchal nature of Islam.

The best anthropological way of studying the veil and its meaning would be to observe a range of practices in a variety of places. Current dress in Cairo illustrates the

Muhajjaba in Cairo. Dress form or jilbab (loose, ankle-length, long-sleeve, opaque fabric) and color (austere dark solid) show typical Islamic dress for women in the 1970s and 1980s. (PHOTO BY FADWA EL GUINDI. COURTESY OF EL NIL RESEARCH © 1995.)

variety of "Muslim-looking" dress options available to women, as I observed in Cairo in Summer 2000. A 1982 film by Elizabeth Fernea, *A Veiled Revolution,* carefully documents the range of dress styles and ways of thinking about dress among middle-class women of Cairo, and subsequent studies (Ahmed 1992; El Guindi 1999) have delineated the complex social and religious meanings attached to dress choices.

First we need to discard the word *veil* and distinguish among various types of clothing. The Arabic word *hijab,* or "barrier," is used in many Muslim countries to refer to Islamic dress or modest dress in general. Several types of garments can be combined in different ways within an Islamic dress repertoire, and, further complicating matters, many different Arabic terms are used to refer to various items. The dress may include headcoverings (*khimar, 'abayah*), face covering veils (*niqab, burqu'*), or an all-enveloping garment (*milayah, jellabah, burga'*). (But these words have different meanings depending on time and place.) And each item comes in a variety of types. A headcovering, for example, might be a simple scarf, a hood-like item, or part of a single garment. A veil may be highly transparent or completely opaque. A long dress may cover all or some of the body or be replaced by trousers and a tunic. It may be accompanied by gloves and socks (El Guindi 1999).

All these items come in a variety of colors and styles, from black through shades of beige, to blue and green, to multicolored, and all have specific associations. Black tends to be worn by lower-class women and is seen by them as the most modest color (as is true in some other non-Muslim parts of the Mediterranean world). Green is believed to be the Prophet Muhammad's favorite color; in some countries (Malaysia, for example) this association leads to a profusion of green, while in some others (Iran, France, and Indonesia, for example), it does not. By the 1980s women in many Muslim societies began to wear "high fashion" outfits of silky materials, with elaborate jewelry and matching accessories.

But women also draw on a repertoire of dress items in different situations. Yemeni women, for example, have two types of headcovering for indoor wear, and two for outdoors (Makhlouf 1979, 30–34). For indoor wear, women can choose between a garment that is draped around the head and that can be pulled down or up to cover the face, and a tied scarf, more fashionable, used for visiting. For outdoors, the *sitara* combines a large scarf draped over the head and a batik cloth covering the face but allowing the wearer to see out. The alternative is the *sharshaf,* a three piece garment consisting of a pleated skirt, a waist-length cape, and a thin black face covering. The choice among possible coverings is shaped by and reveals social status. High-status women tend to wear the *sharshaf,* lower-status women the *sitara,* with those in the middle alternating between the two. Covering may also be used to indicate a kin relation. In parts of northern India studied by Ursula Sharma (1980), for example, Muslim women marry out of their natal villages into their husbands' villages and mark their new status by their veil. The wife's use of face covering depends on her husband's place in the village kinship system: she covers her face in the presence of men considered to be senior to her husband, such as his older brothers and cousins, but not before his inferiors. And she does not cover her face before men of her natal village.

Fadwa El Guindi (1999, 103–114) points out that women and men often use head- or face coverings to indicate status, authority, or respect, noting the specific use of a veil by the widow of the Prophet Muhammad, 'Āisha, who became politically active during the reign of Muhammad's successors. Following the murder of a successor, Uthman, 'Āisha appeared at the mosque in Mecca and, standing on the spot where Abraham was thought to have laid the foundation of the original sanctuary, ceremonially veiled herself and addressed the crowd. Her act of public veiling claimed her a position of political authority, and El Guindi (1999, 112) compares it to the Prophet's act of donning a black headcovering that covered much of his face on his triumphant return to Mecca.

Dress and Feminism in Cairo

The city of Cairo offers illustration of how a multitude of meanings conveyed by head and face coverings have changed over time in the Middle East. Cairo of the 1910s and 1920s was experiencing rapid cultural change, with cinemas, new newspapers, rising rates of literacy, and higher education. Its citizens chafed under British colonial control, and women in particular resented obstacles placed in their way by the colonists. It was the British adviser to the Minister of Education, not an Egyptian, who tried to prevent a woman from obtaining her secondary school certificate. (The Egyptian student finally succeeded in 1908.) Women were contributing to newspapers and attending schools in increasing numbers and were forming intellectual and literary associations. They were also creating hospitals, founding political organizations, and demonstrating against the British. Women were publicly and politically active at the center of nationalist, anti-colonial movements (Ahmed 1992).

Among the leaders was Huda Sha'rawi, who made the lifting of the face covering an act signifying women's liberation. In May 1923, when Sha'rawi and her colleagues arrived at the Cairo train station from an international women's conference in Rome, they publicly and ceremoniously removed their face coverings (*burqu*'), though not their headcoverings. Women of the upper class had already been unveiling in great numbers, but her act gave the trend momentous political and cultural significance by representing women's causes as culturally linked to Europe, despite the women's opposition to European domination.

Two streams of feminism emerged from these activities. One, led by Huda Sha'rawi, urged progress toward a European way of life. The other, led by Malak Hifni Nassef, wanted to place the feminist cause within the struggle for Islamic renovation and reform. Nassef's views were different from Sha'rawi's. Though she equally opposed polygamy and rejected the view that Islam demanded that women cover their heads, she cautioned Egyptian women against slavishly following European ways before they had received the education that would allow them to make intelligent choices. She saw the real problem for Egyptian women as male domination; only education would allow women to overcome their subordination (Ahmed 1992, 179–184). Nassef's early death meant that the former stream predominated until the 1980s, when new Islamic feminist voices began to be heard.

Women advanced to college in record numbers during the 1950s and 1960s and began to move the general program outlined by Sha'rawi into new territory, advocating changes in domestic relations, women's access to contraception, and better medical attention for women. Leila Ahmed (1992) argues that women adopted Islamic dress as a way to combine their feminism with an increase in religiosity that happened during the same period. She points to the rapid rise during the 1960s and 1970s in the number of women who migrated to Cairo, often as children, and received dramatically higher levels of education. In 1953 men outnumbered women in the universities by 13 to one, but by 1976 the ratio had dropped to 1.8 to one. By 1982 women held 26 percent of the jobs in professions and science (Ahmed 1992, 210–211). They trained their new skills on social problems: the maltreatment of women and children, male domination in Arab society (whether Muslim or Christian), illiteracy.

The "open door policy" of the 1970s increased both economic inequality and the visibility of Western consumer products and Western middle-class behavioral norms, particularly freedom of interaction among men and women. But in the 1970s things changed dramatically. In 1967 Israel had defeated Egypt in the Six Days' War. Feeling humiliated and perplexed, many Egyptians turned to religion as a source of strength. Many Muslims joined Sufi orders, which offered activities of chanting and meditating. The most striking event, however, was when many people said they saw the Virgin Mary appear near a Coptic Christian church, under a tree where Mary had rested with Joseph and Jesus in their flight to Egypt. Thousands of Muslims and Christians flocked to the site to see her (El Guindi 1999, 131–132). For these people and many others, the apparition gave a religious meaning to the military defeat, namely, that Egyptians needed to rediscover their piety. Egypt's subsequent military victory over Israel in the 1973 war only added to the growing alliance between feelings of religious piety and national identity.

From then on, it was the "religious movement" (*mitdayyinin*) that developed in Cairo. Students seeking to promote an Islamic model of comportment also advocated Islamic dress for men and women. El Guindi (1999, 134) describes the women's Islamic dress that began to be worn in the 1970s not as a return to any traditional dress form, but as "an innovative construction." The students and other activists made the new garments in their homes. Men and women in the movement wore *jilbabs,* loose full-length, solid-colored gowns of opaque fabric. Men also wore baggy trousers and shorts, and grew short beards. Women wore headcoverings called *khimar.*

These men and women argued that the Qur'ân supported their new dress, citing verses from two chapters of the Qur'ân. In one (Qur'ân 24:30–31), God instructs all female believers to use their khimar to cover their cleavage and to "display their beauty" only to their close relatives. In another (Qur'ân 33:59), God commands the Prophet Muhammad to tell believing women to put on their jilbabs (El Guindi 1999, 139).

Ahmed argues (1992, 222–225) that women and men adopted Islamic dress as a response to a contradiction between their culture of origins and the new urban situation in which they found themselves. Surveys taken in Cairo in the late 1970s showed that these men and women tended to come from conservative backgrounds, with parents who often were less educated and of rural origin. They themselves had achieved university-level education. Adopting an outwardly conservative Islamic dress may have been a way to cope with the tension between the values and norms of the new urban, highly educated classes and those of their parents and helped them deal with their parents' failure to understand their new lives. The new dress styles also helped them feel part of a community of religious-minded people at a time when they may have felt adrift and confused.

In a more positive vein, Ahmed sees both the early feminism of Sha'rawi and the later adoption of Islamic dress as equally the efforts of women to achieve autonomy, under different circumstances and for different social classes. In both situations women have used dress to create a public space for themselves. Islamic dress may offer practical advantages to working women, a point made by the Cairene women who discussed their dress choices in Fernea's film (1982). The women said that when they adopted Islamic dress other men and women accorded them more respect and that they also felt more self-respect. These garments protected them from unwanted advances by men, some said; they were good for working women because one didn't have to dress up, and were more practical for work involving bending down or working on the floor.

These women also saw wearing Islamic dress as a public expression of one's own strong will regarding Islam, keeping the faith, having love for God, preserving Islam. Precisely because they attributed these meanings to the garments, some women said they did not yet feel ready for the burden of wearing these clothes.

Women's Islamic dress can also serve to render more acceptable their roles outside the home. Arlene MacLeod (1991) views this response in a more negative light than does Leila Ahmed, observing that adopting such dress may be a married woman's way of coping with not being able to both work and tend well to her family. MacLeod (1991, 102–107) adds the valuable perspective of working-class women to the story. Before the religious movement of the 1970s, these women wore smocks and kerchiefs, topped by a black overdress when visiting or shopping. But women who reached the middle-class working stratum had generally adopted Western dress, which served as a badge of upward class mobility.

Karima's story exemplifies the conflicts experienced by some working women as part of what MacLeod calls the "new veiling," the revisions of dress that took place from the 1970s onward. Karima was married and had small children when MacLeod spoke with her in the mid-1980s. She also worked in an office. She said that taking on the hijab (*muhajjaba*) after the birth of her first child helped her feel at peace, even as she felt caught between the conflicting, tiring demands of work, child care, and homemaking. "When I wear this dress, it says to everyone that I am trying to be a good wife and a good mother" (MacLeod 1991, 118–124).

Ahmed and MacLeod interpret the meaning of the new forms of dress in slightly different ways. Ahmed, writing mainly about middle-class women, and especially students, emphasizes the autonomy that adopting the hijab can bring. MacLeod's study of lower-middle-class women focuses on the hijab as an expression of the contradictory pull between home and work, conservative and modern social norms. Ahmed points to the instrumental value of the veil in carving out public space, MacLeod to its role in expressing a set of feelings. MacLeod also suggests that it might be seen as an "accommodating protest": protesting even while adapting to their uncomfortable situation.

The differences in MacLeod's and Ahmed's interpretations reflect not only class differences but also the ambivalence many women have expressed concerning the adoption of Islamic dress. The hijab defines its wearer in certain ways that can both promise autonomy and restrict a range of options. The decision to adopt this dress can be felt both as a free choice and as a result of social pressure.

Comparisons

Adopting Islamic dress may have very different meanings for women in other countries and, just as in Cairo, may vary according to social class and religious ideology. In Iran before 1979, for example, wearing the black, fully covering garment called the *chador* was a way for women to protest against the rule of the Shah. It was for them an expression of a desire for freedom, including but not limited to religious freedom.

But since the 1979 revolution enforcement of a strict dress code by religious police has made many women ambivalent about these dress forms. Many women now combine brightly colored dresses with more somber outerwear. If Iran continues to liberalize its cultural policies under President Khatami, Islamic dress styles may continue to diversify.

Controversy has arisen in some countries over the wearing of simple headcoverings by girls attending state high schools. In each country the controversy has had different roots and thus different meanings. Indonesia, as we saw in Chapter 3, has more Muslims than any other country and Islam is state-supported. But the state ideology is pluriconfessional, meaning that all citizens are supposed to follow a recognized religion, though one is not favored over another and all are supposed to be subordinate to allegiance to the state. When in the 1970s some girls began wearing headcoverings to public schools, state officials viewed the headscarves as signifying allegiance to Islam taking precedence over allegiance to country, and banned them. (The ban was later lifted.)

In both Turkey and France, scarf-wearing took place in a context of state secularism, but with two very different histories. Turkey came into existence after World War I under the leadership of Kemal Ataturk, who, in abolishing the Ottoman caliphate (the successor state to Muhammad's political leadership) also abolished Islamic law. He worked to make Turkey a European country, outlawed Sufi brotherhoods, and required that worship be in Turkish rather than Arabic. The army continues to see itself as the guardian of Ataturk's legacy, and vigorously opposes any visible signs of Islamic politics, including the wearing of Islamic dress in public schools or in the Parliament.

French politics are founded upon the opposition between the agents of secularism and the Catholic Church, an opposition dating to the Revolution but renewed at the beginning of the twentieth century by laws separating religion from public affairs and by a concerted effort to create a nationwide, secular school system. When in 1989 some Muslim schoolgirls wore scarves to school, their action was seen by some as an attack on the principle of secularism. As of 2004, French law prohibits wearing clothing that clearly exhibits a student's religious affiliation, but the widespread objections to the law will mean continued negotiations and confrontations in schools (see Chapter 15).

The hair and the head are frequently invested with important social, spiritual, and sexual meanings, particularly with respect to social transitions. An act such as shaving the head may signal that one enters a state outside of normal social life. In Thailand, for example, men shave their heads upon joining a monastery for a period in their lives and regrow their hair upon leaving. When Muslim men or women have made the pilgrimage, they wear white caps or scarves to mark their passage to the special status reached by the person who has completed his or her religious duties. In other cultures those with long hair may be especially powerful (Samson, forest monks, St. John the Baptist, for example) or less powerful (intellectuals, hippies), but they, too, are different.

6

Patterns, Powers, and the Self

*T*hroughout the world, people look for ways to explain what happens to them in everyday life: the good, the bad, the apparently lucky or unlucky. We all would like to have greater control over what happens to us, and, when we cannot have that, reasons for why things happen. Religion in the broadest sense of the term offers solace, reasons, and resources for controlling the social and natural world.

Magic, Patterns, and Causes

*E*arlier students of religion sought to identify the fundamental features that lay behind beliefs in magic. The nineteenth-century anthropologists Edward Tylor and James Frazer thought of magic as a pseudoscience, what primitive people did instead of science. Magic for them was just like science in that it sought to act directly on the world, in a technical or instrumental way, but it was empirically false in its assumptions. Magic was a set of spells and techniques acquired with more attention to their effects (the practical side) than their principles (the theory).

Likeness and Contact

In his massive work on myth and folklore, *The Golden Bough* (1981), Frazer isolated two ideas that he saw as the basis for magical thinking: like affects like; and things that come into contact affect each other. The first he called "homeopathy," the second, "contagion." Homeopathic magic makes use of similarities, either natural or human-made, to reach its end. One kind of similarity is in the appearance of an object, so dolls or pictures of a person, when altered in some way, will, because like causes like, cause a corresponding alteration in the target person—the proverbial "voodoo doll" with the pins stuck in it. But there are other ways similarities are drawn on for practical ends. One can transfer the properties of any object to someone for a good or ill purpose. Gayo people use leaves that feel cool to the touch to bring down a fever on the assumption that the patient will feel cool because the leaves are cool.

Actions, rather than objects, can also have efficacy through the logic of likeness. Take the *couvade,* for example, a ritual first remarked in native North America wherein a father-to-be imitates the process of giving birth while his wife is experiencing labor pains. By his enactment of the successful birth he is supposed to push the process along and make it easier. (Perhaps this way of thinking underlies Lamaze birthing procedures in which the woman's companion performs blowing and counting exercises along with her.) A more complex logic underlies the "cosmic balance rituals," long called "increase rituals," in native Australia (Swain 1995, 25–28). Aboriginal groups recognize a particular plant, animal, or other object as their protective totem. They act out the birth of their totemic animal or plant and thereby increase its number. The additional special relationship between totem and people then leads to their prosperity.

The second principle is contagion, that contact between two objects means that action upon one of the objects will produce effects on the other. The hair or nails of a person, or clothing, may be used to work magic on the person. During the beginning of my fieldwork, several neighbors were concerned that I might become the victim of illness-causing magic and warned me not to hang up my wash outside. A shirt could be used to work magic on me, they said. Of special interest to societies around the world are discarded body parts, from fingernail clippings to the placenta. Because it is born along with the child, the placenta is treated in some societies as the child's brother, and how it is treated can affect the child's fortune. Some people bury it, to ensure that the child will always return from a trip; others store it away. The history of contact with the person gives the placenta its importance.

But "magic" is not limited to marginal activities or small-scale societies. The history of the Christian Church is inextricably bound up with what, from the perspective we take here, we would call "contagious magic." The power held by relics of saints, after all, derives from the relic's history as a part of the saint or as something that came into contact with the saint. For several centuries new churches had to be founded on a relic. Certain portraits, such as Our Lady of Czestochowa in Poland, draw special power from the contact with a saint (Saint Luke in this case). And of course the Shroud of Turin's special claim is not its likeness of Jesus but the supposed contact with Jesus's face. From the point of view adopted by Frazer, "magic" is less a type of practice than it is a psychological basis for making certain claims about power and efficacy. We find the ideas of likeness and contact compelling, and so we are especially likely to accept claims made on their bases.

Magic and Anxiety

Frazer's view of magic as replacement for science too neatly divided the world into "primitive" and "modern" societies. "Magical thinking" is in fact part of religious life and everyday life in all societies. The anthropologist Bronislaw Malinowski (1954) argued that science and magic are not substitutes for each other, but in that all societies they cooperate to create a psychologically satisfactory life. For all people, argued Malinowski, our ability to control our environments stops at some point, far short of what we would like. At that point magic comes in. It allows us to act on the areas of life filled with uncertainty, thus reducing our anxiety and allowing us to get on with life.

Contrary to what Frazer claimed, Malinowski said that no people in the world confuse technical or scientific knowledge with magic. People everywhere realize that their knowledge and control over the world has limits. Within the limits of that knowledge and control, practical, empirical science and skill is sufficient, and one does not find magic. Malinowski offered examples from his fieldwork in the Trobriand Islands, part of present-day Papua New Guinea. For Trobrianders, most everyday activities are fully under their control and therefore do not involve magic. A Trobriander knows how to make a basket or a pot with little chance of breakage and how to fish in safe areas, within the lagoon, for example, with no danger and little uncertainty. These activities are not accompanied by magic. On the other hand, activities that do have a certain degree of uncertainty, risk, or danger connected with them are likely to have magic. When Trobrianders venture out into the open sea to fish, they must use more chancy methods of fishing and face much more danger; it is then that they use magical spells to ensure a safe and successful venture.

Malinowski's approach gives us clear predictions of when we will find magic and when we will not. To state the argument abstractly: in any particular domain, activities that involve the most uncertainty are also the most likely to be accompanied by magic, that is, by practices that do not have technically or scientifically apparent effects but are believed by the actors to help their chances of success.

George Gmelch (1978) provides an example from American baseball. There is a clear division in baseball between activities in which players are expected to succeed nearly all the time and those in which they are not. Fielding is an example of the first, where failing to catch a pop fly ball will be counted as an error and not as an expected, common failure. Pitching and hitting are clear examples of the second category, where players have much less control over what happens. A player who hits one-third of the time is very successful, as is a pitcher who throws strikes only half the time.

Is Malinowski's prediction right for baseball? It appears so: pitching and hitting, where so many things can go wrong, are accompanied by magic; fielding is not. Players practice magic by experiment and correlation. They try wearing an outfit or eating a certain food; if they do well on that day, then the clothes or food become "lucky" and a required part of their daily preparation. Gmelch himself, a former player, ate pancakes on mornings before games after he had won games on pancake days. Or they may decide to abstain from sex (as did an entire Canadian team during the 1996 Olympics), or the opposite, before game days.

Baseball magic can, as Malinowski stressed, relieve anxiety and build confidence. But once a player starts relying on magic he starts to require his magic to keep up his confidence. Magic can create anxiety as well as resolve it—a point made by a contemporary of Malinowski's, the anthropologist A. R. Radcliffe-Brown (1965).

One might say that for Malinowski, magic was a kind of psychology, not science; it arises out of one's awareness of one's own inability to control a situation but a desire to be able to control it. Magic is close to wish fulfillment or daydreaming. Malinowski's approach is an important corrective to Frazer's in providing a richer portrait of why people make use of magic. For example, the couvade, where the father imitates the birthing process, was explained by Frazer in terms of "like affects like." But why do we find magic for this event, giving birth, and not for many others? What drives people to make use of "like affects like" here? Malinowski would say that the couvade gives the father a feeling of participation and accomplishment in a situation in which he otherwise has little to do. In the United States, at least, the joke used to be that the father would be sent to boil endless pots of water, ostensibly to sterilize equipment but in fact to channel his nervous energy. The couvade-like techniques of Lamaze and other birthing exercises are, from Malinowski's point of view, more refined forms of magic.

Seeing Patterns in Sports

Does Malinowski's insight work for all instances of sports magic? Let us consider the notion of luck, good and bad, how you can change it—and most importantly, how you perceive it. Consider wearing the number 13 on your jersey: does it bring bad luck? It sure looks that way once you start to consider examples of players who did so, as does one popular writer (Morrison 2003). In 1999 baseball pitcher Jeff Fassero wore it for two teams and compiled the worst earned run average since 1937. Reaching back to 1951 one finds pitcher Ralph Branca in number 13 and surrendering "the shot heard round the world" home run by Bobby Thomson. I looked through the list of 13-wearers and saw our St. Louis Rams quarterback Kurt Warner, who had a few great seasons and then collapsed—unusual for football, and requiring explaining. Hmmm, maybe so?

My reaction is common: once you find a few examples that fit the pattern it is human nature to believe in the pattern. We do look for patterns; we are pleased to find them—in the skies, in our lives, in sports. But what if I had come across Kurt Warner's name in 2001, when he was completing long passes left and right? I probably would have read down the list until I found another name that fit the pattern.

One pattern many players find in their game is "hot hands." Known best in basketball, "hot hands" designates a winning streak, one ball going in the basket after another. The psychologist Amos Tversky (1988) interviewed players, dedicated fans, and statisticians of basketball, and found that the more deeply they knew their sport the stronger their belief in the reality of "hot hands." And yet when his research team analyzed every shot sequence for all games played by the Philadelphia 76ers over a season and a half, they didn't find that a hit was likely to be followed by another (what the "hot hands hypothesis" would predict) but that a hit was slightly more likely to be followed by a miss! Now, there were strings of hits, as one would predict even if hits and misses occurred randomly, and it probably is the memory of a few of those strings that lead people to believe in the hypothesis. And, of course, strings of hits also are the product of players being alert, in their stride, and so forth—it's just that when we look at the overall picture these strings occur randomly. (See one "hot hands" site at: *www.hs.ttu.edu/hdfs3390/hothand.htm.*)

Many of the most common ideas and practices about luck and rituals in sports depend on perceiving some patterns, like the cases of "hot hands" or truly unfortunate 13-wearing pitchers, and ignoring others, like successful 13-wearers or season-long random patterns of hits and misses. Chicago Cubs fans blame the curse of Murphy the Goat for their long history of losing key games. In 1945, a saloon owner named Billy

Goat Sianis tried to bring his billy goat Murphy onto Wrigley Field. P. K. Wrigley denied the goat entrance, saying it stunk, and Sianis replied, "Cubs, they ain't gonna win again." They didn't, and fans have since blamed the curse, forgetting that they hadn't won for 37 years before the curse either!

These are many examples. Does appearing on the cover of *Sports Illustrated* jinx an athlete? Some athletes think so, and they cite the many cases of athletes who suffered disastrous streaks shortly after being featured in the magazine. *Sports Illustrated* editors thought the rumors potentially damaging enough to hire some statisticians to study the subject (Wolff 2003). They found that a *Sports Illustrated* cover appearance did jinx players 37 percent of the time (and therefore did not do so 63 percent of the time) and that the rate was significantly higher for players of individual sports. Did the appearance have an effect? It is, of course, very difficult to simulate non-appearance by these players, but the difference in terms of type of game suggests that some players may get nervous after expectations have been raised by their appearance—a "clutch" phenomenon—or even that worry about the jinx effect itself affected their play, a reverse placebo effect.

Our tendencies to read causality into patterns make sports magic an empirical science of sorts. Players who are doing well often respond by wearing the same clothes, eating the same food, or doing anything that they happened to be doing when their successful streak began, hoping or wishing that this behavior will keep them "hot" on the field. Sometimes they disconfirm their own actions, as when University of Kansas oarswomen Lauren Royall began wearing a black sports bra to every meet, because she had once worn one and won. The first time she lost wearing the black bra she was furious, and swore off magic entirely. "Now I try not to pay attention to what I put on" (McNearney 2002). The search for causality may explain the famous (and illegal) corked bats used by hitters, which got Sammy Sosa into trouble in 2003. The cork seems to add nothing to performance but was likely adopted when some players happened to hit well with such a bat.

Explaining Misfortune

Most likely, all societies provide some way to explain misfortune by postulating unseen forces, either personified agents such as spirits and devils, or abstract forces such as original sin or karma. These unseen forces are usually invoked when more everyday causes are unavailable.

Karma in South Asia

The idea of *karma* is that one's actions in the past, including in past lives, affects one's life today. The idea can be called on to account for misfortune.

The idea of karma is most widespread in South Asia, where it is interpreted in a variety of ways and is subject to debate between social classes. In particular, views held by some religious authorities of the Brahman priestly class contrast with many popular ideas about karma (Babb 1983). In one Brahmanic view, at least, a great deal of the misfortune of life is due not to a deity, who might be propitiated or recruited through sacrifice or worship, but to one's own actions in an earlier life: that is, due to karma. Under this notion of karma, there is little or nothing that a person can do to change what his deeds in his previous life have preordained. Some Brahmans also invoke karma to explain why they are sitting on top of the caste hierarchy.

Other people reject some of these views about karma, though not the idea itself. Unsurprisingly, people of lower castes are skeptical that Brahmans are on top because of their past good deeds. More generally, as with the strict Calvinist views of predestination that we consider in Chapter 11, "just sit and wait" has less popular appeal than "try something." For these reasons, most village Hindu people have modified the Brahmanic view of karma. The idea that you can do something has strong religious as well as psychological roots. Even the classical Hindu literature portrays people who, through their devotion to the gods, are saved from the consequences of their past lives.

Some people view karma as applying to a group of people rather than only to the individual, and as applying mainly to one's actions in this lifetime. In this view, karma implies that certain categories of people will get their just rewards or punishments during their lifetimes. Susan Wadley and Bruce Derr (1989) give the example of a fire in a north Indian village, which villagers blamed on the bad actions of the Brahman landowners. The fire itself was seen as having singled out for destruction the homes of certain offenders: those who were "eating the earnings of sin" by oppressing the landless laborers. Those Brahmans who escaped did so because of their counterbalancing merit, their good deeds.

The idea of a balance sheet kept between merit and demerit does have some support from classical religious texts. It is widespread in popular culture in South Asia. As one Tamil man in southern India told Sheryl Daniel (1983), karma works "like a bank balance" in that good and bad deeds cancel each other out. This particular man worked as a local temple priest, where his frequent acts of worship brought him much merit. But he also had a number of extramarital affairs, which he needed to offset. (His own calculation was that he was still ahead.) But Daniel reports that for most misfortunes people did not invoke karma. Karma instead served as a background set of forces, much like "fate" in some Western traditions, that can be mentioned when no other explanation is at hand.

Much more commonly invoked as causes of misfortune are the actions of sorcerers, who work through deities and spirits, and a notion of simple fate, brought on by ritual omissions or other unknown events. *Fate* implies no moral responsibility on the part of the people concerned, whereas *karma* implies that their past misdeeds led them to either suffer or commit an undesirable act. Sorcery, however, can be dealt with directly, by countering the sorcerer's malevolent actions through rituals of exorcism and possession.

These various accounts of an event may be invoked with self-interest in mind. In a case of chicken stealing reported by Daniel (1983), the friends of the accused thieves blamed the event of chicken theft on simple fate, thereby attributing no fault to anyone, whereas the other side, favoring punishment, chalked it up to the bad karma of the thieves.

And of course, Hindus, like people everywhere, rarely hesitate to attribute someone's misfortune to laziness or stupidity. As Lawrence Babb writes (1983, 167), "[t]here is little evidence, in short, that Hindus are any more inclined than other peoples to ignore the evident proximate causes of human fortune."

Suffering as Part of God's Plan

Many Christians explain the tribulations of their lives as part of "God's plan." Nancy Ammerman (1987) studied a Fundamentalist church in New England whose members talked to her about their certainty that God has a plan for them, both as individuals and as a moral community of saved people. They view their lives as an extensive contract with God: if I behave according to his plan, then I will be rewarded. Church members refer to 7,834 promises from God to be found in the Bible, covering everything from personal health to child rearing. As one church member put it: "He makes the decisions for me, and that is great!" (Ammerman 1987, 40–51).

Ammerman describes the ways these Christians attribute some misfortune to the basic sinfulness of humans, on whom the original sin in the Garden of Eden is visited. Satan, too, is present in this world, and sometimes someone who suffers is said to have participated in Satan's activities. If he or she drank or smoked, for example, this kind of account seems reasonable to these people. Moreover, Satan may strike down the most righteous people as well as the obvious sinners.

But when these Fundamentalists cannot find a specific reason for suffering they may despair, and some have turned away from God. Sometimes they recount their own spiritual histories as a despairing in God followed by a returning to God. They mention Christ's experience of suffering as a source of strength for them: "My savior suffered for me; who am I not to suffer?" (Ammerman 1987, 68).

Seemingly random events provoke considerable thought. Once, a freak tornado devastated homes and stores in a nearby suburb (Ammerman 1987, 70–71). What could its meaning have been? The rarity of such a tornado here led people to think that it must bear a divine message, but they could not decide what that message might have been. Men and women attending an adult Sunday school class held shortly after the event pondered this problem, proposing several explanations and then revising them after discussion. One man noted that his store, in the affected suburb, had been spared: God was rewarding him for his own righteousness, he concluded. But then another person mentioned that a righteous woman, recently saved from sin, had been endangered by the storm. This fact forced the first man to revise his story; it could no longer be about God sparing the faithful and damaging the damned. Perhaps, he tried again, his store was saved to give him the chance to witness to others about God's power. This interpretation could not be refuted.

It was very important to these people to find divine purpose in the event. It was not troubling to them that that purpose was hard for mere humans to discern.

Chinese Geomancy

Throughout Asia, directions and features of the landscape are thought to shape one's good or bad fortune. In China and Korea, experts in geomancy, which in Chinese is called *feng shui* (wind and water), determine the most favorable locations and orientations for buildings based on directional diagrams or compasses (Weller 1987, 147–155). In the ideal configuration of natural objects, mountains and rivers encircle a central place; cosmic energy, or *chi,* will be concentrated in the center and give positive energy to those who reside there.

Cardinal directions also confer good or bad luck: facing south confers and signifies sovereignty, for example. Directions are also associated with animals—the west with the tiger, for example. Landscape features that resemble animals ought to be located in that direction from the place being studied—tiger-looking hills ought to be to the west for luck to be good. The appropriate sites and direction for graves, towns, and temples are determined in this way.

Geomancy is strongly listened to even in commercial Hong Kong. The shipping tycoon chosen by Beijing to run Hong Kong under Chinese rule, Tung Chee-hwa, selected a site for his new government offices only after consulting a geomancer. The feng shui expert considered the placement of doors and windows, the balance of light and dark in the rooms, and even the angles of desks, before approving one place, two floors in an office building. He had earlier rejected Government House because neighboring tall buildings blocked chi from reaching it (Gargan 1997). Not everyone in Hong Kong follows feng shui; one bank publishes an annual list of feng shui predictions that did not turn out.

Indian *Vastu*

Corresponding to feng shui in India and among the Indian diaspora is a science called *Vastu shastra,* said to have been taught by the original man, Mayan, 13,000 years ago. Numerous Web sites treat Vastu, and they range from the mystical in tone, featuring the healing power of pyramids and pictures of long-bearded sages, to the very modern and scientific, some of which give readers instructions for designing their houses so as to accord with the order of the universe. Vastu Design Studio (*www.ads-vastu.com*), for example, offers an on-line introduction to Vastu and, on CD for purchase, a step-by-step tutorial on how to design building sites and interiors. It also sells the professional services of its architects. The Iowa-based firm is led by Deepak Bakshi, who has emphasized the use of renewable energy sources and earth block design for maximum insulation.

So far, pretty harmless. Within Indian politics, however, any science or craft that claims Ancient Vedic bases, as does Vastu, is likely to become part of the broad program of Hindu Nationalism (see Chapter 15). Hindu nationalists have called for the teaching of "Hindu ways of knowing," which they present as the indigenous alternative to Western science (Nanda 2003). These include "Vedic mathematics" and Vastu shastra. Nanda (2003) shows how the nouveau riche in Delhi and Bombay build their houses to maximize the "positive energy" of the earth, but also how this science has entered into political decisions. In 1997, the chief minister of Andhra Pradesh consulted a Vastu expert and was told that his political fortune would improve if he used the eastward door to his office building. Unfortunately, that door gave onto a slum through which it was difficult to drive. The minister thereupon ordered that the slum be demolished. For Nanda, this episode illustrates how what may seem to be innocuous amusement can become dangerous pseudoknowledge once intellectuals adopt a culturally relativistic approach to science.

The New Age

What are referred to as "new religious movements" in Europe, North America, and Asia nearly always involve a focus on the powers available to the self through proper training, meditation, and access to knowledge. (See Chapter 7 for a Japanese example.) Among these are movements and practices associated with the "New Age."

The term *New Age* refers to contemporary religious movements in Europe and North America that emphasize individual self-realization, a harmonious relationship with the natural world, and an exploration of both non-Western religious traditions and pre–Christian European ones. New Age movements include card reading, dowsing, crystal healing, and other practices that challenge conventional American ideas of religion (Brown 2000).

New Age movements are the latest in a history of American efforts to improve oneself through religious practices. In the early nineteenth century Methodism achieved enormous popularity by promising its adherents self-perfection and salvation. Today, Christian Science and self-healing books claim to be spiritual companions to medical science. Many New Age movements go beyond perfecting and healing the self to emphasize communication with spirits, which also has deep American roots. It all depended on how the religious authorities of the day interpreted the events. We see that possession, unusual speech behavior, and transcendant religious experience continue within contemporary Pentecostalism through practices of glossalalia or "speaking in tongues." New Age movements add some new elements, including a search for sacred places that are centers of energy, often the very same sites considered sacred by native North Americans.

The social organization of New Age religious movements ranges from loose networks and fissiparous small groups to cults, such as Scientology (if one places it in this general category) or the lesser-known Church Universal and Triumphant (CUT) under Guru Ma (Elizabeth Clare Prophet), a cult formed around the charisma of the leader. The apocalyptic message of some New Age leaders can be translated into survivalist actions, as in the case of the CUT, which in the late 1980s stockpiled assault rifles and armored personnel carriers in anticipation of the imminent end of the world (Brown 1997, 126–129).

New Age has also introduced "channeling," seances where humans give voice to ideas and experiences of the long-dead or sometimes the inhabitants of other worlds. For several years in the early 1990s, Michael F. Brown studied channeling. He begins his account by describing the ability of West Coast channeler J. Z. Knight to bring to life the prehistoric man Ramtha. Ramtha delivers messages from another age, which already is sufficient to attract the curious, but he also predicts that, after floods and earthquakes, the world will soon enter a new era in which humans will realize their true potential. He promises that classical American dream, individual self-perfection.

Women are drawn to channeling for the possibilities it offers for imagining other ways of life. Typically, women serve as spirit mediums more often than men across cultures. Brown found that channeling tended to emphasize androgyny, a mixing of male and female elements, in contrast to the women-only emphasis of many Wiccan groups.

Like shamanism and earlier forms of spiritualism, channeling offers direct communication with sources of truth. Distinctive of channeling are the enormous gaps in time and space involved: men or women from thousands of years ago and alien creatures are the commonly invoked speakers. Some channelers enter a trance or trance-like state, a feature that lends them greater credibility and may also increase the attractiveness of the experience for channelers seeking altered states of consciousness. Others operate much less dramatically. Brown describes Bay Area channelers, David and Sarah, with links to spiritual beings called, collectively, "Michael." They work by means of "conscious channeling," which involves the merest hesitations in speech between talking-as-David and talking-as-Michael (Brown 1997, 33–37).

The conscious channelers see themselves as tapping into wisdom shared by everyone—in a sense bringing their own intuition to the fore. In contrast, trance channelers see themselves as relaying messages from a distinct self. We can see these two types of channeling as bringing into this specific practice two distinct streams of American religiosity: the drive for self-perfection, as when the conscious channeler adds intuition to other thought processes, and the contact with spirits.

In their messages to listeners, channelers sometimes borrow ideas from other religions. In the morally relativistic context of the channeling world—everyone doing their own spiritual thing—karma, the idea that some actions will bring about later retribution (either in this or another life), serves as a plausible source of morality, and is particularly attractive because of its non-Western source.

Wicca or Modern Witchcraft

*P*ractitioners of Wicca or modern Witchcraft distinguish themselves from the New Age, although outside observers might see in the shared emphasis on techniques for cultivating the powers of the self, and the shared references to esoteric lore long forgotten or repressed, important common elements. North American practitioners of Wicca often prefer the term *witch* to refer to themselves, highlighting its old meaning of "to bend" reality. This use both distinguishes North American movements from the older European movements, who use the term *Wicca,* and underscores their sense of inheriting an experience of persecution at the hands of patriarchal European religions, particularly in the burning of witches. North Americans may use Wicca in more public settings to avoid the negative associations of Witchcraft, however (Salomonsen 2002).

Wicca provides an excellent example of how a variety of practices can be packaged as a "religion" in the modern sense of the term, with creed and canons, leaders and followers, and a form of organization something like a church. The historical foundation for Wicca seems to be a long legacy, mostly in England, of crop planting and harvesting rituals. People who grew up in those traditions generally thought of them as merely things that one did, not as part of something called "Witchcraft." Margot Adler (1986, 72–73), a true "participant–observer" as both a journalist and Wicca devotee, quotes a Wisconsin woman whose father's parents brought these traditions to the United States from Scotland and Wales. Adler wrote that "to them Witchcraft was a *practice*" (1986, 72); their theology was simply that the earth was the female principle and the oak tree the male principle. As one Witch explained,

I was shown how to do certain things, practical things. How do you make your garden grow? You talk to your plants. You enter into a mental rapport with them. How do you call fish to you? How do you place yourself in the right spot? How do you encourage them? (Adler 1986, 73)

Eventually some people in England became more self-conscious about these practices and baptized them as the English "Family Traditions." Writers began to claim that they were part of an unbroken legacy of the Craft, or Wiccanry, traceable back to an ancient time before the rise of Christianity in Europe.

The founder of the contemporary tradition of Wiccanry is Gerald B. Gardner (1884–1964), an English colonial planter and later civil servant. In about 1939 Gardner was initiated into Wicca in England. This initiation would have likely taken place undercover because Witchcraft was still prohibited in the United Kingdom. After the last of the Witchcraft Acts was repealed in 1951, Gardner began to write about Wiccanry. He set out what became its standard history and doctrine, claiming that it was an ancient religion, focused on the cult of the Goddess and of nature, that had survived underground in Europe through millenia of oppression.

Gardner's claims that Wiccanry had an ancient lineage provoked a great deal of controversy (nicely set out by Alder [1986]). The basic idea that contemporary Wicca practitioners were reviving pre-Christian, proto-feminist, ecologically sound ideas has survived intact, and has continued to animate most practitioners of the Craft in the United States and elsewhere. Wiccanry leaders have drawn on a number of elements to construct a synthetic version of the cult: the older farming practices mentioned earlier, Masonic and Rosicrucian teachings about mysteries and ancient, pre-Judaic religious practices, the Spiritualist ideas of communication with the dead that were popular throughout Europe and the Americas in the early twentieth century, and popular practices of divination. The basic unit of Wiccanry is the coven, a voluntary association of women and sometimes men, which meets to celebrate its lineage and to perform rituals.

Chapter 3 discussed how the Japanese created Shinto out of elements of ritual practice so as to have a religion that would be equivalent in form and structure to other religions. Wiccanry reflects precisely the same process taking place in twentieth-century United States and Britain. With the rise of the idea that the assorted and diverse "magical" practices found in rural areas were in fact the fragments of an ancient "religion" came the impulse to define that religion's elements. Congresses of Witches were held in different locales in the United States to attempt to define the elements of Wiccanry and a Covenant of the Goddess was signed by 13 covens in California in 1975. A major figure in the formulation of Wiccanry, Aidan Kelly, modeled the Covenant on the charter of the Congregational Church, which offered a decentralized model of church governance.

Despite these efforts to create a religion and an established church of Wicca, Wiccan groups are continually forming and changing, with several distinct ideologies. One is feminist, sometimes called *Dianic*, after the goddess. These groups draw particularly on the writings of Starhawk, a West Coast coven leader. They stress their links to ancient Pagan religions that worshipped the goddess. Another stream emphasizes the writings of Gerald Gardner, and hence can be called *Gardnerian*. The organizations that follow this stream are the most formalized of all Wiccan groups, and include an idea of succession to leadership positions for women. Janet and Stewart Farrar's book *The Witches' Way* describes the Gardnerian rituals. A third stream is *traditionalist;* its covens consider themselves to be continuing the traditions of specific places of origin, usually Wales, Ireland, or Scotland. Each coven tries to incorporate into its rituals legends from that country.

Starhawk's book, *Spiral Dance,* probably the most influential work among North American Wiccans, proclaims Witchcraft "perhaps the oldest religion extant in the West" (1989, 16). According to Starhawk's history, male shamans and female priestesses presided over European human societies beginning 35,000 years ago. In the name of the goddess the shamans enticed game to their death and the priestesses guaranteed fertility. As agriculture was discovered, the priestesses brought forth the regenerative power of the earth. Nothing changed in the way humans related to nature until the invasion of the Indo-Europeans who brought patriarchy, metals, and war. But the Old Religion lived on in rural areas to become the practices of the Druids. With Christianity, the figure of Mary was regarded as another form of the goddess; and Christ, of her child who was sacrificed and reborn. In the fourteenth century persecutions began, but most witches escaped; some fled to America, some joined with slaves and Indians, finding commonality in their practices. Only recently has the Craft, the Old Religion, Witchcraft been free to emerge and reorganize into loosely organized covens and practitioners (Starhawk 1989, 15–30).

This multicultural history and nonhierarchical approach to the Craft fits the attitude of the most receptive readers in twenty-first-century North America. In the United Kingdom and North America today are a proliferation of organizations and associations difficult to label, reflecting the creativity of Wiccanry. Indeed, Wiccans stress that they are simply reviving and maintaining ancient practices, or the Craft.

Wiccans also emphasize their freedom from doctrine. "It's a religion of ritual rather than theology" wrote Aidan Kelly (Adler 1986, 170). What then are those practices? Contemporary American Wiccanry eschews centrally prescribed ritual form, though there are certain constant elements within a multiplicity of practices. Wicca ritual usually includes hymns, chants or songs that evoke several goddesses and gods and the power of nature. The participants, sometimes nude, meet and often move in circles.

Wiccan or Witchcraft movements show a great deal of variation. Many in North America refer back to 1979, when two feminist witches, Starhawk and Diane Baker, formed the Reclaiming community of pagan witches in San Francisco. The ideas and practices later spread to other communities in North America and Europe. Although all these communities have underscored feminism and the specific characteristics of women, they differ in composition. Some of the communities are limited to women; others have a mixed membership. Some of the women-only communities are lesbian, whereas others are mixed in sexual orientation. Starhawk's own orientation and thus that of Reclaiming was feminist but not exclusively lesbian, and although she participated in women-only groups, the Reclaiming community she founded included men.

San Francisco Reclaiming introduces people to Witchcraft through classes, rituals, and membership in covens. Classes teach practices rather then doctrine, thus how to communicate with the goddess rather than goddess theology. Students learn a range of ritual practices sufficient for them to form covens. Rituals include celebrations of solar calendar "sabbats," such as the solstices and equinoxes, with hundreds of celebrants, lunar rites celebrated in small, gender-segregated covens, and rites of passage for birth, puberty, marriage, menopause and aging.

Loretta Orion (1995) studied Wiccanry in the 1980s and participated in the 1983 Pagan Spirit Gathering held at the summer solstice in Wisconsin. Before the central ritual, Orion learned about dowsing and the proper way to ask an herb's permission to be picked. Participants evoked or "drew down" a multitude of Greco-Roman, Norse, Celtic, South Asian, and African deities, sent blessings to Starhawk (who was at that moment leading a demonstration against a nuclear power plant) and, to the accompaniment of drums and flutes, moved in a counterclockwise circle while chanting the names of goddesses, singing, and eventually cheering, howling, and laughing.

The moving circle was followed by the full moon ritual, an elaborate event celebrating the great mother goddess represented by a pregnant woman carried in a chair; she was followed by 12 women dressed as different aspects of the goddess, including Kali, Hecate, Discordia, and a generic Amazon figure. A priestess invoked the full moon and promised fertility and men dressed as forms of Dionysus planted seeds in the soil with a "swimming, squirming, spermlike dance," wrote Orion (1995, 140).

Wiccan rituals combine several ritual elements, as the description of the solstice celebration illustrates. They usually involve movement or chanting designed to create a sense of a collectivity. In this respect they resemble the Australian Aboriginal dances that inspired Émile Durkheim to identify the birth of religion in energetic group dance. Durkheim focused on the moment when collective action creates a consciousness of a collective power. Wiccans themselves speak of the creation of a "cone of power" at these moments (Orion 1995, 128–140).

Second, the rituals invoke pre-Christian deities to connect humans to the natural elements, especially to the earth and its fertility. (Recall the origins of the Craft in agriculture.) The rituals continue the idea of ancient mysteries that have attracted people to Masons and Rosicrucians. The prominance of female deities celebrates many Wiccans' belief in a protohistorical period when women ruled. Wiccans disagree about whether an ancient matriarchal period can be proved, but they do agree that matriarchy can provide an idea of female freedom (Adler 1986, 196).

Finally, Wicca rituals link fertility to human sexuality. Sexuality is more or less present in coven activities but should be understood as part of the total complex of ideas, in which it is seen as a way of liberating oneself from patriarchal Christianity.

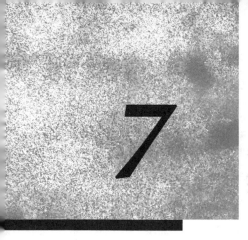

7

Healing through Religion

*I*n the last chapter we considered a range of ways in which people draw on religious ideas to explain or shape the world around them. Now we focus on the ways in which people try to heal themselves or others through religion. In the United States, healing through prayer is widely accepted. A 2003 *Newsweek* poll found that 84 percent of Americans believe that their prayers can help someone else heal, what is known as "intercessory prayer" (Kalb 2003).

Prayer, Faith, and Healing

Christian Science

Faith healing abounds in Christian denominations, and a belief in the power of mind over body made a particularly strong entry into U.S. bookstores and minds in the 1990s. This amalgam of religion, science, and self-healing has its longest-lived representative in the Christian Science Church, founded in 1879 by Mary Baker Eddy. From the enormous Mother Church in Boston emanate the *Christian Science Monitor* and high-quality radio news programs. Adherents are found mainly in the United States and Protestant areas of Europe.

Christian Science healers, called "practitioners," and laypersons can cure themselves and others through prayer and by reading from the religion's two key books: the Christian Gospels and Eddy's book, *Science and Health*, reissued in a new edition in 1996 by the church. This book tells followers that humans are spiritually perfect, though morally far from perfect, and that they only need realize they have the power to abolish sickness. The miracles performed by Jesus are nothing but instances of God's law, available to all humans. Sin, sickness, and death are closely related, and the pure life brings health with it. These beliefs resemble Indian notions of *dharma*, the concept of natural and moral law, where one's moral actions (*karma*) have a direct effect on material events in the world, including one's sickness and health.

Christian Science advocates often relate anecdotes about a recovery through prayer that doctors thought impossible—beginning with Eddy herself, who was inspired by her own recovery from a bad fall on the ice. One writer describes a serious automobile accident in South Dakota, after which he foreswore all medical treatment but called a Christian Scientist practitioner in New York who applied "absent treatment," praying at a distance (Leishman 1958, 127–133).

Science and Health suggests how to pray for health and urges the patient to "mentally contradict every complaint from the body." It contains no secret formulas; but fixed prayers do take on "magical" qualities. The practitioners studied by Bryan Wilson in England recited the following phrase each morning as a defense against the malevolent forces of "animal magnetism":

Malicious animal magnetism does not know where I am or what I am doing: it does not know God's plan or purpose for me, nor the work that God has given me to do; nor can it perpetuate any lies about me; for I live, move, and have my being in God, in Spirit, in the secret place of the Most High. (Wilson 1961, 130)

Mary Baker Eddy herself once flirted with hypnotism as a remedy for illness, and later strongly denounced it, leaving a trace in this prayer and in the general suspicion of mental suggestion as a source of illness and sin. Practitioners admit that the common cold may afflict people, but argue that it spreads only if we so believe. We must repel the "aggressive mental suggestion" that colds spread, thereby keeping ourselves from catching them.

In theory Christian Scientists oppose trying to mix medicine with prayer, arguing that the two remedies are so different that they cannot be combined. In some cases Christian Science parents have refused medical treatment for their child. A Minnesota couple and practitioner who let an 11-year-old boy, Ian Lundman, die of diabetes in 1989 were successfully sued for 1.5 million dollars in compensatory damages, an award later upheld by the U.S. Supreme Court. But other Christian Scientists do wear glasses, enter hospitals, seek dental treatment, and allow doctors to treat broken bones and infections (Fraser 1996).

Does Prayer Heal?

*T*he medical effects of religious practices have come in for a great deal of scientific study in the past decade. The claims and studies bear on two separate questions: What are the health effects when a patient prays, attends church, thanks or blames God, and so forth? And what are the effects, if any, of "intercessory prayer," meaning prayer by someone else for the patient. Although these two practices often are mixed together in articles, they imply two quite distinct mechanisms. If the first set of practices leads to significantly better health, the results can be attributed to a range of psychophysiological mechanisms—for example, the influence of confidence and optimism on the immune system, in essence the same as a "placebo effect." If intercessory prayer leads to greater health, the results are attributed to God.

A number of scientific studies of Christians in the United States support the claim that praying, believing in God, and attending church make people healthier and longer-lived than people who do not practice a religion. Studies have been done on large samples, often balanced between white and black Americans. Some studies focus on patients and their post-operative outcomes, others on blood pressure levels, and still others on mortality rates in the general population. Current research reports from mainstream medical journals are listed on the Duke University Center for the Study of Religion/Spirituality and Health (*www.dukespiritualityandhealth.org/ recentreports.html*). In one National Institutes of Health–funded study (Helm et al. 2000), over 3,000 North Carolina adults were surveyed in 1986 and then monitored over the next six years (1986–1992). The researchers controlled for social support and health behaviors, and found that lack of private religious activity continued to predict a 47 percent greater risk of dying.

Religiosity does not necessarily promote health, however; more important seems to be the relatively positive or negative way U.S. Christians approach a relationship to God. One group of researchers (Pargament et al. 2001) studied what they called "negative religious coping" among black and white patients, a concept that they attributed to patients who wondered whether God had abandoned them, felt punished by God for their lack of devotion, or decided the Devil had made them ill. People who believed these statements experienced 19 percent to 28 percent greater mortality during the two-year period following hospital discharge. Positive religious coping, however, has consistently been shown to promote mental and physical health (for example, Koenig et al. 1992). Frequency of church attendance is a powerful predictor of health in many of these studies, for example, of a strong immune system, indicated by low levels of plasma interleukin-6, an immune system messenger that appears in higher levels among people with chronic illness (Koenig et al. 1997).

Although some of these studies attempt to control for the amount of social support the study subjects enjoyed, it also seems that the social side of church attendance contributes to the positive effects of religion on health. The role of organized religion in offering solace during illness may be particularly important in the contemporary United States, given the mobility of its residents and the tendency to rely on institutions for support for elderly relatives. Prayer also "gives patients something to do so that they don't feel as helpless," notes Harold G. Koenig (2002), one of the Duke investigators. Prayer also may lead to greater relaxation that reduces muscle tension (ibid.).

Even within the medical community, debate has arisen about the mechanisms or pathways that link prayer to health. Writing to comment on Koenig's analysis quoted here, a physician and theologian stated that it was the "spirit of God" that provided the healing because of the patient's prayer (Flynn and Fulton 2002). In so doing, they implicitly link prayer by patients to prayer by others on behalf of patients, or "intercessory prayer," prayer to God to intercede on someone else's behalf.

A small number of medical researchers have designed studies to test the idea that if a team of "intercessors" prays for patients, patients will do better than will patients not receiving prayer from the team. These studies have been controlled, in that patients were assigned in random or near-random fashion either to a prayer-receiving group or to a non-prayer-receiving-group, as well as "double-blind," meaning that neither the patients nor the medical personnel knew which patients were in which group.

In one such study, conducted in a coronary care unit in Kansas City, about 1,000 patients were assigned to the two groups (Harris et al. 1999). Fifteen prayer teams of five people each were asked to pray for patients identified by name. Intercessors all agreed to the statement that God "is responsive to prayers for healing made on behalf of the sick," that is, that God intercedes. The intercessors prayed for 28 days for each patient (a time chosen to cover nearly all patients' hospital stays). The researchers then faced the problem of how to measure outcomes. Because the prayers were for a general speedy and complete recovery, they needed a measure of overall goodness of outcome. They devised a scoring system, on which complications added points: the higher the score, the worse the outcome. They then calculated the association between prayer and outcome, using t tests and accepting $P<.05$ as significant for most tests. Both decisions follow accepted procedures, but were the source of much critique afterwards, as we shall see.

The investigators found an 11 percent reduction in the outcome score for patients who had received prayer, with $P=.04$, thus meeting their conditions for significance. The length of stay was not different between the two groups; the study thus agreed with earlier similar studies. The investigators were able to gain exemption from hospital Internal Review Board (IRB) rules for informed consent on the grounds that simply knowing of the study might create anxiety about not being treated with prayer, and because no clear harm could result from no prayer. They note that because half the patients stated a religious preference, there likely was "background prayer noise" caused by relatives praying for control-group patients, so that the study measured the effects of "supplementary intercessory prayer."

How could such prayer work? The study's authors refrain from suggesting mechanisms: it could be God, or it could be unknown physical forces caused by prayer. They defend themselves against the (correctly) anticipated charges of studying relationships without proposing causal mechanisms by citing the pathbreaking clinical trials conducted by James Lind in 1753 aboard the HMS Salisbury, which determined that eating lemons or limes cured sailors of scurvy. He did not know why this was so, they state, but his observations were sound. Cautiously, they conclude: "It was intercessory prayer, not the existence of God, that was tested here."

Well, as one might imagine, a storm of protest appeared in this and other journals. Some questioned details of the study; others stated that $P=.04$ is more acceptable if a causal mechanism is known or proposed than otherwise (a point made widely in the social sciences as well); most argued that science and faith were two different kinds of knowledge and should be kept that way. A few entered into the theological implications of such a study: if God indeed favors people for whom strangers choose to pray, over others, then is he a capricious rather than an all-loving God? (You can continue to follow the thread of these debates on: *http://archinte.ama-assn.org.*)

The cautious entry of medical science into these waters threatens some because it could legitimate studies that show other kinds of practices to have medical effects despite the absence of known causal mechanisms: homeopathic medicine, which features potions containing minute traces of supposedly effective elements, is the most obvious candidate. Other physicians find the mixing of science and religion ipso facto distasteful. Still others find it enormously welcome that they can speak with patients about the patients' religious beliefs and practices—indeed, most of the medical centers or institutes devoted to religion and healing focus on clinical care and not scientific research.

Mapping the Brain

Another approach from medical science to studying religious experience has been by way of brain mapping rather than experiments. Much of this research has focused on determining how the brain state correlates to states of calm achieved through meditation. People who become adept at meditation report common themes, among them a sense of great calmness, a diminishing of the boundaries between the self and other, and a sense of union with the universe or with God.

Andrew Newberg and his colleagues (Newberg, D'Aquili, and Rause 2001) have used single photon emission computed tomography (SPECT) to measure the blood flow patterns in the brains of Tibetan monks during meditation and Fransiscan nuns while in prayer. The subjects were instructed to give a simple hand signal at the peak of their meditative state. At this signal, a radioactive marker was released into the bloodstream. As the marker passed through the brain, images of the peak moment's effects on the brain were captured.

Most often, the measurements showed marked changes in brain activity during meditation or prayer, and these changes were related to the subjective changes reported by the subjects. In particular, the meditation affected the posterior section of the parietal lobe in the cerebral cortex, an area that receives input from several senses and produces the experience of a three-dimensional self oriented in space. Normally this area exhibits extremely high degrees of activity. However, at the peak moments it experienced very low activity levels, as indicated by reduced blood flow. These were precisely the moments that the monks and nuns said were characterized by the sense of a diminished self or a union with God.

Narratives and Pain Relief

*M*ore generally, stories and activities that a patient believes have a beneficial effect may have that effect, either through the calming effects of the story-telling, or the belief that the story or practice has a direct relationship to healing, or merely because of the presence of a medical helper.

Giving Birth in Panama and Malaysia

Consider two examples of birthing magic, one from Panama and one from Malaysia. In both, midwives and shamans help the mother in moving the baby down the birth canal and out into the world. But they do so by drawing on very different sets of images and values. Cuna society, in Panama, holds high the culture of heroes and battles (Lévi-Strauss 1963b). There, a shaman, who can be possessed by spirits, sings to help childbirth. He sings a story of how Muu, the spirit that forms the fetus, has exceeded her usual domain and captured the woman's soul, thereby preventing her from moving the baby down the birth canal. The shaman must carve small figurines, the spirits of which he then leads up the birth canal to overcome wild beasts and defeat Muu and her allies. In his song the shaman describes in painstaking detail the events leading up to his own arrival at the woman's house—the woman experiencing pain, the midwife coming to call him, his own arrival—and then the journey of the friendly spirits. The journey is in the same concrete detail as the mundane events and, in Claude Lévi-Strauss's analysis, the woman is thus likely made to feel the entry of the spirits as real. She now can identify her pain with specific, well-described animals and spirits lodged in her vagina. The detail makes the journey psychologically real to the woman in pain, giving her a language for her pain and difficulties, organizing her perceptions and feelings.

Now contrast the chants recited by a healer in a Malay village studied by Carol Laderman (1983). As with the Cuna, the ritual specialist only intervenes when the midwife can no longer cope with the difficult birth. Malinowski's idea that most people work on a commonsense basis until they reach the limits of their capacities and knowledge, and only then reach for magic to extend their grasp, thus once again seems to work well. The specialist, called a "bomoh," recites a story about God's creation of the world and of the first couple, and then about the creation of the individual human. These stories follow generally available Muslim lines. They provide a story for the woman that takes place out of ordinary time, placing the woman's suffering also out of ordinary time and giving it a sense of order, naturalness, and harmony. Just as Cuna culture highlights battle, Malay culture stresses the importance of harmony and control.

Even if the woman does not hear every detail of the story, women do know the story's general outline beforehand, says Laderman, and are soothed by its familiar references to the creation story, listing of prophets and mythological figures, and litany of the sequence of days leading to birth.

The story responds to a general cultural emphasis on harmony with the universe. But what happens in the individual? Drawing on work in U.S. hospitals as well as Malaysia, Laderman argues that the psychological response to hearing the story creates a biological response, producing endorphins that reduce pain and also reduce anxiety. Endorphins are chemicals found in several areas of the brain, which appear to be responsible for "placebo effect" pain reduction. Not only do these effects benefit the mother, but because anxiety can prevent proper cervical dilation, the reduction of anxiety may directly lead to more productive contractions, and a quicker, easier birth.

Of course, the ways in which imagery, narratives, beliefs, and emotions affect bodily states, from levels of pain tolerance to changes in the immune system, is a topic under considerable current research. On the one hand, fear can lead to death, as Walter Cannon (1942) observed; more recent research suggests that the "fight or flight" adrenaline response induced by fear, though useful in the short term, is debilitating over longer periods, weakening the heart and the immune system. On the other hand, dissociation (the mechanism involved in trance and hypnosis) and positive imagery reduce pain levels. Just how "magic"—and the many other curing techniques now used in the United

States and therefore not so labeled—works on the nervous and immune systems is far from being understood, but it is now widely accepted that such mechanisms do exist.

The "placebo effect" is surely part of the explanation for a number of approaches to curing. Sometimes it is even recognized by practitioners, as in the following case. Americans dramatically increased their interest in voodoo in the 2000s. In New Orleans, the grave of a nineteenth-century "voodoo queen," Marie Laveau, has become one of the most visited graves in the United States (Kinzer 2003). Laveau was a free woman of mixed Native American, African, and European descent, and she has come to stand for a mixed heritage of religion, power, and geographical roots similar to that of Brazilian Candomble. As in the Brazilian case, many adherents profess themselves Catholics, and one practitioner stated that Catholic priests come to him for help. Why this recent rise in popularity? Some ascribe it to post–9/11 searchings for meaning; others to the constantly shifting search for healing and power. One voodoo priest working in New Orleans for over 20 years said that he performed ceremonies to help people but did not know how they worked. "Have you heard of the placebo effect?" he said (Kinzer 2003).

Trance, Possession, and Healing

*H*ealing practices often turn on the idea that a spirit has possessed the patient and is causing the illness. The cure then involves putting the patient (or sometimes a curer) into a trance state, investigating the reasons for the spirit's actions, and driving out the spirit (or *exorcising* the patient).

Afro-Brazilian Trances

In Brazil today, healers draw on Afro-Brazilian religion traditions to carry out their art. Afro Brazilian religions, variously called "Candomblé," "Umbanda," or "Macumba" (and related to Haitian "Voudun" and Cuban "Santeria"), developed when people living in West Africa were forcibly brought to the Americas as slaves (see Chapter 9). Forced to conceal their own religious ideas and practices, they developed a blend that appeared Catholic but contained elements of West African religion. Today these traditions have changed in various directions, some emphasizing African sources, others Native American elements, still others the ties with Catholicism and with European Spiritism (Brown 1986; Goodman 1988, 42–51).

In the Brazilian trance-healing practices called Macumba (Richeport 1985), trance is employed in varied settings to aid in healing. In sessions involving "professional mediums," specialists sit in a separate, cordoned-off part of a room. They are dressed in white and are already in a trance. They each have special "spirit familiars" with whom they communicate. Patients deliver to the staff slips of paper containing their questions; usually the questions are about their own illnesses. The mediums then ask for answers from their spirit familiars and relay these answers back through the staff. These sessions are calm, although sometimes a supplicant will slip into trance, and in such cases he or she may be approached about becoming a medium.

A second type of session involves mass trances. Dozens or hundreds of people gather together for evenings of trance, dancing and music, and consultation. These large-scale sessions also employ mediums, but they walk and dance around on the floor, mingling with other people who wish to attend. Rather than having personal spirit familiars, all the mediums cycle together through several standard spirit types during the evening. Each type represents both a familiar cultural figure of the Brazilian environment and a kind of emotion. When the mediums are possessed by the "old black slave" spirit, they sit, smoking pipes, and dispense this old man's wisdom to those attending (who are often relatives or friends). When they take on the flashily dressed woman called *Pomba Gira*, they are seductive and loose, enjoying this break from normal behavioral restrictions. When they are the child they scamper about eating candy. (There is also an Amazonian equivalent of these sessions in which Indians act the role of whites, drink champagne, and act terribly refined.)

Use is also made of trances at clinics for the mentally ill. Patients are encouraged to enter a trance state and act out their emotions and frustrations; often they, too, take on stereotyped roles such as those mentioned previously.

Shared Healing in Southern Africa

The Kung people living in southern Africa once lived entirely from gathering and some hunting. The great variability of rainfall and thus food in their lands led them to develop norms of sharing and exchange. Sharing distributes risk and gives people a source of food during periods of drought and scarcity.

Healing follows similar lines of thought. The Kung heal those who have fallen ill by assembling in a group at night around a fire and dancing to reach a trance-like state of transcendence called "kai," reached by tapping into the energy, *num*, that everyone has in the pits of their stomachs. About half of the men tap this energy, and about one-third of the women. (They tend to be people whose parents did so. Larger percentages try, and somewhat smaller percentages become active healers.) Num energy is not a limited good, but is given by God to individuals and benefits everyone in the group when people tap it.

Reaching the state of kai can be dangerous and painful. An older healer described the feeling in terms of death and rebirth.

Your heart stops. You're dead. Your thoughts are nothing. You breathe with difficulty. You see things, num things. You see spirits killing people. You smell burning, rotten flesh. Then you heal, you pull sickness out. You heal, heal, heal. Then you live. Your eyeballs clear and you see people clearly. (Katz 1982, 45)

When your own num has begun to boil others feel it and they, too, begin to dance.

Healing takes place in three stages. The healer, once his or her num is boiling, can see the num in other healers and the spirits causing illness. Then the healer pulls out the sickness, laying hands on the ill person to put num in and draw out illness, and then shaking the illness out into the darkness. The healer begins to sweat as his num boils;

Kung healing dance at dawn, Botswana. (COURTESY OF RICHARD KATZ, *BOILING ENERGY*, p. 33.)

this sweat is the num and he or she rubs it into the patient to forcibly expel the illness (Katz 1982, 106–108).

Then the healer, in a heroic confrontation, does battle with spirits and gods. Usually the illness has been caused by spirits of the dead. Sometimes they have specific complaints about the living person they are bothering; sometimes they are just looking to stir up trouble. But they are also messengers from the great god, Gao Na, a capricious god who may destroy humans should he find them annoying.

Healers may argue with the spirits or even journey to the god's home. Others at the dance hear one side of a dialogue between the healer and the spirits or god, a dialogue of cajoling or threatening. The healer may hurl insults at the spirits or reason gently with them, telling them that they gain nothing from bothering humans.

Kung trance-healing is collective in spirit and in practice because the source of healing power, the num energy, is more powerful the more it is shared.

Modern Magic in Japanese New Religions

*I*n Japan, new forms of healing and worship bring trance mechanisms together with the Japanese cultural heritage to heal patients suffering from what we would call psychosomatic illnesses. These New Religions developed in response to new life situations, particularly in response to the new illnesses and anxieties felt by many newly urban Japanese. Those millions of Japanese who have moved into cities since the

1950s have found themselves cut off from their accustomed places for ritual practice and sources of religious strength. They also found themselves living in a radically new era, with new kinds of pressures on the job and at home.

The New Religions range from the nationally important Soka Gakkai, with its millions of adherents, its own newspaper and university, and its strong ties to a major political party, the Komeito, to smaller sects and cults. Between 10 percent and 30 percent of Japanese are estimated to follow one of the New Religions. But these New Religions and their healing practices draw on elements from Japan's older religious traditions.

One such religion, studied by Winston Davis (1980), is Mahikari, meaning "True Light." It was founded in 1959 when a man of lower-class origins in Tokyo recovered from illness and debt and received a revelation from God that he was to change his name and bring light and health to the people of Japan. This man, now known as Okada Kotama, began to heal people through the use of amulets (a method he had learned from another group), and the sect grew rapidly in popularity. By the late 1970s Mahikari had more than 150 dojos (buildings for practicing spiritual disciplines) and somewhere between 50,000 and 100,000 active members. Close to half a million had received its amulet.

Purification and Apocalypse

The major activity engaged in by people who join Mahikari is called "okiyome" (purification). The process of okiyome is designed to rid the body of spirits that have possessed it. These spirits may be those of ancestors, or of other people, or of animals, especially foxes and badgers. The process involves divination and then exorcism of the spirit.

People generally come to be healed at Mahikari because of a physical complaint, the roots of which are often psychosomatic: cramps, back pains, headaches, and so forth. In their theory of causes of these illnesses, the healers join physical and psychic explanations. Consider one account of illness:

"There is much poison around us," said a Mahikari teacher. (Indeed, in the main river in the city where Davis studied Mahikari, fish introduced to the river die within 3 minutes from industrial toxins!) "We eat poisoned food and the poisons build up inside and cause illnesses. But," he then asked, "why did we eat the poison? Or, given that bacteria can be carried in food and then eaten by us, what led us to eat the infected food?"

The Mahikari world view offers to supplement the scientific world view by bringing the laws of natural cause and effect down to the level of the individual and his or her suffering.

The answer to our suffering is that we are possessed by spirits. Indeed, according to Mahikari, nearly all illnesses are caused by spirits. Each person has an astral spirit, which must burn off its impurities on the astral plane. (Here we see echoes from Buddhism of the planes of existence and the idea of karma.) Burning off impurities is not fun, and many of these astral spirits seek refuge in humans or torment humans for one reason or another.

The power to exorcise spirits derives ultimately from the High God, "Su-God," and also from a Shinto god he created, called Miroku, identified with the bodhisattva figure Maitreya, here called the "Buddha of the Future." Mahikari sees itself as a supplement to other religions. It recognizes that all religions worship lower deities and prophets created by Su-God; some of them have lost their healing powers, however, which Mahikari offers to restore.

The Mahikari ideology also places the individual's suffering on a grand world-historical plane. In its version of history, mankind once was united on the lost continent of Mu, where people existed in five colors. The yellow people were dominant, and within the yellow group, the Japanese. Mu had all the technological advancements of today: telephones, airplanes, and so forth. It was ruined when the races began to intermarry. The present world then developed, but is about to be destroyed.

This story combines an apocalyptic vision of coming disaster with a way out. Because of human wickedness, Su-God has recently put strict gods in power, and signs of this change are to be seen in recent earthquakes, droughts, and so forth. Humankind is to be subjected to even greater torments, and only those possessing the amulets of Mahikari will be saved, to become the "seed people" of the next era.

These kinds of disaster-plus-solution texts appear throughout human history and are often called "millenarian movements" (see Chapter 13). Each of these movements appropriates a set of already widely accepted ideas and traditions—for example, the role of a Buddha or Christ in ensuring salvation—and harnesses them to a small-scale organization, to which are attracted people looking for spiritual guidance or discipline or health. These movements take the promise of salvation seriously, and set out to get it here and now.

Amulets and Ancestors

Consider in greater detail how healing works for Mahikari adherents. People come to the sect to be healed; they learn why they suffer; and the ideas they learn are an important part of the healing process. They learn that their souls are polluted by spirits and by material pollution and that Mahikari offers them both a temporary, personal solution through healing and a way to prepare for future destruction through continued membership in the sect. People are satisfied that they understand why things have happened to them, that it is not their own fault, and that they can do something about them.

The healers diagnose the patient's ills by detecting the auras around their bodies. Bodies give off electromagnetic waves, they are told, and the shape of these waves can be detected by an "aura meter." Auras come in different shapes and colors. Healers can also detect spirits around the body. But the main activity of the healer is to channel energy into the body that will heal and also will ferret out spirits bothering the patient.

The healer wears an amulet, a small locket worn on a chain, with a piece of paper inside that has a symbol written on it. This locket is "plugged in" through the central Mahikari organization to God—indeed, the objective properties of the amulet are explained in ways that draw on electric and electronic imagery. If the amulet gets wet it may disconnect, healers are told, and apology money must be paid to Mahikari for it to be reconnected. Monthly dues must be paid, which are offered to Su-God "to keep the line connected for the next month."

The healer, wearing the amulet, raises his or her hands over the patient's body, concentrating rays from God on the body. The healer begins with the patient's "primary soul" and then looks for parts of the body that seem to need attention, perhaps massaging the body to detect such parts. The healing power of okiyome also works for inanimate objects, such as automobiles or movie projectors. (Of those people belonging to Mahikari who were surveyed, 42 percent had repaired their television sets with okiyome; 29 percent had used it to fix their wristwatches.)

In the case of people, spirits usually are responsible for their ailments. The healer must find out the identity of the spirit and then convince it to leave the patient. The patient must enter a state of trance. The healer chants over him or her, and the patient usually begins to move and cry out in ways indicative of the spirit's identity. The patient's hand movements may be characteristic of a particular animal (serpentine movements indicate a snake, and so on). Or the patient may write out words or names on a tablet.

But the healer usually talks to the spirit as well, asking it if it is human, when it died, and, most importantly, why it is possessing the person. The healer scolds the spirit: "Go back to the other world and leave her in peace."

The most common explanation of specific ailments involves relationships with ancestors. Events may have caused an ancestor's spirit to possess you, for one of two reasons. First, you may have neglected the altar of the ancestors in your house. One man's ancestor came back to possess him because the altar was on a filing cabinet and the spirit was disturbed by the noise. In the Mahikari sect people study proper altar care to avoid these problems. Nothing must be above it (so it must occupy the top story of the house), its flowers must be arranged properly, and it must have proper lacquered tablets and be supplied with food every day. Recall that in rural society the altar was the site of the protective household god, and so the anxiety of ordinary people about neglected altars makes sense.

Second, events that happened to ancestors, or to yourself in an earlier life, may have caused your misfortune and caused you to be possessed by an ancestral spirit. Healers draw on the logic of karma from Buddhism to explain how this works. One woman had been the wife of a warrior (samurai) in a previous incarnation, and when she married he grew jealous and came to bother her. Samurai often appear as the ancestors responsible for possession because they tended to commit all sorts of bad deeds and would be expected to bring misfortune.

But sometimes another kind of spirit is involved: that of a fox or snake, for example. Here, too, there is an explanation of what event caused the spirit to possess the person. One man with cancer of the face was found to be possessed by the spirit of a snake. When he was a boy he had cut off the head of a snake, and the spirit had chosen appropriate revenge.

Trance Psychology

Central to the patient's experience of being healed is the state of trance into which he or she enters. Trance, like any other altered state of consciousness, begins when one dissociates, or withdraws from ordinary states of consciousness (Davis 1980, 132–144).

We have all experienced dissociation during daydreaming, when different, sometimes odd thoughts and images wander into one's consciousness. But in the kind of structured trance settings found in Mahikari or elsewhere the patient has been trained to expect certain specific symbols, images, or actions to emerge. Mahikari patients study books of spirit images beforehand; some also rehearse the hand movements of different spirits. They then *project* their fears, anger, sadness, or specific problems onto the symbols that have been made available to them. They respond to questions posed to them about ancestors or animals, and can introduce into their answers their own life problems. Finally comes the moment of release, or catharsis, when the person collapses onto the floor and experiences a strong feeling of relief. (Aristotle used "catharsis" to refer to the moment in a drama when pent-up emotions in the audience are released.)

The psychology of the trance-healing session is not specifically Japanese; Felicitas Goodman (1988) documents trance and possession worldwide. Its particular form in Japan draws on older culturally specific practices, however. One is the duet form of the healing: the process always involves an exorciser and a subject, who then exchange roles (rather than, for example, a single healer and many patients). This duet form is found in much older spirit possession–healing cults in Japan and is familiar to patients. It is especially effective in the way it taps the Japanese emotion of "dependence" on another, *amae.* This emotional relation has its prototype in the dependence of a child on his or her mother, and underlies relations to teachers, employers, and, in the past, the emperor. When the emperor was demoted to the role of ordinary human and state symbol after World War II, psychiatrists (Doi 1986) noted that some people became depressed by the loss of a pole for their dependence emotions.

The healing session helps to draw out longings for someone to depend on, in this specific, highly charged sense, and also longings to be depended on. The alternation of roles allows the person who is missing these roles in everyday life to better assume them. For example, one housewife had become so concerned about pollution in food that she could not bring herself to cook for her family. She then became immobilized out of guilt for not doing so, for no longer being depended on. These feelings emerged during trance, and repeated sessions gave her a way to speak these feelings as well as a new setting for dependence–role playing.

Mahikari combines universal psychosocial processes (such as trance) with culturally specific features (such as the focus on ancestors). Simply by participating in a group, regardless of its content, some people gain a stronger sense of the value of their lives. Members also have a legitimate reason to meddle in other people's lives. But, remembering Malinowski, we might pay special attention to the way the process adds confidence and certainty to the making of difficult decisions.

Take the case of Winston Davis's teacher, Yoshida Sensei, and his wife (Davis 1980, 52–63). Yoshida's father had died in the hospital, even though he had asked his son to take him home to die. Several years later, their daughter died in the same hospital. Later, Yoshida's mother died of a stomach ailment, and Yoshida himself developed ulcers. They joined Mahikari and began to be possessed by a number of ancestors and relatives, and through the exorcism procedure learned the causes of their various misfortunes.

Yoshida's father appeared in the form of a badger. He complained of dying in the hospital and said he had caused the daughter's death as revenge, and added his regret that Yoshida had sold off their land. (Yoshida remembered that he had had trouble selling the land and now knew that his father was behind these troubles.) Yoshida taught his father that he must be a spirit and not trouble them in the earthly world: "Apologize to God and return to the astral world to continue your austerities," he demanded. His father's spirit wept at this. They then agreed that Yoshida could sell some of the land, since it was difficult to farm and surrounded by buildings, as long as he bought some other land as a hedge against inflation. After that the father appeared as a human spirit; he had progressed up the spiritual ladder.

The process addressed the several sources of guilt faced by Yoshida and his wife, explained the series of illnesses, and finally exorcised the guilt by leading Yoshida through a series of emotionally charged sessions. Finally, it legitimated his further action, allowing him to sell off land with a clear conscience.

Who Joins the New Religions?

Women make up 60 percent of the participants in Mahikari; many of these women are unmarried and in the traumatic period after high school during which society views them as in transition to their next state, marriage. Employers still see most women as temporary employees, biding time until marriage. But some women either wish to pursue careers or have not found suitable husbands, and many psychosomatic illnesses occur then.

Healing can explain why marriage is difficult, perhaps because of possession by a jealous husband from a past life, and can also provide an outlet for repressed emotions and desires. Consider several cases discussed by Winston Davis (1980, 161–200). Tanio lived in fear of men. Her own father was often drunk and violent, and she was raised by her mother. In trance the spirit possessing her declared herself to be that of a woman whose husband she stole in an earlier life. Nakata never married because, trance revealed, she was possessed by spirits of aborted children. Eiko was happily married but her family resisted her joining Mahikari. Her own ancestors torment her whenever she worships her husband's ancestors. (Here emerged the classic problem of changing ancestral allegiances.)

These women and men found power in an environment of their own general powerlessness. Inside the sect people experience possession and curing. But outside, as well, they experience miracles. Only 12 of 688 members interviewed said they did not experience such miracles. They found social status within the group. And they found an ideology that explained much of what was happening around them, gave them a way to muddle through it, and promised future salvation.

Whatever we might think about these groups, they are a response to urban ills. Some of them are clearly destructive (and some think even Mahikari to be so). In March 1995, canisters containing the nerve gas sarin exploded in a Tokyo subway, killing 10 and injuring more than 5,000, and the attack was linked to the sect Aum Shinrikyo. Aum Shinrikyo's leader, Shoko Asahara, preaches much the same apocalyptic vision as does Mahikari's Okada Kotama. Aum hands out battery-powered headgear to followers so that they may communicate directly with their leader. (The headgear also attracts recruits from the sciences.) Its teachings combine Buddhism and Hinduism—especially the god of destruction, Shiva. Aum followers had to renounce ties with the outside world and donate all their goods to the cult (Sayle 1996).

The history of state Shinto and its ties to militarism have made the Japanese state very wary of interfering in these sects, even when evidence of criminal actions emerges. In 1989 Asahara was named responsible for killing a lawyer helping to return children kidnapped by the sect. And yet Aum was recognized as a religious body the same year and no steps were taken against its leader. One legacy of state Shinto is thus an extraordinarily lenient attitude toward the new sects.

Magic and Religion

Those practices that we might call "magic" have differing relationships to religion. Some, such as baseball practices, are not based on any belief system whatsoever. Others, such as Trobriand spells, do imply beliefs in spirits but little else. Still other practices, such as healing in Japan, Brazil, and Malaya or among the Cuna of Panama, draw on extensive bodies of knowledge about how spirits work. In all cases some of the older insights by Frazer and Malinowski about the logic and functions of magic can still help us understand why people are attracted to certain practices. Malinowski's notion that all people use science plus magic, with the latter added on to the former, continues to make sense. The forms of magic differ greatly: memorized spells, possession and exorcism, narratives about creation or battles, or about God or the effectiveness of medicine. But each such practice gives the person a sense of control, or understanding, or certainty greater than what was enjoyed before the event. Each practice also seems to reduce anxiety (although once it is relied on, its absence may create anxiety).

These features of "magical" practices all concern their effects. To understand their contents and why Japanese, Brazilians, and Cuna do things differently, we have explored the linkages between each practice and the dominant forms and motifs of the culture in which it is found. Recall the paths taken by healers. Cuna healers seek to reduce a woman's pain by telling a story of battles; Malay healers, a story about cosmic harmony; U.S. healers, a story about breathing techniques and medicines. Japanese healers draw on ideas about the ever-watchful ancestors, the culture form of the duet, and Buddhist religious traditions to construct a convincing combination of texts and practices.

Institutions built on notions of magic can take on functions of healing, religion, and even community. Their practices can provide confidence insofar as they fit general cultural expectations, and this confidence and assurance can cause physical changes in a patient. For better or worse, they can furnish the basis for close-knit relationships in a disorganized world. Far from being merely a set of mistaken ideas, magic continues to be a powerful force in the real world.

8

Sorcery, Witchcraft, and Modernity

*H*ere is an anthropological stock in trade: all over the world, people think that unseen powers, usually manipulated by humans, cause illness, death, or just plain randomness in everyday life. Anthropologists have used the words "sorcery" and "witchcraft" to refer to these ideas and practices. And here is an anthropological dilemma: many people do not consider these unseen powers as always harmful; indeed, often the same person draws on the same powers to heal or harm. Sometimes terms for "sorcery" also refer to a range of healing practices. Consider the many people in Europe and North America who follow "witchcraft" in order to find spiritual energy or ways of healing (discussed in Chapter 6) and recall the figure in Disney's "The Sorcerer's Apprentice"—hardly an evil character.

Part of our problem with these terms lies in European and North American associations of "witchcraft" with harm, evil, and Satan, thanks to efforts made in the name of Christianity to demonize heretics and control congregations. Do we retain terms that are so ridden with these powerful negative meanings? How do we translate the many ways of talking about the unseen found across the world into a single language of anthropology? Things are still more difficult, because colonialism introduced European terms for "sorcery" into occupied lands. Thus in Cameroon, western Africa, many people use the French word *la sorcellerie*, which corresponds to both English "sorcery" and "witchcraft," to refer to their own ideas about the unseen, ideas that are morally ambiguous.

What do we then do in writing about these things? Most anthropologists writing today use the terms *sorcery* and *witchcraft* (or cognates in other languages), acknowledge the problems that this use poses, and then describe as best they can how things work in the places where they have worked. In fact, this is what we do regarding much of social life: terms such as *kinship, politics,* and, of course, *religion* are not so straightforward either!

La Sorcellerie *in Cameroon*

*A*ccordingly, the best way to understand the logics of sorcery and witchcraft is to jump into an account of one society, and then describe how things differ elsewhere and how they change over time. We will begin with the Maka people, who live in the southeastern, French-speaking, forested part of Cameroon. The Maka survived German efforts to extract rubber from the region, and equally coercive French efforts to force people to plant coffee and cocoa. After World War II, rising producer prices led some Maka to plant more of these crops, and some of them became wealthy and powerful.

Throughout this period Maka have spoken of an unseen power called *djambe,* a force that lives in the belly of some humans in the form of a small animal, like a mouse or a crab. A myth tells of the introduction of the djambe to human society. A hunter found a djambe in the forest. It asked him to give it a little meat and he did so. That day he killed many animals. Every day he did the same, feeding the djambe and enjoying success in hunting. But then his wife followed him into the forest and spoke to the djambe. It entered into her body, promising to make her rich, but then demanded more and more meat. She killed their animals to feed it, and ended by feeding it her children.

As the ethnographer Peter Geschiere (Geschiere 1997) explains, the myth establishes links between greed and killing, particularly of close kinsmen, and it blames women for causing the djambe to become destructive. Maka say that certain people, called *njind-jamb,* "bring out their djambe," which means that they leave their bodies and join others of like mind at nighttime rendezvous. There, ordinary social rules are reversed: men have sex with other men, and women with women, and they finish by eating the hearts of kinsmen. These kin are certain to die if they do not obtain the aid of a healer (*nkong*).

The djambe concept lies at the heart of two problems for the Maka. The first concerns one's kin. The djambe represents the "dark side of kinship." Although if you are to trust anyone it will be your kinsmen, some people, those who "bring out their djambe," eat their kinsmen's hearts. Stories about djambe bring to the surface the possibility that kin may betray one another, a possibility that one sees in everyday life, when kin feel jealousy toward one another and enter into quarrels.

The djambe also brings out the ambivalence of power. One can only have access to power through the use of djambe. No one who exercises authority in the village could do so without having protected himself by drawing on his djambe. Healers, who can counteract harm done by djambe, also gain their powers by way of their own powerful djambe. In the past, healers had to sacrifice kinsmen in order to fully obtain their powers. Indeed, if a boy or girl shows signs of having an active djambe—for example, if all one's younger siblings die—then a teacher might try to teach her or him to channel that power into the practice of healing, so that she or he becomes an *nkong*, a healer.

The ways of talking about djambe illustrate general human problems: do we trust or mistrust our close relatives? Can someone who obtains power be presumed to use it only for good, or is its use for evil inevitable? In each society in the world people articulate and develop these problems in particular ways; often they call on ideas of sorcery or witchcraft to provide language for these anxieties.

Geschiere tells the story of Tsjume to illustrate the "vicious circle of djambe" in Maka society. Tsjume, an elderly man, fell ill and his third wife died. People attributed these misfortunes to djambe, and rumors pointed at Nanga, Tsjume's first wife. She, too, became ill, and most people said she was the victim of her own djambe use (although others said she suffered from fear of djambe attack). But then she died, after being taken to her natal village, and now Tsjume was accused of having caused the deaths of his wives. Nanga's and Tsjume's family quarreled violently over the matter of where Nanga would be buried. A few weeks later Tsjume's second wife died. Tsjume now began to accuse openly a woman who lived in his compound and who enjoyed a spotless reputation. Geschiere heard her reply: "People who know so well what the witches do are the first to leave their bodies in the night."

Tsjume eventually recovered his strength and the matter ended. People assumed that "the witches had settled the whole affair among themselves." The series of accusations showed the social shaping of fear and suspicion in Maka society. People assumed that if a death occurred in the household, that others in the household must be responsible. But how could you decide who is responsible? In the case of Tsjume, people could follow the logic of Maka djambe ideas to decide. They could infer from the fact that Nanga's illness followed closely on that of her co-wife that sorcery was responsible: she was either responsible for the misfortunes or next on the list of victims. Most people thought she was causing the illness until she died, at which point the second possible position, that she had been a victim, became the majority view. Tsjume's final accusations, of a woman who otherwise was above suspicion, elicited a reply that tapped into a key Maka idea, namely, that those who best understand the doings of djambe are those who bring out their own djambe, that is, who attend nighttime revelries and use their powers for ill.

The slipperiness of accusations rests on the postulate that everyone in the society might well have a djambe. What is at issue is not what is inside you but how you use it: do you develop it, and bring it out for use against others? Do you draw on it to become a great healer, or a powerful government official? To exercise power or achieve greatness depends on having "a full belly," meaning that you have an active djambe. Or do you just go about your business and trouble others as little as possible?

Sorcery ideas imply that particular individuals are responsible for misfortune, or that others experience rapid success through use of their inner force. In other words, it explains success and misfortune by pointing to characteristics and actions of individuals. And the specific characteristics of djambe—the uncertainties and ambiguities created in its "vicious circle"—fit with Maka local politics. Maka village affairs are set out and, sometimes, resolved in village meetings, at which the greater persuasiveness of some people over others determine the day. People attribute these powers to djambe, but djambe's inherent ambiguity means that such authority is fleeting. One elder, Mpal, could cut off others in debate. It was said that he did this by tightening their throats so that they could not speak. But one day he was challenged on grounds that his overly active djambe had caused the deaths of several boys. On that occasion another man was able to counter Mpal's powerful djambe by the power of his own indignation.

The moral ambiguity of djambe reminds us of the difficulties of using the English words sorcery and witchcraft, or the French *la sorcellerie*, a word that encompasses both English terms, because of the sense of evil, or at least maliciousness, that these words convey. The difficulty is further compounded by the fact that Maka use *la sorcellerie* to refer to djambe, and *sorcier* to indicate someone who makes use of his or her djambe, for whatever purposes. A man giving testimony in a court case involving sorcery accusations might give his occupation as "*sorcier,*" a self-description that indicates that he has the knowledge and experience to testify, not that he admits committing malicious acts against others. Geschiere notes the problems and in the end uses *la sorcellerie* to refer to these ideas and practices on grounds that the terms fit reasonably well, and in any case they have entered into Maka use.

Azande Oracles

*A*nthropological studies of sorcery and witchcraft nearly always refer back to the pioneering work carried out in the 1930s by E. E. Evans-Pritchard with the Azande in central Africa. Evans-Pritchard underscored the logic of experience, explanation, and proof that underlies these ideas. In this respect he followed his teacher Malinowski, who argued that people everywhere are rational in their everyday behavior. However, Evans-Pritchard examined much more thoroughly than had Malinowski how it is that the institutions of everyday life reinforce a specific set of beliefs. In his 1937 book, *Witchcraft, Oracles and Magic among the Azande*, he paid particular attention to the social logic of oracles, or how Azande would interpret the results of divination through the lens of their knowledge of their society.

The Azande case continues to be cited by philosophers with respect to the "problem of rationality," and we will focus here on the logic of Azande practices as Evans-Pritchard studied them. Azande say that some among them have inherited a substance that lives in their small intestine, called *mangu*. Mangu can give forth emanations that cause misfortune, and this can happen, at least sometimes, without the knowledge of the person in whose body it exists, as a direct consequence of feeling envy or hatred. In this respect Azande ideas differ from Maka ones, although in both societies people focus on the use of these powerful substances rather than the mere possession of them.

Although Azande will point to natural or social causes for unfortunate events, they cite mangu to explain why it was this person who was the victim. Using an arresting idiom, they say that mangu provided the "second spear" of explanation, thrown after the first to clinch the matter. A man hanged himself after a quarrel, but people quarrel every day without killing themselves, so the force of mangu is called on to explain why in this case the man committed suicide. People are killed when a granary collapses on them, and it is clear that termites had weakened the structure, but why it had to be these people who died is referred to the causal logic of mangu.

Sometimes Azande simply say "it must be mangu" and leave it at that. When they decide to accuse someone of causing misfortune, they choose the likely targets: people likely to have hated or envied the victim. How is an accusation evaluated? Usually an oracle of some kind is consulted by an expert. Oracles form a hierarchy from the most common (and least expensive to use) to the most tightly controlled (and most costly), but the form of consultation is the same. You have the expert put a question to the oracle.

The question might be: "Did so-and-so cause my son's illness?" but it might also be on a non-witchcraft matter such as: "If I build a house in this clearing will I fall ill?" Among widely available oracles are the stones that when rubbed together either stick or glide in response to questions and the termites that eat parts of a stick pushed into their mound. On the top of the oracle hierarchy is the chicken oracle controlled by princes. When this oracle is consulted, a handler, who works for the prince, administers a strychnine-type poison to the chicken. He then poses a question, directing the chicken to die (or live) if the answer is "yes." The chicken then dies or lives. Sometimes the answer is verified by putting the question the other way around (using a second chicken). Thus, the first time the handler asks the chicken to live if the answer is "yes"; the second time to live if the answer is "no."

How does this oracle, the most important and beyond which there is no appeal, work? Presumably, if the oracles gave random answers to questions they would come to be perceived as unreliable. There must then be some degree of positive correspondence between outcomes and what those involved already know or suspect. Part of the answer lies in what is asked of the oracles.

Some questions will concern matters about which most people already have some knowledge and about which there is already a great deal of suspicion, such that either answer, yes or no, will fit what people think they already know. For instance, a couple was accused of a specific act of adultery, and the oracle came out against them. They had protested their innocence (and may have indeed been innocent this time) but were known to have been carrying on an affair for some time. Upon being confronted with the oracle's decision, the man blurted out: "It must have been another time!" Still claiming his innocence of this act of adultery, he surmised that the oracle had detected a previous adulterous act on his part. In his eyes (assuming his outburst reflected his thoughts), then, the oracle was mistaken but not disconfirmed. Other questions cannot easily be disconfirmed. A person might ask an oracle: "If I build my house in such and such a place, will I die?" If the answer is yes, he will not build there and there is no test; if the answer is no and he does build there, chances are low he will die soon. Similar is the question "If I marry so-and-so, will she die within a year?" If they do not marry the oracle is untested; if they do marry, the chances that she will die soon are again low, and were she to die an additional explanation could be sought in, you guessed it, witchcraft!

Even if we assume that the handlers do not influence the result by varying the amount of poison administered to the fowl, then, the oracle will appear not random but in accord with common knowledge. And of course some bias may enter in, although Evans-Pritchard claimed he could detect none.

What are the consequences of being found guilty? They can be quite severe; once, Evans-Pritchard was told, a man could be put to death for certain offenses. Today a person or couple might be put to work for the prince or fined. But even more commonly, the offender will merely be ordered to make things right. How he or she does so sheds important light on what this business of oracles and mangu is all about. For when one is formally accused of witchcraft—one is presented with the wing of a fowl that died—the correct response is to blow out water and say: "If I possess witchcraft in my belly I am unaware of it; may it cool. It is thus that I blow out water."

Today, younger people are counseled by their elders that even if they are sure they are not guilty, they should just blow on the wing to show that they bear no ill will. The matter is not about guilt but about setting things right, smoothing over the hurt. Of course sometimes the oracle is right on the money, or only slightly off, as in the case of the adulterous couple, and then a spontaneous confession may result.

In analyzing the Azande system we are better off considering witchcraft first and foremost as a set of social practices rather than a pseudoscientific system of knowledge claims (as philosophers often do). Individual Azande may or may not be completely convinced of the truth of each statement uttered about witchcraft and oracles, but the overall effect of the way questions are put, the range of responses, and the focus on restitution rather than guilt, is to make the set of practices believable.

This way of looking at it helps to solve the "rationality problem": the set of statements about and practices of Azande witchcraft is a discourse about social problems, one that gives the members of the society a relatively socially harmless way of talking about conflicts and dissatisfactions, bringing them to light, and also resolving those problems. The moment when water is blown by the accused is a moment of catharsis. Tensions between the parties may be released and somewhat relieved. The overall system of power receives an ideological reinforcement, as the prince's oracle has revealed the truth.

Sorcery and Modernity

*I*deas about sorcery are neither limited to a particular society nor static. Let us return to Cameroon, where the societies that lie in the same forested region as the Maka share a set of ideas about sorcery. One of the major languages of the region, Ewondo, has provided a lingua franca term, *evu*, to designate concepts that correspond to the Maka *djambe*. These societies also share a basic political structure; they are what anthropologists call "segmentary," meaning that they consist of small kinship-based groups, related more or less closely to one another, and much of their political activity is based on these kin ties.

The relevance of local political form for understanding sorcery becomes apparent if we contrast these societies with those lying to the west, in the grasslands portion of Cameroon. These societies were and are organized in a more hierarchical fashion, with chiefs and notables. People living in these societies also believe in an inner force that can be used in a range of ways, but their chiefs have the power and responsibility to ensure that the force remains under control and that it works in the interest of the good. The chiefs can declare when someone is using sorcery in a harmful way, and in the past they could execute them (Goheen 1996). Their power allows them to cut through the "vicious circle" of sorcery force. Of course, they declared their own powers to be beneficial.

In many African societies, sorcery ideas have provided ways to understand contemporary politics and economics. In Cameroon (as elsewhere), the authoritarian character of colonial rule government has continued into the postcolonial period. Intrigues and feuds among national politicians have led to sudden twists and turns, climbs to success and falls from grace. One way to explain these events is through the logic of sorcery. As Geschiere observes, much as Americans continue to search for complete explanations of the assassination of John F. Kennedy, so do Cameroon people try to explain these otherwise opaque fortunes and misfortunes.

Sorcery ideas also may be invoked to explain how some people accumulate riches, and why some of the rich then suffer for it—all the modern houses have gravesites in front of them, noted one man. The phrase coined by Jean-François Bayart (1989) to describe African politics, the "politics of the belly," points to the idea that power comes from "eating" wealth, whether that wealth comes from the outside, in the form of aid or export revenues, or from villagers. It also refers to the means of accumulating those riches, namely, through sorcery, the djambe that lives in the belly. Because sorcery power engenders jealousy and, often, misfortune, sorcery ideas have often caused people to refrain from accumulating visible wealth—even planting coca trees could trigger sorcery consequences.

People also create new sorcery ideas to explain new forms of great wealth, and the existence of wealthy people who appear to live contentedly with their riches. One new idea has been that of the sorcerer who turns people into zombies to work for him. This practice is called *ekong* in the port of Duala, one of the centers of new commercial wealth in Cameroon and also a center for these new ideas. Someone seeking this way to wealth may dream and in his dreams visit a prosperous estate. The owner will offer it to him on condition that he offer the life of his mother or another close relative. The victim—the poor mother, for example—will dream that she is led away with her hands tied. It is then time for her to consult a healer to counter the sorcery (de Rosny 1992). These self-described victims usually are people who live in cities and who are experiencing problems with their families. Healers understand these social sources of the ills and the fears, and their work is a type of family therapy, bringing to light family tensions. But, as the circular logic of sorcery implies, these same healers might themselves be responsible for ekong practices. People turn to ever-new possible sources of powerful assistance, whether new healers, chiefs (in the western region), or the state.

As we saw above, chiefs in the western regions can neutralize harm, and this power also allows them to "launder" new wealth that is suspected of having been earned through ekong. Presenting wealth to a chief allows a newly rich person to be accepted by others, as they presume that the chief will work to ensure that the power behind the wealth works only for the good.

Since the 1970s, the Cameroon state increasingly has intervened in sorcery, as have other African states. State prosecution of sorcerers began in the eastern part of the country, where sorcery is reputed to be the most common and where the absence of chiefs has provided the state with the possibility of a new role. These prosecutions were at the behest of local notables—farmers, village officials, party leaders—who thought they had been the victims of sorcery. In most cases neither a confession nor material proof is offered. Judges, assisted by a prosecutor, hear the cases, and most of the time they find the accused guilty. Judges do not make use of healers to see whether the accused does indeed have active sorcery inside him or her, but rely on testimony of accusers and of healers. In other words, the courts cut through the local practices of accusation, counter-accusation and divination. Healers function, not to aid the accused or the sick, but to advise judges on the guilt or innocence of a suspected sorcerer.

Throughout Africa, ideas about sorcery incorporate ideas about social tensions and power, and they have changed along with broader social transformations. Even in precolonial times, accusations of witchcraft were made against women much more often than against men. Some cases of rapid social change exacerbated the attacks on women. In Nigeria, for example, the development of the cocoa economy in the 1940s and 1950s led to the rapid proliferation of women traders, many of whom left the traditional patrilocal compound to pursue their activities elsewhere. These women passed on trading capital to their daughters, bypassing traditional inheritance lines that ran from fathers to sons. Local witchcraft ideas already targeted women; the rapid social and economic change in this period led to an increase in witchcraft accusations and to the 1950–1951 Atinga cult of witch finding that accused thousands of women in Nigeria as witches, forcing them to confess, pay a cleansing fee, and eat a substance that would kill them if they ever practiced witchcraft again. In Andrew Apter's analysis (1993) of the movement, newly powerful male traders financed the cult in part to persecute the women traders with whom they competed.

Accusations of witchcraft continue to be a part of modern urban life in many parts of Africa as a way of talking about evil, particularly the evil brought by strangers (Auslander 1993; Bastian 1993). Tabloids and other newspapers carry witchcraft stories across regions of West and Central Africa. Witches in Zambia and South Africa are accused of causing barrenness and AIDS, sickness and economic failure. Witch finders, in southern Africa often associated with the Zionist churches, are recruited by young men to cleanse their villages by identifying the elderly women and men who are preventing the younger people from advancing economically. Witches are not killed but cleansed by having potions rubbed into cuts on their bodies. And yet, an exception to this general pattern, young militants in South Africa have used the "necklace"—the burning tire used to kill suspected informants during the struggle against apartheid   as a weapon against accused witches, leading one chief—significantly, a woman—to create a new town as a sanctuary for the accused.

Sorcery and Reciprocity in New Guinea

In 1998, when the ethnographer Bruce Knauft last visited them, about 600 Gebusi were living in the forests of southwestern New Guinea. The Gebusi once lived in a world of sorcery, but one that was strikingly different from that inhabited by the Maka. Gebusi were known for their absence of warfare and their overall sociability. And yet, until the mid–1980s they had one of the highest rates of homicide in the world; about one-third of the deaths occurring in the period 1940–1982 were from killing, and the overwhelming majority of these deaths were in retribution for a suspected death or illness from sorcery (Knauft 1985). These killings were all within the group, but, contrary to what one might expect to find, they did not engage in particularly great amounts of internal conflict or backbiting. Clearly, a different cultural logic from that we have studied for Africa was at work here.

Knauft explains how Gebusi social life is shaped by the idea of "direct reciprocity": I give you something and you give me its equivalent in return. Anthropologists find that in many societies two modes of reciprocity underlie many social norms and values, regarding agriculture, material exchange, marriage, relationships with spirits, and general sociability. In direct reciprocity operating in Gebusi society, the movement of goods, a service, or a person in one direction is supposed to be countered by a movement of a similar good, service, or person in the other direction. In marriage, it means that if my village receives a woman (or a man) from another group, we must make sure that a woman (or man) from our group marries one of them. In the case of "generalized reciprocity," giving something to another group will eventually be reciprocated, but perhaps from a different group, in a chain-like fashion. My group might take a spouse from one group, and give a spouse to another group. If direct reciprocity implies closure, generalized reciprocity implies an opening toward the outside.

For the Gebusi, both marriage and sorcery involved direct reciprocity. Marriage was supposed to involve women moving between groups in balanced fashion, and if a marriage in one direction was not followed by one in the other, tensions resulted—and sometimes these tensions led to sorcery accusations. Sorcery itself was structured along the lines of direct reciprocity, for if a woman was the victim of sorcery, then a female sorcerer had to be discovered and killed, and that killing put an end to the matter. Discovery was accomplished through divination and the use of mediums. Mediums also allowed the living to communicate with the spirits of sorcery's victims, who lived in the forest as beautiful birds and animals, the spirit familiars and protectors of the living.

The severe consequences of being suspected of sorcery meant that no one seems to have practiced it, and Gebusi refrained from claiming positions of leadership for fear that their actions would be seen as typical of sorcerers. By the late 1990s, sorcery accusations had nearly disappeared. Most Gebusi had joined one of several local churches and now faced the highly powerful spirit, God. All the people who had acted as mediums to ascertain the identity of sorcerers had died or given up their ties with spirits. If someone did level a sorcery accusation, he or she could be hauled into court and charged with slander. Many people continue to believe in sorcery, but in some places, at least, the practice has ceased.

Why is this so? The contrast with the African cases discussed earlier provides some clues. Maka and other people saw in the accumulation of riches and emergence of inequalities a threat, and sorcery has provided a way of talking about, and sometimes acting against, that threat. The Gebusi with whom Knauft has lived have welcomed the introduction of "modernity" in the form of consumer goods, schools, churches, and protection against warfare. They see abandoning sorcery as a way toward that modernity. Many of them did a "direct exchange" between the older spirits and the new God, and see sorcery practices and churchgoing as incompatible. Their new lives bring them into constant contact with people from other ethnic groups at the large station area; these contacts radically alter social life, which now includes a large, depersonalized domain of social interactions at school, office, church, or sports events. The modernity experienced here is attractive, individualizing, but also passivizing—Gebusi now receive lessons, speeches, sermons, all of which instruct them to supplicate and hope for the best.

This outcome was contingent on the particular experience of the Gebusi and differed across New Guinea societies. Knauft suggests that such locally important elements as the relatively friendly character of the local police and the tolerant attitude of church officials made it seem attractive to Gebusi to ally themselves with these local officials. In the case of the police, this reliance contributed to the decline of sorcery accusations, because accused sorcerers now were sent off for jail terms or released for lack of evidence rather than killed. The legitimacy of these state institutions, itself due to this set of contingent factors, then led to sorcery's decline.

Sorcery and Sacrifice in Sri Lanka

In the healing practices associated with Buddhism in Sri Lanka, human agency is assumed to lie behind most illnesses and other misfortunes of everyday life. People spread illness and misfortune through malicious talk, through poisons and effigies; ill will toward others may cause harm even when the perpetrator is unaware of what he or she is doing—an idea we have just seen with the Azande. Expressions for sorcery refer to the sorcerer "binding" the victim to the sorcery to create the kind of intimacy otherwise associated with kinship or sexuality. Sorcery may result from feuding among the spirits of deceased kin that continues down through the ages.

In one case reported by Kapferer (1997, 41–42), a hospital worker who had become seriously ill underwent a series of exorcisms in order to discover the cause of the illness. In trance, the victim described a land dispute that had begun when two sisters of his great-grandfather had not been given the land they deserved at the time of their marriage. It was the spirits of these sisters and their descendants who were behind the man's troubles. His illness was "the monstrous forming of the accumulated anger growing within a body of kin through the generations" (Kapferer 1997, 42).

As in Africa and New Guinea, then, Sinhalese sorcery strikes often among kin and expresses suppressed angers and resentments. A range of anti-sorcery rituals and specialists are available to counter the work of such spirits and persons and to restore health. The force of sorcery is represented and embodied in a demon and deity that exists within and in tension with Buddhist ideas and practices. The term *Huniyam* or *Suniyam*, connoting emptiness, refers to the sorcery force and to the demon/creator. The ambivalence of Suniyam runs throughout anti-sorcery rituals, and recalls a similar tension between sorcery and healing in Cameroon society.

The master anti-sorcery rite is called the Suniyama. An expensive ritual, it requires the sorcery victim or his or her sponsor to build an elaborate structure said to be the palace of the first human King, Mahasammata, and his Queen, Manikpala. The palace represents earthly desires and sources of envy, which have brought on the victim's misfortunes. As the ritual unfolds, the victim moves from outside the place into its bedchamber, also said to be the center of the world and a space of the Buddha, a place of enlightenment. The victim, whether male or female, plays the role of the Queen, who, at the beginning of history, was the first human to be struck down by sorcery. As the victim moves toward the center of the palace, he or she leaves behind all thoughts of desire. A series of sacrifices are performed, and at the ritual's end the palace is destroyed (thereby destroying the reasons for sorcery). Thus the Buddha's power is invoked to regenerate the victim, but paradoxically by means of sacrifice and destruction.

The ritual was created by a sorcerer, Oddisa, to save Queen Manikpala from illness caused by sorcery. Performing it not only cures a victim, but also enacts Buddhist ideas and, in effect, the history of Sri Lanka. The ritual therefore is very attractive to new elites. The ritual's dual function of curing and enacting also helps explain the emergence of a deity, Suniyam, worshipped in urban temples and shrines in Sri Lanka (Kapferer 2003). These shrines are located in boundary areas of cities, and in areas plagued by violent crime. They are visited by people suffering from a wide variety of ailments, or by those who seek help in business or schooling, or to hurt competitors, to stop the police from making an arrest, or to exact revenge. Kapferer (2003, 122–123) stresses the association of the god Suniyam with violence: during the insurrections of 1989–1990, when thousands of young people were killed or jailed, the shrines were crowded with parents seeking either revenge or the return of their children.

Witchcraft as Satan versus God

*I*n early modern Europe and North America, misfortune was thought of in a dualistic framework, where God and his followers confront Satan and those in his grasp. Witch hunts in various parts of Europe resembled those in Africa today, except that the source of the witchcraft was not the individual but her or his ties with Satan.

In the United States, witchcraft is surely most closely associated with the celebrated 1692 trials held in Salem, Massachusetts. I would argue that witchcraft ideas in New England once functioned much as they do in Azande society, to encourage confession and purge the society of its fears and tensions. But rapid social changes of the late seventeenth century created new fissures in village society that were given strong moral and emotional colorations by Puritan preachers and church members. Much as in contemporary Africa, older tensions were exacerbated and witch hunts grew in importance.

New England Puritans

The Puritans of seventeenth-century New England held strong religious ideas about the church as a community and about the immanence of evil in the world. A church in this society was not a building or even an association to which one could freely belong. In its narrow and most compelling sense it was a community of people who felt themselves elected by God, as "saints," who had joined in a covenant that bound each to the other. Church members were responsible for one another, such that the sins of one person would lead to misfortune for others (Miller 1956, 141–152). As John Winthrop put it in his sermon on "Christian charity" delivered to the Pilgrims onboard the Arabella en route to the New World in 1630: "We must be knit together as one man and must delight in each other, make other's condition our own, rejoice together, mourn together, labor and suffer together, always having before our eyes our commission and community in the work" (quoted in Demos 1982, 299).

This sense of common destiny was reinforced by the constant copresence of church members in a village. You encountered your fellow parishioner in his store, where he sold you bread, or near your fields, where you might get along or be embroiled in a dispute over boundaries or water. Common destiny and a shared life worked tolerably well as long as everyone prospered tolerably equally. But sharp differences in economic and social standing had begun to emerge, along with ideas of individualism. These new and dangerous ideas were, ironically, exacerbated by the opportunity afforded in the New World: the abundance of land and the fragility of new institutions.

Puritans also held that a strong line divided good from evil in the world. Evil was incarnate in the witch. As the prominent preacher Cotton Mather put it: "There is in witchcraft a most explicit renouncing of all that is holy and just and good." The witch showed "the furthest effort of our original sin" (quoted in Demos 1982, 304). Witches' meetings were imagined as inversions of all that was holy, involving trampling on the cross and defiling the Host. (And, indeed, contemporary Satanic cults do practice some of these rituals of inversion.) In this respect, witchcraft served to sharpen and perhaps to strengthen the moral boundaries between the community and Satan's forces.

In this context, in which all actions were to be scrutinized for their good or evil, ordinary people understandably could experience a great deal of anxiety about whether their actions and feelings came from God or Satan. Puritans believed in predestination, that God has damned or saved us before we were born, but not revealed to us His decision. Puritans saw the world as full of signs or marks of God's will, so that one might recognize in himself the signs of Election, or of damnation (and indeed becoming a member of the church required that one declare oneself saved). But Satan could be behind such feelings, trying to induce damned individuals to enter the church. Even the most highly placed church member could not easily escape gnawing doubts as to the reliability of his or her own certainty. One story has it that a woman in a Boston congregation, tormented by her uncertainty, threw her child into a well to seek relief of certain damnation. (Hers was, however, an incorrect interpretation of the strictly un-knowable nature of Election!)

Evil and Accusations

In this context of gnawing doubts, the presence of Evil, and the ideal of a morally as well as socially close-knit community, fears of evil within—the witch—were endemic. Throughout the early modern period in Europe, accusations of witchcraft were an expected part of life. England had somewhere between 300 and 1,000 executions for witchcraft between 1542 and 1736. Accusations fit the general pattern already noted. Most of the accused were women; indeed, in one detailed record for the period 1560–1680 in Essex County, only 8 percent of the persons tried were men. The typical English witch was an older woman, perhaps widowed, from the poorer segment of the community. Often she was a beggar. She was usually accused of bewitching someone not only in her own village but in her part of the village. Witches were neighbors. The historian

Keith Thomas argues that accusers were beginning to chafe at the demands of charity, as the ethics of the time gradually became more individualistic. And yet moral responsibility for charity still was preached by the church and probably felt as legitimate by the better-off citizens. Harsh words, even curses, by those whose appeals for financial assistance were denied would have spawned some guilt in the hearts of these newly individual-minded villagers, and to assuage this guilt, argues Thomas, they projected it onto the "witch" (Demos 1982, 298–300).

Witchcraft accusations were brought from England to New England—indeed, in particular from Essex County, England, to Essex County, Massachusetts. In seventeenth-century North America there are recorded 93 witchcraft cases, of which 16 led to hangings, the Salem outbreak excepted. If we count the Salem trials as well, the total rises to 234 cases and 36 executions—an "accusation rate" of seven accusations per 100,000 people in North America, compared to less than one accusation per 100,000 in England, and about 5.5 for the most "active" county in England, Essex. Clearly, then, events in Salem pushed the rate of accusations far beyond their usual frequency (Demos 1982, 11–12).

Accusations functioned in similar fashion to what we observed for the Azande. The activity of a witch could explain why an unexpected event happened, even when the physics of the matter were perfectly clear. For example, a man on maneuvers with his militia accidentally discharged his gun, which ricocheted off a tree and struck another man, killing him. The first man was charged with manslaughter, but people continued to ask why the rather odd accident had happened. In the event, a woman was accused of witchcraft. She had owed money to the deceased and had been his landlord: she was thus close to him and yet in a socially ambivalent relationship to him. But to blame a single individual was insufficient to account for the presence of witchcraft in the community, where everyone was in some way responsible for everyone else. And so, on a subsequent Sunday the preacher widened the field of blame to include the entire community, whose general moral decrepitude, he charged, had permitted Satan to enter among them and do his evil work (Demos 1982, 3–9).

In such a case the matter would rest there, and so it had been in Salem before 1692. Events in that year represent an abnormal, outrageous set of actions. Yet the people involved were ordinary village folk, much like all the other folk peopling the eastern seaboard then and afterward.

The Salem Outbreak of 1692

First, the events. In February 1692, several girls in Salem village began acting very strangely: alternately prancing about and hiding under chairs, making strange, "foolish" speeches that no one could understand, and taking to their beds, moaning and complaining about pains. The authorities of the village interpreted this behavior as witchcraft. One of the first girls to act strangely was the daughter of the village minister, Samuel Parris. As she lay on her bed, Parris and others began to question her, thinking that she might be the victim of witchcraft. The questions put to her and to several other girls were in the form of: "Was it so-and-so?" Much as with the Zande oracle, certain names were put forward and others were not. The girls were urged to name someone, and they did name several women, including Tituba. Three women were then questioned by two members of the provincial legislature, who lived in nearby Salem Town. Tituba confessed to having committed witchcraft; the other two denied the charges.

The accusations snowballed, and the public hangings began in June of that year. Between June 2 and September 22, 19 men and women were hanged, including a minister, the Reverend George Burroughs. The hangings were finally stopped by the intervention of Boston-area ministers who were troubled by the willy-nilly hanging, though not by the principle of hanging witches. On October 12 Governor Phips forbade any more imprisonments for witchcraft, and all prisoners were set free during the following year.

The events raise some troubling questions. First, why were the experiences of the children interpreted as the torment of witches? Were Puritans generally likely to make such interpretations? The nature of the experiences was not all unpleasant, after all. The girls' strange speech suggests the speaking in tongues of the Pentecost spoken of in the Bible and known to the ministers. Indeed, in the very same year of 1692 a Boston servant girl exhibited similar syndromes: spasms, outbreaks of strange speech, and, upon meeting some of the accused Salem women, violent behavior toward them. But in this case, Cotton Mather drew on her behavior to form a group that met with her, chanted psalms, and had similar experiences, which began to be seen as a kind of religious ecstasy.

Later, in the early eighteenth century, the same sort of outbreak in Northampton, in western Massachusetts, was interpreted by the minister of that town, Jonathan Edwards, as a sign of the "pouring out of the spirit of God." This movement led to what came to be called the "Great Awakening," a period during which a wider range of religious experiences and behaviors were accepted (Miller 1956, 153–166).

Second, why were the charges believed? The accusers were young girls, and there was only their own testimony to support their charges. Were the distinguished jurors who found the accused guilty themselves imbeciles? How can we understand their findings?

Finally, why, in this instance but not before or after, did the outbreak expand as it did? Several hundred people were accused, 150 imprisoned, and 19 executed. Earlier outbreaks in New England since 1647 had resulted in a total of 15 executions. Those executed were local people, marginal, following the general pattern: accuse your neighbor if he or she is powerless and likely to be suspected by others on grounds of unpleasantness.

The events in Salem might have been just another minor outbreak. By April, only six people had come under public suspicion of witchcraft. But then the number of accusations picked up and were aimed at people of high status outside the immediate community. The accused included the wealthiest ship owner in Salem Town and two of its seven selectmen, two sons of a former governor, themselves prominent public figures, and even Lady Phips, wife of the governor! And unlike all previous outbreaks, most of the accused were people outside of Salem Village, in the nearby village of Andover (Boyer and Nissenbaum 1974, 22–30).

Salem and Disruption of the Moral Community

The historians Paul Boyer and Stephen Nissenbaum have given us an account of the anomaly of Salem based on the peculiar social tensions of the time. In 1636, Salem Village (today the town of Danvers) was founded but was under the control of Salem Town. The town, not the village, levied and collected taxes and set the prices to be charged for farm produce at the village gate. The village was not legally independent at the time of the witchcraft outbreak (Boyer and Nissenbaum 1974, 37–109).

The town had become a major export center, with a rich merchant class. (Many in China thought the greatest naval power of the day was the "country of Salem" because so many ships bore the name.) By keeping the prices of produce down, the town had prospered for 30 years, and because the town's population had been growing, the farmers had been able to prosper as well. But the population of the village outside the town was growing, too, and the average land holdings per household diminished dramatically at the end of the century, from 250 acres in 1660 to 124 acres in 1690. With less acreage and more farmers, a disparity developed between the amount of food needed by the town and the amount being produced. By the early 1690s, the average income of many of the farmers had declined, and tensions developed between the town and the village.

Not all families fared equally well or poorly in Salem Village. Two families who played leading roles on the witchcraft stage were the Putnams and the Porters (Boyer and Nissenbaum 1974, 110–152). Both had arrived in the 1640s from neighboring parts of England, and both soon became prosperous farming families in the village. But by the 1690s the two large groups of descendants of the original immigrants lived on opposite sides of the village.

The Porters had settled in the eastern half of the village, where they operated two sawmills, sold lumber to town merchants, and eventually married into town families. They and others in the eastern half of the village were able to benefit from townspeople's demand for goods and services. Their land was better for farming as well, and they were also close to the road that ran along the eastern edge. Near them were other small entrepreneurs, traders, and shop owners, all of whom increasingly saw themselves as sharing interests and outlooks with residents of the town. By and large they wished to preserve the close relationship of town and village and feared the future domination of an independent village by the local church. Among other fears was that the church might impose restrictions on the movement of produce outside of the village. The Porters were accused of witchcraft, which they denied. The accusers did not dare to confront the powerful Porters directly, and so they tended to target people who were associated with them.

By contrast, the fortunes of the Putnams were tied up exclusively with the village. Their original grant was of lands in the western portion of the village, where expansion could only be further westward. They were landlocked, with no nearby roads, and with poor, hilly land. They tried to diversify in the 1670s, setting up an iron-smelting plant, but the effort failed. They were fated to stay on the farm, but the farm was getting smaller, as by the third generation the remaining plots were each barely enough to maintain their standard of living.

It was this third generation of desperate Putnams that furnished the leaders in witchcraft accusations. Foremost among them was Thomas Putnam, Jr., his wife Ann, and their 12-year-old daughter Ann. They had been deprived of an estate that had been awarded to Thomas's half-brother (who, to make matters worse, had married a Porter). Several of their children had died. Their frustration and rage was vented at persons who could be attacked in the village and then expanded outward to include outsiders, upwardly mobile, who were insufficiently deferential. The Putnams were involved in the prosecution of 46 accused witches. The daughter, Ann Putnam, was the principal afflicted girl and accuser (Boyer and Nissenbaum 1974, 30–36, 133–152).

For the Puritans, self-interest was the enemy within the body of the community. "Our community are members of the same body," said John Winthrop in 1630 to the first Pilgrim contingent. From this perspective, the town, with its taverns and rich merchants, was to be seen as bringing moral danger to the Church and its community. The minister in Salem village, Samuel Parris, had never been accepted by all villagers, and the Porters were among those whom he saw as his enemies. He felt besieged and insecure, and he channeled his frustrations and anger into his sermons on Judas and on the sense of filth and corruption in the community. And he led the charge against the witches.

Within the village, a remarkable geographic pattern emerged that confirmed the importance of social and economic divisions in the witchcraft trials. Of the 25 accused witches who lived in or near Salem Village, only three lived in the western half of the village and four in the center; all the others lived in the eastern half, most of them along its boundary with Salem Town. (By contrast, of the 32 adult villagers who testified against the accused, 30 lived in the western half of the village.) This distribution of accused witches underscores the degree to which the town was seen as a danger to the community by the accusers. Among the accused was John Proctor, a tavernkeeper who was envied by the Putnams for his success and who was also condemned as too worldly, and John Willard, an outsider who married into the village and then began to buy up coveted farmland in great quantities (Boyer and Nissenbaum 1974, 181–189).

The Porters themselves were of too high a status in the community to be accused by people who would encounter them frequently. But those on the fringes of their circle were accused; for example, a man who had recently married one of their sisters. Other victims were marginal to the community in other ways. Several victims were poor women who were judged as being disrespectful to their benefactors. Cotton Mather had warned that those "who through discontent at their poverty, or at their misery, shall be always murmuring . . . witchcraft is the upshot of it" (Boyer and Nissenbaum 1974, 208).

Historian Beth Norton has added a new dimension to the accusations by pointing out that some of the accusers had fled from villages and towns attacked by Wabanaki Indians in the late 1680s and early 1690s. For example, Abigail Hobbs's confession (on April 19, 1692) marked a critical juncture in the building of Salem tensions. Abigail lived in another village, and her confession signaled the enlargement of the circle of accused beyond Salem. She stated that she had encountered Satan as a "black man," an expression often used for Indians, in Casco Bay and Falmouth, settlements farther north that had been targets of attacks by Wabanakis. Norton argues that Abigail's confession linked witchcraft and Indian attacks in the minds of Essex County residents, and that this linking led to the explosion of accusations that followed (2003, 78–81, 112–132).

Evidence and Confessions

That these people could be witches was not doubted. Everyone accepted that witches did exist. Satan's struggle for the souls of people was evident in the world, and misfortune always had a moral tinge to it. As the historian Perry Miller has written, Puritanism had no room for failure. When failure came, it was due to the work of Satan in the world, and among his favorite vehicles were witches.

What was the evidence for witchcraft? According to the canons of evidence of the day, several kinds were admissible (Boyer and Nissenbaum 1974; Demos 1982). One was empirical evidence, which included behavioral traits: these could be positive, such as great physical strength, or negative, such as the inability to recite the Lord's Prayer all the way through. These signs were largely upheld through the proceedings. The category also included odd physical markings, such as the supposed third "witch's teat," a third breast on women. Such bodily evidence was considered to be God's message to humans, but it was generally rejected in the Salem case as being unreliable.

Of long-standing evidentiary value was the category called "Anger followed by Mischief," that is, when after a quarrel or even a sharp look someone was stricken with a malady. This evidence eventually was rejected because of the difficulty of ascertaining the empirical links between the "anger" and the "mischief."

Finally and most dramatically, there was Spectral Evidence—in this case, when the afflicted girls saw figures of the accused coming to them and harming them. This evidence could, of course, be produced at a moment's notice. Mary Warren, one of the girls, tried to recant her own accusations against previous witches when the other girls accused her master, John Proctor. The others responded to her defection by immediately seeing specters around *her*. At this threat, she retracted her recantation and returned to their side. But when "respectable" townspeople began to be accused, some of the ministers remembered that Satan was capable of creating specters and images to mislead the God-fearing, and at that point spectral evidence began to be doubted publicly. Increase Mather, the leader of Boston's clergy, condemned the use of both Spectral Evidence and Anger followed by Mischief. Mather said that even when one saw a specter, it could be Satan causing mischief and trying to impune the righteousness of a good person.

Of course, many people confessed before the case could come to trial. Those who did confess, here as elsewhere, were not hanged but released. From the perspective of a modern trial court this course of action seems very odd. Why release confessed criminals and hang those who insisted on their innocence? But from the perspective of comparative witchcraft studies it is what we would expect. As in the Azande case, the confession purged the community of tensions and, in this instance, of the deep guilt it felt for straying from the righteous path. As with the blowing out of water among the Azande, the confession gives a language for conflicts, the language of Satan and witchcraft. (Possibly, although this is not documented, some may also have thought, as do Azande, that it was possible to cause evil through witchcraft without intending to do so, just by being angry with someone.)

Here is another way the Salem events went wrong. The first three women to be accused had confessed but after that confessions virtually ceased. Why? Boyer and Nissenbaum argue that a cultural change was just then occurring in New England, one that gave just enough moral sanction to individual pride and "face" that many people were no longer willing to confess for the sake of community. Now they wished to act on their individual consciences. But the logic of accusation and confession had not quite caught up with their new sense of obligation and responsibility. From this point of view the events in Salem are a terrible result of uneven moral and cultural transition, away from one world view, that of the Puritan, toward another, that of the outward-oriented Great Awakening (Boyer and Nissenbaum 1974, 209–216; Miller 1957, 153–166).

In order to understand the events at Salem in the 1690s, we must take seriously a number of competing perspectives. The unusual outbreak in 1691–1692 at Salem Village happened where it did largely because of the unusually high level of tensions that divided the village and set it against Salem Town. The events happened when they did because several rising trajectories of anxiety came together at this moment and place: the social and religion tensions within the village were rising at the same time that fears of Indian attacks from the west and at the same time as a crisis in Massachusetts governance. The accusations had the content they did because of the long history of ideas about witches and Satan; they died down as sharply as they did because of local doubts and debates among influential churchmen about those ideas.

As Mary Beth Norton (2003) argues, these events involved all of Essex County, Massachusetts, and not just Salem Village and Town. Indeed, one of the distinctive features of the 1691–1692 events was precisely the extent to which Salem villagers accused people living in Andover and Salem Town, with whom they had had little or no contact. We might, however, draw parallels between the way in which rising levels of economic tension and anxiety in Salem created a geographically expansive pattern of witchcraft accusation, and the ways in which accusations in some African societies have reached beyond the usual range of kin and neighbors to include the rich and the powerful. In both contemporary Africa and late seventeenth-century New England, new patterns of trade, gain, and political power created new lines of worry, hostility, and resentment.

Note that at the same time that we can see parallel, powerful, psychological changes in two very different times and places, we also explain each set of changes in terms of local ideas and forces. The anthropological insistence on locally based accounts of change precludes easy recourse to vague psychological notions, such as "modernization," or political economic ones, such as "globalization," as if such concepts explained a local series of events. At the same time, the anthropological insistence on comparisons and regional analyses can lead to better understandings of the mechanisms and processes underlying social change. Earlier, we saw an example of such an analysis in the case of Bruce Knauft's studies of sorcery in South Coast New Guinea societies. Knauft first showed the particular set of events that made sorcery accusations plummet in the society he studied. He then pointed to very different trajectories in other New Guinea societies;

these contrasts allowed him to point to the "differences that made a difference" for this region of New Guinea.

For Salem, Norton argues (262–265) that the trajectories of accusations and confessions depended on the specific social character of each village. Salem Village, long racked by internal dissension, produced many who denied the accusations against them, and thus led to the reliance on spectral confessions. In nearby Andover, the site of many accusations, people were accustomed to proceeding by consensus. In that town, many people, especially women and children, acceded to the demands of their male elders that they confess. For example, Mary Tyler later told Increase Mather of the series of pronouncements made to her by her brother-in-law, magistrates, and the Reverend John Emerson that she was a witch; Emerson seems to have tried to beat the devil out of her. She succumbed to these accusations and confessed. Most telling was her brother-in-law's assertion that "God would not suffer so many good men to be in such an error about it" (i.e., her guilt), in other words, not to confess would be intolerable since so many prominent people had stated that she was a witch.

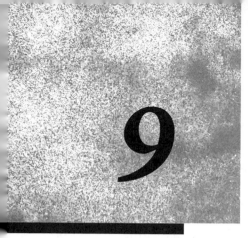

9

Objects, Images, and Worship

Religions involve actions, ideas, and rules, but they also often provide images and symbols around which religious activity centers and coalesces. We have already witnessed the power of objects, particularly images: in the tall bis poles carved by the Asmat to contain and then release their ancestors' spirits; in the enormous statues of Buddhas constructed and honored by Japanese; in the temple statues in India with which the worshiper exchanges vision, *darshan*. We could add masks used in North American, African, and Melanesian rituals, Northwest Coast poles, and Catholic statuary, to make apparent the range and power of religious images throughout the world.

Not all cultures make visual imagery an important part of religious and ritual lives; in most Muslim and Protestant societies, for example, images of people are downplayed, and instead the sacred word is stressed (as we shall see in Chapters 11 and 12). Often people debate vigorously just what an image means in religious terms—is it itself sacred? Does it contain or attract a spirit? As you read this and the next two chapters, consider the question: What kinds of differences does an emphasis on visual vis-à-vis oral media make for religious life?

Conveying Meaning through Symbols

All of the media we use to communicate with one another—words, diagrams, gestures, and so forth—are subject to multiple interpretations, but images particularly so. An image, whether a statue, painting, mask, or other object, has meaning in a way different from a statement that we might utter. If I say, "This is a tree," I have clearly said something about an object and a class of things called "trees." A picture of a tree, by contrast, does not say anything. The picture might be a photograph of a tree (in which case it could be taken as evidence that the tree exists, in a court of law for instance), or a very good painting of a tree (in which case it might be interpreted mainly for the skill of the artist or his or her attention to form). It might be a tree housing an ancestor, or a tree evoking memories of shade and protection.

The tree-picture's meanings come from the larger structure of knowledge, associations, and practices in which it is embedded. Moreover, different viewers, with different histories and experiences, might draw from it very different interpretations and associations.

Such images are multivocalic—"many-voiced" or capable of generating many meanings. Recall the Asmat sago tree. The tree's tall form and spherical fruits suggest the human form and head, and the milky, starchy interior suggests breast milk and nurturing powers. The tree evokes myths about the taking of heads and the origins of the cosmos. Many Indonesians view the huge, spreading banyan trees found throughout the country as evoking feelings of protection, and for this reason the tree was taken to be the emblem of the government's political party GOLKAR. The tree now evokes different feelings and thoughts for viewers depending on their political ideas.

In studying the religious meanings of objects we look for associations and resonances on different planes of human experience, from physiology, to culture, to social structure. Certain such associations have a strong basis in body symbolism, such as the sago tree's evocations of heads and milk, or the ideas of danger often linked to the color red. These associations are often widespread, evoking shared human experiences, although they receive different interpretations in different societies. The anthropologist Victor Turner (1967, 28–30) describes these meanings as the "sensory pole" of a symbol's range of meaning. He contrasts these meanings to those clustering around the "ideological pole," which tie the object to socially specific ideas. The same Asmat trees, when carved into bis poles, stand for the unity of the men in the men's house and the needs of the ancestral spirit to be enclosed and then released by the taking of a head. (Men's and women's ideas about the pole undoubtedly differ, but more fieldwork is required to clarify these differences.)

Turner's way of analyzing symbols allows us to consider the interplay of psychological or bodily associations, which tend to be similar in unrelated societies, with those "ideological" associations that are specific to one society or group of societies, or to one religious tradition. Another perspective on meaning, called "semiotics" and deriving from the logician Charles S. Peirce (1972), focuses on three ways in which an object is meaningful: as an *index* based on direct contact or "pointing," as an *icon* based on resemblance, and as a *symbol* based on historically and culturally specific linkages.

The semiotic approach is particularly useful in pointing out two ways that religious objects convey meaning. The first way is through the *history of physical contact* between an object and a spiritual or sacred being. Sacred relics, such as body parts of holy people, masks originating from spirits, or the bis pole once inhabited by an ancestor, are sacred and treasured because of their history of direct contact with a once-living holy person, a powerful spirit, or a revered ancestor. A second way objects take on powerful religious meaning is through their *resemblance* to a sacred or powerful being. Consider how Catholic images of the Virgin Mary are expected (and are seen by some people) to work miracles: to heal, weep, or speak. (The sense of "icon" as "religious image" is one of its standard dictionary meanings, and has given rise to such terms as "iconoclast," meaning "image breaker" in medieval Greek, referring to people opposed to the use and veneration of sacred images.)

Embodying Deities

In many religions, we find combinations of imagery and contact serving as the bases for worshiping gods. Hinduism freely combines several image types, all of which embody a deity. Some statues are highly realistic and anthropomorphic ("representing in human shape") representations of a deity. The focus of the worshiper's attention toward these statues is the eye: the worshiper "exchanges vision" (darshan) with the deity by gazing on its eyes. Power is absorbed through visual contact. Yet other god-objects are not at all anthropomorphic: Shiva, one of the great gods, is often represented by a simple, phallus-shaped stone called a *linga*. The shape underscores Shiva's cosmic creative energy. It, too, is inhabited by the deity.

Japanese religions exhibit a still wider range of image types to represent and mark the presence of a deity. Buddha statues are of particular Buddhas—Maitreya, or Fudo, or Amida. Each Buddha has characteristic markers, such as the position of the hands or the presence of other objects, but the artist still has a great deal of latitude in how the Buddha is represented. But Buddhas are above the world, so they are not depicted as historical personages. By contrast, the spirits (kami) worshiped at Shinto shrines are tied to the world in one of two ways. Some are spirits of ancestors, and so may be shown in paintings as specific individuals with identifiable dates. Others are spirits of locations; they are represented by natural elements such as a waterfall or a boulder. An ancestor is represented by a plaque, which may be converted into a household god through the logic of direct contact: the plaque is thrown into a river, from which a pebble is selected and added to the pile of pebbles making up the household god's altar. Spirit objects are defined by the fact that they are spirits or contain spirits; Buddhist statues, by contrast, must have certain rituals performed on them before they will be said to contain the particular Buddha they represent.

Religious objects play meaningful roles in two very different traditions. The masks and legends of the Dogon people of West Africa represent the creation of the world in dances. Catholic images of Mary, Christ, and saints are intended to focus worship on the universal message of the Church. Both traditions link the immediate and concrete to the universal, and do so through powerful imagery, with multiple associations. The great disparity in scale between these two cases—one bounded in a small plateau region, the other spread throughout the world—shows how similar forms and practices of religion appear in widely differing contexts.

Masks in West Africa

Masks are used throughout the world to convey ideas of sacred power. They play particularly important roles in certain regions—a belt across the middle of Africa; Northwest Coast America; Melanesia—but they appear most everywhere. In New Guinea, and along the northwest coast of the Americas, masks often depict ancestors, including primordial ancestors, and they dramatize stories of the creation of humans. The famous transforming masks of the Kwakiutl of the northwest coast enact this creative process in themselves: the face of a bear, for instance, may be opened when the wearer pulls on hidden straps to reveal the image of the human into which the bear was changed.

Masks give a timeless or universal quality to real human beings, and for that reason they are often used to represent the cosmos, or the first people or beings, and then they are used to dance out the primordial creation of the world and the establishment of social order. These dances or other uses of masks then affirm and underscore that order in the face of current disorder. Because they are inhabited by people, almost always men, they also represent the social order in a particular way, especially with respect to gender and age-grade or level of initiation. In many societies, particularly in Africa, women are not supposed to speak of the masks or touch them; they mark as taboo the boundary between control of the sacred objects, in men's hands, and the society of women.

The Dogon people of Mali and Burkina Faso (the former Upper Volta) are famous for their elaborate masks and for the extensive study of their culture by a French ethnographic team (Griaule 1965). The Dogon live from agriculture on a cliff and plateau region, under the authority of a council of village elders. Each village owns a large figure of the mythic ancestor Dyongou Sérou, the first being to experience death. Every adult male belongs to a village mask society, the Awa, charged with guarding the village mask, and he also sculpts his own mask, which may be of animals, Dogon people, foreigners, or other objects. He wears the mask during a variety of rituals, including those designed to accompany a spirit of the dead to its resting place, to ward off spells, or to ensure the fertility of crops or of women.

Seventy-eight different types of masks have been identified for the Dogon, each with multiple levels of meaning that correspond to the four degrees of initiation through which males pass (Imperato 1978). For example, a mask surmounted with a tall lattice work is identified on the first level, and to the uninitiated (including early ethnographers), as "the granary door of Amma," the supreme god. On a higher level it is known to represent the phase in the creation of the universe when Amma's collarbones opened up, and on a still higher level, the "egg of Amma" out of which the first beings were created.

The Dogon consider their masks to be capable of defusing and transferring dangerous sacred powers. In their view, all life forms have a vital force or power called "nyama" (Pernet 1992, 53–62). Nyama can flow from one material being to another, but when it leaves its usual resting place, it changes from supporting life to endangering life. It becomes energy out of place. Masks can be used to transfer such "loose" nyama to a safe place, such as a painting. This process is described in the story about the kanaga mask, which depicts a bird in downward flight. The mask has a vertical piece extending upward from the cap, crossed by two horizontal pieces—the lower one with short extension pieces pointing downward, the upper one with pieces pointing upward. Most Dogon understand the mask as the representation of a story about this bird and its nyama. In the story, a hunter killed the bird and carved its image with wood from a nearby tree. But the spirit of the tree lost its resting place when the tree was felled, which caused the hunter to become ill. The hunter then carved a small figure at the very top of the mask to embody the spirit. In a second transfer, he moved the spirit to a painting in red ochre on the wall of a cave, and his health was restored.

Drawing of the Dogon kanaga mask, Mali.

Men who have reached the higher degrees of initiation interpret the mask in a different way, as representing a story about Amma, the supreme god. Amma had twin children through sexual intercourse with the earth. The children are known as the Nommo. One was female and one male, and both had human forms above the waist and serpent shapes below the waist. Amma had other children, and one committed incest with his mother the earth—an act that led to the introduction of death to the world. To cleanse the earth of this polluting act, Amma sacrificed one of the Nommo (Griaule 1965, 130–137). To the men who know this story, the two arms of the mask pointing skyward represent the sacrificed Nommo and his twin; the two pointing downward, the son who committed incest and his twin. (Various alternative interpretations of the carving on the mask's top have been given to ethnographers.) The sacrifice, like the wearing of the mask, turned dangerous power away from society.

We should note two aspects of the mask and its meaning at this point. First, different people viewing the mask as it is danced around in a ritual event will have very different associations and stories come to mind. The mask is multivocalic. Second, the meanings people bring to their viewing of the mask depend on their own social characteristics, particularly on their gender and degree of initiation. The masks call up diverse images in a way that is highly socially structured.

This socially shaped multivocality also applies to the red fiber skirt the dancers wear (Griaule 1965, 16–23). These fibers contain their own sort of nyama. For some viewers (those who have reached higher degrees of initiation), the fibers also recall the mythic fibers Amma gave to his wife the earth. The fibers were reddened by the first menstrual blood, which appeared after the incestuous union described above. Women obtained them and, wearing them, ruled society. Men then managed to wrest them from the women and by virtue of their possession also took over control of society. When men put on the skirts to dance they are thus calling up a complex set of associations in the minds of viewers. Dogon say that the men are dressing as women when they don skirts. Some viewers will find the fibers calling up images of the sun, menstrual blood, fecundity, and death, with different values attached to these images by different viewers. Others will know various versions of the stories of Amma and the fibers, and these stories will further modify their own understandings of the performances.

The masks also accentuate the line between men and women. Women are not supposed to speak of the masks or touch them, nor may a man discuss them with women. The penalty for infringing these taboos is said to be infertility. Men have the masks and the fiber skirts only because they once seized them from women, and they need be on their guard to keep them in their control.

Male monopolies on masks are widespread, but women's masked societies are found in many societies also (Pernet 1992, 136–157). For example, initiates into the Sande women's societies of Sierra Leone and Liberia wear masks, and when these women venture out with their masks, it is men who must remain indoors.

The masks are used especially for funeral rituals and for death anniversary ceremonies called "Dama" and are intended to appease the spirit of the dead by dramatizing the order of the world (for all viewers) and (for the higher-degree initiated) the story of how the world came into being. The dead person's spirit is reminded of how death came into the world through the incestuous act of one child, but also of how people restored and maintain order.

In many Dogon societies these ritual performances have either been abandoned (especially by those Dogon who converted to Islam) or have been transformed into tourist performances. Even in these, some elements of the original ritual have been preserved, especially when the masks are touched to the ground to ask pardon of the deceased. The National Folkloric Troupe of Mali adapts some of the rituals to theater. Even in those performances the actors retain a sense of the stories and associations found in Dogon villages (Imperato 1978). Yet one can imagine a future in which the masked dances survive only as art, no longer as religion or even as lived culture.

The power and meaning of these masks come from their capacity to evoke associations in different ways and on different planes of life. They evoke powerful bodily events such as sexual intercourse, giving birth, menstruation, and death. They also evoke specific mythic personages and events, and they represent in rituals the division of society into groups and by gender. They convey these meanings through representation, as icons of particular ancestors or objects, and thereby bring viewers into the story being told in the dance. But they also signify a history of direct contact with the power of nyama, and this historical relationship makes the masks themselves powerful.

Images and Offerings in Hinduism

*I*n India, sacrifice, offerings, and devotions are directed toward the gods, of which there are many. About 80 percent of India's 800 million people consider themselves Hindus, and most of them, daily and in countless ways (including sacrificial ways), carry out rituals of offerings and homage to the gods (Fuller 1992, 29–56).

Gods: Few and Many

Some gods are entirely specific to a village or district. Others may have locally specific forms but are also manifestations of pan-Indian gods. Particularly important are Vishnu and Shiva, who stand in a complementary relationship to each other—Vishnu the preserver and Shiva the destroyer, Vishnu the king and Shiva the ascetic (renouncer of worldly pleasures), Vishnu at the center of the world and Shiva outside it. (Brahma, less prominent in worship, is the creator.) Because creation is cyclical—creation following destruction in the cycles of cosmic history—both are necessary elements in the world.

Vishnu is usually worshiped through one of his 10 incarnations, most often as Rama or Krishna. The ancient epic of the Ramayana tells of Rama's life as the king of Ayodhya and represents his life as the model for a righteous king's conduct. The Ramayana is known throughout India (and much of Southeast Asia) in various versions, some emphasizing Rama's divinity. It is read or viewed today in the forms of sacred texts, popular stories, comic books, and shadow puppet plays, and during 1987–1988 it appeared as a hugely popular television series—that also raised popular enthusiasm for Hindu nationalist politics (see Chapter 15).

Krishna is portrayed as a warrior or as a mischievous child. His battles are recounted in another well-known epic, the Mahabharata. But he also transcends mere human warfare. In a section of the epic called the Bhagavad Gita, he counsels his cousin Arjuna to remain above the world even as he is forced to continue his battles. Krishna is also worshiped as a youth and remembered for his romance with the cowherdess Radha.

Shiva has many manifestations. He may be represented by a phallic linga statue, or as a human-looking image. Shiva has sons, Skanda and Ganesha, the latter represented with an elephant head. Vishnu's wives, Laksmi and Bhudevi, and Shiva's wife, Parvathi, often are represented by statues in temples, and often their names differ from one temple to the next.

Both Vishnu and Shiva have followers, Vaishnavas and Shaivas, who worship the gods either by these names or in their local manifestations, often alongside other, lesser deities. Each temple in India is, in principle, unique, and each is dedicated to a particular, local form of a deity. For Shiva and Vishnu, this localization of worship means that they are addressed by a distinctive name. In a south India temple devoted to the local

Priest purifies the image of Shiva with water, Shiva temple at Yanaimangalam, Tamil Nadu state, India. (COURTESY OF DIANE MINES.)

goddess–queen Minakshi, for example, Shiva is present as Sundareshwara, Minakshi's consort. At the temple in Benares, Shiva's holiest site on the Ganges in north India, he is addressed as Vishwanatha (Fuller 1992, 37–38).

As with the Virgin Mary, one person and yet also distinct in her many manifestations in the thousands of Marian shrines, these Shivas are many and one. Indeed, some Hindus say the same of Vishnu and Shiva, that they are one, Vishnu–Shiva. Many temples have legends explaining how it was that Shiva or Vishnu came to occupy a spot at that particular temple—after a battle, or a great deed, or to become the consort of a local deity. The idea of one-and-yet-many is thus basic to Hindu religion; however, it is a feature that at least some Hindus find requires an explanation.

The same unity-and-multiplicity is found with respect to the goddess, Devi, who exists in multiple forms. As Durga, she fights off demons; as Kali or Shakti, she is power itself and is supreme over the gods, often shown trampling on Shiva. She manifests herself as a consort of one of the great gods, but also in local forms, where she brings powers of heat, and sometimes disease, but also fertility—all forms of her power, *shakti*. In south India, each local settlement has its own tutelary goddess, known by one name throughout that region. Thus, in much of Tamil Nadu (Fuller 1992, 43) the goddess is Mariyamman: Mariyamman of this place versus Mariyamman of that place—different goddesses and yet also localized forms of the single Goddess.

Hindus also have local deities, and because Vishnu and Shiva, concerned with the cosmos, are unlikely to respond to requests for assistance in everyday matters, worshipers turn to these deities such as the goddess–queen Minakshi mentioned earlier, or still lesser deities worshiped by particular castes. These deities may be ghosts who were enshrined as a means of controlling their powers, or they may be humans, who can be especially relied on to respond to human problems. A village might have dozens of these deities, worshiped by different persons or groups or approached for particular problems.

Thus, some Hindus identify little goddesses (*matas*) that occupy various places in the environment—in a thorn bush, under a three-brick "altar," in a house. They are associated with the Goddess, and their festival is on her day of Navarati, but they are distinct from her. As with the *kami* of Japan, these deities are many and mostly unnamed. They may enter certain men and women and possess them, and through this possession heal a child or answer a vexing question posed by a fellow villager.

At the other end of the deity scale, modern religious and political movements have taken specific gods as symbols for their idea of an all-Hindu India. A prominent Bengali nationalist, Bankim Chandra Chatterjee created a form of the goddess as "Mother India," or "Bharat Mata" (Fuller 1992, 42). In her temple at Benares she is represented not as a personage but as a map of India—a literalistic fusion of the goddess with the nation and the state!

Offerings to Deities

Offerings to deities, or *puja,* may take the form of an informal family rite or that of a village temple festival. You may perform puja to ask a favor from a deity (usually a minor deity; greater ones tend to be above that sort of thing), or when you recite sacred Sanskrit texts about the exploits of a goddess, or when you join a group in singing devotional Hindi songs to Krishna.

A relatively simple puja might be focused on the ancestors of a joint family, of parents, sons, their wives and children (Fuller 1992, 57–82). First snapshot: in a village in Madhya Pradesh, central India, the father regularly worships his agnatic (through males) ancestors in the home. Just before noon he bathes himself, offering some of the water to his ancestors; his wife and sons' wives meanwhile prepare an elaborate meal. He takes a plate of the food, a dish of clarified butter (ghi), and a brass pot with water from the bath, and, in the kitchen, kneels before a piece of flaming cow dung. He sprinkles water around the dung and places some of the butter on the fire. Again he sprinkles water, and this time places some of the food on the fire. After a third sprinkle he bows before the flame, his hands pressed together, touching his forehead. He then joins his family for their meal. Because some of the food has been offered to the ancestors, all the meal now contains the "grace" or *prasada* of the ancestors. Homes also contain altars with images of family deities and teachers; women as well as men worship there daily or occasionally.

Now a second snapshot: in the southern Indian state of Tamil Nadu, in an urban temple a priest is ready to honor Minakshi, the goddess–queen of an ancient kingdom, and her consort Lord Shiva, in one of his many local manifestations. Each of the deities is represented by a two-foot-high movable image set up in the temple complex and draped with white cloth. Musicians play, and their loud drumming signals the close of each ritual stage. A chanter recites sacred formulas (mantras). The priest purifies the

Woman cooking ponkal, *a dish cooked from "raw rice" and suitable for Brahmans, to be offered to the "backyard god" pictured to the left, at Yanaimangalam.* (COURTESY OF DIANE MINES.)

images by rubbing them with a series of liquids, including sesame seed oil, milk, and water that has been infused with divine power through the chanting of mantras. The gods' images are adorned with clothes, jewelry, and flowers, and their foreheads are marked with three stripes of white ash, the mark of Shiva. Food is held out to the deities while water is sprinkled around the offering. The priest waves oil lamps and a candelabra with seven camphor flames in front of the images. People attending the ritual then crowd in to place their hands over the flames and touch their fingers to their eyes and to accept white ash from the priests to place on their foreheads.

This temple ritual may be reduced or elaborated. The images may be purified with water before the ritual, and at its conclusion butter may be poured onto a flame as a final offering. More foods may be offered, and distributed to all worshipers. Or the ritual may be reduced to a presentation of one camphor flame to the deity, with a plantain on the side as an offering. The reduced ritual is still valid (it counts as puja), and the elaborations are not superfluous (they add to what is accomplished).

Forms of offering vary within India and abroad (substantial Hindu communities are found in Africa, Europe, and the Americas, and Hindus make up a large proportion of the populations of some Caribbean islands, Fiji, and Bali). Festivals all revolve around making offerings to the gods. Festivals vary across India but include the springtime Holi,

Worshiper receives from temple priest as prasada *a garland that had been offered to Shiva, Shiva temple at Yanaimangalam.* (COURTESY OF DIANE MINES.)

celebrated in north India to mark the burning of the demonness Holika and the start of the agricultural season, and a sequence of festivals in September and October, especially the festival of lights, Divali, a time for welcoming and escorting departed ancestors.

All forms of offering, simple or elaborate, involve purification, communication, and offering. Purity may adhere to things or procedures. Pouring water over something takes away polluting elements, hence the importance of bathing and sprinkling. Cow products, from butter to dung to the ash of the dung, are pure.

Communication is through multiple channels: chants, music, words, gestures. Before the gods one always shows respect through the gesture called "namaste" or *pranam,* holding the hands together and touching the forehead. It, too, may be succinct or elaborated: a supplicant may merely hold up the hands to the forehead, or may bow down, even touch the feet of the deity. The same range of gestures is used toward people, indicating their relative rank to oneself. Through this gesture one salutes "that bit of god which is in every person." Humans and gods are both arranged in hierarchies.

One also sees the deities—and they see us. This darshan, or vision, is also an exchange of vision, to some people it is the painting of eyes onto the image or a subsequent poke with a chisel that envivifies it. Although the image is not the same as the deity, the deity is in the image and in many different images throughout India at any one moment. Light, the flame, enhances and signals the exchange of vision, and through this exchange the commingling of human and divine essences.

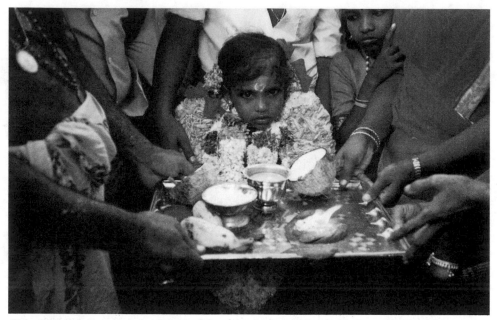

Girl with food that she has offered and received as prasada, *part of an annual offering she makes to fulfill a vow, temple to Murukan, son of Shiva, Pattamadai, Tamil Nadu state, India.*
(COURTESY OF DIANE MINES.)

The deities may also be dressed, sung to, and chanted over, but they are always fed. The food may be anything that people eat, but it is always offered to the deity, taken back, and distributed to those present—family, neighbors, or temple-goers. It may simply be set before the god, or it may be set on fire—"the flame is the tongue of the gods." The consumed food becomes the embodiment of the deity's power or "grace," one literal meaning of prasada, the food offering. Anything that has been placed in contact with the deity and then returned to humans—ash, water, food, flowers—is prasada and conveys that divine power to the human partakers. (In this aspect of puja its transactional character—something given, something received—is most concretely apparent.)

Relics and Images in Catholicism

Catholic imagery also has been based on different types of meaning and multiple associations in the minds of worshipers. When we think of Catholicism we usually think of elaborate representations of saints, Jesus, and Mary. But Catholic images, like masks in Africa and elsewhere, also draw on other kinds of symbolic meanings to become powerful, multivocalic foci for worship and social life.

A famous example is the Shroud of Turin, a cloth held in Turin, Italy, since 1578 that has on its surface an image of a bearded face, said by some to be the image of Christ. The shroud is venerated by many Catholics, not just because it is a likeness of Jesus but because they think that it was produced by direct and miraculous physical contact with his face, in a fashion similar to the process that produces a photograph. This claim of direct contact generates in many pious people a sense of direct communication between the viewer and Jesus. The arguments about the Shroud's authenticity turn exclusively on this issue of contact, not on its resemblance to Jesus. In fact, the iconic qualities of the image on the Shroud, its resemblance to conventional ideas of what Jesus looked like, are precisely what skeptics point to when they claim that it is only a painting. The relative weight of iconic and indexical meanings is thus of great importance for the Shroud's religious status.

Christianity is, after all, founded on ideas of contact and physical presence, in particular the idea of incarnation, the embodiment of godliness in tangible form as Jesus Christ. The central ritual of the Church is based on the worshiper's direct contact with Christ through eating and drinking of his body. Holy Communion enacts the miracle of the Eucharist, in which ordinary bread and wine are consecrated by a priest and, at that exact moment, turned into the body and blood of Jesus. This countlessly repeated miracle parallels the sacrifice Jesus made of himself for the sake of humanity.

The idea that Christ is in the bread and wine was popularly assumed for centuries. It was finally codified in 1215, when the Fourth Lateran Council ruled that consecration does indeed convert the ordinary substances into Christ, or, in the technical language of the Church, that "transubstantiation" takes place. The Council also ruled that Christ was whole in every particle of bread and wine "under two species." This second idea, called "concomitance," responded to the concern, evidently widespread at the time, that when one dropped crumbs of the bread on the floor one was dropping bits of Christ, that chewing the bread was chewing his bones, and so forth.

The History of Relics and the Host

Relics preserve the history of religious miracles through their own history of physical contact with sacred persons or events. They make up an important part of the history of Catholic religious objects—which is also the history of Catholic politics. Religious objects have mediated between the community and the church hierarchy, between local and universal perspectives, between religion and the state, and between cultures.

The central Church ritual, communion or the Eucharist, is based on a miracle of incarnation. In the early Church the ritual of communion was expansive and collective. The priest said "Peace be with you"; the lay worshipers responded in kind and exchanged the "kiss of peace" with each other (men with men, women with women). Worshipers then brought forward their sacrifices of bread and wine to be consecrated by the priest. Communion was thus the Church partaking of Christ and worshipers communing with each other. Christianity drew on its Jewish roots but also broadened them. Communion widened the bounds of the Jewish seder to include the entire community beyond the realm of one's family and friends. Communion thus modeled socially the universal ideal and ambition of the Church (Bynum 1987, 48–69; Feeley-Harnik 1981, 107–168).

Communion recreates for a brief moment what is in effect a direct physical link to Christ. But Christian churches also relied on other kinds of sacred indexes to maintain a sense of connection among churches and among worshipers. As the Church expanded in Europe and North Africa it created a network of churches under the control of Rome. Churches were built on shrines or as shrines, sometimes near or around cemeteries located just outside city walls, where the buried remains of saints sanctified the ground of the new church. There was a practical consideration at work as well—the belief current at the time was that on the day of Resurrection, the first bodies to be taken up to heaven would be those buried near the body of a saint (Ariès 1974).

A Christian shrine or church usually contained sacred objects, an image or relic that gave the shrine its religious status. A relic was a remnant of a saint—a bone, bit of hair, or an entire corpse—or an object that had been made sacred by contact with a saint (or Jesus). It was movable, and so separate from the place itself. Except in Ireland, where the pre-Christian Celtic veneration of places continued unabated, it was the relic, not the place, that was considered sacred.

Saints' bodies, sometimes partially or wholly mummified, have been favorite relics for churches. In the early churches they were often exhibited to worshipers and pilgrims. Today as well, the faithful consider saints' bodies to be capable of working miracles. Some bodies exude healing fluids, such as a marble sarcophagus in the French Pyrenees that accumulates clear water. Throughout the year the water is collected by individuals and used for healing, and the remainder is pumped out each July 30 at a special ceremony. Soil may be taken from the burial place of a saint and used to heal, particularly in Ireland and the Americas. A small church near Santa Fe contains such a miraculous source of earth. Bones are also used as church relics, today usually contained in elaborately sculpted boxes or reliquaries.

The logic of sacrality through contact reaches beyond body parts and sacred soil. Paintings and statues may acquire sacred status from having once been in contact with a sacred person or object. For example, some paintings of the Virgin Mary draw their religious force from their historical ties to what is called the True Icon (*Vera Icon*) of Mary: a painting said to have been made by Saint Luke and considered to be holy because he, a holy person, painted it, and not because of a property of the representation itself. Paintings that are understood as copies of the True Icon are found in Italy, Spain, and most famously in Poland. Our Lady of Czestochowa, the national icon of Poland, is a painting of a dark Madonna, and it is housed in a fourteenth-century church in the southwestern part of the country. It is the object of the major pilgrimage for Polish Catholics. It is said to derive from the Saint Luke painting. Other paintings or statues are touched to the painting in Czestochowa, and from that contact derive a special (indexical, we would say) power. Copies of the True Icon become as effective as the original in working miracles. (At least by the sixth century C.E. we find stories of paintings carried into battle to ensure victory.)

Images versus Relics

By the late fourth century, a lively traffic in saints' remains had developed across Europe. Remains were sent as gifts, sometimes stolen from crypts in Italy. This traffic was encouraged by the idea that remains could be divided up, and the saint became present in each fragment (analogous to the idea that Christ was totally present in every fragment of consecrated bread). As Theodoret of Cyrus proclaimed: "in the divided body the grace survives undivided and the fragments, however small, have the same efficacy as the whole body (Bynum 1987, 48–53).

During the eighth century a rapid rise in missionary activity led the Church to develop rules for creating new churches. In 787, the Second Council of Nicaea declared that a new church had to possess a saint's relic in order to be consecrated. The new rule further increased the demand for relics. People began to scour the Roman catacombs for bone fragments that could be attributed to early Christian martyrs, and a virtual flood of these bone fragments poured forth from Rome out into northern Europe. The hunger for relics turned major discoveries of bones into momentous cultural events. In the early ninth century Saint James' bones were discovered in northern Spain, and the site of this discovery, known thereafter as Santiago de Compostela, became the third most important Christian pilgrimage site after Rome and Jerusalem (Nolan and Nolan 1989, 160–171).

The propagation of relics not only expanded the bounds of the Church but also provided a firm spiritual foundation for the empire created by Charlemagne. From the ninth century onward, the oath administered to witnesses was taken on saints' relics, and read: "May God and the saints whose relics these are judge me that I speak the truth" (Rothkrug 1980).

During the early years of Christian expansion, there were no official procedures for evaluating relics, or indeed for canonizing saints. A local church could declare someone to have been a saint and then build a church around him or her. The remains would be disinterred and placed on an altar within the church. If the body was found to be intact, or in the language of the times, "uncorrupt," this condition was attributed to its holy qualities, which had continued to reside in the body after death. (Note that in this tradition intact bodies were signs of purity; by contrast in the Greek Orthodox practices, discussed in Chapter 3, total disintegration of the flesh is a sign that the soul was received into heaven.)

Many of the relics were, in fact, fakes: countless pieces of wood from Christ's cross circulated throughout Europe, as did chalky stones from the Milk Grotto in Bethlehem said to be colored by milk Mary used to nurse Christ. The market pressures also encouraged theft: one Roman deacon named Deusdona contracted to steal the remains of Saint Peter and to supply them, broken down into small parts, to the Franks. As their authenticity increasingly was doubted, their value declined. (Compare with Gresham's Law in economics: "bad money drives out good.")

The Church responded in two ways. First, it began to exert authority over the status of holy man or saint. It carried out its first canonization of a saint in 993 and gradually gained control over that process. Second, the Church tried to substitute images for relics. Early Christian art (like Islamic art) had been largely decorative. Many people felt that the crafting of human figures would be tantamount to worshiping graven images, a fear inherited from Judaism. In the words of Saint Epiphanius in the fourth century C.E.: "When images are put up, the customs of the pagans do the rest." But popular use of imagery, pictures of saints, developed in the late fourth century and became widespread by the sixth. The Church came to encourage this trend in the interest of promoting universalism. Saints, after all, were many, and their stories often emphasized local miracles and military victories rather than the universal message of Christ that was central to the Church. Basing the legitimacy of a local church on relics underscored the local bases for worship rather than the Church's universalism. To the extent that the Church was able to refocus worshipers' attention toward paintings or statues or other images, it would be able to emphasize the universal figures of Mary and Christ, whose bodies were not available to be relics (Nolan and Nolan 1989, 160–171).

To meet popular objections that only relics were sacred—and the practical point that only relics would share in the resurrection—Church authorities encouraged the crafting of reliquaries: elaborately carved boxes, often with jewels and gold, or statues in the image of a saint that contained minute pieces of the saint's bone. These objects were both relics and images. Images such as paintings or ordinary statues were also said to have had direct contact with a sacred person, or, as in the case of the True Icon mentioned above, to have been painted by a saint, or to have been once physically touched to a painting that was painted by a saint, and so forth, along a historical chain of direct, sacred contact. These efforts drew on popular ideas about contact and sacrality but also promoted universal images.

A More Hierarchical Ritual

The Church's efforts to emphasize its universal message over local sacrality gained momentum in the eleventh, twelfth, and thirteenth centuries, a period of growth in the political power of the Church. What we often call the "age of faith," or, in reference to the great energies devoted to church crafting throughout Western Europe, the "age of cathedrals," also saw a shift in the relationship of people to the institution of the Catholic Church. Rome began to exercise more control over local churches, and in each church priests recast their role vis-à-vis lay persons in a more hierarchical or vertical way.

The eleventh century saw the growth of powerful monasteries, which resisted secular control, the struggle for priority in spiritual affairs over the kings, and the Crusades, which began in 1096. The church became "monumental" in several senses. Doctrine was systematically formulated, most notably by Thomas of Aquinas (1225–1274); the great cathedrals of northern Europe were built; and Rome was able to exert ever-greater control over the behavior of individual churches. It was the great age of pilgrimages to such sites as Santiago de Compostela in northern Spain, to England's Canterbury Cathedral, the site of Thomas à Beckett's assassination in 1170 (and the destination of the pilgrims in Chaucer's *Canterbury Tales*), and the first great Holy Year pilgrimage to Rome in 1300. Many religious orders that promoted pilgrimages—Dominicans, Franciscans, Carmelites—were founded during this period.

All these developments added to the general sense of a Christiandom united by movements of people, the mobilization of popular energies, and a central, controlling power lodged in Rome. In worship itself, these changes led to a great focus on the priest's role, as the representative of Rome, over and against that of the people. Communion and other aspects of liturgy became more centralized, more in the hands of priests and monks. Saint Thomas himself wrote that priests engage in the communion of Eucharist on behalf of others. Saints once had come from the popular ranks, even after canonization became a Church monopoly. Now male saints began to be drawn entirely from the ranks of priests (Bynum 1987, 53–69).

The ritual transformation that most evidently represented this change was the shift from *receiving* communion to *seeing* the Host. By the twelfth century churches had begun to offer communion less frequently and instead to concentrate the attention of worshipers on Christ's presence in the bread and wine at the moment they were consecrated by the priest. Christ could be seen on the altar and adored there. Physical contact was downplayed in favor of, again, the image of Christ, albeit an image of the Host that had become Christ.

As priests emphasized the "adoration of the Host" other changes were made as well. Elaborate containers for the Host, reliquaries, were made and placed so all could see. Holes were made in some church walls so that even horses could commune by viewing the Host. The Host began to be raised up for general view; this practice of "elevating the Host" first occurred in Paris in 1200. Fifteen years later Pope Innocent II declared as dogma the miracle of transubstantiation, the change of bread and wine into Christ's body and blood. In 1264 a new feast day, the feast of Corpus Christi, the "body of Christ," began to be celebrated. By the fourteenth century a new kind of vessel called a "monstrance" ("displayer") was created to display the consecrated Host. As the historian John Bossy (1983) writes, the "socially integrative powers of the Host" were transferred from the mass to the feast of Corpus Christi.

From the twelfth century onward, receiving the Host became something priests did. Already by the eleventh century only priests could take Christ in their hands; others had to receive a wafer directly in their mouths from the priest. The priest once had carried out the consecration of the Host in full view and standing facing the worshipers—after all, in the early church it had been their bread and wine that had been brought to be consecrated. But now the priest celebrated with his back to the people. He took communion for their sake with his back turned. Special "rood screens" were constructed to seal him off from view. In these churches communion became a mystery, a miracle that touched only the priest, who was sometimes venerated precisely because of his privileged contact with Christ. In the words of Saint Francis of Assisi (1181–1226): "He touches Christ with his own hands."

The "two species" of the Eucharist now were treated differently. When communion was offered to worshipers, the consecrated cup was sometimes withheld and ordinary wine substituted. The reason given was that the church feared that a careless parishioner could spill Christ's blood. The wafer now became the focus of this longed-for ritual act. It became a strongly held symbol of the unity of the church and of fears of its being desecrated. Anti-Semitism was often voiced as an accusation that someone had defiled the wafers. Stories circulated of Hosts turning to flesh and bleeding in protest against misuse (for example, by sorcerers) or in an effort to warn churchgoers against an approaching danger (Bossy 1983; Bynum 1987, 53–69).

The Host increasingly became a symbol of the church, rather than a source of redemption for the individual person. Some people protested this church control; these protests included demands to receive the Host "in both species," that is, as consecrated wine and bread. A hunger for the chalice and communion intensified, and ordinary people, particularly women, experienced religious devotions and ecstasies as sensing and eating God.

The central objects that located or founded a church also shifted from relics of saints (with the host as one of many relics) to the general adoration of Christ and the Virgin Mary. In 1150 the pope rejected his former title, "Vicar of Saint Peter" for the new one, "Vicar of Christ," shifting his grounds for authority from the presence of Saint Peter's body in Rome (a relic), to his direct receipt of authority from Christ.

The Church also began to desacralize relics and to replace them with images of saints. It developed the idea of the saints and Mary in the "communion of saints," or "the unity under and in Christ of the faithful on the earth, the souls in purgatory, and the blessed in heaven." Dead souls were enrolled in the new brotherhoods and orders as part of this universal community. This idea of the communion of saints allowed one soul to pray for another. Helping other souls through prayer became a major activity both in church masses and at pilgrimage sites. (Recall the same activity by Gayo Muslims discussed in Chapter 4 and the similar controversies surrounding prayer for the dead.)

Christ Incarnate

The Eucharist, as it became the focus of church activity, is best seen as Christ's incarnation—it gave the worshiper direct contact with Christ. Recall that it was only in 1215 that the Church proclaimed as dogma the eucharistic miracle of transubstantiation. The elevation and adoration of the Host began about then, and Corpus Christi followed in 1264.

These steps addressed what we can think of as the problem of Christ's relics (Nolan and Nolan 1989). After all, according to the church, Christ ascended to heaven 40 days after the Resurrection, leaving no body behind to generate relics. In popular opinion he did leave some relics behind: his blood and the earth that was touched by it; pieces of the cross and nails from the cross; garments worn during the Passion; the Shroud of Turin. The church gradually accepted the idea that his milk teeth, foreskin, and spilled blood could, in theory, have remained on the earth even though he ascended to heaven. Popular pressure was for more relics of Christ, perhaps because of the more difficult access to Christ through communion.

The steps taken by the church in the thirteenth century to promote the worship of Christ may have been responses to this pressure. The doctrine of transubstantiation not only provided an officially sanctioned opportunity for direct contact with Christ incarnate, but it also allowed numerous further miracles, at least in the popular imagination.

Sometimes the Host was said to really become flesh and blood. In at least one shrine, in Lanciano, Italy, are small pellets of blood and a strip of flesh said to have been formed from consecrated bread and water during the celebration of Mass by a doubting monk in the eighth century. Bavaria has a shrine where sacramental wine, spilled on an altar cloth in 1330, formed an image of Christ. Christ could now become real, the object of worship (and sometimes even contact) within a more hierarchical church (Clark 1967, 410–434; Nolan and Nolan 1989, 216–290).

Mary and Marys in European Societies

The church has also promoted the adoration of Mary as Mother of God. This "cult of Mary," which undoubtedly draws on older images and ideas of a virgin mother goddess, first appeared in Turkey in 431 and expanded across the West. At some point a popular idea developed that Mary herself was conceived in her mother, Saint Ann, free from the original sin that everyone else receives by virtue of Eve and Adam's transgression in the Garden of Eden. This idea of "immaculate conception"—conception in the womb free of original sin—spread on a popular level but was not immediately accepted by the church. In the sixteenth century, the Council of Trent declared Mary free of original sin, but only in 1854 did Pope Pius IX declare as dogma that Mary indeed had experienced an immaculate conception.

Marian worship on a widespread, dominant scale dates from about the eleventh century and is due in part to the activities of the Cistercian order, all of whose churches were dedicated to Mary. The popular idea that she was bodily assumed into heaven was officially proclaimed as Roman Catholic dogma in 1950. As with Christ, this doctrine meant that very few relics could be claimed to be available: her sash and veil, a few strands of hair, pieces of milky rock white from her breast milk—slim pickings indeed. More popular were images of Mary, usually as the Pietà, holding the body of the dead Christ.

This image of Mary drew, intentionally or not, on much older notions of a virgin mother goddess who bears a child who later dies in her arms. Inanna, the Queen of Heaven in Sumerian mythology, gives up her son Dumuz to torture and death. The Egyptian Isis nurses and mourns for her son Osiris. (And as we shall see, such pre-Christian images are found in the Americas as well.) Pietà images are especially popular in German culture (70 percent of these images are found there), probably because of the long-standing tradition of imperially founded nunneries. Around 1300, Dominican nunneries began to promote the image of a suffering Mary, a representation of their own direct, personal, at times erotic relation to Christ. The pietà image generally becomes popular during times of sadness and war, because it provides an especially apt image for suffering. For example, many new pietà statues were carved after the trauma of the Thirty Years' War in the seventeenth century, and again after the First World War in our own century (Nolan and Nolan 1989, 191–209).

The numerical analysis of to whom a shrine is dedicated shows how sharp has been the change from saints, usually based on relics, to Mary, always based on a shrine image. In the period before 700 C.E., 92 percent of the shrines formed were dedicated to a saint. That percentage dropped to 20 percent in the "high medieval" period of 1100–1400, and has remained about the same since. The percentage of shrines dedicated to Mary was only 6 percent in the early period, but 73 percent in the high medieval period, and level ever since. Shrines dedicated to Christ have remained at below 10 percent throughout the common era (Nolan and Nolan 1989, 155).

Marian Apparitions and Modern Life

Over the past 150 years, Mary has taken on a new identity in the popular imagination, less as Mother of God and more as an individual who intervenes on behalf of individuals

Pietà of Mary and Jesus venerated at Theirenbach in Alsace, France, c. 1350. (MARY LEE NOLAN AND SIDNEY NOLAN, *CHRISTIAN PILGRIMAGE IN MODERN WESTERN EUROPE,* p. 200.)

in modern, industrialized societies. She begins to appear in the sky to troubled individuals and to offer solace and instructions. Hundreds of such apparitions have occurred in the past two centuries, but seven were approved by local bishops and gained international attention; these occurred in France, Belgium, and Portugal. These visions include the apparitions of Mary at Lourdes, France, in 1858, and in Fatima, Portugal, in 1917. Both were eventually accepted by the Church; most others were not (Zimdars-Schwartz 1991).

In 1917, in Fatima, three children reported a series of appearances of Mary. One of the three, Lucia dos Santos, later discussed in her memoirs her religious upbringing as well as the events surrounding the apparitions. Lucia took her First Communion at age six rather than at the usual age 10. She tells of how the priest told her to kneel before the image of the Virgin and to ask Mary to take care of her heart; when she did so, she saw the statue of the Virgin smile at her, and she heard the Virgin say she would do this for her.

Lucia was 10 when, together with her friends, she saw the Virgin appear on six separate occasions. Mary spoke to the girls, saying that they had come from heaven, and that she would take them to heaven. All three girls reported hearing the same words. Others came to the place where the apparitions occurred. Some of these other watchers reported seeing a small cloud appear over the tree where the girls saw the Virgin and the tree's branches bend.

At the time, the girls reported hearing three secrets from the Virgin. In 1941 Lucia revealed two of them. The first concerned the nature of hell. The second was a prediction of war unless the world became devoted to her Immaculate Heart. Mary further specified that her followers would need to secure the consecration of Russia to her Immaculate Heart and to convert that country's people. If such steps were not taken, she warned, the world would be annihilated. Lucia wrote the third secret down, and in 1957 her note was sent to Rome. In 1977 Pope John Paul I visited with her (Zimdars-Schwartz 1991, 190–219).

Other reported sightings of Mary followed in the late 1940s, and manifested the worries held by many European Catholics about the general loss of faith and the coming clash with communism (Christian 1984). Marian apparitions provided a kind of collective catharsis, a general focusing and release of these tensions, and have continued unabated through the 1990s.

One of the more recent apparitions has been occurring frequently on a hill just outside Medjugorje, Bosnia, since June 24, 1981. Six girls saw Mary on the first day; since then more than 20 million pilgrims have come for a view. The girls moved the place for their visions into the church, until the bishop ordered them out. Since then some people have reported nightly appearances of Mary (Bax 1991; Zimdars-Schwartz 1991, 220–244).

Pilgrims to the site often return with stories of personal conversions and healing. One Irish woman described her visit as at first just a "holiday." But then she saw the concrete cross that had been built on the site, and saw the sun behind it turn blood red, with a small piece of the sun missing after it had moved behind the cross. On her return home she attended a funeral mass and when the priest held up the Host she saw it as "the image of the sun at Medjugorje and I really believed in the presence of Christ—the sun had been the Host with the piece missing like when the priest breaks off a piece—and I was overcome and cried."

Medjugorje spreads. An Italian family bought a white plaster statue of Mary during a visit to the site, and in February 1995 reported that tears of blood had begun running down the statue's face. Crowds began to flock around the family's home near Rome, and the local bishop had the statue removed. CAT scans of the statue showed no hidden mechanisms; laboratory tests showed the blood to be human; DNA matches with the family's blood were proposed. In the end, the bishop became a believer in the miracle (Warner 1996; Bohlen 1995).

In the United States, an American returned home to New Jersey after a visit to Medjugorje in 1988 and reported that he had been healed of a back injury and hearing loss. Mary appeared to him in his backyard six months later, stating that she had work for him to do. In August 1992 he publicly announced when the second visit would happen, and 8,000 people came to witness the event. About the same number showed up in Cold Spring, Kentucky, when a local pastor predicted an apparition (Steinfel 1992).

The Church has been ambivalent about the apparitions. On the one hand, the apparitions encourage popular faith, and their message is in keeping with the interest of the Church. On the other hand, the apparitions occur outside Church control; they challenge the hierarchy of the Church by providing an alternative source of religious enthusiasm to worship in churches. The Church has given official recognition to the apparitions at Lourdes and Fatima, but not to Medjugorje. There, the local Franciscan fathers, who for centuries functioned as the parish priests, have encouraged people to enjoy the special grace provided by the visions. But the Bishop of Mostar, whose district includes the apparition site, has forbidden worshipers to make the pilgrimage and has called the apparitions "theatrical practices." His ruling has been part of an effort, backed by Rome, to wrest control of the parishes away from the friars, and Mary, here as elsewhere, has become a key token in that struggle (Bax 1991).

Religious sentiments in Catholic Europe have always included some resentment of the power and privileges of the clergy. For those visitors to the sites of apparitions who share these anticlerical feelings, the Church's rejection of visions makes the visions even more attractive. The apparitions usually are reported from marginal regions during times of trouble—Bosnia and southern Italy in the 1990s, economically depressed parts of the United States in the 1980s, post–war Western Europe.

Spanish Shrines

As the Church increasingly came to promote Mary as an object of worship, people have made her into a local protector as well as the symbol of Church worship. In agrarian parts of northern Spain, each valley of herders and farmers contains a number of small villages. Each village parish has its own active patron, whose image is in the village shrine and who protects the village as a whole. The shrine may be an isolated chapel at the boundary of several villages or the parish church at the village center.

In the Nansa river valley studied by the ethnographer William Christian (1989) are 14 such village parishes. Of these 14, one has Christ as its patron, three have the souls in purgatory (*Las Animas*), and 10 have a particular aspect or realization of the Virgin Mary.

Thus, in one village the patron is Our Lady of the Queen's Ford; in another, Our Lady of the Light; in a third, Our Lady of the Bridge; and so forth. Each shrine, each saint, protects a particular territory, a "territory of grace," acting as patron to its inhabitants.

Some of the shrines to Mary are located at boundaries of villages or herding districts. In one district, three statues of Mary are found right at the meeting point of three villages' lands, each facing back toward "her own" village. In local stories, the Virgin is said to choose the spot where the shrine is to be built. In one case a shrine was placed at one spot, but during the next night two oxen came and moved the shrine up the hill to the place where she had desired it to be placed. The Virgin keeps the sheep at home, say local herders, and calls down divine power to protect them. William Christian calls the shrines "energy transformation stations."

One of these patron saints is Our Lady of the Queen's Ford, the patron of the village of Tudanca. The shrine is located in a chapel about five kilometers behind Tudanca. The saint's name comes from a nearby ford, but the patron is also identified as Our Lady of the Snows, an aspect of Mary recognized by Rome and given a feast day, August 5. Over the centuries, celebrations of the feast day have waxed and waned, depending both on the level of nearby economic activity and on the attitude of the parish priest toward the shrine. Currently the shrine is visited only by some Tudanca residents; in other decades, however, it has received attention from people of other villages as well. The shrines patronize and protect their own villages, but they may be appealed to by anyone, especially people from neighboring villages.

In the first week of May each year the image is carried down from the isolated chapel to the parish church in town, where it remains for three months and is the center of church devotions. The period when the image is in the church is also the period of plowing and sowing the fields, and its presence may once have been intended to protect the crops. On the feast of Saint James, July 25, the image is carried in a procession of all the villagers, organized in the following order: children first, then lay men, priests with the image, and women. The villagers thus see themselves as a whole composed of parts. "The villagers for once in the year," writes Christian (1989, 70), "see the village as a social unit, abstracted from the buildings and the location that makes it a geographical unit."

It is the women who continue up the mountain to the shrine and replace the image in its resting place. A woman keeps the key to the shrine, and when, on the patron's feast day of August 5, a mass is held at the mountain chapel, even the priest has to wait for her to unlock it. In other villages, too, special roles in the devotion to the patron are handed down from mother to daughter. Women are the chief worshipers at the shrines.

These patrons are firmly planted in the rural landscape. Each exists and acts on her own. Some of the names are unique, appearing nowhere else in Spain. Others do appear elsewhere, but then are given additional local tags to emphasize their individuality. A shrine to Our Lady of Carmel, for example (a common name for the Virgin Mary), will become Our Lady of Carmel of Cosio, or of another village. These shrines have existed for a long time; some may predate Christianity (when clearly they were known and worshiped by other names).

From the standpoint of these "localized devotions"—worship activities focused on a local manifestation of Mary or a saint—Mary appears as many distinct patrons woven together into a general community of sainthood. The Mary of the Snows is an agent distinct from the Mary of the Bridge, despite the fact that all are manifestations of the one Virgin Mary, Mother of God.

Many in One

Recall a similar feature of worship in India. In south India each local settlement has its own tutelary goddess, known by one name throughout that region. So throughout the state of Tamil Nadu, for instance, once finds Mariyamman of this place versus Mariyamman of that place, as different goddesses and yet also localized forms of the single Goddess (Fuller 1992, 43). This many-in-one is quite similar to that found in northern Spain and elsewhere in the Catholic world. Mary exists in both a highly local and a universal form at the same time in the consciousness of some Catholics, as does Mariyamman (the similarity in names is a coincidence) for Hindus.

The parallel stops at the level below Mary, however, for whereas Hindus have local, lesser deities as well as the major gods, most Catholics have only the major textually sanctioned figures to turn to—Mary, Jesus, saints. In Catholicism the distance between God and local, reachable spiritual beings is mediated by proliferating the number of forms of Mary, and remaining entirely within a restricted pantheon.

There is an irony in the fact that the adoration of Mary was encouraged by the church as a way of unifying and centralizing devotion, but that Mary became the vehicle for differentiated devotions and representations. Of course, even in the universal language promoted by the church one has different names or "advocations" (different forms of a deity) of Mary, a variety that in part stems from the very images the church used: Mary of the Immaculate Conception, Mary the Pietà, Mary of the Assumption, and so forth. Mary is shown in different contexts, and these images become signs of different attitudes or emotions. But it also may be that relying on replicable images as the basis for Catholicism (or any other widespread religion) itself gives rise to this dual character, the "one Mary or many Marys" problem. Once the image takes on any local roots it begins to be thought of as the image of a local individual. The very replicability of the image poses a problem: is it one or many? If one, what are all these other objects? If many, are they different actors?

A Japanese Comparison

Just as Catholics have created "many Marys" to provide nearby, accessible images, so have Japanese men and women turned to deities called "bodhisattvas," or "Buddhas-to-be." These deities, who put off their transition to Buddha status in order to help humans, are nearer to hand when one needs help than are the distant Buddha figures.

Especially important among them is the goddess Kannon, who ensures fertility and safety in childbirth. In India, Kannon was the many-armed god Avalokitesvara, and became (via a gender change) the important Chinese goddess Kuan-Yin, and then the Japanese Kannon. The bodhisattva Kannon is capable of rescuing people from earth-

Jizo statues set out to atone for an abortion or to ask for safe delivery of a child, at the shrine to Kannon near Kamakura, Japan. (COURTESY OF JOHN RENARD.)

quakes, fires, shipwrecks, witchcraft, execution, snakes, and thunderbolts, and of giving a woman the child she wishes, son or daughter. She is sometimes depicted as associated with the waterfall because of her power; her many arms are likened to the many different streams of a fall. She also has lesser spirits called *jizo* who act as guardians of travelers and children. Travelers often set out small statues of jizos on their routes, and especially when they are embarking on a pilgrimage. But one may also set out a jizo as a concrete way to take a request to Kannon. These requests are most commonly either for forgiveness for having had an abortion or for safe delivery of a child.

Kannon is both a single goddess and many personal guardians. She can be depicted as a single protector, or as highly individuated. For example, a shrine to Kannon at Kyoto is supposed to contain "60,000" statues of Kannon, one for every face there is in the world; this way of representing her is supposed to guard all the world's people.

A debate has arisen in Japan over the practice of buying jizo statues from a temple to atone for an abortion. Setting out the statue is thought by some to help guide the fetus across the river that separates the world of life from the world of death. These statues, called "water child jizos" (Mizuko jizo), are sold by Buddhist temples for several hundred dollars each. More than 2,000 temples now offer these statues, and temple leaflets warn that failure to appease the spirit of a dead fetus could lead to cancer, heart disease, back pain, rebellion of children against parents, and so forth—a list long enough that anyone who fails to buy the statue will surely find herself victim of the fetus's spirit. Is this service a way the temple serves people's needs or, as one magazine called it, a "business of terror"?

Some women continue to visit the statues for years or even decades after the abortion, dressing them up against the cold or pouring water over them to quench their thirst (WuDunn 1996).

Generalized Devotions

Priests entering the Nansa valley have had to work with the shrines already in place, but sometimes they have tried to discourage devotions at the shrine. In most cases, devotions go dormant, reappearing a decade or more later. The priests bring with them devotional emphases of the papacy, and often of a religious order. They try to refocus the devotions of villagers on universal images of Mary and Christ, rather than on her specific manifestations, what one priest called approaching "to the main doors, not the side doors" of the church.

These "generalized devotions," in William Christian's (1989) phrase, are based on the circulation and promotion of images that are highly interchangeable. In homes and in parish churches one finds paintings, lithographs, pamphlets, calendars, and rosaries. These images could be substituted easily one for the other, or replaced with a new batch, without any loss of religious significance. The images are usually of Mary as the Madonna, and sometimes of the cross, and they are used in family devotions. They often come from Rome or from the religious orders currently in papal favor, and their propagation and use is intended to underscore the universality of the Church. For example, the Dominican brotherhoods have promoted the devotion to the Holy Rosary at home using personal rosary beads. The brotherhoods teach people that saying prayers with the beads will allow one to share in all the prayers said by all members of the brotherhood throughout the world. Other orders, including Capuchins and Passionists, have provided images of saints or Mary that correspond to their particular religious emphases.

Mary has played her part in efforts to reuniversalize worship, both through her interchangeable pictures in homes, and through her role in regional and national shrines. Many villages in the Nansa valley have been visited on trips to the regional shrine to Mary, which was approved by the Vatican in 1954, on the 100th anniversary of the papal proclamation of the Immaculate Conception.

Jesus, Mary, and the Nation–State

Of particular importance in changing local worship practices has been the devotion to the Sacred Heart of Jesus, begun in 1673 when a nun in Paris had visions of Jesus Christ in which he urged her to devote herself to his heart as a symbol of his love for humankind. But it was not entered as general feast of the church until 1856, when it quickly became an image to which popes and rulers tried to rally the faithful. In 1899 Pope Leo XIII consecrated the world to the Sacred Heart of Jesus, and King Alfonso of Spain did the same for Spain in 1919, with the backing of a conservative government. Images of the Sacred Heart entered the Nansa valley about that time as well (Christian 1989, 84–85).

Because of its association with the political right, in the 1930s statues commemorating the Sacred Heart became symbols of the Nationalist forces, the right wing fighting under Franco to topple the government. The national monument to the Sacred Heart was frequently "executed" by the Loyalists, and pictures of the ruined monument were circulated by Franco's side to rally Catholic support.

Elsewhere too, the Sacred Heart of Jesus became a symbol of conservative governments. In late–nineteenth-century France the relation of a largely Catholic people to a secular state (and largely secular capital city) was a continuing source of tension. In 1871 many Parisians rose up against the Thiers government, in part because of the state's capitulation to Prussian forces. The government, which had fled to Versailles, brutally suppressed the uprising, known as the *Commune,* and regained control of the city. Shortly thereafter, in an attempt to underscore the central place of the church in French life, the government constructed the magnificent church on the hills of Montmartre called Sacre Coeur—Sacred Heart. Though much loved by tourists (and many Parisians), the association between the building and the suppression lives on in the minds of many on the left. (I happened to be living in Paris in 1971, the year of the Commune's centennial, and I witnessed Sacre Coeur being pelted with tomatoes and stones.)

At the same time, images of Mary surface as symbols of national resistance. In communist Poland, the national shrine of Polish Catholicism dedicated to Our Lady of Czestochowa has for centuries been associated with national resistance against foreign conquerors. The Polish Primate under communist rule, Cardinal Wysynski, mobilized the nation around the shrine image, beginning with the rededication of the nation to this "Queen of Poland" in 1956, and following with hugely successful annual pilgrimages of the shrine to every single town in Poland.

The state's use of religious imagery underscores the changes in how the Church represents itself. In the ninth century, a person was sworn in on relics as the clear chain of direct contact to local sources of sacrality. By the late nineteenth century the state was staking its claim to loyalty on images of and devotions to Mary or, in particular, to Christ. Christ seems more immune to the differentiation process that has made Mary many. Indeed, the role of Mary in Catholicism as a firm local identity goes far beyond Spain, as we shall see.

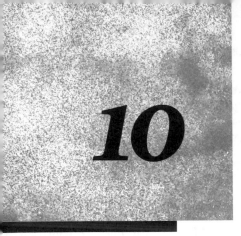

10 Crossing Cultural Boundaries

*T*hroughout this chapter we explore a tension central to those religions that have spread to culturally diverse regions of the globe. The list of such religions is longer than one might suspect. The many forms of Christianity, Islam, and Buddhism come to mind first, but the list would also include other religions, each with relatively few followers, but including people from a broad range of cultures. Consider in this light Mormonism, the Bahai faith, and Hinduism, all having practitioners in North America, Asia, and elsewhere. (Other religions, such as Santeria or Lubavitcher Judaism, are, at least as of today, carried by adherents into new environments but less often adopted by people of different religious and cultural backgrounds.)

The history of all of these religions involved the process of *conversion* as people in new environments adopted them. Conversion has required translating religious elements from a language and culture of origin into a new language and culture and also *adapting* the religion to the new environment. Crossing cultural boundaries continues to involve conversion, translating, and adapting as these religions attract an increasingly diverse set of followers.

All three processes create a tension of "crossing" that has strong psychological, social, and theological elements. On the one hand, proponents of each religion try to preserve something of a core message, or set of practices, or allegiance. Failure to do so may provoke retribution or at least prevent recognition as legitimate practitioners. Notions of orthodoxy and orthopraxy, "correct" belief and practice, are regularly brought into play. But on the other hand, converting people in a new cultural environment requires the bundle of ideas and practices that characterizes it to be adapted to emphasize or minimize particular elements. Indonesian Islam does not have the marked gender separation of Arabian forms, for example, and Islam could not have spread so easily in Indonesia if people had not reinterpreted Islam to fit local norms. But that reinterpretation would have been sharply criticized, even within Indonesia, if it had not taken place within the Islamic tradition of acceptable interpretation.

Converting

Converting to a new religion requires one to make some sort of commitment to it. (Although, as we shall see later, conversion may be thought of more as a choice among alternative social rules than as an act of faith.) And commitment to a religion may require, or indeed may itself be, a kind of conversion. The interdependence of conversion and commitment may be understood most easily with regard to children, who are not expected to become adherents and practitioners of a religion without effort. Children are usually required to study in order to become fully accepted members of a religious community, when they may undergo a ritual of acceptance that includes commitment to the religion of their parents. The acts of commitment required of a child are often the same as those required of an adult convert: learning a text by heart, reciting a statement of commitment, undergoing an initiation ritual.

Adult Baptism among the Amish

Consider the Amish, one of several Protestant religions that underwent persecution in Europe beginning in the sixteenth century (others include Hutterites and Mennonites). They were persecuted mainly because they practiced and preached adult baptism, and thus were called Anabaptists ("to baptize again"). They did so because they believed that only someone who had reached the "age of reason" could make an informed and conscious decision to become a member of the Church.

Today, Amish communities are found in many parts of North America, concentrated in Pennsylvania, Ohio, and Indiana. Amish people live in villages and towns, close to non-Amish people they call "English." They continue to learn and use a dialect of German within the community. Their major religious values are submission to God, humility, and openness. They live according to their values by wearing simple clothing, renouncing those inventions that would separate them from the land and from work, and preventing the outside world from intruding on family life.

A commitment to the Amish way of life means staying apart from mainstream society. Boys and girls make that commitment at baptism, which occurs between the ages of 16 and 21. Candidates take a series of classes that stress the strict nature of the Amish social code, the Ordnung. They are told that it is better to not join the order than to join and then break the code. The baptism itself takes place in front of the congregation after a regular Sunday service. Kneeling, the candidate agrees to obey God and his church, and the presiding bishop drips water over his or her head.

The idea of active commitment, of the seriousness of the vows taken, explains a puzzle in their lives. On the one hand, the Amish more than any religious group in America try to keep themselves cut off from the broader society. Electricity, telephones, automobiles, public schools are all suspect because they plug the community in (literally or figuratively) to the wider sociocultural grid. Telephones are one of many subjects of intense controversy because they provide safety and comfort but they also disrupt family and social life. (One solution is to have telephones in separate buildings, so that they can be used if needed but cannot break up, for example, dinner conversations.) On the other hand, the Amish also permit their teenagers to "flirt with the world" (Kraybill 1989, 138). Indeed, although the Amish churches exercise strict control over the lives of adults, with sanctions that include being shunned by the community, the churches have no direct authority over children and adolescents. Until they are baptized, Amish boys and girls are supposed to be under the authority of their parents.

Amish teenagers typically join one of the several "crowds" of youths in the community (Kraybill 1989, 138–140). A crowd plays sports together, attends films, and travels to cities and to the beach. For their outings they buy and wear clothes similar to those worn by "English" youth. The boys often drive cars and are sometimes arrested for drunken driving or have serious accidents. In the late 1990s several youths were arrested for drug trafficking.

A student of the Amish, Donald Kraybill (1989, 139), writes that this liminal period and tolerated rowdiness serves as a "social immunization" against the subsequent temptations young people face. Having experienced something of the world, they can reject it with knowledge. And though they would find it difficult to leave the Amish world they have been educated for and where their friends live, they believe that they have a choice because they are presented with one. About 80 percent of Amish youth do choose to undergo baptism and remain in the church. There is a psychological soundness to the Amish idea that you can knowingly reject only what you know. For an example of the problem faced by a group of people who have never known such temptation, and are thereby unable to face it with strength when it arrives, one could do no better than to read Mark Twain's classic story, "The Man Who Corrupted Hadleyburg." Hadleyburgians, naive believers in their own goodness, could not withstand the temptation of some easy money to be made through telling a simple lie.

Conversion as Total Social Change

What does conversion entail? It may appear to be merely a matter of changing one's religious allegiance—going to a different place of worship, perhaps wearing different clothes or eating different foods or making different friends. It is, then, an individual choice, accomplished fairly quickly, perhaps with some changes in lifestyle (less likely if the conversion is within Christianity).

This idea of conversion, however, only makes sense for those societies that have an easily detached notion of "religion." If particular spirit beliefs permeate all aspects of one's life, then giving up all those beliefs for some new set will most likely entail leaving the society altogether and changing one's ideas about oneself.

The experience of the Akha people of highland Burma and Thailand offers an example of how, in many societies, conversion can be a process of near-total social change (Kammerer 1990). In the 1960s when their neighbors were converting to Catholicism and Protestantism in droves, the Akha stood out among the peoples of this region for their resistance to conversion. But by the 1980s conversions were occurring with increasing frequency among the Akha. Why this sudden shift?

The answer returns us to our earlier discussion of what the category of religion looks like in different societies. In the Akha language, the word *zah* is the closest to the English *religion,* but it includes much more—the rules for planting crops, holding funerals, healing the sick, and conducting a marriage. For the Akha, their zah defines who they are. Others have their own zah, and those rules define them. One should not, they say, mix zahs from different people. (This sounds rather like the most extreme statements of "cultural wholes" in American anthropology.) Akha have been less likely to marry people of other ethnic groups, and when they do, often they become one of those people, a Lisu, say, rather than an Akha. Custom and culture (including religion) is seen as an all-or-nothing affair.

The Akha were somewhat more insistent than were their neighbors about changing zah, which would logically initially keep them from converting. To change zah would be in effect to change one's overall identity, to become something other than Akha. But we are still left with the task of explaining why, at some point, the balance tipped and the Akha began to convert in large numbers. Here, too, understanding their idea of identity helps us to understand what happened. Akha had begun to attend state schools and learn broader Thai ways, and at some point the intricacies of their older zah became too difficult to learn and practice. Because Akha saw their zah as a unity of practices, and not any better or worse than other people's zahs, it made sense to change zahs entirely, to convert to another kind of people, those who practice "Jesus zah" rather than "Akha zah."

Kammerer (1990) points out that Akha never say they "believe" in new or old zah, Akha-ism or Christianity. For them conversion is a matter of exchanging older practices for new ones, for pragmatic reasons. For the Akha conversion is neither a change of heart nor a sitting on the fence.

External and Internal Conversion

A different case study shows us that conversion may also turn out to be something quite different: not an all-or-nothing choice of social life, but a long-term process of reworking and reinterpreting social practices. John Barker (1993) studied the Uiaku Maisin people of the Oro province in northeast Papua New Guinea. The Maisin people have been Christians since the early 1900s, when they were converted by Australian Anglican missionaries. But Barker observes that conversion continues to take place, and does so in two ways. What he calls "external conversion," associated with the mission station, has to do with trying to acculturate local people to relatively cosmopolitan ways. By contrast, "internal conversion" takes place in villages, where people debate and adapt their ideas to new circumstances. The advantage of Barker's perspective is that it locates distinct conversion processes in two distinct social environments. People have no trouble separating the two, because each addresses distinct concerns.

"From the mission station," writes Barker (1993, 208), "Uiaku appears a Christian community." The church is the center of social life, for sports, women's groups, and for celebrations of saints' days. Bells mark the hours for church and school attendance. Avenues are wide and straight. The church council encourages church attendance, urges people to grow cash crops, and comforts the sick. Councilors fly to other cities in the country to meet with delegates from religious, political, or other organizations.

But village hamlets are organized along quite different lines, one that mark a continuity in social and cultural organization. People build houses near birthplaces.

Elders preside over dispute-resolution sessions and have the power to strike through sorcery. Not that things in the village have not changed over the years—villagers added God to the list of powerful spirits in the cosmos, for example. They also stretched older ideas they held to become the equivalents of Christian ideas taught by the missionaries. For example, the term Barker translates as *amity* probably once referred to a peaceful condition that resulted from balance in the exchanges of goods and services between clans. As missionaries taught about Christian "universal brotherhood," people stretched their idea of peace-inducing balance to translate the new idea.

But these stretchings were more than just translations; the new cultural categories, once in place, could serve as moral foundations for criticizing contemporary practices. Barker relates how the extended notion of amity was mobilized by the church deacon (a local man) to condemn some people who allowed the period of mourning to continue too long, so that it was disruptive. In response, some subsequent deaths were met by much shorter periods of mourning than ever before. Villagers understood this change not as an adaptation to Western norms, but as a more consistent pattern of behavior in terms of their own social norms, *their* idea of amity.

This "internal conversion" is thus a kind of moral ironing-out of everyday and ritual practices in terms that are seen as local, but that have been transformed as a result of the process of "external conversion." Villagers participate in both worlds (see Hefner 1993).

Missions and Civilization in South Africa

Another case study of conversion as a long-term process comes from the work of Jean and John Comaroff (1986, 1991, 1997). The Comaroffs study the dual British colonial project of converting "natives" in South Africa to Christianity and creating a socially modern and disciplined colonial society. They describe how Protestant evangelical missionaries failed to realize their dreams of constructing a unified black Protestant church but succeeded in reshaping the way Africans carried out their lives. Their study focuses on the lives of the Tswana people of South Africa and Botswana and on the activities of the Methodist London Missionary Society beginning in the 1820s.

The Comaroffs point out that Methodist missionaries (and, in varying ways, other Christian missionaries) measured their effectiveness not merely by obtaining formal conversions, but by their success in changing natives' ways of behaving. French sociologists, among them Marcel Mauss and Pierre Bourdieu, have termed the ways an individual acts, responds, speaks, walks, and so forth, his or her *habitus*. South African Methodists were bent on teaching the Tswana the "arts of civilization," which included the arts of cultivation. Missionaries urged the adoption of the plow, which, because only men tended cattle, had the effect of raising the value of male labor relative to female labor. They also taught that natives should live in monogamous households arranged in rows and squares rather than in circles and arcs. The church clock and the church calendar now regulated social life. And as the hourly base for figuring wages, time was now used to measure the value of an individual's labor.

But the Methodist message contained the seeds of destruction for the colonial project. Central to the Wesleyan idea of self-perfection preached in the churches was the equality of people and their freedom to perfect their natures. This message was blatantly contradicted by the realities of mining labor in the nineteenth and twentieth centuries. It also gave ammunition to those within particular churches who would resist any kind of central control, leading to the subsequent proliferation of churches, as dissatisfied factions set out to found new denominations (Comaroff 1985).

The Comaroffs present the encounters between missionaries and Tswana as part of an ongoing conversation. Each side incorporated the other's messages into its own way of thinking, and yet also changed its religious practices slightly as a result of the encounter. The control of water was a matter of survival, for example, but also a political and cosmic matter (Comaroff and Comaroff 1991, 206–213). It was the ruler who brought on rains, and the rainmaking rituals, carried out at his direction, that ensured the rains' arrival.

The missionaries regarded these rituals as the height of superstition and thought they should be eradicated. But they themselves were caught in a contradiction, proclaiming that rain was a matter of nature and scientific meteorological detection, while saying that rain was ultimately in God's hands. The Tswana concluded from this missionary double-talk that their scientific instruments were merely their version of rainmaking devices, which worked through their deity.

Consider how the Tswana people's firm grasp of missionary logic shaped the following dialogue between a mission medical doctor (MD) and the rain doctor (RD).

MD: . . . you cannot charm the clouds by medicines. You wait till you see the clouds come, then you use your medicines, and take credit that belongs to God only.

RD: I use my medicines and you employ yours; we are both doctors, and doctors are not deceivers. You give a patient medicine. Sometimes God is pleased to heal him by means of your medicine; sometimes not—he dies. When he is cured, you take the credit for what God does. I do the same.

The rain doctor is simply calling the medical doctor's bluff: if he really believes, as the missionaries did indeed claim, that all is in the hands of God, then how could he or any other European claim that his human science had cured someone or predicted rains?

The Tswana version of how rain arrives was in fact fairly complex. Rainmaking rituals did not work in some automatic, mechanical way; they required that the community be in a state of "moral recitude, of 'coolness' (*tsididi*)" (Comaroff and Comaroff 1991, 210). Therefore, the ritual expert's primary task was to remove social pollution that might be preventing the heavens from unleashing the rain. It was thus fully within Tswana logic when they later blamed the presence of the Europeans for the failure of rainmaking rituals. For their part, Europeans began to include rain services in the church calendar, the more effectively to combat the natives' view. The conversion effort thus became an extended exchange of and change in the views of both sides.

Translating: Mary in the Americas

We saw in the last example the extent to which projects of conversion also involve attempts to translate across belief systems. Now we look at this translation process from the center outward, and follow the images and ideas of the Virgin Mary as she (and other saints of the Catholic Church) became part of religious complexes in the Americas.

The nurturing and tragic image of Mary has served as a particularly powerful figure in translating Catholicism into other cultures. Not only are there universal resonances with her story, but one also finds very specifically similar stories about a sacred and virgin birth or an assumption to heaven in other cultures.

The story of Mary in the Americas exemplifies the logic of religious syncretism, or the blending of two or more traditions. Syncretism occurs when people adopt a new religion but attempt to make it fit with older ideas and practices. The process usually involves changes in both or all of the traditions. As we saw in Chapter 3, Japanese religious history is virtually defined by syncretism, as Japanese have combined elements from Chinese Confucian political ideology, Buddhist teachings and practices, Christian ceremonies, and the older practices called Shinto. As we have seen in Chapter 9, places already sacred before Christianity became the sites of shrines to Mary. The meaning of the places changed when this happened, because they were no longer entirely local, but linked worship to a larger religious tradition—the images in the shrines were carried to the common parish church for feast-day worship, for example. But the meaning of Mary was also changed, in that she became locally specific and concerned with rendering assistance in local affairs, and not just a remote semi-deity. (More examples of these changes in the meaning of Mary are offered later.)

The Virgin of Guadalupe

In Mesoamerica, today's Mexico and Guatemala, the Mary of Guadalupe has served as a symbol of nation and people, sometimes in opposition to foreign rule. During and after the Spanish conquest of the region, from the mid-sixteenth through the late seventeenth century, the native Mayan people of eastern Mesoamerica organized rebellions. These rebellions soon incorporated the symbols of Catholicism, reworked in Indian terms. The insurgent movements often included figures anointed as Christ or king. In some cases, villagers were visited by the Virgin Mary, who then instructed them to start a new church organization. She would leave proof of her visit in the form of an image that she created either on cloth or as a statue (Lafaye 1976; Wolf 1956).

The two most influential cases involved the Virgin revealing her image to a peasant (in both cases, as it happened, named Juan Diego) during the sixteenth century. The first apparition, in which Mary left her figure on a cloak, took place in 1531 in Tepeyac near Mexico City and became known as the Virgin of Guadalupe; the second, known as the Virgin of Ocotlan, occurred about 10 years later in Tlaxcala state, when Mary imprinted herself on an ocote tree.

The Virgin of Guadalupe was to become the master symbol of Mexico. The Mexican War of Independence was fought under her banner, and her shrine at Tepeyac became the major Mexican shrine. In the official story of the events, the Virgin addressed a Christianized Indian named Juan Diego in 1531, 10 years after the Spanish conquest of the area. The Virgin commanded him to go to the archbishop of Mexico and tell him that she wished a church built in her honor on Tepeyac Hill. Juan Diego tried twice to win the archbishop's approval, but was unsuccessful. Mary then performed a miracle. She told Juan Diego to gather roses in a dry spot where roses never grew, and then to present them to the archbishop. He did so, but when, standing before the archbishop, he unfolded his cloak, there appeared from inside, not roses, but the image of the Virgin miraculously imprinted on the cloak. The bishop immediately acknowledged the miracle, so the story goes, and ordered a shrine built on the spot where she had appeared.

This particular spot was not, however, a random choice. It had once been the site of a temple to the goddess of fertility Tonantzin. Tonantzin, Our Lady Mother, is associated with the moon, as is Guadalupe's image. Indeed, for at least the next 50 years worshipers called her Tonantzin as well as Guadalupe, and this still is the case in parts of Mexico. Stories about Tonantzin continue to be told in Mexico: in one, she intervened when God wanted to punish his children, by challenging him to try to produce milk so she could nourish her children.

These associations or "syncretism" are not unique to the New World, of course. William Christian speculates about preexisting deities where there now are shrines in Spain. In Ireland, in particular, statues of the Virgin often are erected in spots formerly considered sacred because of an unusually shaped rock formation or a sacred grove. And in the Church of Saint Germain in Paris, a black image of the Egyptian goddess Isis was displayed as the Madonna until 1514.

Guadalupe and Mexican Resistance to Spain

In later centuries, rebellions against Spanish control frequently formed around cults of the Virgin Mary. In 1721 in Cancuc (Chiapas), the Virgin appeared to a young girl and asked her to place a cross in her hamlet, build a chapel around it, and offer incense. A local Mayan leader then claimed to have ascended to heaven where he spoke with the Virgin Mary, Jesus Christ, and St. Peter, and was told that the people were to appoint their own officials and no longer had need of the Spanish. This man, Sebastian Gomez, then appointed bishops and priests, all using the symbols of the Catholic Church.

Devotions in the local church had already become "localized" in the sense in which we used the word earlier: worship focused on locally specific images of the Virgin that were understood as protecting the village. Services consisted of giving offerings and prayers to these advocations of Mary and to other localized saints, rather than addressing prayers to God. Gomez and his followers now renamed Cancuc "Jerusalem" and referred to the Spaniards as "the Jews who persecuted the Virgin Mary." Although the movement was suppressed, it illustrates the ways in which local opposition to Spanish rule was elaborated in what were once the conqueror's own images, the sacred images of Catholicism itself.

By choosing Mary and the saints as key images, those local movements that did not reach the stage of open rebellion managed to insulate themselves (and popular religious practice generally) against charges of heresy. The Spanish Inquisition investigated these religious movements and looked for evidence of idolatry, in particular prayers said to images that asked them to directly heal illnesses. The Indians whom the inquisitors interrogated denied that they acted in this way, claiming that they merely appealed to the patron saints and to the Virgin Mary for help. Because the Spanish Church accepted as legitimate both the cult of the patron saint and the possibility of visitations by the Virgin, the inquisitors were unable to find solid ground to prosecute Indian religious leaders (Lafaye 1976).

Why was it the Virgin Mary (and not Christ) who became Mexico's national symbol? The answer is in part due to the way the Church itself portrays Mary and Christ, and perhaps in part due to local family dynamics. The Virgin is associated with struggle and life in Mexico, while Christ is associated with defeat and death. On the religious plane, these distinct associations stem from the crucifixion of Christ, on the one hand, and the nurturing role of the Virgin, on the other. The anthropologist Eric Wolf (1956) argues that on the family plane, the associations grow out of the distinct sentiments the child forms toward his or her mother and father, in both Indian and Mexican families. The child experiences a paradise of closeness to his or her mother, and sides with the mother in her struggle against domination by the father. Mary thus brings out a wealth of early pleasant memories; Christ, the object of struggle. Sentiments formed in the family are expressed in the culture through the symbols of the Virgin and Christ.

On the plane of politics, the Virgin Mary, in the specific advocation of the Virgin of Guadalupe, is associated with the struggle against Spanish military and religious colonization. Many Mexicans interpreted Guadalupe as the goddess Tonantzin who has returned to liberate Mexico. This interpretation follows an indigenous logic of cyclical history, in which gods depart only to return later. Mexico appears as a new paradise, to which came the Virgin to herald independence. In one seventeenth-century text, the Virgin of Guadalupe is linked to the woman portrayed in the Revelation of John, "arrayed with the sun, and the moon under her feet, and upon her head a crown of twelve stars," and who is to realize the prophecies of Deuteronomy. Not coincidentally, the image of the Virgin of Guadalupe in the shrine today is adorned with a sun and moon and the twelve stars.

The Virgin of Guadalupe thus links family (mother), politics (liberation) and religion (salvation). Against the background of these linkages we can understand how it was that in 1810 the patriot Father Miguel Hidalgo y Castilla began the revolution for Independence with the cry: "Long Live the Virgin of Guadalupe and down with bad government."

The political and religious associations have continued in full force into this century. In the early twentieth century, the church, trying to render more uniform the devotions of the faithful, attempted to replace the Virgin of Guadalupe with the Sacred Heart of Jesus from Rome. This attempt was perceived in Mexico as an effort to supplant a Mexican figure with a European one, and it was strongly, and successfully, resisted. And in 1996, the Bishop of Guadalupe, speaking to a reporter in Italy, declared that he considered the peasant Juan Diego to have been a mythical figure (*St. Louis Post-Dispatch*, September 7, 1996). The remark led to his immediate removal from office!

Africa to Brazil: The Role of Images

The example of Guadalupe and Tonantzin suggests that religious imagery can be effective in translating a new religion into an older cultural and religious context: Mary made sense to Mayans who already venerated Tonantzin. Sometimes this process involves a literal translation across deities. Such is the case for religions found in the Americas but derived from West African religions. In Brazil, Cuba, Haiti, and elsewhere, Catholic deities provided useful cover for slaves who wished to continue to practice their own religions, but had been forbidden to do so. As this need for subterfuge decreased, Americans have been free to explore both the African roots of the traditions and the appeal these traditions have to a wide range of Americans, including those of European descent. Known now by the names *Umbanda, Candomblé, Santeria,* and *Voudun,* these Afro-American traditions have formed a distinct religious stream alongside, though at times intermingling with, Catholicism (Murphy 1994). (We examined healing practices within Umbanda in Chapter 7.)

The slave trade brought large numbers of African people to the southern and central portions of the Americas as well as to the colonies in North America. Slavery lasted longer in the southern regions—until 1888 in Brazil. Many of the Africans were taken from what is today Nigeria and Benin. In particular, Yoruba people were brought to Brazil and Cuba, and Fon people were brought to Haiti. Slave traders and slave owners tried to wipe out cultural traditions and mixed slaves from different regions in an effort to prevent Africans from organizing rebellions (Walker 1990).

Because slave owners prohibited the practice of African religions, Africans translated some of the ideas and deities of West African religions into the images and language of Catholicism. Slavers thought that they were imposing Catholicism; Africans understood that they were preserving older traditions.

In Brazil these traditions today are called "Umbanda" and "Macumba" in Rio de Janeiro and "Candomblé" in the northeast region of Bahia. They combine, in different proportions, African qualities, especially in Bahia, and Brazilian innovations, especially in Rio, with Catholic imagery and ideas from a Euro-Brazilian movement called "Spiritism."

In Rio a woman presides over services in a small storefront center (centro) called the Spiritist Tent of Granny Maria Antonia of the Congo, one of many places to which people come to worship and seek help from the spirits (Guillermoprieto 1990). In this center, as in many others, there is a particular "patron" spirit, Granny Maria Antonia. She is understood to be a woman who was born in Africa and was brought as a slave to Brazil, where she died. She is of a recognizable type of Afro-Brazilian spirit, the "Old Black Woman" (and as such replicates the one deity/many deities relationship we have been discussing).

Also exhibited in the center are statues of Christian figures: the Virgin Mary, Jesus, St. George (of dragon-slaying fame), and others. Each resembles corresponding statues in, say, European Catholic churches. But each also corresponds to an Umbanda deity called an "Orisha," and can be traced back to its original in Yoruba society, West Africa. Today people freely offer the Orisha as well as the Catholic name for each image; a century ago any but the Catholic identity would have been strongly denied to outsiders.

In this schema of cross-religious translation, God is Olorun, the creator of the world. The image of Jesus is also identified as Oshala, the creator of human life. Saint George, depicted slaying a dragon, corresponds to Oshossi, the hunter god, and St. Lazarus, protector of lepers, to Omolu, a deity governing disease. Mary is identified with Yemanja, the mother of some of the other Orishas. Furthermore, and here note the parallel with our Spanish valley, other Orishas who are mothers are also identified as manifestations of Mary. These maternal deities are associated with the water and sea as well.

The lifting of the veil surrounding this momentous project of religious translation was not followed by the crafting of new, original statues. In Yoruba and Umbanda, the Orishas have no concrete form; they are forces and principles rather than personages. Thus, the process of rendering African deities in Catholic form added a new visual and individuating dimension to worship, and the Catholic images remain as foci for Umbanda worship.

The identification extends to ritual occasions as well. People observe the Catholic feast days that apply to their "translated" deities, but do so in a way that corresponds to the Afro-Brazilian meaning of the deity. For example, Yemanja (Mary) is identified with the sea, so people flock to the sea on the Catholic feast days for Mary, and once there they offer gifts to Yemanja, wading out into the water and letting the sea carry them away.

Umbanda and Candomblé in fact bring together three religious traditions. Alongside Catholic and Yoruba religions is the doctrine of Spiritism or Kardecism, popular among the elite in Europe and Brazil in the late nineteenth century, and today adhered to by millions in Brazil, either as part of Umbanda and Candomblé or on its own. As we saw in Chapter 7, Spiritism provides a means of healing people from physical and mental afflictions. The doctrine attributes a wide range of events in the material world to the desires and actions of spirits. Sometimes spirits possess people, and when they do they can cause the person to suffer illness. Specialists can communicate directly with these spirits, ask what their wishes are, and restore the person to health.

Umbanda in Rio

Umbanda was in fact born as a revolt against the elitism of Spiritism in Rio (Brown 1986). By the 1920s, Spiritism had become a highly intellectualized and European-oriented set of practices. Lighter-skinned Brazilians (Brazilian color coding of individuals contains many categories, from very dark to very light, rather than a simple black/white dichotomy) controlled the seances. They were speaking with the likes of Voltaire and Plato. If an Indian spirit appeared, possessing a darker-skinned person, they would refuse to allow him to speak.

In the 1920s a middle-class Rio man, Zelio de Moraes, suffered an illness that left him partially paralyzed. His father, a real estate agent, was a Spiritist and took him to his group for healing. There he was visited by the spirit of a Jesuit priest, who revealed that the illness was spiritual, and that he had a mission, which was to found a truly Brazilian religion that would be dedicated to the worship and propitiation of Brazilian spirits.

These spirits included *Caboclos,* spirits of Brazilian Indians, and *Pretos Velhos,* spirits of Africans enslaved in Brazil.

Zelio received additional messages from other spirits. The "Indian of the Seven Crossroads" told him the new religion would be called "Umbanda." Zelio then did as he was told, and founded the first Umbanda center, today called the "Mother House." This center, the Spirits' Center of Our Lady of Piety, attracted a largely white and middle-class clientele. But the spirits that spoke through the participants were those of Indians and Africans, giving them the voice denied them by the Spiritists. The movement grew rapidly, attracting a diverse range of participants.

The social and political role of these movements has changed dramatically in this century. At first tolerated, it was repressed as heretical in the 1930s, 1940s, and 1950s by the Catholic Church, with support from the Brazilian state. State repressions began to loosen in the 1960s, and since 1970 people have enjoyed relative freedom to worship openly. The initial reason for this tolerance was political, as politicians seeking office sought support from the large communities of Umbanda-Candomblé followers. But the change also has been motivated by social and cultural changes (Walker 1990). In the past 30 years many Brazilians have sought their "roots," and some, including many of lighter skin color, have found them in the links back to Africa. Many of these people, mostly of the middle class, have found these links through the experience of possession by an African spirit. In doing so, they have moved away from the Catholicism that once was virtually required of those seeking high social status. Being known as a follower of Umbanda or Candomblé is no handicap to political office, and participation in the movements can be combined with a range of political and social doctrines. The Brazilian Secretary of Public Works in the 1980s, for example, calls himself a "Marxist–Spiritist," believing in both reincarnation and Marxist–Leninism.

These movements also have become part of a broader popular culture in Brazil. On New Year's Day, the major newspapers in Rio run the Umbanda seers' forecasts for the next year. In Bahia state, the home of Candomblé, pop singing groups have risen to the top of the charts with songs based in Candomblé; new wave filmmakers have drawn on the Orishas for their subjects, as in the popular film *The Amulet of Ogun.* The Orisha named Esu, who controls roads and pathways, has been adopted as the patron deity of all communications facilities, and a statue to him stands in front of the post office in Salvador, Bahia's capital (Murphy 1994).

The urban poor are also drawn to these movements. Two million of Rio's 6.5 million people live in squatter settlements called "favelas." For them, "survival calls for imaginative solutions, and Umbanda is nothing if not the triumph of imaginative thought," writes the reporter Alma Guillermoprieto (1990).

Let us return to the Granny Maria Antonia center mentioned earlier. The center is a two-story house located in a lower-middle-class neighborhood in central Rio. A black woman named Stella Soares runs the center. Stella, a former nurse, insists that all who attend don white uniforms; this measure makes everyone more nearly equal, she says. Certain specific spirits visit the center and possess those who attend its services. They are the spirits of individual Indian and African people rather than Orishas. They include the Indian of the Seven Crossroads, the Indian of the Coral Cobra, and the "Indian who tears up tree stumps with his bare hands." They speak; they embody the local identity of black and Indian Brazilians, and through the experience of being possessed the worshipers can experience several identities, several sides of themselves. Her clientele includes dozens of mainly white, middle-class initiates, who go into trance, but also many very poor black clients. "Once they have changed into their white clothes," she says, "you cannot tell the difference."

Are these religions part of Catholicism? Catholic priests call on people to abandon Umbanda, claiming that it has nothing to do with Catholicism, and some practitioners (probably an increasing number) consider themselves to be followers of Umbanda and not, or no longer, Catholics. But many other Umbanda followers claim status as Catholics. They point to a number of close relationships between Umbanda practices and Catholicism. The images in worship are all Catholic. Some Candomblé priests require initiates to be baptized Catholics before they can join in the rituals. The story of how the first center was founded also underscores the connection with Catholicism—it was, after all, the spirit of a Jesuit priest who commanded Zelio to open up his center. Catholic feast days are observed, and many Umbanda practices reinforce the link to the Catholic Church. For example, on August 16, the feast day for Saint Lazarus, Umbanda priestesses drive by churches where the mass is held and sprinkle popcorn on all so that they will receive benefits from Omolu, the deity associated with the saint.

Catholic images, and especially the image of the Virgin Mary, have served to mediate translations of religion across vast social and cultural divides, first within Europe, and then out across seas with the expansion of the church. But the very capacity of the image to carry multiple meanings—what I have called the multivocality of the image—has allowed subordinate groups to contest the dominant meanings. Spanish villagers insist on their own Mary's capacity to protect and nurture; Mexicans, on the Virgin of Guadalupe's role as a national symbol; Brazilians, on Yemanja/Mary's powers over the sea; Christians throughout the world, on Mary's willingness to appear to them and to deliver messages of hope and struggle. Each set of claims to Mary is asserted over and against official counterclaims that underscore the unity of Mary and Christ and the single authoritative voice of Rome.

Adapting: Islamic Sacrifice in New Cultures

Islam requires a number of practices of its adherents. Among them is the sacrifice of an animal at the Feast of Sacrifice. This requirement is observed worldwide, but how it is observed and how it is interpreted varies, reflecting the way practice and discourse are adapted to local conditions. The examples that follow focus on the role played by ideas about gender and about ritual efficacy (how a ritual "works") in leading Muslims in particular societies to inflect and reshape the ritual, even if slightly.

As with other ritual events, Muslims see their performance of sacrifice as part of their obligation to submit to God's commands as revealed through the Prophet Muhammad. (Indeed, *Islam* means *submission* to God.) Islam does not have an international hierarchy of religious authorities (as do Catholicism and Mormonism). It is thus striking that the ritual life of Muslims worldwide is as uniform as it is. Muslims everywhere agree on the importance of completing ritual prayer five times daily, fasting during the month of Ramadan, undertaking the pilgrimage to Mecca if they are able, and so forth. This degree of uniformity in the general norms of ritual practice results from the agreed-upon central importance of the Qur'ân, the word of God as revealed to Muhammad, and the hadith, collections of what Muhammad said and did. Islamic scholars base their interpretations, decisions, and law codes on these scriptural texts.

And so Muslims throughout the world often begin an account of why they perform a certain ritual by referring to a place in scripture where God gives a command. For example, we can safely say that all Muslims agree that a Muslim should observe the Feast of Sacrifice (in Arabic, *îd al-adhâ*) each year. The feast day commemorates the willingness of the prophet Ibrâhîm (in English, Abraham) to sacrifice his son at God's command. God's command to sacrifice to him and to him alone is contained in the Qur'ân in Chapter 22 (verses 34–38) and again in Chapter 108, and is the scriptural touchstone for this ritual. Moreover, the collection of reports of the Prophet Muhammad's deeds and statements, the hadith, specify how Muhammad carried out this command during the month of pilgrimage. These reports have become the basis for the annual pilgrimage to Mecca, the hajj.

Now, despite this general agreement on text and command, Muslims have developed strikingly varied ways of observing the command, and sometimes they vigorously debate the propriety of these ways. We start with village practices in the Gayo highlands, then examine alternative practices followed in the nearby town, and finally consider how the ritual is carried out at the other end of the Islamic world, in Morocco. Even when, as in this case, there is a clear and explicit text for ritual, that text may be subject to many interpretations. This multiplicity of interpretations and ritual practices is due in large part to different ideas about the relationship of humans to God, and different ideas about social relationships, especially those between men and women and between rulers and ruled.

Gayo Observances

The Gayo case illustrates how both religious interpretation and social ideas, particularly ideas about gender and family, shape ritual. All Gayo Muslims observe the annual sacrificial ritual. They do so with a keen awareness that they are part of a global celebration. Each year upward of 100 Gayo undertake the pilgrimage, and those who stay behind in their Sumatran highlands homeland often talk about the sacrifices the pilgrims are carrying out simultaneously with their own. I recall in 1989 sitting with a Gayo religious teacher night after night following shortwave radio reports from Malaysia on the daily events of the pilgrimage in Mecca and Medina.

But people also carry out their own personal obligations for each household to sacrifice something on the feast day. In the community of Isak, where I have done most of my work, households sacrifice various kinds of animals: chickens, ducks, sheep, goats, or water buffalo. The person carrying out the sacrifice itself takes care to do it in the correct manner, cutting the animal's throat quickly to minimize pain, and pronouncing

Men preparing to sacrifice a water buffalo for the Feast of Sacrifice, Isak, Sumatra. (COURTESY OF J. BOWEN.)

the formula, "In the name of God, the Merciful and Compassionate." Just before cutting the animal's throat, the sacrificer speaks softly near it, dedicating the animal to one or more relatives, who receive religious merit from the sacrifice. Who actually cuts the throat is not of great importance; a man may delegate the job to someone else, but the ritual must be performed properly, by an adult Muslim. When it is a buffalo that is sacrificed, the animal is first purified by being washed with the fruit of a citrus called the *mungkur* that is thought to rid the animal of its impurities and dedicate it to God.

As in most of Southeast Asia, Gayo gender relations are relatively equal. Women inherit property, manage household finances, and work alongside their husbands in fields, offices, or shops. The household is the unit of production and consumption: all its members work and eat together. Not surprisingly, then, the sacrifice is carried out in the name of the household, not just the male household head. Women as well as men speak of "their" sacrifice, and couples decide jointly on a list of people who will receive its merit. In the case of a buffalo, the beneficiaries usually include parents on both sides, and daughters as well as sons. Widows also carry out sacrifice (without being socially redefined as men), although a man will cut the animal's throat. When a wealthy female trader in Isak sacrificed a buffalo, others tended to speak of it as her sacrifice, not her husband's. She had generated the wealth, although he was part of the household.

Following the sacrifice, households host ritual meals, called *kenduri*. At each such meal, prayers to God are recited by all present. Depending on whom you ask, blessings, or merit, or just prayers are sent to the spirits of the deceased. These ritual meals are central to many events in the highlands and elsewhere in Indonesia. Sometimes a household will host a meal for everyone who wishes to attend. During each of the four years when I was present for the *íd al-adhâ* in Isak, three or four households sacrificed a buffalo and sponsored such a village-wide feast. At these feasts men and women chanted Qur'ânic verses and statements in praise of God far into the night. These special kenduri were intended to send extra merit to the host's ancestors. Recitations please God, say villagers, who then relieves the torment of these ancestors. (At these events, as at the feasts held after a death that we studied in Chapter 3, the number of guests times the number of repetitions yields the overall benefit.) The learned man who leads the guests in chanting will have been given a list of the people to whom the merit should be transmitted; he then embeds these names in a long prayer (sometimes saying the names very softly), thereby directing the evening's merit to the intended beneficiaries.

Not only do the words sent to God generate spiritual benefit for deceased relatives, but the sheep or buffalo that has been sacrificed by a household also provides a future material benefit. On the Day of Judgment, the persons named as sacrificial beneficiaries will be able to ride on the animal to the place of judgment. Only one person can ride a goat or sheep to this place, but seven can ride on a buffalo. A buffalo sacrifice thus provides the opportunity to bring together parents, children, and grandchildren on the back of the afterlife vehicle, and if they have the resources, most Isak households will stage a buffalo feast sometime during their lives. (With the sands of the Holy Land in mind, they also say they wished they had camels to sacrifice.)

The ritual meals and the sacrifice that precedes them all involve the transmission of a ritually purified animal in the name of God, the communication of an intent that the merit of the sacrifice (and of the chanting at larger feasts) be attached to certain specific persons, and the expectation that God will indeed grant these benefits.

Objections to Ritual Efficacy

But Gayo (and other) Muslim reformists object to these practices. As we saw in Chapter 4, reformists hold that one can only benefit from one's own actions, and therefore ritual meals during which people intend to send merit to a spirit contradict the proper understanding of God's statement: "People shall have only as they have labored." Now, some reform-minded scholars in Indonesia actually support the idea that sacrificing in obedience to God does generate merit for yourself. But Gayo reformists, who tend to live in the town and mingle with non-Gayo people, try to distinguish their own interpretations and practices as clearly as possible from those of the villagers. (Other scholars, who call themselves "traditionalists," defend some village practices.) In part this is because townspeople's identities are based on their rejection of the past—they live as self-styled "modern Muslims"; in part it is because of their own religious convictions.

Certainly religion has been the main idiom for, if not the entire substance of, townspeople's ways of differentiating themselves from villagers. Town friends told me on many occasions of how villagers remained in "pre-Islamic days" (*jaman jahiliya*),

Men and women at worship on the Feast of Sacrifice, Isak, Indonesia. (COURTESY OF J. BOWEN.)

evidenced by their reliance on kenduri. They stated that before the coming of Islam people worshiped stones and spirits, not God, and did so by sending them gifts, sometimes food gifts, in return for their assistance in hunting or sorcery or to achieve other ends.

Village religious practice includes the idea that rituals, often in the form of ritual meals, can send merit, communicate with spirits, and accomplish other practical ends. In order to maximally distinguish themselves from villagers, town reformists have focused their efforts on ridding town observances of any indications that rituals can do these things. In the case of the Feast of Sacrifice they have tried to eliminate any signs that killing and eating together make merit or send blessings to ancestors.

In 1989 I observed the celebration of the Feast of Sacrifice in a reformist stronghold in town. When asked about the purpose of the ritual, town residents invariably referred to God's command in the Qur'ân to follow the example of Ibrâhîm. (Villagers, by contrast, usually mentioned the importance of providing a vehicle for the afterlife.) For these reformists, to follow the example of Ibrâhîm means to adopt his attitude of selfless and sincere devotion, or *ikhlas.* One scholar explained that one receives merit from the sacrifice only if it is done with the proper intent, "for the sake of God and not for a worldly reason." He called the notion that the sacrifice becomes a vehicle for the afterlife "amusing."

In recounting the story of Ibrâhîm, townspeople emphasized his prior decision to give something away in devotion to God, not the moment of sacrifice itself (which would bring up village ideas about the purpose and result of sacrifice). The killing of the goat or other animal was sometimes left for someone else to perform, privately, effectively downplaying killing and eating in favor of other public events: street parades, congregational worship, and chanting in the neighborhood prayer-house.

Townspeople did eat in the prayer-house, but referred to the meals as "eating together" and never as kenduri. Friends of mine gave away food on the feast day, and mentioned prominently the invitation given to town orphans to eat in the prayer-house as proof of the event's real character. The meal was about self-sacrifice and not about creating merit. (The fear of mistaken understandings of what the eating meant sometimes leads to extreme reactions. I recall one teacher who reacted in horror when cookies were passed around a classroom after he had delivered a homily to the students about the meaning of sacrifice.)

Town religious practice has thus developed in part as a reaction to earlier models of sacrifice. Because villagers emphasized ritual meals and the efficacy of the sacrifice itself, town modernists avoid any association between the killing of the sacrificial animal and eating together. The value of selfless sacrifice is instead underscored.

Certain elements of the Feast of Sacrifice, for example, are shared by Gayo villagers and town reformists alike. Women are active participants in the rituals. They may perform sacrifice. They are members of a household unit that is directly involved in the activities: in the villages, when they gather together for a ritual meal (and in images of the family, holding hands, being saved because of their wise decision to sacrifice animals to God); in town, when the family gathers for tearful confessions of their shortcomings and of their love for each other. These elements of female and family involvement are also found in other Indonesian societies and in the writings of Indonesian religious scholars. For example, the possibility for women to carry out a sacrifice is explicitly defended by influential reformist scholars. Are these elements generally true of Muslim societies, or specific to Indonesia? Or to a wider belt of Asian Muslim societies?

Moroccan Muslim Sacrifice: Reaffirming Male Dominance

To answer this question we can appropriately start by searching for the maximal contrasts, the differences that will aid us in constructing a field of possibilities. As it happens, we can begin with Morocco, at the other end of the Islamic world, recently studied for its forms of sacrificial ritual practice by M. E. Combs-Schilling (1989). Here, in contrast to the family-oriented practice and ideology found in Indonesia, patriarchy is accentuated through ritual. Each year on the feast day, the king, who claims descent from the prophet Muhammad, publicly plunges a dagger into a ram's throat, reenacting Muhammad's ritual practice and underscoring his tie to the Prophet. Combs-Schilling shows that the sacrifice also reaffirms patriarchal power in the family and embodies a notion of male fertility. After the king has accomplished his sacrifice, male heads of household throughout the kingdom follow suit. Each publicly kills a ram, the size and virility of which is commented on as a measure of the man's own virility. In village and town settings, the other men of the household stand erect to witness the sacrifice; women and children are either absent or in the background, seated. Women play only the role of passive observers to the sacrifice; after the killing they may dab some of the victim's blood on their faces to "share in the power of sacrifice."

This public enactment of patriarchy accords with Moroccan cultural assumptions about the opposition of male reason versus female passion. More generally, the fixed male/female opposition is just one instance of the belief described by Lawrence Rosen (1989) that one can read from social characteristics of persons to their attendant mental states. The Moroccan view asserts that persons have essential differences in their mental characteristics, depending on such critical social differences as gender and place of origin. This theory underpins not only gender segregation and patriarchy, but also legal processes of determining a reliable witness.

This maximal contrast brings out two major cultural differences between Morocco (and perhaps other North African societies) and Indonesia (and perhaps other Asian societies). The first is the salience of the killing event in the former, but not in the latter. Whether on Java, coastal Aceh, or highland Sumatra, and whether reformist or traditionalist in religious orientation, Indonesians downplay the act of killing in favor of other aspects of the ritual. This tendency tinges all other aspects of the ritual, including the second axis of contrast, that of patriarchy's greater or lesser centrality. As Combs-Schilling emphasizes (and others support her account), the ritual is publicly, officially interpreted in Morocco not just in a gender-segregated way (as one might find in parts of Muslim Asia) but in such a way as to underwrite the domination of women by men.

Other Moroccan Forms of the Sacrifice Ritual

The contrast between Morocco and Gayo (and some other Indonesian) ritual practices thus points toward broad cultural contrasts that also shape, differentially, the way Muslims interpret scriptural commands. This maximally broad contrast is especially important in preventing us from assuming that particular features observed in one place are true of Muslims in general.

But it turns out that within Morocco one finds variant forms of the ritual much as we saw for Gayo society. And, just as with Gayo reformist self-differentiation from villagers, some of these other forms of ritual appear to be constructed in explicit distinction to the public, state-backed patriarchal form of ritual. Abdellah Hammoudi (1993) describes observances in a village near Marrakesh, where women play a ritually central role in purifying the sacrificial victim. They gather its blood not just to share in its power but for use over a long period of time to guard the home and to combat illnesses. Moreover, over the longer ritual cycle (found in parts of Morocco, Algeria, and Tunisia) the Feast of Sacrifice is followed by a series of carnivalesque processions and masquerades in which characters representing women, Jews, workers, and other figures flaunt sexuality and, in classic ritual-of-reversal fashion, violate the sanctity of the sacrifice by wearing the skin of the sacrificial victim. The masquerade highlights the social contradictions between classes as well as those between male and female. These representations of cultural difference contradict the rigor of all-male purity that the sacrifice tries to impose. Stressing the resemblance with European forms of carnival, Hammoudi argues that these rites are part of the overall process by which Moroccans made Muslim sacrifice their own.

The publicly patriarchal character of sacrifice and the explicit links to the Ibrâhîm myth, emphasized by Combs-Schilling, are also documented by Hammoudi. But these public forms now appear as pronouncements that disguise the activities and counter-representations made by women. Moroccan ritual activity, at least in some places, is not the unambiguous proclamation of patriarchy but a structured combination of official patriarchy and other forms, either domestic (such as the healing blood gathered from the victim) or interstitial (such as the masquerades). In these offstage events the socially necessary activities of women gain voice.

Together, the Moroccan and Gayo cases show how Muslims have shaped a particular set of ritual duties in sharply contrasting ways, with cultural foci that do not derive in any direct way from Islamic scripture, but rather, are the products of adapting, elaborating, and transforming scriptural and other elements in directions that make sense locally.

11

Sacred Speech and Divine Power

*I*t is hard to think of a religion in which set ways of speaking—spells, prayers, recitations—do not play central roles. Humans are talking animals, and we use our powers of speech to understand and shape events in both the visible and invisible worlds. Most rituals we have examined so far have had certain speech forms at their center: invocations of ancestral spirits (in Africa, Sumatra, or New Guinea), stories and spells that heal (in Japan, Panama, or the United States), and pronouncements that channel the meaning of images (in the Catholic mass or Dogon masked dances).

Some religious traditions place particular emphasis on the centrality of the spoken word to religious practice. For the Navajos of the American Southwest, the world was brought into being by the Gods when they spoke and sung it into existence. Speech and song bring this creative power into the present world, for good or evil. So, too, for the Dogon, who understand the world as having been spoken into being. In both Hindu and Buddhist traditions, the word that is spoken and heard has primacy over that which is written and read—in the latter case a direct chain of transmission is broken. It is not only in the European traditions of Moses, Plato, and Jesus that writing has been understood as secondary to speech (mistakenly so, argues the philosopher Jacques Derrida), but in other religions, of greater and smaller scale, as well. Written scripture may play an important role in these traditions—"scripture," after all, means "writing"—but it does so as the written record of what was originally an act of speech.

Certain religious movements portray their own distinctiveness by contrasting their emphasis on the spoken word to the reliance of competing faiths on images. In seventh-century Arabia, Muhammad and his followers contrasted the word of God, which they followed, to the images of polytheists, which they condemned. Moses responding to Aaron's setting up of the golden calf, or Joseph Smith and Brigham Young leading the Mormons across the United States, both condemned the worship of "graven images" and urged their followers to focus on the word of God. Luther chastised the Christians of his time for following the Church rather than scripture, and the "letter of the Bible" has been the watchword for Protestant movements of reform ever since. Each of these leaders has accused other faiths of forgetting or ignoring God's words.

But speech, like images, can be meaningful in more than one way. When we speak we refer to concepts, and through them to things in the world. We also call up associations in the minds of our hearers, associations linked to their memories of hearing such words before, or to the style, rhythm, or voice tone of the speaker. Thus, the way in which a sermon is delivered or a hymn sung can be as meaningful to worshipers as the manifest content of the sermon or hymn. We also understand some speech as directly accomplishing something, as having force as well as meaning: a marriage vow seals a pact; a spell compels a spirit to act. Within a religious tradition people often discuss and debate how best to understand their own speech. Is a sermon better if it is carefully crafted beforehand (as clearly a human product), or is it better if it is spontaneous (allowing the Holy Ghost to offer direct inspiration)? Can a prayer, or a mass, or the recitation of a verse work directly on the universe, or is it only a request to a deity or god?

We consider the relationship between ways of speaking and divine powers in three religious traditions: Islam, in which God's speech sets out a proper path for humans to follow; Navajo religion, in which humans draw on the creative powers of the first beings when they sing prayers of blessing or healing; and several Protestant religions, in which God reveals his word through scripture and spontaneous, inspired speaking.

The Qur'ân as Recitation of God's Speech

For Muslims, speech is sacred and powerful mainly as the source of commandments from God and as the vehicle for carrying out, through prayer and worship, those commandments. Muslims' sacred book is the Qur'ân, a word that comes from the Arabic root meaning "to recite." The Qur'ân is the collection of verses spoken to Muhammad by the angel Gabriel, who conveyed them from God. The revelation of these verses took place between 610 and 632 in Mecca and Medina, in Arabia. The Qur'ân preexisted these revelations as God's speech—indeed, most Muslims regard it as eternal (Graham 1987, 79–115).

The revelations were handed down orally long before they were first written down, and even today Muslims consider it important to memorize and recite these words of God. In its written form, the Qur'ân is arranged as 114 chapters, each divided into verses, and arranged, not in the order in which they were spoken to Muhammad, but, by convention, from the longest to the shortest.

Unlike the Hebrew Bible or Christian Gospels, the Qur'ân is not a collection of long narratives. It contains brief parables and stories but mainly consists of directives and exhortations to Muhammad and his people. Muslims learn the fuller stories of the prophets and of Muhammad's life from other narratives, not from the Qur'ân itself. Much of the Qur'ân is about how Muslims ought to live: values, social norms, and what we generally call "law." These guidelines for living are called sharî'a, "the way." (Law in the narrower sense of enforceable jurisprudence is designated by the term *fiqh*.)

The following passage, from the third chapter of the Qur'ân, exemplifies the way in which several kinds of messages are typically combined. It reads:

Say: 'God has spoken the truth; therefore follow
the creed of Abraham, a man of pure faith and no idolater.'
The first House established for the people
was that at Mecca, a place holy, and a guidance to all beings.
Therein are clear signs—the station of Abraham,
and whosoever enters it is in security.
It is the duty of all men towards God to come
to the House a pilgrim, if he is able to make his way there.
As for the unbeliever, God is All-sufficient nor needs any being.
(Qur'ân 3:90–92)

A lot is contained in this passage. Muslim children and adults will memorize it in Arabic, learn its meaning in their own language (if they are not Arabic speakers, as most Muslims are not), and then be taught the ways to understand it by a religious teacher. Most Muslim children begin to learn the Qur'ân at a young age, and as they grow up they will likely attend Qur'ân interpretation sessions in the local prayer house or mosque.

The passage is addressed to Muhammad, as are all Qur'ânic verses. It shows him precisely how to admonish and guide the people of Arabia, some of whom had become his followers. God directs him to say a certain passage to the people, a passage that identifies Muhammad's mission as pulling people back to the true path of worship of God from which they have strayed. How that path is identified is important: it is the "creed of Abraham," the same creed delivered to Jews and later to Christians. These people had their own "messengers," similar to Muhammad: the Jews had Moses, to whom was revealed the Bible, and David, to whom was given the Psalms; Christians had Jesus, to whom was revealed the Gospels (in this, the Islamic view of Christ's mission). Jews and Christians are "people of the book," and have been accorded special treatment in Muslim-held territories. Muslims believe that Jews and Christians eventually strayed from pure monotheism (the doctrine of the Trinity is a particular target) but that people of all three faiths worship the same God. *Islam* means "submission [to God]" and is intended as a return to an old faith, not the creation of a new one.

The passage then refers to a historical event, the construction by Abraham of the Ka'ba, the large, cubic, black-draped structure in Mecca around which Muslim pilgrims process during the annual religious pilgrimage. The duty to make the pilgrimage, for those with the means to do so, is based on this passage in the Qur'ân, short though it may be, and the fact that Muhammad made such a pilgrimage in 632, the year of his death.

The final sentence in the passage implies a warning to the unbelievers, those who do not yet accept God, and reminds them that God does not need them, but, it is implied, they do need to heed his call.

Islamic calligraphy in the Congregational Mosque in Isfahan, Iran. The inlaid tile design shows both cursive and geometric styles; the inscriptions include Qur'ânic passages and, in this Shi'i setting, invocations of both Muhammad and 'Ali. (COURTESY OF JOHN RENARD.)

The Qur'ân is treated not just as a book to be read, memorized, and studied, but also to be celebrated through song and calligraphy. Contests of Qur'ân melodic recitation are held at regular intervals throughout the Muslim world, in which the beauty of the voice control and melodic interpretation, as well as the fit of melody to content, are the basis for judging winners. (Indonesia and Malaysia, two non-Arabic speaking countries, routinely win prizes at the international finals.) Much Islamic art is based on the artistic interpretation of the form of the written Qur'ân, and intricate writings of the names "Allah" and "Muhammad" are found on almost every conceivable surface in Muslim societies. Many Muslims also believe the spoken and written words have the power to ward off evil or heal people of illness.

The Qur'ân is God's major gift to humans, analogous to the presence of Jesus among humans in Christian understanding. It is an exact replica of the words spoken to Muhammad; therefore, the forms of the spoken and written words themselves take on sacred value. It is also evidence of direct historical contact between God and Muhammad. This direct contact is crucial to Islam's religious foundation, and explains two areas of study within Islam: one that proves that Muhammad was illiterate and could not possibly have created the Qur'ân, and a second that shows the Qur'ân to be inimitable in grammar and rhetoric. These lines of investigation, taken together, prove that the Qur'ân is from God. (Contrast the lack of importance to most Christians of the original sound and shape of the Greek words in the Gospels.)

But Muslims debate among themselves about what the implications of the Qur'ân's divine source are for everyday life. Many Gayo Muslims, for example, consider prayers (do'a) that include Qur'ânic verses to be directly effective in healing, or giving one invulnerability, or harming one's enemy. One of my friends, for instance, used a passage from chapter 61 of the Qur'ân as the beginning of an invulnerability spell:

And He will give you another blessing which you love:
help from God and present victory.
Give good tidings, O Muhammad
to believers.

To which he would append a plea ending in the lines:

Let my blanket be from God,
my cloak from God,
my shawl from God.

My friend thought that when he uttered the prayer, God gave him a cloak and shawl, as the material realization of God's promise to give "help from God and a present victory." In his own memory, these divine gifts had served him well during battles fought in the 1950s, making bullets and knives skip off his clothes as he fought. But in the 1980s others pointed out to him that the Qur'ânic passage had been revealed to Muhammad as a message of peace, to stop fighting. One scholar objected to my friend that reciting the Qur'ân could not automatically confer any power on the reciter; that all power came from God and that He knew all that happened in the world anyway and would do as He pleased, regardless of what mumbo-jumbo ordinary men and women chose to recite. All that we can do, he said, is to live good lives and worship God, and then perhaps He will choose to reward us.

The Creative Power of Navajo Speech and Song

*T*he view that speech directly confers power, limited within Islam to one, often criticized view about the Qur'ân and God, flowers fully within Navajo religion. Like Muslims, Navajo place speech at the center of religion, but as the source of creative power rather than as the source of divine commands.

In Navajo tradition, the individual human being has the power to change the world through language (Witherspoon 1977). A person can do so because the world itself was created through language, when First Man sang the song known as Blessingway. Among the first creatures, the Holy People, were Long Life Boy (thought) and Happiness Girl (speech), to whom First Man said: "You two will be found among everything." Indeed, their names are found in nearly every Navajo prayer and song as signs of the powers to create. They also are the parents of Changing (or Earth) Woman, the being who is associated with the earth's fertility.

The sung prayers known as Blessingway tell the story of creation. They also reenact creation each time they are told (Wyman 1970). They may be performed as a separate ritual—for example to bless a house—or be incorporated into other rituals in which, by invoking the events of creation, they endow the ritual with that same creative power. Navajo sand painting also draws its powers from the story of creation. After the Holy People built the first house, they decorated the floor with bits of shale, rock, and mineral dyes. They drew all the forms of life that they eventually were to create, depicting them in the forms of holy people. They then recited a long prayer to these holy people, and in that act created a causal pathway between sand paintings and the sacred powers of creation.

Blessingway and many other prayer cycles identify and associate everyday people and conditions with the Holy People and the events of creation. Blessingway contains many lines that link powers given to the Holy People to powers desired by the speaker, such as:

May the power that enables you to inhale also enable me to inhale.

Let the dark flint which arises to protect you always arise to protect me.

Often these sections of the prayer provide long catalogues of body parts and powers, underscoring the identification of the Holy Person's body with that of the prayer reciter. These identifications are intended to transfer the properties of the Holy People to that of the person who is the object of the ceremony. For example, Navajo singers will help ensure a good birth for an expectant mother by performing a Blessingway ceremony that identifies the Holy People of the Earth, themselves associated with fertility and life, with the mother and child (Gill 1981). The singer will collect earth from a cornfield and water from a flowing stream, both nurturing life, and apply them to the woman. The prayers recited include the Earth's Prayer, which underscores these identifications through passages such as the following:

Earth's feet have become my feet by means of these I shall live on.

Earth's legs have become my legs by means of these I shall live on.

Earth's body has become my body by means of this I shall live on.

Earth's mind has become my mind by means of this I shall live on.

Earth's voice has become my voice by means of this I shall live on.

. . .

It is the very inner form of Earth that continues to move with me, that has risen with me, that is standing with me, that indeed remains stationary with me.

Now it is the inner form of long life, now of happiness that continues to move with me, that has risen with me, that is standing with me, that indeed remains stationary with me, surprising, surprising. (Wyman 1970, 136)

The pair of terms *long life* and *happiness* are the principles personified in the Holy People Long Life Boy and Happiness Girl (Wyman 1970, 19–46). They are linked to all the components of the earth. The effect of these pairings is to transfer to the mother and expected child these two essential qualities, long life and happiness.

Prayers such as these are used for healing when Holy People are thought to have been responsible for the illness. If a person has trespassed on a holy site, the Holy People may place a spell on that person; the Holyway ceremony is designed to induce them to remove the spell. The singer addresses a particular holy person by name and makes an offering of tobacco smoke to him. In the Holyway stories associated with the ceremonies, the holy person is sent tobacco, smokes, and then agrees to help cure the patient. The holy person addresses the patient as "grandson," placing himself in a relationship in which he can be compelled to aid the ill person, his "grandson." The prayer draws on the knowledge contained in these stories by demanding, not requesting, that the holy person cure the patient:

This very day you must remake my feet for me,

This very day you must remake my legs for me.

The prayer ends by asserting that the cure has occurred:

With my body cooled off, I am walking about,
with my body light in weight, I am walking about,

. . .

As one who is long life and happiness I am walking about

Pleasant again it has become,

Pleasant again it has become! (Gill 1981, 128–129)

In this, its concluding section, the prayer performs the act of bringing the patient to health. The verb is in the progressive mode—"I am walking about"—indicating that the patient will continue to enjoy health. Most importantly, the prayer identifies the patient with Long Life Boy and Happiness Girl: he or she has become "one who is long life and happiness."

Speech and Grace in Protestant Churches

So far we have considered ideas about how speech relates to power; now we introduce a third concept, that of the grace of God. Ways of speaking found in many Protestant churches introduce the idea that speech by everyday people can, when accompanied by God's grace, be divinely inspired.

In the sixteenth century, several Christian scholars, notably Martin Luther (1483–1546) in Germany and John Calvin (1509–1564) in Geneva, protested against certain Church teachings. The worship movements that Luther, Calvin, and others established thus came to be known generally as "Protestant" because of this series of protests. Although differing strongly among themselves, these movements shared the dual conviction that, first, people could be saved only through faith and by the grace of God and, second, that scripture, not human institutions, was the ultimate source of religious authority. As the billboard outside the Lutheran Church near my home in St. Louis proclaims today: "Only by Grace; Only by Faith; Only by Scripture."

Protestants make the claim that faith and grace connect individuals to God in opposition to the Catholic claim that the Church, through its sacraments, creates that connection. For the Catholic, the miracle of the Eucharist means that Christ is produced in the bread and water of the Mass. For most Protestants (and, from at least the ninth century onward, for some Catholics), the objects of a mass are signs of, not the substance of, Christ. Moreover, for them the ritual of the Eucharist does not automatically confer merit or salvation or grace on the individual worshiper. Nor do chants said on behalf of the dead aid the dead in their struggle through purgatory to heaven. The individual has free and direct access to God, and God may bestow grace on anyone. The gift of the Word of God thus may reach anyone at any time and place and in unpredictable ways. Faith is all that is required (Clark 1967, 99–115).

In the wide array of movements and churches that followed Luther's break with Rome—Methodists, Baptists, Lutherans, and so on—this emphasis on universal access to God's grace and revelation of grace through speech and hearing led people to develop many and varied ways of worship. Quakers and some Baptists have stressed the universal nature of the minister's role, that anyone may be visited by the Holy Ghost and moved to preach. Charismatic and Pentecostal churches (and certain movements within Lutheranism) have encouraged worshipers to let the Holy Ghost visit them and lead them to speak in tongues, as did the apostles after the death of Jesus. But other movements denied the universal access of people to grace and salvation. John Calvin argued that God has predetermined who is to receive his grace and be saved, and who is to be condemned to hell. This doctrine of *predestination,* held by the Puritans in early North America as well as Calvin's followers in Europe, implied that one's good works had no bearing on one's fate after death.

The Letter and the Spirit of Scripture

The ultimate authority on all religious matters for Protestants is scripture, and not the teachings of a church or pope.

But what is "scripture"? One interpretation of the Protestant slogan "only scripture" (sola scriptura) is that the written text is paramount. Luther was indeed an outstanding biblical scholar, learned in Greek, Latin, and Hebrew, and did argue for the importance of the scholarly interpretation of the text as written. Early Protestant preaching never strayed far from the text of the Bible. What came to be called "Fundamentalist" movements, but might more correctly be called "literalist" emphases on the literal meaning of the text, follow from this focus on the written word.

For some Fundamentalist churchgoers in the United States today, literal truth resides in the 1611 King James Version of the Bible. Some of these Christians call modern translations "perversions." KJV is the Bible "as it is written" (Ammerman 1987, 53). Rather than considering the Bible as a whole, and worrying about contradictions between various parts, Fundamentalists (along with many other Christians) tend to refer to a verse or a phrase, on which they then elaborate, both in sermons and in discussing everyday life. People turn to individual verses that they have memorized, and they also use the language of some of those verses in everyday conversations, speak of their sicknesses as "suffering in beds of affliction" or having "a thorn in the flesh" (Ammerman 1987, 87).

This literalism can lead some Fundamentalists to a point at which they are nearly using the Bible for divination, as in the case of a man who decided to order a tent from Sears and Roebuck Company because he found listed among the permitted foods in 14 Deuteronomy the "roebuck" (Ammerman 1987, 54).

This interpretation of scripture can, of course, be used to underwrite claims of special authority grounded in learning. But these claims are often countered within the tradition of Luther and Calvin by appeal to a second understanding of scripture. Luther, Calvin, and other reformers looked beyond the text to the divine message it conveyed (Graham 1987, 141–154). They placed no special value on the original languages of the Hebrew Bible or the Greek Gospels, and indeed Protestant reformers have encouraged translation as the best way to spread God's word. In this respect they differ from Muslims, for whom there can be only one Qur'ân, the Arabic-language speech of God. (Indeed, most Muslims consider it impossible to "translate" the Qur'ân; English and other versions are usually called "interpretations" or "renderings.")

For the Protestant reformers, then, speech and writing was best thought of as a window to God's word, transparent to its referent. It is the Word, not the particular letters, that is holy. The Bible as preached, translated, interpreted, and witnessed in one's life is the key to the proper understanding of God, not the scholastic analysis of the Hebrew or Greek constructions. The Word of God is thus the meaning of scripture. It can take different forms, including the presence of Christ himself in the world, as the Word made flesh.

God can thus communicate his word in very different ways. Luther underscored the importance of inner communication with God, communication that did not depend on learning. He wrote that "no one can understand God or God's word rightly unless he receives it directly [literally, "without mediation"] from the Holy Spirit." And Calvin wrote that "all of scripture is to be read as if God were speaking," and that the spirit of scripture was more important than the letter of scripture. In their view, God can communicate with ordinary people through many media: the revelations recorded in scripture, the embodiment of the divine in Christ, and the visiting upon any of us of the Holy Ghost (Graham 1987, 143, 147).

Because these inner modes of communication—hearing with help from the Holy Spirit—must accompany the reading of the Bible, Luther linked speech and hearing to the central value of faith:

If you ask a Christian what work renders him worthy of the name Christian, he will not be able to give any answer at all except the hearing of the word of God, that is, faith. Therefore the ears alone are the organs of the Christian person, who is justified and judged a Christian not by the works of any member, but through faith. (quoted in Graham 1987, 141)

The writings of Luther and others thus could be taken to give to individuals the right to hear God's word, no matter what statements were made by the authorities of a church. This radical giving of spiritual rights to individuals surfaces time and again in subsequent history.

Election and Signs

Most Protestant Christians would agree that God bestows his grace where he sees fit. But how and when does he see fit? Can our actions bring on grace?

The struggles over this issue within Christianity trace back to the very roots of the religion. On the one hand, Christianity drew from Judaism. It began, after all, as a sect within Judaism, where obedience to the Law determined the fate of individuals and of the universe. The idea that good works redeemed one's soul were developed by the Church into elaborate doctrines of penance, masses, and salvation. Many Protestant traditions also incorporated such a notion, Methodism among them.

But Christianity became, not a sect within Judaism, but a new religion, and did so in large part by adopting ideas from Hellenism, the world view that pervaded the Mediterranean world (Jaeger 1961). Hellenism included the idea of divine grace that is visited upon humans rather than achieved by them. This concept accorded well with the idea of an all-powerful God, and indeed with the unpredictability of the God of the Hebrew Bible. After all, if God does not need humans then he will dispense grace in ways that fit his plans, not our works.

The idea that God's grace is entirely independent of human actions finds its most eloquent exposition in Paul's letter to the Romans, in a section where Paul is distinguishing between the older idea of the Jewish "chosen people" from the Christian idea that God chooses, or elects, some people (and not others) both from among the Jews and from among the Gentiles.

. . . [W]hen Rebecca had conceived children by one man, our forefather Isaac, though they were not yet born and had done nothing either good or bad, in order that God's purpose of

election might continue, not because of works but because of his call, she was told, "the elder will serve the younger." As it is written, "Jacob I loved, but Esau I hated."

What shall we say then? Is there injustice on God's part? By no means! For he says to Moses, "I will have mercy on whom I have mercy, and I will have compassion on whom I have compassion." So it depends not upon man's will or exertion, but upon God's mercy. For the scripture says to Pharaoh, "I have raised you up for the very purpose of showing my power in you, so that my name may be proclaimed in all the earth." So then he has mercy upon whomever he wills, and he hardens the heart of whomever he wills.

You will say to me then, "Why does he still find fault? For who can resist his will?" But who are you, a man, to answer back to God? Will what is molded say to its molder, "Why have you made me thus?" Has the potter no right over the clay, to make out of the same lump one vessel for beauty and another for menial use? (Romans 9, 10–21)

Just as the potter may select some pots for greatness, and others for quick destruction, without the pots having the right to answer back, how can we, God's creations, question the will of God, our Creator?

The doctrine of election formed a central part of the teachings of Saint Augustine in the fifth century (Burns 1994). Because original sin cost humans their free will, he wrote, all our fortune, good or ill, is due to God's grace. In the sixteenth century, John Calvin developed this argument into the idea of predestination, which became founding doctrine for the Presbyterian Church. As inscribed in the Westminster Confession of 1647, which the English Parliament accepted the following year, the doctrine was stated in the form that "some men and angels are predestined unto everlasting life, and others foreordained to everlasting death" (Weber 1958, 98–101).

This doctrine left its adherents with a radical uncertainty about their future. Calvin taught that no one can know whether he is saved (although Calvin apparently thought he was), because the damned can have all the mental states possessed by the saved except for the final state of trust in God. So although a strong feeling of faith in God is necessary for salvation, it is insufficient as a source of reassurance about salvation.

This uncertainty has one opening, in the "doctrine of signs," that even if we cannot know with certainty about our salvation, we can see signs of it. These signs could be in one's ability to succeed in the world. Some Protestant theologians argued that one had a duty to assume that one was saved and act accordingly. Individual psychology led believers in the doctrine toward intense worldly activity in the hopes that leading a rational, systematic life for the greater glory of God on earth would itself be a sign that one has been called to serve God—has been elected. Some added an additional tenet that helped close the logical circle: that only the elect had faith strong enough to keep them hewing to this path. Thus, success and profit are themselves signs of election.

Although this line of thinking brought even Calvin's heirs back to a position in which good works counted for something on the religious plane, it was not a return to Catholic doctrine. The Calvinist still has no possibility of absolution; if he is damned then there is still nothing he can do about it. Furthermore, in the idea that a life spent for God was a sign of election, it was the whole life that mattered, and not the individual work, as in the Catholic calculus of sin and absolution.

Max Weber (1958) drew on these religious responses to develop his theory that what he called the "Protestant ethic" provided a psychological push for the development of modern capitalism in Europe. He noted that the pioneers of modern capitalism in Europe were mainly Protestant rather than Catholic, despite the fact that Protestant theologians were far more restrictive regarding what we might call the modern business necessities of interest and competitive pricing than were their Catholic counterparts. Luther, for example, wrote that "the greatest misfortune of the German nation is easily the traffic in interest. . . . The devil invented it, and the pope, by giving his sanction to it, has done untold evil throughout the world."

Weber's idea was that Protestantism spurred on the development of capitalism, not directly through its doctrine but through the psychological consequences of that doctrine. Men tormented by the unknowability of election were spurred on to succeed in the world, to build edifices of successful businesses as monuments to their worldly success. Weber called this cast of mind "worldly asceticism": denying pleasure to oneself but doing so in a life very much devoted to this world. The capitalist experienced loneliness, since no one could save him and God was distant; had a hatred of material, sensuous life, since it had no positive religious role and tempted people to idolatry; and threw himself into a social life that was solely work for the glory of God.

Weber advanced his thesis by studying the sermons and diaries of Calvinist theologians in the seventeenth and eighteenth centuries. Richard Baxter, for example, served in Cromwell's government as well as in the Puritan Church. He preached hard, methodical work as a religious labor (and opposed sports). The divine quality of this work will be "known by its fruits," he wrote. As a consequence, these men preferred specialization and the division of labor for the greater returns to labor they brought, and thus the greater indication of their own personal election.

The doctrine of election—or "particular election" as it came to be called—was by no means universally accepted by Protestants. An especially widely effective treatise written by Jacobus Arminius in 1608 and called *Declaration of Sentiments* argued that God wishes all people to be saved and gives them the means to do so. Living the good life, stated Arminius, can bring one to God's grace. This position (often called "Arminianism") implied that humans are "perfectible." This argument was taken up in the eighteenth century by John Wesley. The movement he founded was named Methodism for the methodical life he urged Christians to lead. Methodists and other movements accentuated the emotional work required to bring about certainty of salvation and to lead the person into the state of grace.

Baptists gained their distinctive position within the array of Protestant churches through their argument that only those who had gained their faith should be baptized into the church. They thus rejected infant baptism. But Baptists themselves split over the issue of election, with some teaching that Jesus died for everyone; others, that he died only for the elect. Those who held the first view were called "General Baptists" and included the group that left England for Holland in 1607, some of whom then journeyed to Plymouth, Massachusetts, in 1620. Those holding the second view, called "Particular Baptists," founded churches in England and also sent groups to America. Today, some Presbyterian and Reformed churches in Europe and the United States advocate the doctrine, but may place more or less emphasis on it.

Singing and Certainty among U.S. Primitive Baptists

One group of churches that has attempted to remain faithful to Calvin are the self-styled "Primitive Baptists" of the southeastern United States. These churches are scattered throughout the Appalachian mountains, but I draw here on a study conducted in the early 1980s by James Peacock and Ruel Tyson (1989) in the Blue Ridge mountains straddling North Carolina and Virginia. In this sparsely populated region, both elders and other worshipers travel from church to church to worship, often staying Saturday nights with friends. Services include hymn singing, one or more sermons preached by elders, and large meals spread out on communal tables. The churches belong to the Mountain District Association.

The Primitive Baptists adhere to the Westminster Confession, and they actively wrestle with the difficulties the doctrine presents. They attempt to uphold election and reject the idea that we can earn our salvation or have certain knowledge of it. As one preacher put it, "every time you feel inspired, it didn't necessarily come from the Lord." But they also hold to the idea of signs of salvation that one can sense in the world. These signs include the experience of community attained through fellowship and church services, "a sweet meeting," such as one preacher recollected in a sermon in the early 1980s. "Oh, my friends, sometimes we've sung songs here that've lifted us up," he reminds them. And the beauty of their singing is a sign, a foretaste of heaven: "Beyond the little foretastes of experience now, ah, in heaven's pure world today there are angels that sing" (Peacock and Tyson 1989, 112).

"Hymns are small sermons," notes one church elder. Peacock and Tyson describe how, concerned with not overstepping the boundary between faith in their salvation and (mistaken) assurance about it, they choose their songs carefully: "Amazing Grace" and "Guide Me O Thy Great Jehovah" affirm God's absolute sovereignty and "In Sharon's Lovely Rose" expresses hope of reaching heaven, but "Blessed Assurance, Jesus Is Mine" is unacceptable because it presumptuously claims assurance of salvation. In their style, too, they express resignation and modest hope, but avoid the joy that could dangerously approach certainty. Upbeat tempos and complex harmonies are avoided; unison singing in a dignified cadence is preferred. Peacock and Tyson recall the tears running down the cheeks of the congregation while singing; their participation in the service is no less emotional than that of their more animated Pentecostal brethren, but it bespeaks a resigned, stoic attitude in the face of God's great and unknowable will (Peacock and Tyson 1989, 114–118).

Sermons pose two related dilemmas for the preacher. Does one prepare an elaborate sermon and risk the sin of pride, or wait for the Spirit to emerge inside one, and risk incoherence? Does one urge people to perform their duties as Christians and risk strengthening the erroneous idea that doing their duties will win them salvation, or refrain from any exhortations and miss the opportunity to guide them along a righteous path?

Preachers do not, in fact, preach from outlines or notes. To do so would be to insult the "Spirit that bloweth where it listeth." Sermons come from the heart. "If I can't feel that power, I ain't preaching the Gospel. I may stand up there and quote scripture and so on, but it ain't the Gospel," remarked one preacher. For, as Luther and Calvin proclaimed, the Bible is the inspired word that emerges in and through humans, not the dead letter of the written book. It was the word of God that produced the Bible and inspires people today as well. Or does not: an elder may rise to preach and after quoting scripture, sit down when he finds he has nothing to say (Peacock and Tyson 1989, 118–126).

In their sermons preachers strive to avoid implying that religious experience is evidence of salvation or that good works can lead one to salvation. Elder Bradley used a sermon he preached in a North Carolina church to trace his own path. His experience preaching and "saving souls" had led him to think that preaching could bring a person to salvation. He realized his error after revisiting the passage in the Letter to the Romans on election. His sermon reminds us how what appears to be an obvious reason for preaching is indeed in error from the perspective of the doctrine of election, and also how the apparent gloominess of this perspective can be in fact the basis for joy:

Finally came to the conclusion that this which I'd been taught, that salvation was dependent upon men hearing the gospel, repenting of his sins and believing on Jesus, that God was using this the preacher to reach the dead sinner, that this was totally contrary to that which was taught in the word of God, but that this salvation depended upon God's own sovereign pleasure and that he made choice of a people in a covenant before time began. And, oh what a joyful sound it was, and how beautiful it was for me then to see things in that order! To see that God planned this salvation, and if God planned something you can rest assured it's not going to come to naught. That which God has planned will be executed. God declared this salvation before men ever had being in himself. (Peacock and Tyson 1989, 122)

The "sweet meeting" that comforts the soul depends on community: preaching, singing, and eating together makes up what these Baptists call "the visible church." But here enters a difficulty: if your group consists of both the damned and the elect, how can you construct a solid community? Two ideas of community have emerged in the Mountain District, roughly corresponding to the contrast between North Carolina and Virginia churches, and these two ideas have consequences for practices of speaking, singing, and gathering in fellowship.

Two Models of Church Authority

For reasons of topography and modes of livelihood, the churches in North Carolina are dispersed in fields and hills, whereas those in Virginia are located in villages (Peacock and Tyson 1989, 87–117). The North Carolina churches are less well attended than the latter group, and worshipers are more likely to live individualistic lives, usually as independent farmers. Charisma, direct divine inspiration, governs the lives of the elders, and it appears in their sermons, which often recount personal experiences. Songs of stoic resignation, sermons about doctrine, moods of individualism, and antibureaucracy sentiments characterize the North Carolina churches.

In contrast to this individualistic structure and attitude, the Virginia churches have created some degree of bureaucracy, and their elders emphasize organization over charisma. The lives of those attending services are more likely to involve work in government civil service or small businesses (although here, too, many farm). Sermons are more likely to dwell on duty. Singing has changed in some Virginia churches, evolving in the direction of mainline Protestant church singing, with major keys predominating and harmonies explored.

Peacock and Tyson recount how the two groups of churches have come into conflict over their differing ideas of authority and community. The North Carolina churches have favored allowing individual churches and members to go their own ways, as the Spirit moves them. Charisma, the gift of grace from God, dominates. Those in Virginia have stressed the importance of following rules and obeying duly constituted authority.

The contrast surfaced in a dispute during the 1980s about the right of a church to exclude some of its members. Churches do exclude members, and members cannot join other churches. Because members and elders rotate where they worship they can effectively keep out the excluded. In this case, one church excluded a majority of its worshipers on grounds that they had associated with a sinner. They had shown themselves not to be of the elect and so had to be thrown out of the church—much as did the Puritan churches of seventeenth-century New England that we read about earlier. The church is responsible for community as a whole, and must exclude sinners.

But the excluded members then formed their own church and asked to be recognized by the Mountain District. The rule-following Virginia churches supported the exclusions and refused to recognize the new church, because doing so would contradict the righteous authority of the church that had thrown them out. The North Carolina churches supported the right of the members to form a new church. They felt called to do so, and who can say they are mistaken in their calling? (Peacock and Tyson 1989, 71–85).

At issue was not just who makes the rules, but who has access to the Word of God. If the Word of God is given to anyone and everyone, at any time and place and in unpredictable ways, then the worship and preaching of anyone should be recognized and attended to. If an individual is called by God, his or her subsequent actions should be respected. But if the right to provide an authoritative interpretation of scripture is held by those persons capable of correctly reading it, then all others should obey that authority. Here the North Carolina churches stood in favor of the availability of God's word to anyone; the Virginia churches, of the importance of a duly constituted hierarchy based on knowledge and the consent of the community acting as a whole.

This tension about authority and community plagues all Christian movements that attempt to structure themselves around the ultimately unknowable grace of God. The Virginia churches have changed as had the Quakers in 1700, toward hierarchy and a "routinized" authority. The North Carolina churches have resisted this pull.

Charismatic and Pentecostal Churches

Other Christian churches in the same part of the United States have maintained an independent stance but have taken different positions on the question of whether we can perceive and experience signs of our own election or salvation.

Many Fundamentalists, such as those in the Northeast U.S. church studied by Nancy Ammerman (1987) doubt that everyone who claims to be saved is so, and they look for signs of salvation, most importantly some outward, noticeable change in the person's life. They should have given up smoking and drinking. They also should show confidence in the Lord; constant worries are signs they have not yet been saved.

Throughout much of the South, Holiness churches are scattered in hills and towns much as are the Primitive Baptists. Preachers and ordinary people often travel long distances to worship. The focus of worship is on the relationship between the individual and God, as in all the movements we have considered so far. But here the role of rather dramatic signs is paramount, for snake-handling is often part of the service. Surviving a snakebite, or a drink of poison, or an electric shock is a sign of God's grace. The women and men who have been bitten sit together in services as the "true believers," or the "true saints." These signs, having survived, are signs, or "charismata" that are given by the Holy Ghost. They are proofs of Jesus' power to save them; cups of strychnine are called "salvation cocktails" (Covington 1995; La Barre 1964).

One church name says it all: "The Church of Jesus Christ with Signs Following." The phrase is in reference to 16 Mark, a key chapter for worshipers at Holiness churches and for many other churchgoers throughout the South—just as the Primitive Baptists and other believers in particular election take their cue from 9 Romans. In 16 Mark, Jesus appears to his apostles and upbraids them for not believing those who said they saw him risen. He then commands them to go into the world and preach the Gospel, and says:

He who believes and is baptized will be saved;
but he who does not believe will be condemned.
And these signs will accompany those who believe:
in my name they will cast out demons;
they will speak in new tongues;
they will pick up serpents, and if they drink any deadly thing,
    it will not hurt them;
they will lay their hands on the sick,
    and they will recover.

Mark continues to relate that these apostles did indeed go forth and do the work of the Lord, and the Lord confirmed the message "by the signs that attended it" or, in the King James Version, "with signs following." Here ends Mark, and from here derives the name of the Holiness church mentioned above.

The relation of speaking in tongues to salvation is further evidenced in 2 Acts, the second key text for Pentecostal and Charismatic churches. It relates, speaking of the apostles:

When the day of Pentecost had come,
    they were all together in one place.

And suddenly a sound came from heaven like the rush of a mighty wind,
*   and it filled all the house where they were sitting.*
And there appeared to them tongues as of fire,
*   distributed and resting on each one of them.*
And they were all filled with the Holy Spirit and began to speak in other tongues,
*   as the Spirit gave them utterance.*

Because these events took place on the Pentecost (the Greek name for the Jewish Feast of Weeks), religious movements that seek to experience what the apostles did are called Pentecostal, or Charismatic because of the adherents' desire to receive the charismata, the gifts of grace visited upon them by the Holy Spirit. Participants in these movements believe that their own speaking in tongues and ecstatic experiences are signs that they are saved—they have renounced the doubt that plagues those who adhere to particular election, and embrace the idea that anyone may be saved—and yet these signs of salvation are still required.

Perhaps it is the strong need to overcome strong doubt that explains the great lengths to which some worshipers go to prove their salvation to themselves and their fellow worshipers. Some handle snakes; others swallow poison. Snakes may have been chosen precisely for the shock the handling delivers to outsiders. "Spread the Word! We're coming down from the mountains!" announced one preacher. The Holiness churches in which snakes are handled date only from about 1900. As with the Primitive Baptists, the churches value their independence. They are usually scattered throughout rural areas and are visited by a series of preachers. They first practiced snake handling in 1909, in Tennessee. Apparently it was not until 1918 that someone died from snakebite, and he was denounced as a backslider, someone who had lost his faith, when he died (La Barre 1964).

Snakes are typically brought out in their cages partway through the service, after a sermon and singing have taken place. Sometimes music continues, usually on a guitar, and worshipers begin to dance and enter trance states, at which time someone may pick up a snake and handle it before dropping it back into the cage or passing it on to someone else. The handling may take place in a more subdued setting, the snake passed from one person to another. Women and men handle the snakes. Perhaps 20 or more people are known to have died from snakebites in Holiness meetings; some state governments have responded by forbidding the use of poisonous snakes.

The Church of Jesus Christ with Signs Following in Alabama received national attention in 1992, when the church's preacher, Glenn Summerford, was accused of attempting to murder his wife by forcing her to put her hand in a case filled with poisonous rattlesnakes. She claimed he was trying to kill her because he could not divorce her and retain his position in the church. He claimed he did it to prove her innocence and that the snake bit her because she was backsliding. He was convicted and sent to jail, and his church, lacking any institutions for succession, disbanded. Other preachers soon began to hold outdoor snake-handling services, however (Covington 1995, 1–63).

But snake handling is just the most spectacular (at least to date) of a wide range of practices intended to bear witness to the divine presence within oneself. It is itself the most visible sign of the powerful need to bear witness in a striking and public way to God's grace, to the presence of the Holy Spirit in oneself.

Much more widespread than snake handling are practices of speaking in tongues. Even the relatively staid Lutheran churches of suburban St. Paul, Minnesota (near where I grew up), have begun to encourage members to speak in tongues. Some report a sense of release and of grace as the incomprehensible words flow out of them. They do not speak of the experience as like a trance, but as an experience over which they have some control.

Charismatic movements are growing within Roman Catholicism as well, and in 1981 John Paul II met with Charismatic church leaders and gave his approval to their movement. Worldwide anywhere from 50 to 75 million Catholics can be considered to be Charismatic. And Pentecostal churches are growing rapidly throughout the world, particularly in South America and Southeast Asia. In Brazil, where Umbanda and Macumba had become popular as supplements or alternatives to Catholicism, many are finding that Charismatic churches that focus worship on God but offer the opportunity to speak in tongues combine the best of both worlds.

All these movements are seen by participants as bringing the divine into themselves through the mediation of the Holy Ghost. The religious experience provides a material sign that God has accepted the worshiper and that he or she can hope or know of salvation. This particular emphasis on the individual's avenue to grace through personal experience—often spoken experience—is a key characteristic of Protestantism. The individual's relation to God through the inspirited Word is markedly different from the idea that contact with God is through the miracle of the Eucharist, itself mediated by the priest. Protestantism relocated God's miracles, his charismata, signs of grace, from communion and the icons of Mary and Jesus, to the individual's ways of speaking. Doing so made possible new forms of community and authority based on those ways of speaking, of which the churches discussed here are but a few instances.

In these religious traditions—Islam, Navajo, Protestant—speech is linked to power through the individual. The speaker who speaks truly and clearly is able to do so because of a relationship with the divine. This relationship is complex and debated, but across religious traditions an idea emerges that sacred speech, in its utterance, places the speaker in contact with the divine. Reciting the Qur'ân is repeating God's own words and can confer power on the speaker. Chanting Blessingway reenacts the events of creation that accompanied the first chanting by the First People. For some Protestants, a true worship service requires speaking in a holy way—in tongues, or when called by the Holy Spirit to preach, or when reading from the Bible in a state of inspiration. This inspirited speaking is in some respects the equivalent of the worshiper's contact with an image—the drawing in of power through an "exchange of vision" with a Hindu statue is probably the closest equivalent. Catholic, Hindu, Japanese, and other traditions also rely on prayer for worship, of course. But the traditions studied in this chapter have taken the spoken element of worship and made it into the privileged element. When this is done—and it is done in different ways in each tradition—the subjective state of the individual also becomes a matter of increased concern. If an object is the center of worship, its objective qualities—its separation from the worshiper—give the process of worship an air if not a doctrine of objectivity: the worship succeeds if certain steps are taken. The Catholic mass is objectively efficacious even if the priest or the worshipers have their minds elsewhere. But once the words uttered by the worshiper become the whole of worship, those daydreamings endanger the very idea of worship. "Thought is the inner form of speech," say the Navajo; "no actions are effective without the correct intention" echo Muslims. Speech is close to thought, or ought to be, and words uttered must be accompanied by the proper state of mind if they are to reach their destination. Subjectivity now takes center stage.

Religion on the Web

*T*hese examples mainly concern people talking in "real life." Yet recent years have seen a dramatic rise in the use of electronically mediated religious activity. Do prayer, chatting, or visiting Web sites constitute qualitatively new types of religious activity? Thousands of Web sites devoted to advancing or discussing religious beliefs and practices now exist. (Some are mentioned in earlier chapters.) E-mail lists and chat rooms facilitate long-term debates about religion and society. And Internet users also favor religious Web sites. A 1998 study estimated that of the 100 million Americans on-line, 25 percent used the Internet for "religious purposes" each month (Leibovich 2000).

Some of those users are looking for information, but most, according to the 1998 study, use the Internet to communicate with other people about religious ideas or experiences. Some sites function as virtual worship sites. Beliefnet (*www. beliefnet.com/*), for example, gives users the opportunity to create virtual prayer circles. When Judy Spiegal's father died in 2000, she started such a circle. On the first day, a dozen people of different faiths posted prayers on the site (Leibovich 2000). A temple in Calcutta, India (*www.maakali-kalighat.com/*), offers Hindus a way to worship online, with the option to request different levels of puja (offerings), for free, 10 dollars, or 90 dollars. As the Web site puts it, "You can thus partake of the holy supplication without actually leaving the comforts of your distant home."

These two examples represent different characteristics of the target audiences—multireligious America, the Hindu diaspora—but they share the basic feature of allowing worship at a distance, anonymously if so desired. The Web sites also create a sense of the network or "community," of those who use the service. Much of Ms. Spiegal's comfort came from the sense that people out there were supporting her. One of the effects of the Hindu temple site is the created sense of a community of worshippers around the world. This virtual community may address specific needs: for example, the Cathedral of Hope in Dallas (*www.cathedralofhope.com/*) advertises itself as the "world's largest gay and lesbian church," a claim it can make because of the online participation in services that it offers.

This kind of Web site offers primarily to mediate—among individuals (as in the prayer circle) or between individuals and religious institutions (as in the virtual temple and church). The sites differ in the kind of audience they target, from "narrowband" to "broadband." Some sites are linked to specific churches, temples, mosques, or other highly local bodies, and are intended mainly to provide a service (in two senses) for current, potential, or virtual worshippers. Even here there is a good bit of variation, between the site that is merely a convenience for those who physically attend a site of worship anyway, and the virtual religious site. (The Cathedral of Hope is probably halfway between these two points.) Other "narrowband" sites are intended for the followers of one particular religion or set of beliefs (such as the different Jewish sites listed earlier in this book.)

"Broadband" sites attract a wide audience of people with differing beliefs and practices and so they broadcast a fairly tolerant and catholic (in the sense of encompassing diversity) message. Their design varies: some have a menu format (Catholics click here, Muslims there); some offer humor, like the Beliefnet site mentioned earlier, whose December 2000 homepage features a picture of the Pope twirling a basketball. The "religions" link on this site takes users to a page featuring columns and discussions about interreligious issues: interfaith marriages, the place of religion in schools, comparing religions on various topics, and noting the overlapping celebrations of Christmas, Hanukkah, Ramadan, Yule, and Kwanzaa. (Yule refers to the "modern pagan" celebration of the Winter Solstice.)

Here the specific characteristics of Web sites are exploited to good advantage: on the home page one senses the celebration of all religions together, which at times takes on a synthetic "world" characteristic (as in "World Sacred Music," a musical sampler available as a download). But the many links on that page take users to religion-specific sections, some of which are intended to be acceptable to practitioners of each religion. A question-and-answer section features a spokesperson for each of several religions: Father Ted informs fellow Orthodox Christians how to fast; Rabbi David Wolpe urges the Jew who seeks to follow Law not to lose sight of people, and so forth.

The Beliefnet site also takes advantage of the interactive properties of the Internet in two ways. First, it features, as right-hand columns, letters submitted to each of the many linked subsites. Second, it features (center-front, first "religions" page) a quiz in which the user picks his or her religion, and then answers a series of diagnostic questions about beliefs, obervance, behavior, and so forth. Based on the answers, the user is then told whether he or she is (in the Muslim case) a secular Muslim, spiritual seeker, progressive Muslim, or traditional Muslim. The reader who is classified as a traditional Muslim learns that "the Qur'ân plays a role in your daily life as a Muslim" while the progressive Muslim learns that "you probably interpret Islam historically and might believe that *ijtihad* (individual interpretation of scripture) should be reopened." Among the practices that would classify you as traditional is fasting and praying during Ramadan, considering killing Salman Rushdie, saving sex for marriage, and planning on marrying a Muslim.

One has no idea where these correspondences come from. The idea that ijtihad and everyday use of the Qur'ân would be associated with distinct types of Muslim has little relationship to the social lives of Muslims I know or know of. More interesting, perhaps, is the sense of audience implied by this site. Who would take this quiz? Perhaps the Muslim student in a non-Muslim land who feels a need to identify who he is through one of these available labels? Surely not the fellow who threatens Rushdie in a dark alley (the site's scenario). The quiz also suggests books appropriate for each of the four categories (oddly, the traditionalist is referred to a book decrying the influence of "Islamists" in Cairo—perhaps the real intent of the list is to subvert the categories!).

The other current broadband strategy is a more synthetic New Age theology combined with heavy marketing, best illustrated by the new site SpiritChannel.com (*www.spiritchannel.com/*), which bombards site visitors with a heavy-beat song about "there's only one religion." (The site's founder is Isaac Burton Tigrett, who created the Hard Rock Cafe and the House of Blues.) It pronounces itself a "for-profit" site, marketing "information, data, guidance, entertainment, products and services related to spirituality and health—all via the Internet, traditional media and in three-dimensional locations."

Grafting cyberspace onto traditional rituals, with their own notions of effectiveness, poses new problems of theology and sociology. Consider the Cyber-Seder, which is held somewhere IRL ("in real life") and simulcast on a Web site. In 1998, the "real life" event was held in Lincoln Center in New York City and cybercast on *www.jewmu.com/cyberseder/*. Now, the seder has a formal structure that also allows for variation. In the retelling the story of Exodus, participants ask and receive and answers about the meaning of the foods served and the event celebrated. The 1998 Cyber-Seder was enlarged to include the readings of poetry by Allen Ginsberg, a reading by Lou Reed, and a shofar and clarinet duo (Brasher 2001, 74). Most interesting was the chat room activity that proceeded before, during, and after the seder. Those logged on exchanged tips as to how best to obtain good sound and video feeds, and debated whether they were participants at the seder or merely onlookers. They forwarded the question to the ritual's organizer, who was unable to decide.

Ashley, a Christian engaged to a Jewish man, logged on to the seder in 1998 to learn more about Judaism (Brasher 1001, 72–78). She used the name Sarah in the chat room, implicitly identifying herself as a Jewish woman. She found the cyber-ritual at the same time broadly reaching out to engage non-Jews, through the use of nontraditional (and non-"Jewish") material, and at times excluding, as when some participants on the chat room slipped into Hebrew to discuss the ritual in greater detail. Six months later, she converted to Judaism.

Creole Spaces

If we think about them in real space and time, then we can profit from Jon Anderson's (1999, 43–44) characterization of many religious Web sites as "creole" spaces. Anderson means that these sites, like the populations in the New World mixing Spanish or French with local languages, mediate between older institutions (associations, governments, churches, schools) and a global public. They are both local, responding to needs, fears, and hopes of a particular group of site creators, and global, in their electronic spatial reach.

Daniel Miller and Don Slater (2000) are anthropologists who have studied Internet use in Trinidad. They found that the religious Web sites are both highly local in their concerns, and yet also attempt to "expand back" (2000, 178) into the larger realm that they see themselves as rightly occupying . What do they mean by this? For the religions they studied, adherents see themselves as part of a much larger community than the

Trinidadian one. Trinidad Catholics see the Church as universal, and they have long believed that the common experience of Caribbean peoples makes a regional Catholic theology desirable, something now much more likely to develop through region-wide electronic communication. Hindus on Trinidad see themselves as part of a global network of Hindus, in India, of course, but also in North America, on Fiji, and elsewhere. The Internet makes communication among members of that network vastly easier.

These sites are shaped by very specific, locally grounded networks of communication and influence. The Hindu site is maintained by Sanathan Dharma Maha Sabha, the major Hindu organization in Trinidad. This organization represents the community as under threat from Christians. The major links from the Web site's home page, for example, include texts such as "Jesus Lived in India" and "Hinduism Under Attack." Miller and Slater (2000, 175–176) point out that militant Hindu nationalists, mainly in their North American branches, have actively used the Internet to alert Trinidadians to negative stories about Hinduism, so that they can then negate those stories on their own Trinidad Web site. Internet communication has also instructed Trinidadian Hindus about the differences between their forms of religious life and those found in India, through the decline of caste and the influence of Christianity in the Caribbean. Thus, the site is dynamically located in a network of Hindu nationalism as well as within a network of Trinidadian concerns.

A very different example of the mixing of languages and genres cited by Anderson is presented by MyQuran.com (*www.myquran.com*), an Indonesian site for Muslims with an English title and English phrases. It is part of a MuslimNet Ring, a grouping of sites with links to each other, and its content and links are overwhelming. One can hear an entire Surah of the Qur'ân (on December 20, 2000 it was al-Lail) with RealAudio Player, and link to downloads of other chapters. One can also search the entire Qur'ân in one of 15 languages (although some of the attempts reached not yet working sites). A user can download a call to prayer (adzan) with RealAudio and have a choice among calls from Mecca, or Medina, or one by the late Shaykh Muhammad Rifat of Egypt, or from the Istiqlal mosque in Jakarta.

The site's "eMuamalah" (social affairs) section contains Islamic eCards, an Islamic bookstore associated with Amazon.com, and several networks (*jejaring*), including one for academics. I am a fan of Indonesian Islamic music so I went to that link, where I was offered the chance to download about 50 songs by various religious-oriented Indonesian groups, plus the latest songs by Yusuf Islam (the former Cat Stevens) and links to other Islamic music collections. Each visit to the site also pops up a Hypermart window with an ad unrelated to Islam (during my visit, they were for free E-mail, Amex cards, and the latest U2 song).

This site and others like it are extremely user-friendly in more than one way. They have a modern, secular, even consumerist feel to them. They indicate nothing about a particular religious message or orientation. They serve as a portal in a theological as well as technical sense. They communicate a meaning about tolerance toward religion through their very form.

12   *Pilgrims and Places*

*I*n previous chapters we have examined the religious roles of rituals vis-à-vis doctrines, rites of transition, healing practices, sacrifices, taboos, religious objects, and ways of speaking. All these topics involve religious events; they all *take place* in a particular place and time. Such is true of all religions, but some religions give to specific places a special significance. A religious place may be conceived as an origin point for a prophet or people; as a place where gods or spirits reside; or as a spot where a notable event occurred. Places may be unique (Mecca, Jerusalem) or multiple (Mary's many apparitions), or even rather commonplace (graves). They may be natural (a sacred mountain), or made by humans (a holy city), or supernatural (a vision site).

Religious places may organize life far beyond their boundaries. For those whose religion covers a vast territory, the sacred spots may provide a shared orienting direction and thus a spatial sense of community. Mecca is the most striking example, but so are Jerusalem and Benares or, on a slightly smaller scale, the Ise temple in Japan or the Guadalupe shrine in Mexico. But places may also differentiate people into small communities, each with their own temple or altar or ancestral grave. Graves, in particular, link people to place through their dead: the corpse is where ties of descent meet ties to the land. (Some religious traditions, of course, place relatively little emphasis on places, as with most of the Protestant movements examined in Chapter 11.)

Centers and Directions

*W*e find some general associations between features of the natural geography and features of religions that appear in widely scattered societies: that the gods live in mountains; that centers are more powerful than peripheries; that the cardinal directions determine one's fate. But each religious tradition selects and interprets such general associations in its own terms. Consider the cardinal directions. The apparent movement of the sun across the sky creates a natural east–west axis that people use to orient themselves. (The movement of rivers provides another such axis.) The north–south axis bisects this axis to create four cardinal points. This four-way division of the sky provides a handy scheme to sort out many other features of the universe, giving people a sense of understanding and even control over nature and spirits.

For example, the Zuni Pueblo people of the southwestern United States assign to each cardinal direction a season, type of weather, set of animals, color, and social function (Bunzel 1992; Durkheim and Mauss 1963). North has associated with it the winter wind; the grouse, pelican, crane, and the evergreen oak; the color yellow; war and destruction. Some of these associations have natural bases: northern winds are colder and forceful and appear to bring winter, and the evergreen oak is remarkable for its ability to remain green throughout the winter. But other assignments seem more arbitrary and are the result of classifying the world into sets of fours: the colors blue, red, yellow, and white, each assigned to a direction, form the primary colors plus their fusion into white.

These assignments not only appeal to a human love for ordering the world, they also provide a plan for carrying out certain rituals. For example, along with the animals already mentioned, each direction also has a "prey animal": for the north it is the mountain lion (which is yellow, thus fitting animal to color). If people desire to increase their chances of hunting "northern" animals (say, the grouse), they ask the spirit of the mountain lion for help, who then preys along with them. Zuni also divide their social world according to this scheme. Each direction has assigned to it three clans, each of which is named after one of the cardinal animals. Thus, to the north are the clans named after crane, evergreen oak, and grouse. The clan's name animal is also its totem; the clan members stand in a special relationship to it.

Many societies have narratives in which gods or spirits or the first people journey across the natural landscape. These narratives invest sacred power in that landscape. For the Navajo, for example, one of the very first actions taken by the First People was to conduct the first Blessingway ceremony to make the first house, or hogan. They built it facing east, with each of the four directions pointing to one of the four sacred mountains in the Navajo homeland. The directions themselves are not of great significance; what is important is that the creation story locates cosmic events at specific places in the everyday landscape. The directions hold down the cosmos in the world. Narratives about various gods and events always situate their birthplaces, travels, and battles in specific local spots. They also direct contemporary Navajo people about where they will find the correct plants or objects to perform different healing or purifying rituals (McPherson 1992).

The core Navajo ceremonial, Blessingway, contains speeches by gods in which details about each sacred mountain are recited (Gill 1981). The Holy People themselves lived in specific earthly places. For the First Woman the people "made a nice trail leading south from the entrance of First Man's hogan, and along the side of Huerfano Mountain they prepared a nice place for her." Changing Woman orders the people: "at the base of this Huerfano Mountain on the west side you will build a hogan for me, my children, my grandchildren, leaving the entrance toward the west." "At the base of Mount Taylor there is a place called Tree Circle, where Rock Crystal Talking God happened to live." And so on: mythic events, repeated in Navajo ceremonials, can also be located in the everyday world. (One can then understand the vehemence with which Navajo oppose plans to mine ores in the mountains or build new towns along the slopes.)

Dimensions of Pilgrimage

Sacred places also draw people to them as visitors or, especially, as pilgrims, and here we turn to pilgrimage as a type of religious practice. Through the attitudes, ideas, and practices of the visitor one gains a deeper sense of how the place is meaningful.

We can define pilgrimage as travel to a sacred spot for an act of religious devotion. Depending on the attitude and intention of the individual, a wide range of actions might be pilgrimages, from a visit to your grandparents' graves, to a trip to see the Liberty Bell in Philadelphia, to a visit to the Grand Canyon. If a sense of awe and of a reality that transcends the everyday makes an experience "religious," then these events could be considered pilgrimages. But our focus here is on events that are explicitly designated as pilgrimages within the broader context of a religious movement or institution.

Let us consider the various dimensions of a pilgrimage (compare Turner 1974). One might ask, first: What is the primary purpose of the pilgrimage? (There may be a host of secondary reasons, ranging from status-seeking to lunacy, that fall outside the religious domain.) These primary, explicit reasons include general obligations and individual needs. Pilgrims may be responding to a god's command, as when Muslims carry out the pilgrimage to Mecca. Or they may have a specific individual purpose, such as fulfilling a vow or seeking a cure. They may address a more diffuse set of spiritual needs without being commanded or even recommended by religious authorities. Pilgrimages to sites of Marian apparitions fit in several of these categories: people may travel to Lourdes to seek a cure, or to refresh their spiritual lives, or to fulfill a vow made when ill.

Second: Is the primary emphasis the journey itself, or reaching a particular place? We often assume that pilgrimages are usually about going somewhere and then returning, and certainly this is uppermost in most pilgrims' minds when they set out for Mecca, or for Santiago de Compostella in Spain, or for Benares along the Ganges in India. And yet the journey may also be valued, either explicitly within the religious tradition or as part of the broader experience. As the Shikoku pilgrimage described later shows, in some cases the journey may be emphasized, and no particular spot prescribed as the goal. In Western literary traditions that reach back at least to Bunyan and Dante, the pilgrims' wanderings, albeit toward a particular destination, served as an allegory for personal growth and the passage through life. The *Canterbury Tales* concern pilgrims to Canterbury Cathedral in Kent, southeastern England, but are really about the journey itself. Or consider the following from Rabbi Abraham Heschel:

Faith is not the clinging to a shrine but an endless pilgrimage of the heart.

The goal of some pilgrimages contains a mini-pilgrimage within it. As we shall see, the Islamic pilgrimage hurries the pilgrim around the Ka'ba, down the road to 'Arafat, back to Mina and then to Mecca, around the Ka'ba again, and then home. What the pilgrimage is really about is commemoration of Muhammad's actions, not the visit to the holy places, which, unlike the pilgrimage proper, can take place at any time of the year. Some Christian shrines are devoted to the stations of the cross, the path undertaken by Christ that led to his crucifixion, and thus are representations of his own journey.

Finally we should ask about the topography of sacred places. Where is the place located—in the center of a city, or on the periphery of human settlement—and what significance does the location have? How did the pilgrim's goal come to be a sacred place? Consider the classic urban sacred places: the Hindu temples along the banks of the Ganges in crowded Benares city, Mecca at the crossroads of Arabian trade, Jerusalem, and Rome. These places are centers for great institutions: temples, mosques, churches. From these sites come centralized and centralizing claims to authority and knowledge, conjoined with trade and politics.

One also finds sacred places located in remote spots: places where Mary appears to schoolchildren, temples to female Hindu deities, monasteries, centers for Sufi learning, places for lone Japanese pilgrims to wander, forests where Buddhist monks meditate in isolation. These places are sites for marginality: meditating, protecting, reassuring those who are not in power, warning those who are. The distinction between centers of power and its margins is often replicated in the places where pilgrims gather and the faithful worship. (On a small scale, this center/periphery distinction appears in the opposition of parish church/isolated shrine in the Nansa valley in Spain discussed in Chapter 9.)

Let us gain a better understanding of variation across pilgrimages by looking more closely at three pilgrimage traditions: first the Islamic pilgrimage, the hajj, for an extended analysis; then two other examples, the Japanese pilgrimage around the island of Shikoku and the pilgrimages by Hindus to temples in Benares.

The Pilgrimage to Mecca

*E*ach year during the pilgrimage month of the Islamic lunar calendar, more than a million Muslims from throughout the world gather in the holy places in and around Mecca. These men and women have traveled to Mecca to carry out their religious obligation to make the pilgrimage. All the pilgrims must carry out a series of very specific actions, moving and worshiping together, before completing their task and returning home. The principal goal of the pilgrimage is to obey God's commands, as they were made clear to humans through his messenger, Muhammad.

Following the Footsteps of Muhammad

We have already seen that Muslims consider the Qur'ân to be God's major gift to humans, and in this respect the Qur'ân's role is similar to that of the Torah for Jews and that of Christ for Christians. But Muslims also consider as divinely inspired the actions of the Prophet Muhammad—not because he was divine himself, but because he spoke and acted as God's messenger. The collection of reports about his statements and actions are called the "hadith." These reports supplement the Qur'ân as the second basic source for guidance and law in the Muslim community. Much of Islamic ritual as well as everyday life is based on what Muhammad did as contained in these reports, and it is in this way that Muslims developed the pilgrimage, or hajj.

The pilgrimage is meaningful for Muslims in the first place as a repetition and commemoration of the Prophet's actions, "following in his footsteps," as many returned pilgrims said to me. But it was also dictated by God in his revelations to Muhammad. Several years after Muhammad and his followers had fled from Mecca to Medina to escape persecution, came the first revelation concerning the pilgrimage, quoted in the last chapter of the Qur'ân:

The first House established for the people
was that at Mecca, a place holy, and a guidance to all beings.
Therein are clear signs—the station of Abraham,
and whosoever enters it is in security.
It is the duty of all men towards God to come
to the House a pilgrim, if he is able to make his way there.
(Qur'ân 3:90–92)

The house mentioned in this passage is the large cubic structure called the "Ka'ba," which is draped in gold-bordered black silk cloth. The Ka'ba is the centerpoint of the religious world for Muslims. It is toward the Ka'ba that Muslims worship five times daily, and it is around the Ka'ba that they walk when they make the pilgrimage.

In Islamic tradition the Ka'ba dates back to the prophet Abraham, who journeyed to Mecca with his son, Ishmael, and Hagar, Ishmael's mother. (In the Islamic version of the sacrificial trial of Abraham, it was Ishmael, not Isaac, whom he was ordered to sacrifice.) Abraham built the Ka'ba on God's command. The angel Gabriel then brought down a black stone to place in its corner. The stone, it is said, was white, but turned black on contact with the sinful world.

By the seventh century C.E. Mecca had become a trading center in the Arabian peninsula, and it was here where Muhammad was born, grew up, and received his first revelations. His triumphant return to Mecca from Medina marked the victory of Islam over the polytheistic Meccan elites, and his first pilgrimage, in 632, the year of his death, became the model for all pilgrimages since (Peters 1994).

Making the pilgrimage is one of the five ritual obligations, or *rukns* (pillars), of Islam. The pilgrimage has always attracted Muslims from throughout the world, but the development of steamship travel in the nineteenth century and air travel in the twentieth has led to a boom in pilgrimage activity. By the mid–twentieth century about 30,000 people made the journey each year; today about 2 million pilgrims, from the 60 or more countries with sizable Muslim communities, arrive in Mecca each year. Pilgrims come from near and far: the largest delegations are from Nigeria, Pakistan, Turkey, and Yemen, and then Iran, Indonesia, and Iraq. Some pilgrims stay on to study and teach; most return home bringing new ideas and trade goods. Islam was founded by a trader amid vast networks of desert caravans; the contemporary pilgrimage enlarges those networks of trade and communication to the scale of the entire world.

Precisely because these holy cities occupy such a central place in the Muslim popular imagination, they have sometimes been the targets of political movements. During the 1979 pilgrimage, an armed group seized control of Mecca's Grand Mosque and broadcast denunciations of the Saudi government over a citywide loudspeaker system. Iranian anti-American demonstrations at Medina in 1982 led to arrests and revived debates about whether religion and politics could legitimately be separated in Islam. Since then the Saudi government has prohibited delegations from making the pilgrimage when they feared political disturbances (or health risks, as in the 1996 ban on Nigerians during an epidemic in Nigeria).

Although the details of the hajj are taken one by one from accounts of that first pilgrimage, the steps can be sorted into the three stages of rites of transition that were discussed in Chapter 4. Indeed, Victor Turner (1974, 182) argues that in larger-scale societies pilgrimages perform some of the same social functions that are filled by initiation rituals in smaller-scale societies, in providing the place for a religious experience outside the bounds of everyday social life. The pilgrim separates himself or herself from ordinary social life, enters a liminal stage in which distinctive everyday identities are exchanged for the shared identity of the pilgrim, and then returns to the social world. Each transition point is marked by clear religious duties.

Rites of Separation

Although a Muslim may visit the holy places in Mecca and Medina at any time during the year, the pilgrimage itself may be performed only on the eighth, ninth, and tenth days of the last month of the Islamic lunar calendar—the pilgrimage month, Dhu'l-Hijja. (Because the lunar year is 11 days shorter than the solar year, the pilgrimage season cycles back through the solar year.) Unlike pilgrimages made by Christians, Jews, or Hindus to their holy cities, the hajj is a series of ritual actions performed together, simultaneously, by all the Muslim pilgrims for that year (Ruthven 1984, 23–48).

Weeks or even months before these key days, pilgrims have been gathering and departing from villages, towns, and cities all over the world. In Indonesia, as in many other countries with large Muslim populations, each group receives an official send-off from a local government official. As recently as two generations ago, departing pilgrims from the Gayo highlands received a different kind of send-off. They were fed at a ritual during which prayers for the dead were recited on their behalf because most who made the journey were older, and many would not survive the two- or three-month sea voyage. The ritual was held before they left because otherwise they would not receive one.

Travel, whether by land, sea, or air, is for much of the way a secular affair. Only when approaching the port or airfield of Jiddah must pilgrims take steps to enter the state of consecration, or *ihram*. Each pilgrim announces his or her intention to undertake the pilgrimage, renounces shaving, cutting the hair, and sexual intercourse, and changes clothes. The new pilgrim's clothing consists of identical, simple, white seamless garments. Men leave their heads uncovered, and women must not have cloth touching their faces. Some pilgrims even ride roofless buses once they approach Mecca. Each of these measures maintains an unbroken physical link between the pilgrim's head and God, and signals his or her surrender to God.

Moving in the Liminal State

Wearing identical clothing, renouncing normal relationships to their bodies, and concentrating their lives on worshiping God defines the pilgrim's position during the days of pilgrimage. In the liminal state, between their previous lives of various occupations, nationalities, wealth, and status, and their future lives as returned pilgrims, these men and women live and move as equals, sharing some rudimentary Arabic, simple accommodations (for most pilgrims, anyway), and the same daily objectives.

The clothes mark the fact that all pilgrims are religiously equal. As Muhammad's grandson Husayn stated, "The pilgrim offers himself to God as a beggar." Pilgrims mingle with one another even while onboard ship or plane as pilgrims, leaving ordinary social status aside.

Once in Arabia they gather in groups by country and are led through the pilgrimage steps by a group leader, usually someone from their country. For many pilgrims this is their first international experience, rubbing shoulders with others whose language they cannot understand. Arabic prayers and a few short greetings are usually the only form of verbal communication across these groups. Even the American Black Muslim leader Malcolm X (1973, 339) was shocked by this universalism, as he wrote in a public letter to his mosque in Harlem. "For the past week, I have been utterly speechless and spellbound by the graciousness I see displayed all around me by people *of all colors.*"

Pilgrims arrive steadily at Mecca. As they do, they make seven lefthand circles (*tawaf*) around the Ka'ba. Indeed, the root meaning of *hajj* is "to describe a circle." Huge masses of pilgrims move slowly around the silk-draped structure. Each tries to touch or kiss the black stone set into its eastern corner. The Iranian scholar Ali Shariati (1977, 31) described the experience of the tawaf as that of "a small stream merging with a big river. . . . Suddenly, you find yourself floating and carried on by this flood. You have become part of this universal system. Circumambulating . . . Allah, you will soon forget yourself."

The Ka'ba already served as a holy site before Islam, but its guardian was the deity Hubal, whose statue was kept inside the structure. Many other deities were worshiped as well, and the circumambulation was part of worship. Muhammad retained this practice and the veneration of the black stone when he undertook the first pilgrimage, and his followers, though surprised that he did so given the stone's association with paganism, followed suit. The rigorous logic of following the Prophet's actions won out, here as elsewhere.

After the tawaf the pilgrim does the *sa'y,* "running," which does indeed consist of simply running (or, for the older, walking) back and forth, seven times, along a street in Mecca. The running commemorates the time when Hagar was abandoned under a tree at Mecca by Abraham. When her food and water ran out she began to run wildly between two high points, pleading with God for help. When Ishmael raised his hand, there was a well, which became known as the well of Zamzam. The well marked the spot where Mecca was then built. Pilgrims collect water from the Zamzam well and

Major rituals and places of the **hajj.** (COURTESY OF RICHARD T. ANTOUN, *MUSLIM PREACHER IN THE MODERN WORLD,* p. 173.)

bring it home with them; often diluted with rainwater, it will be used to heal or bless others. The running covers about two miles, and some pilgrims must be pushed in wheelchairs.

The circumambulation, also called the *'umra,* is sometimes performed separately out of season as the "little hajj." Travel agencies throughout the Muslim world offer umra packages—a Muslim may travel to Saudia Arabia at any time of year, circumambulate the Ka'ba, visit the holy sites, and return home.

The Hajj Proper

Pilgrims then begin the events that constitute the pilgrimage proper, the events that are performed only on the prescribed days. They must travel to the plain of 'Arafat by sunrise on the ninth day of the month. It is at 'Arafat, a barren plain about two miles from Mecca, where Adam and Eve were reunited after their expulsion from heaven. Here, too, Muhammad delivered his final sermon in 632, in which he set out most of the details of the hajj. A vast tent city is erected on this plain on the days before to the ninth, and there the pilgrims are assigned quarters.

At 'Arafat the pilgrims spend the ninth day in prayer and meditation, gathering around the Mount of Mercy at the edge of the plain. After performing the midafternoon worship, the millions gathered together stand, awaiting sunset, shouting cries of "God is great." This standing (*wuquf*) is the central event of the hajj proper. The special status enjoyed by this rather unspectacular (relative to the tawaf that precedes it and the sacrifices to follow) event comes from its role in replicating Muhammad's final sermon, and from the shared sense pilgrims derive from it of showing humility before God.

Pilgrims then disperse and return toward Mecca, stopping to spend the night in the city of Muzdalifa, where they are to rid themselves of all resentments toward others. There, too, they collect pebbles, which they use the next day to throw at three pillars near Mina, on the return road to Mecca. This *rajm*, or stoning, of the statues is understood to be a stoning of devils. No mention is made of it in the Qur'ân; as with the veneration of the black stone in the Ka'ba, it is performed solely because Muhammad did it on his pilgrimage. As interpreted by most participants, it commemorates Abraham's resoluteness to obey God, for it was on this spot that he prepared to carry out God's command to him to sacrifice his son. The devil appeared to Abraham, and tried to instill doubt in his heart about the sacrifice. Abraham stoned the devil until he fled. After the crowding and rushing of the previous two days the stoning also undoubtedly releases tensions. Some commentators have harnessed the energies visible during the stoning to religious mission; Ali Shariati urged pilgrims to think of the pebbles as bullets used to kill one's enemies.

Pilgrims then carry out a sacrifice in memory of Abraham's submission to God's will. Usually they buy a goat on the spot and arrange to have its throat cut. The meat is distributed to the poor, much of it immediately frozen on the spot by Saudi authorities. The day after this event is called the *yaum an-nahr,* or day of sacrifice, and, as we noted in Chapter 10, it is celebrated throughout the Muslim world by similar sacrifices. The pilgrimage is thus both a duty for all Muslims and the occasion for a worldwide ritual observance.

Reintegration to Normal Life

The pilgrimage proper is complete at this point, and the pilgrims gradually make the return to normal social status. They begin by cutting some of their hair. Women snip off just a bit, but men often have their heads shaved. Now all prohibitions are lifted except for that on sexual intercourse. Pilgrims return to Mecca, perform another circumambulation of the Ka'ba, collect Zamzam well water for the return trip, and now can again engage in sexual intercourse. They are urged to spend several days in "eating, drinking, and sensual pleasure." This urging emphasizes that the pilgrims are now leaving the state of consecration and returning to normal society—the rite of passage has ended.

Those pilgrims who return home immediately find themselves enjoying a new status, that of hajji (male) or hajjiyah (female), someone who has made the pilgrimage and returned to society. Many now wear white for everyday activities or when they attend the mosque to signal this new status. Their status may lead to other achievements: they are probably looked on with greater favor by their local bank; they may be chosen for office. They certainly have much to tell about from their journey. But they also enjoy a sense of religious accomplishment, having fulfilled the most difficult of God's commands.

How Is It Meaningful?

Ordinary Muslims undertake the pilgrimage for a variety of reasons—they are obeying a divine command; they are fulfilling a duty expected of them socially; they may be advancing their own social status. But is this all we can say? In what ways is the pilgrimage with its many component actions meaningful?

The pilgrimage presents a challenge to our usual ideas of the meaning of a religious act. It is not performed with a separate goal in mind, such as atonement or cleansing. The religious historical event that is commemorated in each segment of the ritual is sometimes but not always clear. The only overall, uniting idea of the pilgrimage is that it is made up of actions that were performed by Muhammad on his first (and only) pilgrimage.

Scholars do suggest parallels with earlier rites, either those performed on the same spot as a contemporary ritual and taken over by Muhammad, or parallel rituals within the Semitic ritual tradition that were adopted by Muhammad as properly monotheistic. For example, the wuquf, or "standing," was part of earlier Hebrew practice. Muhammad made the entire plain of 'Arafat a place of standing before God. The 'umra was originally a sacrifice of firstborn livestock and was held in the early spring, much as with Passover, in the month of Rajab (at that time the lunar calendar was made concordant with the solar, so that Rajab always occurred in the spring). The sacrifice was carried out at the Ka'ba. As late as the twelfth century C.E., local Muslims were still carrying out this older sacrificial 'umra in the month of Rajab.

In fact, although the 'umra is thought of as a little hajj, 'umra and hajj were once distinct events. The essence of the 'umra is the tawaf, the circumambulation of the Ka'ba, while the essence of the hajj is the standing before God at 'Arafat. In origins, the one is sacrificial, the other is an act of submission to God. Muhammad then tied them together in one long series of events.

This kind of explanation may provide a historical account for why certain events became part of the overall pilgrimage. They do not account for the meaning of the rite for those people who take part in it. Muslim commentators have offered several broad lines of interpretation.

One interpretation links the performance of the hajj to the overall meaning of Islam as *surrender*. According to the important twelfth-century theologian Al-Ghazali, devo-

Man returned from the pilgrimage proudly displays his new clothing, Isak, Sumatra. (COURTESY OF J. BOWEN.)

tion to God demands self-abnegation, surrender to his will. Therefore, God has imposed on the Muslim actions that in themselves have no emotional or intellectual appeal, such as the running back and forth between two points, or sa'y.

A second interpretation identifies symbolic or iconic meanings for each individual place or object that the pilgrim encounters. The Ka'ba is the House of the Lord. You will meet God in a seamless shroud, so you meet him today wearing such garments. The tawaf resembles the movement of angels that encircle the Throne of God, which itself is situated directly above the Ka'ba in heaven. Ali Shariati (1977) sees the "running" as standing for purposeful activity on the earth.

A third line of interpretation seems to me to be closest to the ways in which pilgrims themselves interpret their experience. This approach locates meaning not in the events but in their historicity, as commemorations of past events. The running commemorates the moment when Hagar was looking for water for Ishmael and Gabriel created the Zamzam well. The stoning marks the moment when Abraham stoned the devil. The sacrifice commemorates Abraham's willingness to sacrifice his son. At the very least, every event commemorates Muhammad's pilgrimage—and this insight returns us to a key element of Islam, that practices and texts constantly refer back to the life of the Prophet for their authenticity.

And what is the specific goal of the pilgrimage? Despite the fact that worship is always conducted facing the Ka'ba in Mecca, and that "Mecca" has become a shorthand for a central place or goal, in fact the central event in the pilgrimage, the standing at 'Arafat, takes place outside Mecca itself, as does the sacrifice, both in places that are virtually uninhabited during the remainder of the year. Within the hajj framework, for instance, the pilgrim is never still, but is hurried around the Ka'ba, down the road to 'Arafat, back to Mina and then to Mecca, around the Ka'ba again, and then home. What the pilgrimage is really about is commemoration of Muhammad's actions, not the visit to the holy places (which, one should again note, can take place at any time of the year).

Pilgrims expand this sense of historicity from particular commemorations to a more diffuse sense of being in the place where their religion was born, being "at the source." "Everywhere," writes the Pakistani religious leader al-Maudûdî of the typical pilgrim, "he sees the relics of those who lived God, and sacrificed their lives for His sake. Every grain of sand witnesses the glory and grandeur of Islam, and every piece of stone declares: 'This is the land where Islam took birth, and whence God's word rose high'" (quoted in Cragg 1980, 60). As the leader of U.S. Muslims Waris Deen Muhammad said in conversations in St. Louis in 1996, "on the pilgrimage you come near to God; you are visiting Him."

Contrasts in Pilgrimage from Japan and India

*T*he hajj has certain distinctive features that no other pilgrimage tradition shares completely: its script dictated by Muhammad, the temporal limitations on its performance, its decidedly worldwide quality. Two other examples, from Japan and India, illustrate other ways that pilgrimages are constructed and understood, other ways that elements of journey and place, and a variety of motives and purposes, can be combined.

Circling Shikoku

Each year more than a thousand Japanese pilgrims travel around the island of Shikoku in southwest Japan (Reader 1991, 112–116; Statler 1984). The trip takes the pilgrim by many temples and shrines, where requests can be made and spirits venerated. In a society noted for its group characteristics this pilgrimage is highly individualistic: the lone pilgrim may begin anywhere on the island and stop where he or she wishes, for whatever reasons and with whatever goals in mind that she or he might have. Purposes include healing and self-discovery; the emphasis is on journey over goal, and the place itself is very peripheral to Japanese society.

This pilgrimage grew out of a particular movement within Japanese Buddhism called Shingon. The founder of Shingon Buddhism, who also invented the Japanese writing system, was named Kukai, called after death Kobo Daishi (774–835 C.E.). In China he had studied the teachings of Gautama Buddha pertaining to the Buddha Dainichi, who emphasizes the source of salvation to be found inside every man and woman (and the same Sun Buddha who was made the center of the state cult). Salvation may be achieved in this world, taught Kobo Daishi. But the path to salvation is less a matter of accumulating merit than finding an individual path to inner awareness of the true nature of the world.

Shingon Buddhism made ample use of methods for developing awareness that evolved in India and Tibet within tantric Buddhism, whose methods are designed to help an individual better control his or her mind. The writings about these methods were called *tantra,* hence the name for the practices taken together. Some of these practices involved chanting single syllables, called *mantras,* meaning literally, "true word"; meditation; and sexual union. This last practice led rulers to discourage or even persecute tantric groups; but the teachings spread to China, where they became known as *Chen-yen,* the Chinese translation of *mantra,* and this name was carried with the practices to Japan, where it was pronounced *Shingon.*

Kobo Daishi taught that truth had to be reached through inner concentration; it could not be attained through study. (His teachings thus reinforced the general Mahayana Buddhist point that anyone, not just scholars or monks, can achieve salvation.) One of his verses speaks of the ultimate "darkness" lying at the end of study:

Unknowable, unknowable, it is completely unknowable;
about the Buddha and the non-Buddhists, there are
    millions of scrolls.
Dark, dark, it is very dark;
of the Way that is spoken there are many paths.

What is left, when the copying and chanting of scriptures stop?
No one knows, No one knows, and I too do not know.
Though they consider and speculate, even the wise do not know.

The other side of this darkness is the hope that through meditation and concentration one can find enlightenment, find the Buddha-nature that is in everyone, within one's own lifetime. Kobo Daishi personified this path to enlightenment; his legends tell of him covering Japan with temples and shrines and practicing an austere life of meditating and traveling. On the Shikoku pilgrimage the pilgrim not only reenacts part of Kobo Daishi's life, he is also accompanied by Kobo Daishi.

The pilgrimage takes the pilgrim to 88 temples devoted to Buddhist worship, as well as to unofficial places for Buddhist worship and many other shrines to spirits. The

Pilgrims resting near Kyoto, Japan. (COURTESY OF JOHN RENARD.)

thousand-mile journey around the island's circumference, stopping at each official temple along the way, takes about two months for the healthy and longer for men and women who are ill. The pilgrimage is always made clockwise. One may begin anywhere and stop when one has reached the initial point, closing the circle. The circle has no beginning or end (although the temples are numbered 1 through 88), making the circuit the point of the pilgrimage. The pilgrim is fed and housed in the temples and receives alms from people he or she passes on the way. About a thousand people each year make the journey on foot; many thousands more take two-week package bus tours or travel by train or car. Others travel to the island intermittently, eventually visiting all the temples.

Because the saint Kobo Daishi accompanies each pilgrim, alms given to the pilgrims generate merit for the givers. A gift made to a pilgrim is a gift made to the saint. Indeed, the pilgrim, embodies some of Kobo Daishi's saintly qualities in his physical contact, so that people will ask a pilgrim to lie down on their bedclothes so as to physically bless them. (The pilgrim is a kind of walking, temporary relic of the saint.)

But the purpose of making the pilgrimage is not to earn merit but to purify and better understand oneself. "The path is the goal itself." Pilgrims give a variety of reasons for making the arduous journey, but they all have to do with self-improvement. Many are seeking better physical or mental health, either from the Daishi, or from specific deities enshrined at temples along the way. The nature of the ailments has changed. As one priest put it: "In the old days many who were ill made the pilgrimage; lepers, for instance, were numerous along the path. [Indeed, some came to die on the journey.] Nowadays the physically ill go to hospitals. But these are times of strain and mental illness, and so today the benefits of pilgrimage are greater than ever." Today victims of corporate down-sizing are more likely to be found on the path. One such middle-aged former computer management worker made the journey in 1996 to decide what to do after being fired. He made the journey relatively quickly, in 32 days, and resolved during his walking to spend more time with his family (Pollack 1996).

Like the Muslim pilgrim, the person who circles Shikoku is temporarily leaving this world for a liminal world. Also like the pilgrim on hajj, he or she wears the white garments that serve as burial shrouds, signifying both a willingness to die on a pilgrimage and a temporary renouncing of the normal world.

But the elements of the two pilgrimages also point up important, general contrasts in the two religious traditions. Notice how "circling Shikoku" differs from "circumambulating the Ka'ba." The Islamic practice is prescribed, collective, and fixed on a center point that lies directly under heaven itself. The Japanese practice is optional, individualistic, and has no center, or even starting and ending points. As a lesson in how wrong we would be to generalize from supposed facts about a culture to its religion, ponder the highly individualistic Shikoku pilgrimage in a Japan known for its orientation to the corporate group, and contrast it with the highly collective Islamic pilgrimage in an Arabia known for its argumentative style and qualities of schism and fission.

Indeed, it may be precisely because Japan is as society- and group-oriented as it is that individualistic religious practices emerge as essential to human spiritual growth. Not that these practices are asocial—the pilgrim often makes his journey to become a better member of society. But they do respond to a value of self-cultivation that suffuses all Japanese religions, old and new. The ascetic, who undergoes severe deprivations to purify himself and to find merit and spiritual power, is a central figure in the Japanese popular imagination. Monks at a Buddhist center near Kyoto practice a thousand-day austerity, each of those days making a 20-mile journey, living on little food, and depriving himself of sleep. The ordeal ends in a nine-day total fast during which he must refrain from sleep entirely. Having drawn near to death, the ascetic has thrown off his former self and become one with the Buddha figure Fudo. Many ordinary Japanese practice lesser austerities, such as bathing in ice water or fasting. Waterfalls located along the pilgrimage routes are favorite places for cold baths; these baths purify the pilgrim and augment his or her spiritual powers (Reader 1991, 116–128).

Bathing at Benares

If the Japanese pilgrimage stresses self-discovery on a journey as a counterpoint to a collectivist everyday sociability, its Hindu equivalent, similar in many respects, emphasizes multiple power-bringing visits to temples. The pilgrim's goal is to have "exchanged vision" (darshan) with the gods many times in many places. Pilgrimage in India thus involves multiple goals strung out along a journey. Each site is called a "crossing place, ford" (tîrtha) to somewhere beyond; a pilgrimage is tîrthayâtrâ, journey to a ford (Fuller 1992, 204–223).

The prototypical goal is Benares, in north central India (Eck 1982). Called by Indians "Kâshî," the City of Light, Benares lies alongside the Ganges, a river said to have descended from heaven to earth. More than 70 landings, or *ghâts,* line its banks, some containing temples to Shiva, who makes Benares his earthly home. Benares has always been an earthly crossing, the place where the old northern Indian trade route crossed the river Ganges. As with other places of pilgrimage, it is also a spiritual ford, where earth and heaven meet. Here the dead may be assisted in crossing over the Ganges to the condition of *moksha,* liberation from rebirth, the ultimate goal of the Hindu. Here, too, the gods may descend from heaven to earth. Shiva lives in the city's many temples but also in its ground and buildings: "The very stones of Kâshî are Shiva," goes the popular saying.

The gods descend and pilgrims cross at many other fords, throughout India. Of the thousands of places where Shiva, or the hero Rama, or the goddess Durga have emerged to split rocks or have crushed enemies, a few cities are particularly favored. Some are associated with Rama, and in particular his capital at Ayodhya (the recent political importance of which we consider in Chapter 15). Others, including several associated with Krishna, are on mountains; still others mark the four corners of India.

Benares is the most widely acclaimed of all, however. To many Hindus it is the center of the universe (as is Jerusalem to some Christians, Mecca to some Muslims, Beijing to some Chinese)—located directly under the heavens. Benares also encapsulates worship in India: temples from other parts of India, from the Himalayas to the southern tip of the subcontinent, have replicas in Benares. One may visit these temples and exchange vision with their deities without leaving the city. The city has absorbed their power. And in one new temple the devotion is of Mother India, Bharat Mata, represented in the form of a relief map inside the temple where the image would usually be. The map shows the major pilgrimage places, which pilgrims can view (and "exchange vision" with) all at once! Benares is itself replicated elsewhere: hundreds of temples called "Shiva Kâshî" are scattered throughout India, and at each one a pilgrim or other worshiper exchanges vision with Shiva (Fuller 1992, 208–209).

Our notion of "goal" or "site" thus has to be rethought for Benares: deities are here, in this city, but they are also elsewhere—gods, and God, the spiritual force behind all the gods—is indeed everywhere. (One pilgrim, longing for the black stone dedicated to Shiva near his village home, remarked: "I miss God.") Nor does any deity command pilgrims to visit Benares.

To understand pilgrims' purposes we must return to the way in which Hindus approach the image of a deity. Contact between the deity and the worshiper is exchanged most powerfully through the eyes, through seeing or darshan. When Hindus go to the temple, writes Diana Eck (1982, 20), they do not say "I am going to worship" but "I am going for darshan." And in the temple, in the city, the Hindu sees many images, all of which act as lenses through which he or she can perceive divinity. (Recall the many-in-one quality of sacred images that we discussed in Chapter 9.)

When Hindus travel on a pilgrimage they are engaged in "sacred sight-seeing," a rich process of exchanging vision with deities—and with sacred places themselves. For places are dwelt in by deities, as Benares is by Shiva, so by "taking in" the city's sites they are also "taking in" Shiva himself.

Benares also attracts pilgrims to bathe in its particularly sacred waters and to cremate their dead. The variety of alternative activities and places for worship distinguishes the

Benares pilgrimage from the highly prescribed and channeled activities of pilgrims to Mecca, and the focus on the journey itself for pilgrims around Shikoku.

The pilgrim's first duty is to bathe in the river on one of its many landings. Pilgrims bathe in the Ganges to partake of its purifying powers, brown and replete with ashes and bacteria though it is. Indeed, usually they take the popular "Five Fords" trip along the riverfront, where they bathe at each of five landings, or *ghâts*. At each stop, the pilgrim recites a statement of intention, that he or she is undertaking this pilgrimage, and if the pilgrimage is made to fulfill a vow or with a goal in mind (which is not necessary) a statement to this effect is added, such as, "I am making this pilgrimage in hope of bearing a son." Each stop has stories of kings and gods associated with it, and nearby are temples, or phallic linga statues devoted to Shiva, or even a mosque (Eck 1982, 211–251).

The last bath is taken at the landing of Manikarnikâ, at the center of the three-mile-long waterfront. This bath is the most important. The site has a cremation ground and a large sacred well nearby. Shiva is in the temple, but Vishnu built the well as the world's very first tîrtha. And a manifestation of the Goddess, or Devi, here called "Devi of Manikarni," guards the well. This site is called the "burning landing" because when seen from the river one sees the plumes of flames from the crematorium located among the temples.

Those who die in Benares are cremated by the Ganges and their ashes are scattered over the waters. Some who die elsewhere have their ashes brought, or even mailed, to Benares. When one's ashes lie on the Ganges, one's spirit crosses over from earth to liberation. But failing this, pilgrims will say prayers for the dead, offering balls of rice while saying their names. These rites ensure that the ancestors will dwell in heaven. So important are these rites that when long-lost ashes from the cremation of Mohandas K. Gandhi's body were discovered nearly a half-century after the event, they were carried to the Ganges to be poured into the waters (Burns 1997).

Newly arrived corpses are placed by the river's edge before being dipped into its waters for their final bath and then hoisted onto the funeral pyre. The eldest son circumambulates the pyre, lights it, and when the burning is finished, walks away without looking back. Members of an untouchable caste in charge of the cremation ground throw the ashes into the river, where they are gradually carried downstream.

But just as Shiva is present in many places, so are there other tîrtha that can claim the same effectiveness and power as can Benares. Unlike, say, Jerusalem or Mecca, no one spot in India can claim unique attraction. Temples to Shiva elsewhere are just as suitable as places to worship him as is his Benares temple—but those other temples are likely to exhibit pictures of Benares, attesting to the Ganges site's quality as the prototype.

The religious importance of seeing sacred places and images helps us understand why a rapid bus tour of a large number of sites would be a heightened religious experience for Hindus and not just a way to be the active tourist. Pilgrimage is the major reason Hindus travel, and they do so by the millions every year, on foot, by bus, or by train. They value the journey itself: joining others in travel, making merit by giving alms, "seeing" (darshan) many deities, getting away from normal routines, and experiencing another realm—both another part of the country and a glimpse into the beyond.

Hardship may itself be felt as proof of merit earned through the journey, even if not explicitly sought out.

Or pilgrims may choose a bus tour that, without the hardship of journeying on foot, offers a greater number of chances for darshan with deities. The anthropologist Ann Grodzins Gold (1988, 262–298) traveled by bus with a group of pilgrims from north-western India to the eastern coast of Orissa. The pilgrims were from different castes, and came from town and village settings. The villagers included Brahmans (the order, or varna, associated with the priesthood), Rajputs (traditionally a warrior caste and of the second-ranking Kshatriya order), and people from farming, gardening, and other mis-cellaneous castes. The pilgrimage did not erase these distinctions; indeed, the castes stayed apart; "the fact that we were sharing a pilgrimage did not act as a leveler of rank" (Gold 1988, 269).

On the road, pilgrims sang songs about the deities Ganesha and Rama and about the Sun King, from whom a woman in the song takes darshan each morning. They stopped at one site after another. When reaching a pilgrimage place, a *tîrthayâtrâ*, they would bathe in the waters, view the images in the temples, make gifts to priests and beggars, and occasionally perform a short offering ritual. They traversed the country where Lord Krishna had spent his childhood and observed darshan tableaux of his babyhood. They made a whirlwind tour of Benares's many temples, which left a colorful blur in their minds. The deepest and most favorable impression was made by the sea. "These Hindus had seen countless icons in their lives," remarks Gold (1988, 284) after one pilgrim, emerging from the famed temple at Puri, said with a shrug that "Well, God is God." But, she continues, they had seen "only one sea."

What did the pilgrimage mean to them? None of Gold's fellow pilgrims thought that bathing in sacred waters would cleanse them of bad deeds. Rather, and in a more diffuse way, the entire experience of getting out of everyday routines, taking many powerful darshans of gods, enduring the hardships of the road, and giving alms to beggars would be good for the soul. Hitting the road and seeing the gods lightens the pilgrim of goods and attachments and concerns, bringing her or him nearer to "the deity within himself." Approaching one's inner divinity prepares oneself for the moment, perhaps in some future life, when one will finally attain release or liberation—*moksha*. "Sweeping the road ahead," suggested one widow.

While some pilgrims thought that pilgrimages causally improve one's chances of eventually achieving moksha, others were more skeptical. The differences of opinion resembled the debates we have studied among Christians and Muslims about whether rituals can change God's mind. One pilgrim told Gold (1988, 288) that traveling and bathing could not affect what God determines, although he would reward giving alms: "From what does moksha come? From his own hand, God's, that's from whom. It does not come from wandering. Whatever you give, in whatever place give it. From this comes moksha. What kind of dharma is dirtying the water? But dharma is giving-and-taking."

In scholarly debates as well, Hindus are of two minds about the benefits pilgrimages bring. On the one hand, some commentators on the classic texts assure the pilgrim that "Even if a man be a sinner or a rogue or irreligious he becomes free from all sin if he goes to Benares." But others equally clearly say the opposite, that it is the inner self that must be purified through meditation. After all, observes one scholar, "Fish are born and die in the water (of tîrthas); and they do not go to heaven, for the impurities of their minds are not purified."

The village pilgrims did agree that giving money as alms lightened the soul and brought them merit. Pure giving is easier on the road than in the village—in the latter, one will usually receive tangible or reputational goods in return for a gift, making the gift less pure.

As in the pilgrimage around Shikoku, for many Hindu pilgrims the goal is the journey, and the personal, inner transformations that happen along the way. Indeed, for all pilgrims, in all societies, the journey is important, even where, as in the case of the Muslim's hajj to Mecca, the main emphasis is on performing specific actions. Separating oneself from everyday life, focusing one's attention on the divine, is virtually the defining element of pilgrimage to anywhere.

13

Saints, Visions, and Prophets

We have encountered figures of authority, and struggles over authority in all the preceding chapters: the individuals who founded pilgrimages and New Religions in Japan, rabbis of and converts to Hasidism, and preachers in Quaker and Baptist churches; as well as struggles over who had the authority to interpret texts on Islamic sacrifice, to declare someone a witch, or to certify as valid an apparition of the Virgin Mary.

The beginnings of a religion often lie in the personal authority generated by an individual: a prophet, or saint, or holy man who is treated as truly exceptional among humans. Such authority we call "charismatic." This term originally referred to God's gift of power as understood in Christianity and as evidenced in such gifts of the spirit as miracles, faith, and speaking in tongues. The sociologist Max Weber (1978, 400) used the term in a broader way, as a universal category. In contrast to traditional authority, which relies on inherited characteristics (such as birth order), and legal authority, which derives from characteristics of office (such as a priesthood), charismatic authority rests on the intrinsic attributes of a leader.

Such leaders may draw their authority from different kinds of sources and claims, and we have discussed many sources of authority in previous chapters. Some may be considered to have special ties to spirits, or to be powerful sorcerers. Speaking in tongues is a sign of God's grace for some Protestants.

Shamanic healers may claim to be possessed by spirits or deities, and to derive their power from this possession. The speech of spirits that leaps from their mouths brings together the individual needs of the patient with the general norms and values of the society. In some societies these healers may become community leaders. In the Wana society of Indonesia they become the poles around which people gathered to form settled communities. In urban Japan they become the nuclei for new religious organizations that meet social and psychological needs of their followers. Healing may also involve other types of internal power or access to the divine. Mary Baker Eddy's popularity and the success of her Christian Science movement rested on her claims that all humans had within them the power to heal themselves.

This chapter examines the role of individuals in initiating religious movements, and the relationships between individuals' sources of authority and the history of new religious movements. First we consider the roles of the saint as a moral exemplar to others and as a source of power and assistance. Then we explore the diverse social forms religious prophecy can take, from Oceanic "cargo cults" to large-scale revivalist movements. We look at two examples—the Mormon Church of Latter-Day Saints and Islam—to illustrate the problems of leadership and continuity in religious movements as they expand over time.

Saints as Exemplars and as Sources of Assistance

One kind of religious authority is the saint, or holy person, who provides an example of how to live a holy, or virtuous, or religiously focused life. The saint is an "exemplar" (P. Brown 1987): a model of the ideal way to live, which may be appropriately reflected on by everyone, even if living the ideal is beyond the reach of most people. Many religious traditions have stories about such exemplary people—Christian martyrs, Jewish holy people, or tsaddiqim (such as Hasidic rebbes), Muslim walî, "friends of God," the followers of Gautama Buddha in India, or of Lao Tze in China. In a broad sense, stories about virtuous ancestors in any community serve the same purpose of instructing the living on how best to live.

In some traditions the exemplary life *is* the major teaching. Christianity is in many ways about Christ's lived example; Islamic teachings rely on Muhammad's life as well as on God's commands. *How* the religion's prime exemplar lives in some respects defines the major thrusts of the religion. Gautama Buddha's turning away from the world to find enlightenment through meditation became the paradigm for the monk and the lay person, especially in the Theravada Buddhism of South and Southeast Asia. By contrast, the exemplary life of Confucius in China is based on harmony within the community and is defined through the relationships people have with others in their families and with their immediate society and in their relationship to the state. This ethic of harmonious worldly involvement defines the virtues to which everyone should strive.

The idea of harmony or balance is also the basis for Haitian Vodou. Karen McCarthy Brown (1987) views the ritual practices of Alourdes, a Vodou healer who lives in New York, as providing a moral exemplar to others in her community. Alourdes's role is, in the eyes of participants, passive, as the "horse" ridden by the spirits who possess her. The spirits embody conflicting aspects of life for these Haitians: courage and childishness, or caring and capriciousness. Alourdes dances among different such spirits, being possessed by one after another. Her possession performances intensify and clarify the clash of such forces in the world. For those who watch her, writes Brown (1987, 167), "the moral problem is not evil but imbalance, both within and among persons." In her possession by different deities, Alourdes exemplifies how to maintain such a balance.

Vodou reminds us that spirits and deities can also serve as moral exemplars, and that as a plurality of beings they can define different points in a moral space, different aspects of the moral universe. Alourdes dramatizes this plurality of spirits and ways of acting, as does the polarity of Vishnu and Shiva in Hinduism, with Vishnu as the preserver and king; Shiva as the destroyer and ascetic. Christianity provides not only the polarity of God and Satan, but also the different kinds of examples provided by Jesus, Mary, and distinctive saints. Gayo Muslims, like Muslims in other societies, not only tell of the lives of prophets, but also understand the world to be populated by good and bad spirits, who live in societies resembling human societies. These spirits embody "good" and "bad" traits more definitively than do complex human beings. They also illustrate the virtues of community: the good ones cooperate and thrive; the bad ones quarrel because of jealousy and hatred.

Saints and other kinds of holy persons provide *practical assistance* as well as moral examples to ordinary people. People pray to Christian saints for help, or they place the medallions of those saints in homes or automobiles. Muslims and Buddhists also ask the spirits of holy people to help in a variety of ways. Living saints, such as the Buddhist and Hindu examples discussed below, may produce talismans or amulets, objects containing some of the saint's power, for people to take home with them. (Writing can also serve as a talisman; Jewish and Islamic scriptures may be placed in a position to guard the home.)

The power to help wielded by saints and by talismans is a secondary power, deriving from their intermediate role between a deity and an ordinary person. Muhammad, Mary, or the healer Alourdes all serve as intercessors and go-betweens. Because saints do not own their power, they can distribute it to others, through prayer, talismans, or dreams. In this respect they resemble the shamanic healer who channels the power of a spirit through his body and voice, or the group of Kung people gathered to boil their internal energy together, through dancing, and heal the entire community.

The holy man's ability to receive and distribute power may come from his personal disinterest in it. The ascetic, the individual who renounces worldly pleasure for the sake of spiritual enlightenment, is a figure in many religions, from St. Francis of Assisi to the forest-dwelling Buddhist monk, to the Nuer prophet Ngundeng of the Sudan, discussed later. Ngundeng's trance-like behavior and eating of filth placed him outside of ordinary society and gave his words added force. Mohandas Gandhi innovated saintly asceticism (Fox 1989) by drawing both from traditional Hindu ascetic practice and from international exemplars, including Jesus, St. Francis, and Tolstoy.

The holy man as renouncer, as ascetic, illustrates how the two features of sainthood—example and assistance—can present a paradox or tension. In the Hindu and Buddhist climates of South and Southeast Asia, the saintly man cuts off contact with the mundane world in order to achieve salvation. But others flock to this saint precisely because he is powerful (Tambiah 1976). Furthermore, he comes to depend on the offerings given by these devotees. How can a world renouncer also be the leader of a movement? This paradox is even more acute today, when some "renouncers" attract millions of followers, not only in South Asia but in Europe and North America. Two examples of these saints are a forest-dwelling Buddhist monk in Thailand and a Hindu "god-man" who uses jet arline transportation but also urges followers to return to Hindu traditions.

Acharn Man, a Buddhist Forest Dweller

In Thailand, monks are known as either "forest dwellers" or "town dwellers," with the first specializing in meditation and the second in book-learning. (Many monks combine aspects of the two categories.) Some forest monks become known as "perfected saints," or *arahants* (Tambiah 1987). Although their powers come from having turned away from the world, they also bless commercially produced talismans distributed to the lay masses. The king and queen of Thailand, along with generals and rich bankers, seek out these forest monks to absorb some of their moral powers.

From where do these powers come? In the Buddhist teachings consulted by monks and royalty, meditation and renouncing material possessions allows the ascetic to ascend to higher than ordinary levels of consciousness and to find there superior powers, or *iddhi,* which enable him to vanish and then reappear, to hear far-off sounds, and to recall his own past lives. But the monk must refrain from enjoying these powers lest in his worldliness he is impeded in his quest for salvation.

The complex life of the saint can be illustrated through the biography of Acharn Man (1870–1943), the most famous exemplar among Thailand's contemporary monks. As with Sufi orders in Islam and lineages of rebbes in Judaism, Buddhist monks trace their spiritual lineages, their sources of inspiration and powers, to earlier monks. Most forest monks today trace their own lineage to Acharn Man.

Man's biography shows him wandering alone throughout Laos and Thailand, but also attracting disciples whom he encouraged to form small monastic cells. In a story analogous to that of Gautama Buddha, Man went through periods of wandering, followed by seclusion and meditation, instructing disciples in villages, and pacifying tigers in the forest. To his disciples Man was primarily an exemplar, but to his circle of lay followers, he was mainly a "field of merit" (Tambiah 1987, 121). Donations of food or other gifts to Man brought the donor religious merit and blessings in return.

After Man's death, some of his disciples joined lay followers in promoting the cult of talismans stamped with his image. Others became forest dwellers in their own right. The talismans are metal medallions with the image of Acharn Man on one side and the lay person or organization that contributed funds for the medallion on the other. A follower of Man blesses the talisman by holding one end of a cord that lies on a pile of the objects, and then engaging in meditation to transfer some of his own powers to the medallion.

Acharn Man's charismatic powers thus continue to be radiated outward to the public through a chain of spiritual transfers. This chain starts from his own person and image, through his followers who themselves have gained higher powers, through their direct physical contact with the metal talismans they bless, to the consumer of the talisman. (Note the similarity to the chains of direct contact created by Christian relics.)

Sathya Sai Baba, a Jet-Age Holy Man

India's contemporary saints are of several types. Some are leaders of large devotional orders, many of them directing worship toward the god Rama. These saints inherited their leadership position from their own teachers, and so on back into time, in a fashion similar to the spiritual lineage of the Buddhist monk. The orders preserve these genealogies of teachers, which tie today's leader across the centuries to the founding saint. One Hindu order, the Ramanandis, dedicated to Rama, consists of both ascetics—some of whom renounce all worldly interests and wander, near-naked—and temple dwellers—who pursue the devotion to Rama through chanting. (These movements have played an important role in current Hindu political activity, as we shall see in Chapter 15.)

While many of these devotionalist orders are centuries old and make their antiquity their warrant of legitimacy, a new kind of saint, the "god-man," makes miracles to show his power and promises salvation to today's middle class. Some of the god-men have attracted large international followings; in the United States these include Bhagwan Rajneesh and the Maharishi Mahesh Yogi. But in India the most famous of these figures is Sathya Sai Baba. He has attracted large followings in the large cities. Some Buddhists in Sri Lanka have also become followers of Sai Baba, seeing him as the Maitreya Buddha.

Sathya Sai Baba's appeal is especially to the English-speaking middle and upper-middle classes, and he is often en route by plane or automobile to meet with his supporters. As Lawrence Babb (1986, 159–201) explains, Sathya Sai Baba is worshiped as a "descent" of God to earth, an *avatâr*. Indeed, his followers refer to him as Bhagavân, "God." At 13 he underwent a prolonged seizure; emerging from it months later he explained that he was the incarnation of an earlier holy man, Sai Baba, who blended Hindu and Muslim traditions. Twenty years later he added, after another seizure, that he was also the deities Shiva and Shakti. He said that after him would be another incarnation of Shiva—this new holy man would be his successor. (He thereby solved the problem of succession ahead of time.) His miracles also became more tightly associated with Shiva: he would materialize sacred ash, a symbol of Shiva's powers, at festivals to Shiva, or materialize lingas (phallus-shaped places of devotions to Shiva) inside his own body, which he would then eject through his mouth.

His followers frequently refer to his miracles as evidence of his divinity. He cures apparently incurable illnesses, raises the dead, accomplishes surgery at a distance, changes sand into religious books, foretells a devotee's thoughts, and, his own particular specialty, materializes objects out of thin air. He apparently can produce any object, but he most often materializes sacred ash, about one pound per day, for devotees to take away with them. He is also said to leave ash footprints in people's houses without every having entered the premises.

This god-man's cult has no formal boundaries, no membership lists, and no centers. It is a loose collection of those who consider themselves his devotees, centered on him alone. But the trusts that exist in his name receive large amounts of donations and use the money to maintain devotional centers, publish books and magazines, and build Sathya Sai Colleges, eventually, according to plans, one in each state. The trusts also sponsor charitable activities, including feeding the poor and working as relief agents during floods or other natural disasters. None of these activities proscribe any special religious rites, and the followers include Hindus and some Muslims. At devotion sessions they sing songs devoted to Sathya Sai Baba and engage in worship at an altar; they may also purchase pictures of the holy man, recordings of the songs, or even life-sized plaster replicas of his feet.

Sathya Sai Baba has special appeal to educated, often rather secularized urban people (and white New Agers) in the United States, and this appeal is at first glance puzzling. These people should be the first to reject magic. But, as we saw in Chapter 7 regarding the followers of Japan's similarly magical healing sects, it is the people who have left many older religious and social practices behind who often feel most in need of new ways to solve personal crises. In India, these people include city dwellers who accept the new conditions of secularism and egalitarianism but worry about the loss of an older life. They find it difficult to maintain religious obligations and find older patterns of authority broken down. Those who come from high castes worry about the pollution they experience in their new lives, where they mingle with people from lower castes in what feels to them to be a disordered way.

The often disorienting conditions of modern life may have led many of these followers to discover their own cultural and religious identity in need of supplement. At times of crisis—illness, loss of employment, family discord—they may be attracted to a new kind of immediately available healing power. Sathya Sai Baba's teachings reinforce their fears at the same time that he offers remedies. He blames Western values and national disorder for much of what ails people, and urges adherents to return to the study of the older Hindu texts. As D. A. Swallow (1982) shows, Sai Baba dramatizes the continuing power of Shiva to deal with pollution and sickness, to overcome pollution and restore health. He embodies Shiva, reassuring his followers of the continuing presence of the god even in this secularized world. His devotees find a way to recover the very religiosity they have left behind, through the visible magic the holy man performs. His cult is not demanding—people can participate in the magic merely by buying a portrait, or reading a magazine—and it may offer something of their more religious past. Indeed, he claims that wealth and liberation go together. He can be experienced as combining the best of old and new: Shiva, health, wealth, and social work.

Prophets and Social Change

When spiritual leaders claim to be entrusted with divine authority, and begin proclaiming divine messages, we call them prophets. Some prophets are also saints; they stake out a path to enlightenment by setting an example, and it is this personal example that remains behind as their primary prophetic legacy. Such was the case for Gautama Buddha in India, and for Kobo Daishi in Japan (the saint in whose name Japanese undertake the Shikoku pilgrimage described in Chapter 12). Max Weber (1978, 447–451) called this type the "exemplary prophet" and contrasted it to the "ethical prophet," whose role is based on the claim to bear specific messages from divine authority. Muhammad, prophet of Islam, and Joseph Smith, prophet of Mormonism, said they were ordinary individuals through whom God relayed a call to return to the proper ways of worship. Moses, of whom we know little, was also an "ethical prophet," revealing commands from an ethical, law-giving deity.

These distinctions are general ones, instances of what Weber called "ideal types." In practice, followers attribute many diverse qualities to prophets. Some Muslims treat all of Muhammad's actions, from the color of his clothes to the manner in which he ate, as if they provided a divine example for humankind. This view moves the figure of Muhammad closer to the status of saint. Others take a different view, considering only certain of his actions—how he conducted the pilgrimage to Mecca, for example—to have been inspired by God and thus intended as examples or models. They emphasize his ordinary human qualities precisely in order to underscore the belief that the Qur'ân came from God, not Muhammad. Such terms as *saint, prophet,* and *charisma* can therefore only be taken as indicators of types of roles and tendencies within religious movements, not clear-cut descriptions of individual leaders.

The Problem of the Prophet's Continuity

Sathya Sai Baba's teachings emphasize a return to older scriptures. But when a prophet has a new message to deliver, how can he or she transmit the prophetic authority and message beyond immediate surrounds and to the next generation? The power of the prophet may be embodied in portable objects (such as the powerful statues found in both Japanese Buddhism and European Catholicism). The message may be transmitted and transferred through verbal reports, or even songs, as with the Nuer people of the Sudan.

These orally transmitted messages may be considered as more authentic than written messages. (Such is the case for religious traditions in India, North America, and in Islam, for example.) When prophetic messages are transmitted, they become subject to radical change, as in the example of the Paiute Ghost Dance we will see later. Variant versions of the original message arise. In many religions, the fact of having many versions of "the same" sacred narrative does not pose a problem. Navajo narratives of the world's origin are told in many ways and in many contexts, and this plurality of versions suits the many uses to which the narrative is put. The story of Beautyway, for example (see Chapter 11), describes world origins and the close ties between speech and thought. Narrating the story brings to life the power of creation and the power of words, to be used in healing or blessing. Different versions of the sacred story can accomplish these goals.

In other religious traditions, however, the nature of the narrative makes such diversity problematic. If, as in Islam or Christianity, the religious message stresses the importance of conformity to divine commands by the community as a whole, then disagreement about those commands will likely lead to divisions in the community. If religious leaders perceive this danger, then they will likely act to create a single version of scripture, commit it to writing, and repress alternative versions of scripture. (They will also likely act to expel religious dissidents.) The creation of a written Gospel, with its four distinct versions of Jesus's life, and of a written Qur'ân, occurred long after the revelations and miracles related in the narratives. In both cases the narratives had been transmitted orally, and in several versions. In the case of the Qur'ân, when the verses were collected in an authoritative version, other written versions were ordered destroyed. In Christianity, books not included in the Gospels were labeled "apocryphal."

This passage from the individual holy person, to multiple memories of his or her life, to an authoritative scriptural text, involves the emergence of a centralized religious authority, and in some cases to state-enforced religious law. Authority becomes less personal and more bureaucratic. Max Weber called the process of transforming religious authority the *routinization* of authority, by which he meant the creation of routine ways of arranging succession to the leadership, structuring the religious organization, and resolving disputes. Even when "routinized," most religious movements are forced to come to terms with other claims to authority, either claims within the movement or assertions of superior authority by external political institutions, especially by states.

The routinization of a movement is one way for religious authority to be transferred. One example of this change of authority is that of seventeenth-century Quakers. The Quaker prophet George Fox had been able to keep the movement together in its early years by virtue of his personal powers of persuasion, but the very ideas that animated early Quakers worked against any centralized control. The spirit, argued the early Quakers, inspires those persons whom it would inspire, so that speaking at meetings, or other social behavior, should not be regulated. The resulting Quaker tendency to pose stark and shocking challenges to established authority—from using "impolite" speech, to refusing to take oaths of loyalty to the king, to going naked as a sign of innocence before God—led to state repression and to turmoil within the movement itself.

Quaker elders eventually came to routinize authority in order to preserve the movement. They established firm rules about how meetings were to be run and how individual Quakers were to speak with other people.

The Birth of Prophecy in the Sudan

Although the Nuer people of the southern Sudan have given rise to many types of leaders and magicians, a new type of "ethical prophet" first emerged in the late nineteenth century. His message has been preserved, transmitted, and used to diverse ends, through the media of song and radio.

Douglas Johnson (1994) calls Ngundeng Bong (d. 1906) the first prophet, the first "vessel of divinity," among the Nuer. As a young man, Ngundeng began to exhibit strange behavior, including wandering alone in the bush, fasting, and eating cow dung. His relatives interpreted this behavior as evidence that he had been "seized" by a divinity—much like the way Sathya Sai Baba was "seized" in his youth. They sacrificed oxen in the hope of propitiating these divinities. After these sacrifices, Ngundeng became normal once again. He reported that he had indeed been seized by a deity, the divinity Deng. He began to teach people prayers to this deity.

Earlier, Nuer had frequently sought help from clan deities, but Ngundeng declared that Deng was a deity for all the Nuer. Many people agreed with him, not because of a crisis in Nuer society, argues Johnson (1994, 327–329), nor because the clash with British armies led Nuer to search for a new leader—indeed, it came before the impact of colonial rule began to be felt. Johnson points instead to the general increase in mobility and dislocation in the late nineteenth century in this part of Africa as the cause of Ngundeng's success. In a way similar to the effects of social mobility on religious consciousness in the first millenium B.C.E., these social changes may have made the idea of a general divinity more appealing to many Nuer. Nuer already were imputing a more active role to clan deities in causing good or bad fortune than they had before, and they were concerned about the power of magic possessed by other groups. Ngundeng's claims thus fit with general changes in religious and social consciousness.

Ngundeng built up his influence and authority through a series of successful acts of religious sacrifice. Before a critical battle with another Nuer group, Ngundeng sacrificed an ox to Deng. His side won the battle. Ngundeng soon gained a reputation for having power over life and death. Merely by looking at him, he caused the death of a relative who had denied him meat. Others who refused his demands soon died, without his having to say or do anything. (Recall from Chapter 8 the related idea among the nearby Azande people that one's witchcraft substance can cause harm without human action.) He was also credited with making many barren women fertile by making sacrifices to Deng. Upon the outbreak of smallpox in 1888–1889, he sacrificed oxen and urged everyone to leave their houses; the incidence of smallpox among the people who followed his urging was relatively low. (One doctor who was present at the time said that the extra meat produced by the sacrifices, together with the act of inducing people to spread out, probably did contribute to a reduction in susceptibility to the disease.)

But Ngundeng was a prophet, not a sorcerer. He was able to turn other prophets and magicians into his disciples. He mediated feuds between clans, usually through sacrifices. He was able to bring together many clans through his prophetic activities, citing messages from Deng. Soon after the smallpox outbreak, he began work on a large earthen mound, said to enclose all evil and disease inside it, and mobilized thousands of Nuer to work on it for more than four years. Sacrifices at the mound were intended to benefit all Nuer, not just the particular clan who had brought the ox. The idea that a religious act or a deity could give general benefits to all Nuer was an innovation over earlier ideas and practices.

The prophet spread his message widely through the hymns and songs he recited, which he said had been created by the divinity Deng. These songs urged Nuer to reconcile with each other and with their various enemies. Even after British raids on Nuer camps in 1902, one of his, or rather Deng's, songs pleaded:

I reject the fight you bring
Divinity and the prophet do not quarrel.

The Nuer have not enjoyed peace in recent years. Relations between the Islamic northern part of the Sudan and the non-Islamic, mainly Christian south, have been violent. Southern rebels have often sung Ngundeng's songs in support of their struggle. He was said to have predicted the wars against the north. But his songs were also sung by Nuer opponents of the rebels. Some of the divisions among Nuer have also pitted Nuer groups against members of a neighboring group, the Dinka. In 1988 these factions finally joined forces against the north, and announced their reconciliation publicly in another Ngundeng song:

Nuer and Dinka
even if you hate yourselves
There will come a time when you will recognize me as your father.

The rebel radio broadcast Ngundeng's songs right after the announcement of the reconciliation, and the legacy of his prophecy continues to animate southern resistance against the north.

Revitalization Movements: Messiahs, Millennia, and Revivals

Many prophets hold out the promise of a "new heaven, new earth," a new kind of world in which the trials and problems of this one are replaced with a just and perfect order. Their promises sometimes lead to movements of people seeking to overturn the present order, or converting others to their beliefs, or simply awaiting the promised transformation. Such movements may develop and grow particularly in times of rapid social change and perceived threats to older ways of life, but they also offer innovations, not just reactions to change.

We find such movements throughout time and throughout the world, and called by many names. Judaism, Islam, and Christianity are all built on such a promise of a future redemption and the return of a messiah. This hoping for a future redeemer can be called "messianism" and such movements "messianic." In the histories of Judaism, Christianity, and Islam there have been other persons claiming to be messiahs or perceived as such by followers, such as Joseph Smith, the founder of Mormonism; the Lubavitcher Rebbe; and the Imam Mahdi of the Sudan. These figures and followers fit squarely within the tradition of messiah-beliefs.

Many Christians believe that Christ will return to the earth and reign for a millennium before the Last Judgment. The belief is called "millenarianism," and it is based on a passage in the book of Revelation (20:1–10) describing the imprisonment of Satan and the "first resurrection" of righteous souls during this period, a great battle with Satan, the Judgment of all souls, and then the creation of a "new Jerusalem," a new heaven and earth.

There are further refinements of this belief, discussed later, but the term has been used to describe beliefs and movements in Christianity and in other religions in which leaders promise a world transformation. Such movements have particular appeal to those people who believe that the entire society needs to be changed and that some great event is needed to accomplish these changes. Contemporary U.S. society produces such figures and their followers at near-regular intervals—David Koresh, or Jim Jones, for example. But so do other modern societies: Mahdis or Imams in Islamic societies, or spiritual healers in Japan. Millenarian movements developed in one context often spread to others, as when the Zion Church of Chicago became a basis for a "countercultural" church in colonial South Africa (Comaroff 1985). Other examples of these movements include modern Melanesian "cargo cults," movements based on expectations of social transformation when native peoples acquire the same wealth or "cargo" as owned by Europeans, and the Chinese T'ai-ping Rebellion, a late–nineteenth-century rebellion against the Ch'ing dynasty that was inspired by the vision of a new Heavenly Kingdom close at hand.

In the discussion that follows I use the relatively neutral term *revitalization movements,* taken from Anthony Wallace (1956, 265). Wallace defines such a movement as "a deliberate, organized, conscious effort by members of a society to construct a more satisfying culture." Although his definition imputes a singular psychology to such movements, it aptly emphasizes that such movements are creative, and aimed toward social and cultural improvement. The term revitalization movements, then, may describe the general category of religious movements that promise a radically changed future. Other terms refer to specific features of such movements. "Millenarian" applies to movements that envisage a thousand-year reign of Christ; "messianic" covers a wider range of reference.

Land, Wealth, and Religious Visions

Even where something short of a millennium was prophesied, a wide variety of revitalization movements arising in colonized parts of Asia and Africa have drawn on the imagery and language of the Book of Revelations, often associating it with the power and wealth of the colonizers (Burridge 1969; Trompf 1995).

Throughout the Pacific Islands, colonization brought rapid and often radical changes to local ways of life. Three transformations stand out. Colonists seized lands that had belonged to local people. Missionaries built schools and hospitals, and through conversion created new divisions among people. Europeans also brought new manufactured goods and encouraged or demanded of locals that they grow cash crops and purchase these goods.

Local responses to these dislocations highlighted the three issues of land, trade goods, and religious innovation. Their particular emphases were shaped by specific local conditions, but they usually featured creative combinations of European and local ideas and practices. Some responses drew on Christian paradigms; others blamed their own neglect of their gods as responsible for current troubles and emphasized the revival of customs or rituals. One variety of these Oceanic revitalization movements was based on the premise that if local people engaged in some European religious practices, then they would receive European trade goods. These movements came to be called "cargo cults," from *cargo,* the neo-Melanesian word for trade goods.

Maori Prophecies in New Zealand

European settlers in New Zealand drove large numbers of Maori people off their lands in order to create room for new colonial settlements. Maori swidden agriculture (crops grown on land recently cleared of vegetation) required large tracts of land to lie fallow for extended periods, and the people gathered important foodstuffs and other materials from the forests. Colonists converted vast areas of fallow scrub land and forest into permanent grassland for grazing their sheep. Depriving Maori of their land also deprived them of the signs of their worth and power, or mana. Maori responded by attacking settlers, and the result was protracted conflict throughout the 1850s and 1860s. Maori united behind a new king, but settler attacks and reprisals continued, and in 1862 there emerged a new movement, this one based on prophetic leadership.

The new movement, named "Hauhau," was led by the prophet Te Ua, who claimed to have been given new revelations by the angel Gabriel. The movement illustrates two conflicting pressures in many revitalization movements: awaiting God's actions versus taking matters into one's own hands. Te Ua advocated remaining peaceful and letting God destroy the settlers on behalf of his chosen people—here the prophet assimilated the plight of the Maoris to the biblical plight of the Jews. Te Ua instigated religious rituals in which he and his followers chanted hymns around a mast salvaged from a British ship.

But Te Ua also reported a revelation that uttering the word *hau* would render them invulnerable and mobilize the many angels waiting to help the Maoris drive the Europeans into the sea. The hymn-chanting also included barking out the word *hau* as they circled the mast. Te Ua staged raids on British military camps. Miraculous powers began to be attributed to him, and his movement gathered supporters from Maori alarmed at the European usurpation of their lands. After some skirmishes, Te Ua surrendered in 1868. Hauhau became a church, and it still survives till today.

The Hauhau adherents linked their loss of land to missionaries' activities. As one man put it in a speech to villagers: "These men, these missionaries were always telling us, 'Lay up for yourselves treasures in heaven.' And so, while we were looking up to heaven, our land was snatched from beneath our feet" (Burridge 1969, 19).

Cargo Cults in Samoa and New Guinea

A movement in Samoa during the 1830s and 1840s was largely motivated by the desire to possess the power and control—mana—that some Samoans associated with European trade goods. Here emerged a cargo cult, intended to produce new material wealth, but also based on a new combination of religious ideas. Siovili, the leader of the movement that bore his name, was an early convert to Christianity and traveled widely on European ships, visiting Tahiti and Australia, among other places. He was subject to trances and traditional forms of spirit possession (Burridge 1969, 22–27).

Upon his return to Samoa, Siovili began to claim that Jehovah and Jesus Christ spoke through him. Some of his followers thought he was Christ. He stated that those who joined him in following these religious practices of the Europeans would share in the European goods. But his movement was also religious, one of many cults found in Samoa in this period that emerged out of the various missionary teachings and immigrants from other islands. Chiefs competed for the manas that the new religious ideas might bring them. Other Samoans joined churches and cults for a variety of motives.

Siovili's followers built churches, brought various books to service, and recited words over them in the hope that these acts would bring Jesus with his material gifts (Trompf 1995, 174–175). One of Siovili's followers claimed that she had become possessed by Jesus Christ and announced that Christ was about to revisit the earth, at which time the dead would arise from their graves. She ordered other Samoans to throw out the crops growing in their gardens, walk down to the sea, and there await Christ's arrival. Christ would cause abundant food and goods to fall from the sky. This woman's followers did wait on the beach for three days, after which time they returned to their gardens to see if they could rescue any remaining food (Burridge 1969, 15–27).

Cargo cults are especially common in Melanesia, the area that includes New Guinea and Fiji, perhaps because of the importance of prestige goods in these societies. Political leadership and social prestige in many Melanesian societies result from success in accumulating and redistributing food and other goods. But the revitalization movements in Melanesia were also religious movements, inspired by new religious ideas and practices.

One Melanesian movement that attracted a particular degree of foreign attention was called the "Vailala Madness," a series of events occurring among the Elema people along the Vailala River in New Guinea from 1919 to 1922 (Worsley 1968, 75–92). As with the Maori, the "Vailala Madness" grew out of a particular conjuncture of resistance to colonial land control, religious innovation, and the desire for new material wealth. Just prior to the "madness," the Anglo-Persian Oil Company had begun drilling for oil in the region; both this company and plantation owners took Elema men away as indentured laborers. Many of the workers died of dysentery. Meanwhile, European authorities were extracting agricultural revenue from the district by ordering the Elema to pay a head tax and to grow rice for sale. Elema had no desire to do either.

The local mission church authorities, from the London Missionary Society, supported the colonial cause but also urged Elema churchgoers to transform their lives through spiritual experience. These Elema did just that: they began to speak in tongues and be possessed by the Holy Spirit. Although church authorities interpreted their behavior as spiritual growth and enthusiasm, colonial authorities came to view the behavior as a dangerous "madness." One observer described local people "taking a few quick steps in front of them, and they would then stand, jabber and gesticulate, at the same time swaying the head from side to side; also bending the body from side to side from the hips" (Worsley 1968, 75). People so possessed said they had been given special powers by the ancestors to divine and to cure.

The leaders of the movement were men who had traveled out of the district; many had been pressed into service in the oil fields or plantations. They abolished traditional practices, burning sacred objects and substituting their own prophecies. The prophet Evara foretold the coming of a new order without the colonizers. Ships would bring back the spirits of dead ancestors (including those who had died while laboring for the Europeans) and considerable cargo, material goods. He and other leaders told their followers to engage in actions that would bring back the spirits. Tables were set up in the villages, with flowers on them, around which the relatives of dead persons would sit, dressed in European style. Some leaders contacted ancestors through the village flag-poles, perhaps on the model of the Anglo–Persian Oil Company's wireless (Worsley 1968, 85). Leaders ordered strict moral codes to be observed, including observing Sunday as a day of rest.

Although after many years the movement gradually died down, some living in the area remembered it as having produced real miracles: messages *had* been received via the flagpoles; the steamers of the ancestors *had* arrived; "the ground shook and the trees swayed" (Worsley 1968, 90–91).

The Ghost Dance in North America

Similar to the Oceanic movements was the Ghost Dance that was begun by Paiute Native American prophets and then spread across the North American Plains. Born in conditions of repression and starvation, the dance has continued its existence as part of a political and cultural heritage for some Native Americans, though with a changing message.

First introduced in 1870, the dance was revived and its message spread widely by a Paiute prophet in western Nevada, Wovoka (c. 1856–1932). During a solar eclipse in 1889, Wovoka fell into a trance, during which, as he later reported, he rose to the other world, where he saw God. God instructed him to remain on peaceful terms with white people and to dance a special circle dance that would place dancers in contact with the spirit world; hence its name. Dancing the dance would hasten the time when the people would be reunited with the dead, he taught. Euro-Americans would be wiped out, and Native Americans would return to their earlier state of plenty. (European-manufactured goods would remain behind for Native American use.)

Wovoka's prophecy was spread both by word of mouth and by delegations sent to see him from other Native American groups. Some delegates returned reporting that Wovoka, as "the messiah," had done wondrous things: made animals talk, descended from heaven on a cloud, and conjured up a vision of the spirit world.

As the message spread into new areas, with different cultural backgrounds and different relationships to the Euro-Americans, it was transformed. In Wovoka's message, the destruction of Euro-Americans was to happen automatically, and less as a punishment than as a means for Native Americans to regain their earlier ascendancy. His prophecy stood in a tradition in this part of North America of myths about the dead returning to life and inaugurating an age of plenty.

In Dakota Territory, however, the Sioux interpreted the teachings in a different context. The culture as well as the economy of the Sioux had revolved around the buffalo: buffalo furnished food and materials for houses and bedding and were the objects of many rituals. The art of hunting was a central part of life. All this was lost when Europeans wiped out the buffalo herds. During the 1870s and 1880s, the Sioux were confined to smaller and smaller territories until, in 1890, they occupied a particularly barren part of the Dakota territory, where, deprived of buffalo, they were supposed to live from crops, cattle, and government rations. In 1888 the cattle were destroyed by disease, and the following year the crops failed, followed by epidemics of measles and whooping cough. In 1890 came another crop failure and a reduction in government rations.

In March 1890, Sioux delegates returned from seeing the messiah, Wovoka, and within a few months most Sioux had begun to practice the Ghost Dance. In their version of the message, the Spirit had sent the Euro-Americans to punish them for their sins but had now returned to their side and had made European bullets powerless against them. To prepare for the coming catastrophe, Sioux must rid themselves of European things, they said. No metal of any kind was allowed in the Sioux dances, and people began to wear "ghost shirts" of buckskin or cloth. Nor was any weapon carried in the dance. (The ghost shirt was not part of the Paiute dance and was disavowed by Wovoka.)

In October 1890, Sitting Bull began to practice the dance at his camp, claiming that he had received a direct message from the spirit world to do so. He urged all Sioux to gather in one place and dance, to advance the coming of the great change. Although he did not urge the dancers toward violence, publicity about the Ghost Dance movement exacerbated Euro-American fears of renewed fighting with the Sioux. Government soldiers were sent to arrest Sitting Bull, and they killed him in his camp. Shortly thereafter occurred the massacre of a band of Sioux at Wounded Knee. Some Sioux killed at Wounded Knee wore the ghost shirts, believing them to be impenetrable by bullets.

After these events, and the failure of the expected resurrection to take place, Wovoka, in Nevada, began to alter his message, stressing the importance of proper living. Other groups picked up the dance and the messages, now shorn of the predictions of a coming apocalypse. In Wyoming, the Shoshone combined the Ghost Dance with a ceremony of thanks to God. During the ritual, shamans would report visions of the dead waiting in heaven to return to earth. The Ghost Dance occupied a place in subsequent Native American religious and political life. Later, Christian converts among the Sioux reconceptualized the messiah of the Ghost Dance as Christ. In the 1970s, as Wounded Knee became, for some Native Americans, a symbol of U.S. repression, the American Indian Movement revived the dance.

Christian Millenarian Movements in the United States

Many early Christians expected the Second Coming in their lifetimes, and millenarian movements flourished in western Europe in the medieval and early modern periods (Cohn 1970). Today as well, some Christians consider the millennium to be near. Believers hold one of two ideas about the millennium, however, and the difference between the two ideas, fine as it might seem on paper, has important implications for the role of the believer in the world. Since the 1940s, the two ideas have defined two different groups of U.S. churches (Casanova 1994, 135–145; Wuthnow 1989).

One group, which includes Seventh-Day Adventists and most groups calling themselves Fundamentalists, follows the idea of "premillennialism," that Jesus will return to reign before the millennium. Before he arrives, the world will grow increasingly corrupt, until finally those who are truly saved will be taken up to heaven in a "rapture," leaving the others to face a time of tribulations. These groups keep separate from the sinful world, as we saw in Chapter 11, building their own schools and universities for their children.

By contrast, "postmillennialists" hold that Jesus will come after the world has experienced a millennium of harmonious existence. For most people in this group, which includes many Evangelical Christian denominations, the task at hand is converting as many people as possible to Christianity, in order to prepare the world for Jesus. Led by Billy Graham and others, and emphasizing conversion, large rallies involve healing and speaking in tongues and worldwide crusades. Jimmy Swaggert, for example, regularly tours the world to address crowds in soccer stadiums and other large venues. In

Brazil, during the 1980s the work of these U.S. evangelists led to new conversions from Catholicism or Afro-Brazilian religions to an Evangelical church on the order of 10 million (Riding 1987).

The tendency of Fundamentalists to separate from the world was challenged in the 1970s, when the Moral Majority movement led by Jerry Falwell urged Fundamentalists to work to change the world. José Casanova (1994, 156) argues that Falwell and others realized that fundamentalism "cannot survive in a world devoid of shared moral meanings and standards, in a postmodern world in which it would become just another quaint subculture, like that of the native Indians or the Amish, to be added to the 'gorgeous mosaic' of American cultural pluralism."

Mormon Prophecy and Authority

T he history of the Mormons shows both how a movement changes the nature of its authority from charismatic (in this case, prophetic) to bureaucratic, and how it adapts to demands made by an encompassing political structure (in this case, the U.S. government).

Joseph Smith, Prophet

The Church of Jesus Christ of Latter-Day Saints, commonly known as the Mormon Church, traces its origins to a man Mormons consider a prophet, Joseph Smith (Anderson 1942; Shipps 1985). In the 1820s Smith received divine revelations concerning certain records that had been written on golden plates and buried near his home near Palmyra, New York. According to his own account, Smith unearthed the plates and translated them "from Reformed Egyptian" to English with the aid of two translation stones. By 1829, two years after he found the plates, Smith had completed translating them. He had kept the plates away from the vision of others, working on one side of a curtain while his scribe—initially his wife—remained on the other. He was then given further directions through divine revelation, and in particular he was directed to found a new church of Christ. In it, he would speak as a prophet and would initiate others, who would also speak God's words. The church would baptize people in a new covenant with God, augmenting the earlier covenants delivered through Moses and Jesus Christ.

Smith published the translation as the Book of Mormon in 1830. Smith was thoroughly familiar with the King James Version of the Bible, and the Book of Mormon is written in the same style, with a similar organization into books and sections. The Book of Mormon tells of a tribe of Israelites who, in about 600 B.C.E., sailed to the Americas. There they built cities and temples and continued to obey the Law of Moses. They were visited by Jesus Christ after his death and resurrection. Christ performed miracles and organized a new church with 12 disciples. But the Israelites fought among themselves. In a reprise of Cain versus Abel, one group, the Lamanites, who had become hunters, disobeyed God's word, but it was they who prevailed over the other group, the peaceful farming Nephites. (The Lamanites' descendants are said to be today's Native

Americans.) The last remaining Nephite prophet was Mormon, who wrote an account of the travels and struggles of these Israelites on gold plates and passed them on to his son, Moroni. Moroni buried the plates for discovery by the people who could restore the church that had once existed in America. It was Moroni's angel who revealed to Smith the location of the tablets. The "Latter-Day Saints" of the church are those who respond to the new direct revelations from God, the first revelations since those delivered through Christ. In the Mormon view, Christianity was misled soon after its founding. God had decided to reestablish his true church, with Smith as its prophet.

Soon after the book's publication, Smith began to attract a small group of followers, a few of whom attested to having seen the gold tablets. The group grew over time, and eventually followed Smith from New York. His success as a prophet must be seen in the religious context of his place and time. In the northeast United States of the 1820s, a diversity of religious faiths and movements abounded. This diversity was due in part to the intensity of the religious emotions following on the Second Great Awakening, a period of religious revival throughout the region that had begun three decades earlier. The revival encouraged religious experimentation and the questioning of established churches. (Adventism also began in this region during the same period.) Many people sought more direct forms of contact with Jesus Christ than those offered through standard liturgies. Joseph Smith himself said he was confused by the diversity of religions open to him, and his first revelation was mainly a message from a divine figure telling him not to join any of the existing churches, but to recover the authentic form of Christianity. As with Islam, Mormonism began as, and remains today, a call to return to the purity of the early worship of God.

Smith's part of New York State was also replete with Native American populations and mounds of ancient origin, and the Book of Mormon responded to a deep curiosity about the origins of Native Americans and the identities of the mound builders. (This curiosity also spurred on early archeological speculation in North America.)

Smith himself already had a reputation as a person in touch with the unseen. Before he received the revelations, he had found a "seerstone," a smooth, egg-shaped stone used to locate lost objects. Indeed, he and his father worked as treasure hunters, benefiting from generally accepted beliefs in the powers of seers. After his first revelation, members of his family stopped attending the local Presbyterian church, and joined him in waiting to found a new church of apostles of Christ.

Relatives and neighbors began to accept Joseph's claims, not despite his reputation as a practitioner of magical arts, but *because* that reputation supported his claims to have found a true treasure. Soon the church had 40 members, with Joseph as its Prophet, Seer, Apostle of Jesus Christ, and Elder.

In 1831 Smith moved the church to Kirtland, Ohio, which he proclaimed was on the eastern edge of Zion, the church's ultimate destination. There he attempted to construct a communal form of economy based on sharing, the legacy of which is the tithe, one-tenth of one's income that members are expected to pay the church. Financial difficulties and local hostilities led Smith to move some of the Ohio Mormons to Missouri. Their partial economic success in Missouri, their perceived socialism and the large numbers of immigrants they attracted, led to local attacks on the Mormons (Leone 1979, 11–16). Smith at one point made explicit the parallel to Muhammad's experience of a call for religious purity followed by persecution, when he publicly proclaimed, "I will be a second Muhammad." This parallel hardly improved his image locally, and in 1838, after renewed attacks on the community, the Mormons moved back across the Mississippi to an Illinois town they renamed Nauvoo.

In Nauvoo, Smith rebuilt the church around the divine revelations he continued to receive. These instructions included the doctrine, written down privately in 1843, that God intended males to take more than one wife. This doctrine, announced publicly from Salt Lake City in 1852, was part of a new vision of the afterlife, in which marriages properly conducted by the church would be for eternity, and a man with his wives and all his progeny would move on to rule new worlds. Taking plural wives would mean a larger retinue of progeny, and it followed the example of the Hebrew patriarchs Abraham, Isaac, and Jacob (Foster 1981, 123–180).

Smith attracted many additional adherents, most of whom, poor, had left unprofitable farmlands or poorly paid factory jobs, and were attracted by the utopian message of the Mormons. The community grew into tens of thousands, with Smith as its leader, now declared to be King of the Kingdom of God. He became increasingly despotic, and in 1844 he destroyed an opposition press, an action that led to his arrest. On June 27, 1844, a mob stormed the jail where he was held and lynched him.

The New Prophet and Conflicts with the United States

As with most prophet-led movements, Smith's death left no automatic successor. Struggles for leadership produced several factions. In particular, two lines of reasoning emerged. One group argued that the Smith's descendants had inherited his right to rule. This group followed members of Smith's family back to Missouri, where they established the Reorganized Church of Latter-Day Saints. This church is headquartered today in Independence, Missouri. A second group, the majority, continued the leadership of Smith's church, arguing that the followers had the right to choose their leader. They chose an elder, Brigham Young, to become the new Prophet and Elder. Young led the community westward, across the Great Plains, to the Great Salt Lake in what is today Utah. (A similar debate over succession, at the break between charismatic and "routinized" authority, occurred in Islam, as we shall see in the next section.)

By 1849, Brigham Young had established an autonomous, theocratic (religion-ruled) state on the lake called Deseret. Hundreds of small communities sprung up in orbit around the lake, extending into today's Arizona, Colorado, Nevada, and California. The need for cooperation in creating irrigation provided a material base for authority in these new communities; the church held them together through an intricate hierarchy of leaders and through its ownership of numerous enterprises.

In 1850 the territory came under U.S. rule, and tensions quickly mounted between the Mormons and a U.S. government toward which Mormons had always felt uneasy. For its part, the government feared that the Mormons might refuse to acknowledge U.S. sovereignty. During the 1850s, armed conflict occurred on several occasions between Mormons and "Gentiles" (non-Mormons), and in 1857 President James Buchanan sent an army of five thousand troops to try to occupy Utah. Polygamy, now made public, become a symbol of the conflict, and in 1862 Congress banned it (Firmage 1991). In 1879 the U.S. Supreme Court upheld the U.S. statutory ban on polygamy, declaring it not to infringe religious freedom but rather to protect the vital social institution of monogamous marriages. In 1890 the Court upheld additional, severe legislation that dissolved the Mormon Church as a corporation and confiscated most major church properties. The Mormon Church president responded to these assaults by advising his followers not to contract plural marriage or polygamy. However, he did not characterize the directive to be a revelation, as most other important directives had been and would continue to be characterized. Some Mormons continued to practice polygamy. By statehood, in 1896, the church was deeply in debt. Mormons had become part of a larger economy of the Western states, characterized by industries of mining, livestock, timber, and railroad, all bankrolled from the East. But since the 1930s the church has regenerated its wealth, building on its tithing requirement, and Mormons have become successful capitalist entrepreneurs.

Authority and History Today

The Book of Mormon continues to serve as a sacred book to today's Mormons, who number nearly 5 million in the United States, and about 2.5 million overseas. The Mormon following expands both through extensive missionary activities and by encouraging large families—children are said to incarnate already existing spirits and to advance one's own standing in the next world. Beginning at age 12, every Mormon male passes through several grades in each of two orders of priesthood. At about age 18, most men also go on a two-year mission for the church and are rewarded by passing into the second, adult priesthood order.

Mormons are grouped into wards of about 700 persons; 10 wards make up a Stake of Zion, headed by a president. The center of Mormon activity is Salt Lake City, where the Quorum of Twelve Apostles manages the church. The senior apostle becomes the church's president on the death of the previous president. Mormons attend local chapels and at intervals also attend services at one of the temples found in different parts of the United States and overseas. Chapels hold Sunday services, centered on a form of communion that is quite similar to that held in Lutheran and some other Protestant churches. Lay persons preside over the service and do most of the talking. Rituals held in the larger temples are kept secret from non-Mormons, but they include services held both for the living and for deceased ancestors of living Mormons.

Mormons attach great importance to the long-term historical record. They do so in part because of their ideas about salvation, and in part because of the particular historical account provided in the Book of Mormon. First, Mormons see themselves as capable of saving the souls of deceased persons. Ancestors of Mormons who lived before the advent of Mormonism may be baptized into the church, with a living person standing in for the ancestor. These souls may then be taken through the successive temple rites that move persons up the ranks of the priesthood. These ancestors may be very far removed, and in theory those who can be aided include a large percentage of the world's people. But to do so one must establish the connection to a living Mormon. Therefore, Mormons carry out extensive research into the family trees of, in theory, everyone in the world. The resulting vast holdings of genealogical records, located in Salt Lake City, are available to non-Mormons as well as to members of the church.

Second, history matters because history underlies the church's claims to authority. The Mormon Apostles see themselves as the direct heirs of God's message to humankind, through the media of the buried tablets and succeeding direct revelations to the church's prophets. The rationale for these revelations lies in the saga of Israelites fleeing Jerusalem, founding a new community, witnessing Christ, and establishing a new covenant with God. Though the community was eventually destroyed, it left its message for the latter-day prophet, Joseph Smith, through whom God's communication with his people was reopened.

History thus provides the rationale, the reasonable account, of why it was that Joseph Smith became a new prophet. The historical record of continued revelations to his successors depicts them, too, as prophets. In the eyes of the outside analyst, the charismatic authority of Joseph Smith was replaced by the bureaucracy of the church in Salt Lake City. In the eyes of the church leadership, however, Smith's successors continue to serve as prophets, seers, and apostles. They continue to receive charisma, divine blessings, from God, in the form of revelations. Charismatic authority is changed but not lost.

This historical account does, however, present Mormons with dilemmas in everyday life, especially in their attitudes toward Native Americans. Believed descended from the Lamanites, the ancient people who disobeyed God and wiped out the obedient Nephites, Native Americans are nonetheless also descended from Israelites. They are thus of the same origins as are Mormons, and for a group that places great emphasis on genealogy this connection gives Native Americans a special status. They are entitled to convert and become full members of the church, a privilege long denied to African Americans. Mark Leone (1979, 174–177) describes a service in an Arizona chapel at which a missionary couple described their experience living for several years on a Navajo reservation. The couple spoke from their experience in business about how Navajo were like anyone else. The couple's talk encouraged their listeners to put aside conflicting attitudes toward the Navajo and to get on with their twin concerns of commerce and conversion.

Muhammad and His Successors

When Joseph Smith announced that he would be "a second Muhammad," he was referring to the special role played by the Prophet of Islam vis-à-vis previous religions. Muhammad, like Smith, saw himself as God's vehicle to perfect and complete the work of revelation. In the views of both men, Judaism and Christianity were indeed the results of God's revelations, but the two traditions' leaders had strayed from the original message.

Islam was also born against a background of polytheism, however, and the statement most often pronounced by a Muslim, called the confession of faith, begins with the dictum: "There is no other deity but God." Islam began in the central desert area of the Arabian peninsula in the seventh century C.E. Trade and social life were organized by tribes, without central authorities. Power resided in one's lineage connections. Arabs worshiped many deities, although trade with Syria had also brought the monotheistic ideas of Judaism and Christianity.

Muhammad's own tribe, the Quraysh, dominated the city of Mecca by its control of the caravan trade. Mecca became a religious as well as a trade center; people came to the city on pilgrimages to its shrines, which included the Ka'ba. Several verses of the Qur'ân berate the Meccans for worshiping many gods and for letting the Ka'ba, built by the prophet Abraham (as we saw in Chapter 12), degenerate into a site of pagan worship. Monotheism remains one of the central emphases in Islam. This emphasis makes especially sensitive the appeals routinely made by many Muslims to other entities (spirits, saints, or prophets) that they intercede with God. These appeals are often branded as polytheism by other Muslims, who cite the Qur'ânic texts originally directed at the merchants of Mecca.

Muhammad as Messenger and Prophet

The second part of the confession of faith reads: "and Muhammad is his Messenger." Muhammad was born about 570 C.E., and was orphaned early in his life. He married an older woman, a trader, and managed her caravan. He began to receive revelations when he was 40 years old, in 610 (Peters 1994). The first verse of the Qur'ân to be revealed reached Muhammad when he was in a cave. The archangel Gabriel appeared to him and said: "Recite, in the name of the Lord who created, created man from a clot." (The first word of this verse is sometimes translated as "read," and quoted as evidence that God intends people to educate themselves.)

Muhammad then began to warn the Meccan people of the errors of their polytheistic ways. A few men followed him; most threatened him, and in 622 he fled or made the emigration (*hijra*) to the nearby city of Medina. The emigration marks the beginning of the lunar Islamic calendar. In Medina, Muhammad became the leader of the community through his skill in arbitrating between its several populations. He joined with the Jews of the city in praying in the direction of Jerusalem; verses revealed during this time stress the similarity of the two religions. (These verses include the dietary laws, for example.) Muhammad's growing group of followers engaged the Meccans in several battles, most notably those of Badr and Uhud, and his victories finally won him the right to make the pilgrimage to Mecca. He died after making the pilgrimage, in 632.

The place of Muhammad in Islam is both as the Messenger of God and as the Seal of the Prophets. As Messenger of God, Rasulullah, he brought a new collection of God's revealed word to humankind. Other messengers in the past had brought other books: Moses, the Torah; David, the Psalms; and Jesus, the Gospels. This lineage of revelation makes Jews and Christians, along with Muslims, "people of the book." (Hindus were later included in this category because of their use of sacred texts.) Because of their special status, members of these two religious communities were accorded special, protected treatment in Muslim-held territories.

As a prophet (*nabi*) Muhammad is the last in a long series of prophets, including the earlier Messengers. Among the prophets mentioned in the Qur'ân are Abraham, Noah, Hud, Salih, Lot, and Shu'ayb. Hud, Salih, and Shu'ayb do not figure in the Hebrew

Bible, but appear in various stories, often as specifically Middle Eastern personages. Shu'ayb warns his people against dishonest business practices, as Moses warned the Pharaoh against preventing the Israelites from going free.

Muhammad was thus human, a normal human being granted the role of God's mouthpiece. What is sent are words, and not Muhammad himself. Because all messengers are said to have this status, Muslims strongly deny the claim that Jesus was the son of God. Nonetheless, many Western commentators on Islam continue to make the error of presuming that the place of Muhammad in Islam is analogous to that of Jesus in Christianity. (Islam once was called "Muhammadanism" in the West.) It would be more accurate to draw an analogy between Jesus in Christianity and the Qur'ân in Islam, in that each is held by the religion's adherent to be God's major gift to humans. Similarly, the Gospels, the accounts of the life and statements of Jesus, are best compared not to the Qur'ân but to the hadith, the record of Muhammad's life and statements.

Who Rules after Muhammad?

Muhammad's authority in the early Muslim community came from his direct ties to God. He was a prophet but would have to be succeeded by someone who was not a prophet. Who was to rule after his death? On what principle should he be chosen? Or in Weber's terms, how was Muhammad's charismatic authority to be converted into a routine mechanism for selecting leaders?

Muhammad had neither designated a successor nor suggested a way of doing so. He had no male heir, but had there been one, it is not clear that this person would have succeeded him. As it happens, upon Muhammad's death in 632, his closest followers in Medina gathered and chose one among them, Abû Bakr, to be the first caliph (*khalîfa*), "deputy" of the Prophet. He in turn was succeeded by another close follower, 'Umar, under whose able rule Muslim armies conquered the rest of Arabia and moved on to Egypt. 'Umar realized the need to create a regular procedure for choosing rulers, and convened a council (*shûrâ*) to select a new caliph. This action legitimated the idea of reaching decisions by council, and the process continues to be followed in the Muslim world. 'Umar's committee chose a weak candidate, 'Uthmân, an early convert to Islam, who was assassinated in his own house by dissident soldiers.

The Development of the Shî'î

The next caliph was 'Alî, one of the key figures in Islamic history. 'Alî was the son-in-law of the Prophet and also his cousin and had a great deal of support because of his kin ties. He was the closest heir available to the community. But he failed to punish 'Uthmân's assassins and revoked some of his decrees and thereby provoked the ire of 'Uthmân's own kinsmen, a powerful Meccan aristocratic clan called the Umayyads. Their own leader, Mu'âwiya, challenged 'Alî's leadership. He called for a new council to select a caliph, and met 'Alî in battle (the dispute was arbitrated). 'Alî's rule began to crumble and he was assassinated in 661. His son Hasan abdicated in favor of Mu'âwiya, who began a new period of Umayyad dominance. But 'Alî's other son, Husayn, grandson of the Prophet, became the champion of dissident Muslims who began to see themselves as the "party of 'Alî." In 680 an event occurred that was to mark the Muslim world forever after: en route to the Iraqi city of Kûfa, Husayn was ambushed and his entire company massacred by Umayyad forces at a place called Karbala. His head was taken as proof of the defeat.

The Karbala massacre became the pivotal event in the emergence and identity of the party of 'Alî. Now known as the Shî'î, or "party," this group conceived of legitimate authority as forever charismatic. The spiritual and temporal authority of the Prophet was handed down through his grandchildren to a succession of spiritually perfect leaders called *imâms*. Born in opposition to the regime in power, the Shî'îs, or Shiites, have continued to stress the chasm between political realities and a longed-for truly Islamic world. Shiite populations, most importantly in Iran, Iraq, and Lebanon, formed communities of teaching and learning divorced from the regimes under whose control they had to live. The date of the Karbala massacre, the tenth of the month of Muharram, 680, is commemorated annually in *ta'ziya*, or martyr plays, that feature the assassination of Husayn. Sometimes the events include processions of men striking themselves with chains to participate in the pain and sadness that characterize the Shiite community's historical self-understanding (Momen 1985).

By contrast, the Umayyads and their successors saw themselves as the majority party and the continuers of the Prophet's ways, calling themselves "Sunnîs," after *sunna*, (the Prophet's) custom or practices. Sunni conceptions of authority return to the first council that chose the caliph. The entire Muslim community, or umma, inherits political authority, which they then bestow on a leader through a council. This way of routinizing authority drew on Arab tribal ideas of succession and loyalty, and also was effective in incorporating new peoples as part of the umma. It has meant that Sunni spiritual leaders have tended to play roles in political life.

Notice how the split in the Muslim world over succession fell along the same lines as did that affecting the Mormon community centuries later. One party elected a leader to follow the prophet, while another chose to follow his descendants. In both cases the "kinship party" refused to lose the charismatic quality of prophetic leadership; they repudiated the routinization of authority. In both cases this party proved to be the minority one.

Masters and Disciples in Sufi Orders

A third type of authority, alongside the council and kinship, is that possessed by the Sufi master toward his disciples. Sufi orders offer paths to greater spiritual awareness and closeness to God, through prayer, chanting, and poetry. Each such order offers a specific *tarîqa* ("way" or "method"). The current teacher or master in the order traces his authority back along a spiritual lineage to his teacher, that teacher's teacher, and so forth, usually back to the Prophet Muhammad and, through him, to God (Eickelman 1976).

The first order was founded by the Persian scholar Abdul Qâdir al-Jîlânî (1078–1166). Abdul Qâdir's influence as a preacher grew so large that followers established a special retreat for him, where people came to study and listen. He taught that to approach God, people would first need to divest themselves of worldly goods; that these goods acted as veils that came between them and God. As in other Sufi orders, he urged people to practice *dhikr:* "remembrance" of God by chanting phrases either aloud or in one's heart. Dhikr chants vary from one order to the next, but often include multiple recitations of "there is no deity but God" (*lâ ilâha illâ 'llâh*), the first half of the confession of faith, and of praise phrases such as "glory be to God" (*subhan Allâh*). These activities of remembrance may also be enhanced by music and dance, such as those performed by members of a Turkish order called the "Mevlevi" (dedicated to the Persian poet Rûmî) and known in the West as "whirling dervishes" (Schimmel 1973).

After Abdul Qâdir's death, people began to ascribe miracles to him, and consider him a saint. His sons, and their sons, and so on, succeeded him as heads of the Qâdirî order. As the order spread throughout Asia and North Africa it gave rise to suborders, each linking themselves back to Abdul Qâdir. These orders were an effective way of converting people to Islam, offering as they did spiritual activities and a well-organized religious structure. Each present-day Qâdirî order has its own spiritual genealogy, detailing the transmission of knowledge back to Abdul Qâdir (and continuing on to Muhammad). These spiritual genealogies connect Muslims in South and Southeast Asia, the Middle East, northern and western Africa, and Europe into an international network of Sufi practice and worship.

The movements we have examined here vary greatly in size, complexity, and purpose—from the Buddhist forest dweller and his followers to revivalist movements of many types, and from Ngundeng the Nuer prophet to the large-scale movements begun by Joseph Smith and Muhammad. In each case we have seen adherents grapple with practical problems of continuity and with their relationship to the outside world. Some have had to ask in the face of crisis, "How shall we continue?" Their answers have involved the creation of routines and bureaucracies, a process remarked upon by Weber, but some answers also involve genealogies and talismans. Alongside the routinization of authority there often continues its charisma: in Acharn Man's medallions, in the powers of the Qâdirî teacher, in the Mormon Elder's revelations, in Ngundeng's songs, which continue to ring out over southern Sudanese radio.

Religious movements and authorities of all forms today are part of modern nation-states, in which they invariably live side by side with others of different faiths and practices. Our discussion of the Church of Latter-Day Saints already touched on the problem of maintaining a religious vision that runs counter to that of a nation's majority; in the concluding chapter we encounter this problem head-on.

14

Religion, Violence, and War

*T*his chapter will be devoted to the question of what role religion plays in the genesis and development of violence and war. At first glance, it would seem reasonable to say that religious beliefs often lead to violence and warfare. Hundreds of recent books and articles about contemporary violence blame religion, whether regarding Islam and terrorism, Hindu violence in India, or conflicts between Catholics and Protestants in Northern Ireland. Case closed, it would seem.

Upon a closer look, however, each case for religion's direct role in violence seems fuzzier. Archeology and ethnography of small-scale societies show no consistent role for religion in the genesis of war. An overview of the anthropology of warfare (Ferguson 1990) argues that a range of material factors, such as competition for scarce economic or political resources, best explain the occurrence of large-scale violence, and that structural and psychological factors, such as political scale or resentment, then channel and shape what follows. Recent anthropological analyses of genocide support these claims, though they give greater prominence to political power struggles (Hinton 2002). Religious loyalties and affinities may lead people to join a cause, or reinforce the resolve of fighters, but so may loyalties to social or ethnic groups, or to a nation or cause. There does not seem to be anything intrinsic to religion that predisposes people toward, or away from, violence or war.

More generally, anthropologists long have abandoned generalizations about humans as naturally aggressive (as in the view promoted by Hobbes) or naturally peaceful (as in the contrary view proposed by Rousseau). It is more interesting to reflect on the fact that everywhere, and in all ages, one finds people engaged in conflict and peace, hostility and acceptance. Hindus may protect cattle from harm, but some have killed Muslims for sacrificing their own cows. Some Muslims have bombed in the name of God, but most draw on their religion for its lessons of patience and submission. Indeed, most of the time people do not fight others on grounds of religious difference.

The more interesting question concerns the social and historical conditions surrounding violence, and the roles that religious ideas and orientations may play with respect to the mechanisms that lead people to engage in or refrain from violence or warfare. This way of putting a general question—focusing on conditions and specific mechanisms—usually produces more interesting answers in the social sciences than do broader questions such as, "does religion promote violence?" Other questions have similarly benefited from such whittling-down. For example, the "contact hypothesis" held that familiarity breeds acceptance. It turns out, however, that it is specific social mechanisms that breed acceptance, such as cooperating on a specific task, and that simple contact has no predictable result (Forbes 1997).

As in previous chapters, we will consider a series of case studies to discern the relevant dimensions to our question. The two types of religious phenomena most consistently linked with images of violence today are the small-scale movements often called "cults" and politically active forms of Islam, and we will consider each in turn. Elsewhere in the book we have considered specific acts of violence, for example, those committed on persons undergoing initiation (Chapter 4) and the killing of people accused of witchcraft (Chapter 8).

Cults, Sects, and Violence

*A*mong the many new religious movements appearing in the past decades in Europe, North America, and elsewhere, most conduct their affairs as peaceably as do more established religious groups. Those that commit acts of violence, directed toward themselves or toward others, thereby become widely known. These acts contribute to a popular sense that a "cult" or "sect" is likely to involve brainwashing, terror, and physical violence, despite the fact that these features occur relatively rarely. We consider two recent movements that did involve violent acts and then ask what is true of them that is not true of other, peaceful movements.

Aum Shinrikyo

The Japanese movement Aum Shinrikyo at first resembled many other Japanese New Religions in promoting meditation and ascetic practices under the leadership of a charismatic person, in this case the the blind Asahara Shoko (Reader 2000). Asahara earlier had joined a religion called Agonshu, whose adherents practiced yoga and meditation and sought special psychic powers. Like many others in Japan, Asahara was attracted by the movement's teaching that the world was threatened by environmental or nuclear disaster. He left to form his own group in 1984, which began by setting out goals and ideas that were similar to those of other Japanese religious movements (Davis 1980). Members sought greater psychic powers, perhaps through contacts with ancestors, in order to purify themselves or to solve their everyday problems. Like other such religions, Asahara's saw people as being reborn according to their karma, and most people as falling into undesirable rebirths.

Starting in the mid–1980s, Asahara began to preach a coming conflict between good and evil, but at first he saw his mission as purifying the world to avoid conflict. He urged followers to form *sanghas,* using the word for Buddhist monasteries. His demands were strict: those who would join the sanghas had to break off all ties with their families and friends. Even under these conditions, over 1,000 people did join a sangha, and perhaps 8,000 more joined the movement. As with other Japanese new religions, many of the recruits were educated young professionals. Asahara offered them the chance to engage in research, much of it aimed at giving them superhuman powers; some of it consisting of fabricating amphetamines and hallucinogens along with poisons and explosives. The recruits practiced ascetic regimes and meditation along a path set out by Asahara. Disciples could purchase containers of what was supposed to be the guru's bathwater, or vials of his blood, which would give them his special DNA (and which probably produced effects through the addition of hallucinogenic drugs). They had to rent a helmet that would connect them with the guru's brain waves and enable them to reach his state of meditation (Hall, Schuyler, and Trinh 2000, 76–110).

The stated purposes of these practices changed over time. At first they were supposed to give practitioners personal powers and thereby enable them to save humanity. But as Asahara failed to reach his own goals of massive recruitment, his disillusionment led him to turn toward a more dramatic form of apocalyptic preaching, in which he said that mass destruction was coming and only a few people on earth would be saved. In itself, this doctrine is not so different from that adhered to by many Christians in North America who believe that at the coming moment of Rapture only a few saved souls will be brought up to heaven to avoid the destruction that will follow on earth. But (as readers will be quick to add) doctrine does not determine people's ideas or practices. In this case, Asahara responded violently to his failure, blaming the world for what had happened. He turned inward, demanding complete obedience from his followers, and set an example by having his wife beaten until she complied with his demands to lead an ascetic life. He had others beaten and forced to follow regimes involving near-starvation or other extreme practices, and in 1988 one of his followers died after a regimen involving repeated immersion in baths. Asahara was waiting for legal recognition of his movement as a religion and covered up the death; worse, he ordered the killing of a follower who was about to defect and tell the authorities of the death. The murder changed Asahara's writings and preaching; now he warned of Satan corrupting some in his movement, a logic akin to that of the Salem witchcraft accusations.

The violence escalated, as did opposition from families of those who had cut their ties to the outside world in order to join one of Aum's sanghas and from some disillusioned adherents. Asahara ordered the murder of an opposition group's lawyer and his family. His entry into electoral politics in 1990 failed miserably, adding to his humiliation, and leading to a decision to destroy large numbers of his opponents. He may have ordered as many as fifty people killed. His efforts to develop weapons of mass destruction culminated in the sarin gas attack on the Tokyo subway in 1995, which killed twelve people and injured thousands, leading to the arrest of Asahara and many of his followers.

Order of the Solar Temple

The Order, or OTS in its French version, came to the world's attention in 1994, when police investigating the burning of vacation villas in Switzerland and Québec found that they contained bodies neatly arranged on the floors and killed with bullets to the head.

The dead turned out to be successful men and women from Switzerland, France, and Belgium—among them a nuclear engineer, a mayor, and wealthy businesspeople. A year later more people died in the same manner near Grenoble, France. Letters sent out the day of the 1994 deaths explained that those who died were in fact in "Transit" to another world. It turned out that some had killed themselves, while others had been "assisted" in their journey. Some dissidents had been outright murdered.

The Solar Temple Order developed in the 1970s from the partnership of Joseph Di Mambro, a French former member of Templar and Rosicrucian orders, and the Belgian homeopathic doctor, Luc Jouret. Di Mambro had earlier joined a movement in France that saw itself as the successors to the medieval Knights Templar, and some survivors of the massacre-suicides compared the fate of the Order to that of the knights (Hall, Schuyler, and Trinh 2000; Introvigne and Mayer 2002). The Knights Templar was formed during the Crusades in the twelfth century in order to protect Jerusalem. Their order was chartered directly by the Pope. During the twelfth and thirteenth centuries they succeeded brilliantly both in combat and in amassing and investing wealth from donations. They established parallel lay organizations that functioned as shadow churches with their own rituals. Their secrecy, success, and activities in the financial world aroused envy and suspicion, and once they failed on the battlefield, the Church and the King of France, Philip the Fair, moved together against them. In 1310, Philip had 54 knights burned at the stake for heresy.

The mystique of the knights has propelled them into literature (most recently in *The Da Vinci Code*), and into the popular imagination. The red (or "rosy") cross they wore gave the name to the Rosicrucian order, and Masonic orders claimed descent from both Templars and the Rosicrucians. Hundreds of such "neo-Templar" and Rosicrucian orders have formed over the past two centuries, each combining mysticism, chivalry, secrecy, and promise of delivery from death. The Vatican II reforms that lessened the sense of mystery and tradition associated with the Catholic Mass gave a further boost to the creation of such orders (and to New Age movements generally).

It was out of this cauldron of movements and mysticism that the Solar Order emerged, based on ideas about a "Solar Christ" and the existence of "Ascended Masters" who move in and out of historical existence. Jouret had been ordained as a priest by a dissident Roman Catholic priest, and became the Grand Master of the Solar Order. Drawing on his homeopathic medical background, Jouret lectured throughout the French-speaking world, linking health concerns to the Order's ideas, and selling cassettes, books, and lecture tickets in health food stores and New Age bookstores. Jouret's lectures were by all accounts spellbinding, and he had clubs for people to join—on nutrition, gardening, music, and so forth. His message was that a vital essence in ourselves was troubled when we felt sick, and that the same essence in our environment was troubled, a line of thought leading him to predict ecological apocalypse. His appeal was in his ability to link together a number of New Age themes: astrology, health and environmental consciousness, a mixing of science and faith, and to tie these to the mystical countercultural Catholic traditions, in which francophone Catholics disaffected by the liberal reforms of Vatican II could rediscover history and mystery.

Even as he was predicting that humans would find it difficult to make the crossover from this age to the Age of Aquarius, Jouret came under suspicion in France, where active anti-cult organizations watch out for such movements. He developed a new center in Québec, where the Order's initiation ceremony happened to be videotaped by a member. The tape shows how the internal structure of the Order worked in a ritual. The Order was governed by an inner group, below which were three degrees of initiation, each with three internal ranks. In the videotaped ritual, initiated members wearing white robes with red crosses enter an outer room, line up, and raise swords toward the light emanating from a single candle. A priest blesses a new member, at which point Jouret emerges from behind a door to bless the group. Behind that door was the inner sanctuary where a few initiates would be admitted to witness images, which probably were holographic projections but were experienced by the initiates as visitations by Ascended Masters. They saw apostles of Christ, grand Templar masters, Moses, and other world figures. Di Mambro himself was considered to be the reincarnation of the Pharoah Akhnaton, Osiris, and Moses.

The Order demanded the members donate money and sought a high degree of control over their lives, to the point of rearranging marriages in order to produce "cosmic children" who would create a New Age. Some rebelled at these measures, and dissidence increased when it became known that the spectral appearances of Ascended Masters were the result of technologically sophisticated image projections. By the early 1990s, police and anti-cult groups had begun to investigate the Order. In 1993 Québec police raided an Order building, found weapons, and arrested Jouret and others; they eventually were convicted of weapons charges. The trial added to the group's negative publicity and built up their feeling that the outside world had conspired against them.

The group's leaders responded by declaring that cosmic messages indicated the need to make a "Transit" out of this world and into another (specifically, to the star Sirius). They then took the steps that led to the murder-suicides of 1994 and 1995 in Switzerland, France, and Québec. Would the massacres have taken place had there been no outside intervention against the group? It is hard to say, and it did not take much to push the leaders over the edge, but letters sent by the group pointed to police raids and arrests as the reason for their decision to embark on the Transit at the moment they did so.

French and French-speaking authorities were quick to apply the standard analytical framework used in these countries to denounce "cults" (*les sectes*): the members were gullible people, marginal to their societies, who had been brainwashed by dangerous leaders. However, most followers of the Order were solid, middle-class citizens. Why, then, did this group march toward destruction, and why did many of its members willingly commit suicide?

As with Aum Shinrikyo, the best account of the group's "success" focuses both on their internal social and psychological dynamics and on the effects of external pressures on the group. Even by the late 1980s, the group's message of apocalypse considered the end of the world to be part of a long-term cycle of birth and death, the idea of 6,000-year cycles found in Hinduism. These events would develop naturally, without any need for the group to take action. In this respect, the Order resembled Aum Shinrokyo at a similar, early stage of development. The group amassed money and arms for survival in face of a coming catastrophe, not in order to kill others, and in that respect resembled the mainly peaceful activities of survivalist groups in western parts of North America. Apocalyptic beliefs thus do not appear themselves to be a sufficient cause of violence.

It was a combination of perceived threats and fears that they were losing their hold on their followers that led the leaders to move to a new stage of killings and suicides. By the early 1990s, Di Mambro and Jouret had begun to express desires to leave this earth. At the same time, police investigations of Order finances and firearms procurement combined with dissent within the movement to create a sense of external threat in the minds of the leaders. Of course, that they responded by killing dissidents requires a further psychological explanation. The members' reasons for maintaining their involvement also are unclear, but most likely had to do with that enjoyment of being in on a secret, being one of the few to know what really is going to happen, that adds strength to secret societies around the world, whether in Masonic temples or New Guinea societies. If we can believe the letters sent out just before the mass suicides and killings, the members of the Solar Order saw themselves as leaving a sullied world for a purer one. Whether they would have followed through with the Transit even without outside opposition is difficult to say, but surely their drive to do so came initially from within themselves, through a conviction nourished by age-old narratives of Christian martyrdom, mysticism, and dispensed salvation, maintained through rituals of access to wisdom, and reinforced by contemporary concerns for psychological and environmental purity.

The series of events that led to the destruction of the Order appear in a number of other cases of small apocalyptic groups, such as Heaven's Gate, whose adherents committed suicide near San Diego in 1997, and the Peoples Temple of Jim Jones, living in its communal settlement in Guyana, South America, where 918 people died in 1978. All three groups believed that they had come from, and would return to, another world. They felt persecuted, and were particularly threatened by defectors and dissidents. Attacks on some of these groups added to this sense of persecution: the fate of the Branch Davidians convinced many cult leaders that they were next in line to be destroyed. In their efforts to restore authority, reclaim charisma, and remove themselves from their persecutors, they took violent action against themselves and others. These actions also were statements to the world. The Order and Heaven's Gate sent out press releases before destroying themselves. Jim Jones said: "We've got to be in the history books."

These and other groups that ended in violence had apocalyptic expectations about the soon-to-arrive end of human history. Their expectations led them to engage in practices intended to deliver them from catastrophe, but that had the indirect effects of promoting strong norms of internal solidarity and loyalty. In the society at large they were confronted by a strong group of cult detractors whose efforts to expose, oppose, and sometime destroy cults reinforced their feelings of persecution.

Persecution does not in itself lead to violence, of course. Scientologists have been subjected to more governmental scrutiny and harassment than was, say, the Order of the Solar Temple and, although Scientologists may have carried out revenge actions against dissidents, there has been nothing approaching the behavior described above. The difference lies in part in the internal ideas: even though Scientology does demand secrecy and conformity from adherents, it does not (as far as we know) organize its activities around the idea of an impending apocalypse.

But then again, the belief in an apocalypse does not necessarily lead to violence either, as is evidenced by the millions of (relatively) peaceful churchgoers in the United States who believe that the end of the world is near, the "dispensational premillenarianists" discussed in Chapter 13. One could believe that the world will end and draw a wide range of consequences from that belief: that one should better the world to attract a savior, that one should lead an ethically correct life so as to achieve salvation, or that one should convince others to do so as well in order to save the largest number of people. For a movement to move from apocalyptic beliefs to violence demands additional internal elements as well as a perception of external repression. Movements such as those described in this chapter moved from a simple belief that the world would terminate in an apocalypse to a drive to either to flee the world or bring about its end. This turn toward world-ending or world-fleeing action was led by a small number of individuals, whose charisma and paranoia allowed and drove them to carry it off.

Struggle and Authority in Islam

*A*pproaching ideas by viewing them in a social context is nowhere more important than when we consider doctrines of large-scale religions, such as Islam or Catholicism. Each has doctrines that can be drawn on to justify violence and war, such as the Catholic doctrine of the just war (Regan 1996), or the Islamic idea of the jihad, to which we now turn. What role do these doctrines play in conflicts: do they cause them, mobilize people, or play roles at certain specific moments?

Historians note that Islamic ideas of jihad (Arabic jihâd, from the verb jâhada, to struggle or strive) have developed in response to particular sets of social norms and practices. In eighth-century Arabic, war between tribes was expected and ongoing, and most scholars interpret the Qur'ân's statements on jihad in that light (Peters 1996).

Multiple Approaches to Scripture on Jihad

The Qur'ân contains two kinds of verses with respect to war. One set of verses explicitly limits legitimate war to situations where Muslims are first attacked, such as chapter 2 verse 190, which says "and fight in the way of God with those who fight you, but aggress not: God loves not the aggressors." Other verses mention no such conditions, such as chapter 9 verse 29, "Fight those who believe not in God and the Last Day and do not forbid what God and His Messenger have forbidden—such men as practice not the religion of truth, being of those who have been given the Book—until they pay the tribute out of hand and have been humbled." Even this second set, however, links fighting to the expansion of the Muslim political and religious community, the *umma*, and the subjugation and payment of tribute by neighboring peoples. Indeed, maintaining control over armies before and after the beginning of Islam required periodic raiding of neighboring tribes, if not expansion of a community's borders, in order to retain soldiers' loyalty by redistributing wealth (Berkey 2003).

Early jurists confirmed the idea that the umma, led by a caliph, a rightful successor to Muhammad, had the collective obligation to urge other peoples to convert and join the umma, or to submit to Muslim rule and pay tribute. This obligation gave rise to the idea that the world was divided into the *dar al-Islâm*, the world of submission to God, and the *dar al-harb*, the world that was subject to warfare and conquest. These jurists also developed laws of just war, including the rights of enemy combatants and of noncombatants, rules regarding when attack was permitted, and norms concerning how to fairly divide the spoils.

In the modern period, jurists have developed several quite distinct sets of ideas about jihad. Modernist Muslim thinkers writing from the late nineteenth century onward drew on the first kind of Qur'ânic verses mentioned above to argue that the normal state of relations among nations, Muslim or non-Muslim, is the state of peace. War is justified only when necessary to defend oneself. Furthermore, they said, God wants people to come to Islam out of study, reflection, and conviction, and not under force of arms. The Qur'ânic verse, "there is no compulsion in matters of religion" (2:256) is often quoted to buttress this argument. This line of thinking has been continued by such influential Muslim figures as the Egyptian jurist Sheikh Yûsuf Qardâwî, and by Sheikhs of al-Azhar University in Cairo.

A second, opposed line of reasoning was put forth by Islamic groups seeking to fight their own Muslim governments and seeking religious justification for their attacks. Sayyid Qutb (d. 1966), for example, argued that armed aggression against the Egyptian government was justified because Egyptian leaders, although they professed Islam, in fact had left the faith and thus were legitimate targets for attack (Qutb 1978).

As in so many matters, Islamic texts and traditions may be cited to support a wide range of actions. Many contemporary Muslim scholars underscore this quality of Islam (a quality shared by all religions). However, there is a different tendency that one finds in all religions that depend on a scripture, a tendency that one might call the "retreat to literalism," whereby one claims that scripture has a single, unambiguous meaning. Interestingly, this has not been an important position among Muslim jurists, who generally have held that either there is no single correct Islamic position on legal matters, or that there is, but that humans, imperfect as they are, cannot be expected always to arrive at it. Under these two views, differences in interpretation of the Qur'ân and the hadîth either are planned by God, or are forgiven by Him (Abou El Fadl 2001).

It is, rather, Muslim public intellectuals who have invoked their claims as to what Islam "really says" to advance particular stances. One saw this "retreat to literalism" practiced, very understandably, by Muslims in the United States just after the destruction of the World Trade Center towers on September 11, 2001. Some scholars were featured in media coverage as saying that "Islam is a religion of peace" and that it "could never approve of such attacks." Similarly, verses from the Qur'ân promoting peaceful coexistence among peoples and attacking those who kill were cited widely, as if they, and not the statements coming from terrorists, represented true Islam. Rare were the authorities who stated that scripture contains lots of messages, and that one can find verses and interpretations of them that support attacks on unbelievers, as well as the peace-oriented verses more widely quoted.

Of course, the weakness of the "retreat to literalism" was immediately apparent when other Muslims quoted verses that urged Muslims to fight infidels, or that spoke in a highly negative fashion of the Jews. The appropriate response to this practice of citing out of context was to speak of the historical circumstances in which these verses were received, and of the interpretive traditions and alternatives built up around them. But this way was closed to those who had begun the debate by their own literal, and thus ahistorical, way of interpreting scripture.

The problem in searching for a single "Muslim position" on jihad, or even regarding particular actions, is that the major ways in which legal opinions, *fatwa* (pl. *fatâwa*) are produced is in response to a specific question. The choice of question can shape the answer. For example, shortly after the invasion of Afghanistan in the fall of 2001, influential U.S. Muslim scholars posed a question to Sheikh Yûsuf Qardâwî, the Egyptian scholar living in Qatar, whose broadcasts on the television station al-Jazîra are followed by Arabic-speaking Muslims throughout the world. The scholars asked whether Muslims serving in the U.S. armed forces ordered to fight in Afghanistan ought to obey their orders. Qardâwî answered that they should, because they had taken an oath to do so. Subsequently, others put a different question to him: should Muslims bombard women and children in Afghanistan? Qardâwî answered that they should not. Looked at in two different ways, the same actions could be judged as advisable or reprehensible.

Throughout Islamic history, the idea of jihad has provided a justification for unifying against an enemy, and in many cases it has provided the basis for a new political system. In West Africa, for example, the norm of jihad was instrumental in expanding the realm of Islamic rule and constructing stable and prosperous communities. The "chain" of jihad spread through the region over two centuries, from the 1670s in the far western Sahara, to the anticolonial movements of the late nineteenth century.

West African jihad movements responded to a difficult question for Muslims then and now, namely, in the absence of a single Muslim ruler, a caliph, who is it who has the authority to create an Islamic polity, or to declare jihad? In West Africa of the eighteenth century, established Muslim political authority was weak and distant, consisting of an Ottoman Empire effectively confined to the Mediterranean, and an independent Moroccan authority with little reach below the Sahara (Robinson 1985). It was thus new leaders who took it upon themselves to announce the combat against non-Muslim rulers and colonial powers.

Commenting on the contemporary struggles among Muslims over political authority, Gilles Kepel (Kepel 2002) has argued that recent instances of terrorism under the banner of jihad are not signs of the strength of political Islam, by which he means political projects to create Islamic states, but rather signify the decline and defeat of such projects, a thesis first argued by Olivier Roy (Roy 1994). Violence by armed Islamic groups occurs when an earlier movement for political Islam, which was supported by an alliance of a devout bourgeoisie and young Muslim groups, rejects extremist Islamist projects and opts instead for projects of multiparty democracy and focusing on Islamizing civil society. Violence thus is the result of the combination of the preexistence of a cultural repertoire which includes a doctrine of jihad, the development of highly controlled movements with goals of establishing an Islamic state, and rising external resistance to and rejection of those goals by mainstream Muslim populations.

Competing Authorities in the Afghan Struggle

The history of recent struggles in Afghanistan underscore the connections between varying ideas of jihad and struggles over political authority. From the beginning of the resistance to the Soviet-backed regime in the 1970s, to the victory of the Taliban in 1996, Islam has provided a repertoire of ideas of authority, on which various individuals and groups could call in order to rally people behind them. In this respect, the question of jihad has been subsumed in broader questions of political authority (Edwards 2002).

The traditional social forms for armed combat in Afghanistan were tribal. Tribes fought under their own leaders, sometimes perhaps allied with each other, particularly if they spoke the same language. In a place with many different ethnic groups and language families, centralized authority never has been easy to develop. When, in the late 1970s, Afghan tribes began to form armed groups, or *lashkar*, to attack the troops of the Soviet-backed government, the most effective rhetoric for gaining intertribal unity was that of Islam. Various actions taken by the regime could be cited as defiling Islam, and thereby provide a rallying cry for all groups. An intertribal "jihad council" took collective responsibility for actions, preventing tribal rivalries from fractioning the antigovernment coalition.

Eventually, tribal and larger ethnic rivalries stymied efforts to mount a unified military front. But in their efforts to do so, rival claimants to lead the resistance or to govern Afghanistan called on different elements of the Islamic tradition to justify their claims. The three most important kinds of religious claims were saintly lineage, the prestige of a foreign religious education, and the promise of a "return to village religion." None was decisive, but each was legitimate in Islamic terms as a basis for claiming the right to lead the jihad.

Claiming descent from a saint, or better yet, from the Prophet Muhammad, attracts followers in most, if not all, Muslim societies. Continuity through direct contact over the generations is a general feature of Islam, as we saw in Chapter 10. The Prophet's statements are only valid if an unbroken chain of reliable witnesses has transmitted them. Relations of teachers to students create a chain of spiritual learning. Descent from parent to child is a particularly accepted basis for claiming to have inherited a mantle of religious authority. In Afghanistan, the strong tribal norms that bind people together based on patrilineal descent reinforce the appeal of these claims.

One man making such claims was Hazrat Sibghatullah Mujaddidi. Mujaddidi came from a family that claims to have descended from Sheikh Ahmad Sirhindi, a central figure in the development of Indian Sufism in the seventeenth century. The family was invited to Afghanistan in the late eighteenth century by the first Afghan king, and established a political base among Pakhtun tribal groups (the largest ethnic category in Afghanistan). These tribesmen became their disciples in a Sufi order (Edwards 2002, 253). The family enjoyed considerable power in making and breaking subsequent kings. Mujaddidi increased his own authority when in 1953 he earned a degree in Islamic jurisprudence from al-Azhar University in Cairo. This combination of lineage and a prestigious degree gave him considerable legitimacy in the eyes of Pakhtun Afghans. In 1979 he sent letters out to his followers throughout Afghanistan calling for mass uprisings against the government. In Herat, 200,000 people responded to his call, saying, as he himself recalled it, "Oh, this man is the right man. We shall start." The uprising was brutally suppressed by Soviet troops, a failure that considerably lessened his capacity to mobilize people for jihad. In any case, ties of loyalties to Sufi leaders (*pirs*) had weakened considerably in the course of the twentieth century.

The chief beneficiaries of this weakening in the struggle to lead the jihad were the new Islamic political parties. The legitimacy of claimants to lead these parties rested on their early involvement with party organizations and their foreign Islamic credentials. A key source of legitimacy was a professor of Islamic law at Kabul University, Ghulam Muhammad Niazi, who in the late 1960s was the principal sponsor of the Muslim Youth Organization, the origin of later Islamic movements. Two of the most important contestants for Afghan jihad leadership, Ustad Burhanuddin Rabbani and Engineer Gulbuddin Hekmatyar, based their claims in large part on their respective ties to this professor. Rabbani claimed that he had been Niazi's chief assistant at the university. Hekmatyar countered that it was another man from the Niazi tribe, Abdur Rahim Niazi, and not Rabbani, who was Professor Niazi's true heir, and that Abdur Rahman Niazi had worked closely with Hekmatyar in the early days of the Muslim Youth Organization. The Rabbani–Hekmatyar rivalry was ethnic as well as purely political: Rabbani was a Persian-speaking Tajik, whereas Hekmatyar was a Pakhtun. Their respective parties became increasingly polarized along ethnic lines in the late 1970s and 1980s.

Why were their ties to a university professor so important to these two rivals? Professor Niazi was acknowledged as the first Afghan to have studied with members of the Muslim Brotherhood in Cairo, and to have brought their ideas to Afghanistan. It was Ustad (a religious honorific) Rabbani who had translated works by the Brotherhood figure Sayyid Qutb into Persian, but Professor Niazi's status as the first to have learned the new ideas of the Brotherhood underscores the importance of precedence in determining authority in Afghan society. It also shows how the older ties to Sufi teachers and other Afghan scholars had diminished in importance, supplanted by a new kind of genealogical tie, that to prestigious foreign, and presumably better, formulators of Islamic knowledge (Edwards 2002, 239).

The rivalries among Hekmatyar, Rabbani, and other leaders led to the destruction of Kabul, murder and plunder in towns and villages throughout the country, and the rise in the mid–1990s of a new movement, the Taliban, or "students." Their claims to legitimacy in leading a jihad against the tribal rulers and party leaders were, again, based on religious norms, but this time norms having to do with the ideal of an indigenous Islam of the Afghan village. The Taliban argued that this ideal had been corrupted by the work of the parties and by the predominance of Kabul University. The Taliban warriors had grown up in refugee camps along the frontier and in Pakistan, and had attended religious schools, *madrasah,* in Pakistan. They held out the possibility of a restoration of an earlier Afghan Islam and the rejection of all foreign influences, whether Soviet, Western, or Arab. Ironically, it was their subsequent naïve welcoming of Saudi and Egyptian members of al-Qaeda that led to their destruction and the return to power of the regional tribal leaders. But much of their original appeal to Afghans was their refusal to follow either tribal loyalties or city-based party politics.

David Edwards's scholarship shows how we can understand calls for jihad as part of specific struggles for autonomy and power. The traditions and literature around jihad form part of a number of distinct cultural repertoires on which Muslims can call; these repertoires differ across societies, such that the resonances of and alternatives to jihad are quite different in Afghanistan than, say, in Indonesia or North America. Edwards shows that the Afghanistan repertoire includes several sets of values and actions centered on genealogy, honor, and tribal loyalty. In Indonesia the "jihad repertoire" does not reflect those concepts, but instead has associations with long-standing Christian-Muslim tensions over missionary activities and conflicts over power and resources in local contexts. In North America and Europe the concept of jihad has no local purchase, but can only be used to refer to conflicts occurring elsewhere, for example, in Palestine and Chechnya.

Indonesian Jihads

A brief look at recent violence in Indonesia will help to distinguish between the causes of violence and the factors that make it last and grow in strength. Muslims make up the large majority (around 85 percent) of Indonesians, but Christians occupy important positions in society, and in several regions of the country they form the local majority. Although open conflict between Muslim and Christian groups has been relatively rare in Indonesia (attacks on Chinese being determined by a different set of tensions), in the late 1990s bloody conflicts between Muslim and Christian groups did arise in the eastern island area called the Moluccas. What caused this sudden change in Muslim-Christian relations?

Christianization is a centuries-old phenomenon in eastern Indonesia, but much of the conversion in Maluku took place in the nineteenth century under Dutch rule. Some Muslims had lived in the region, especially in the largest city of Ambon, for centuries, but many more began to arrive from the large island of Sulawesi beginning in the early 1990s. These newcomers took over many informal sector jobs, such as market-place sellers and pedicab drivers. They drew on relatively tight social networks to dominate these sectors, as do new immigrant groups throughout the world. Tensions between Muslims and Christians rose after the economic crisis of 1997, when the control of jobs became a matter of survival. In Ambon, patronage networks stretch all the way up to the highest offices, with the governor, high-ranking army officials, and a former mayor of Ambon controlling both employment opportunities and local gangs.

In 1998 a small incident involving a bus conductor and an obstreperous passenger touched off fights between rival gangs (whose numbers had swelled with recent arrivals from Jakarta). Unlike other conflicts that had exploded elsewhere in the country, in particular in Kalimantan and Aceh, here the lines of social cleavage corresponded to nationwide divisions between Muslim and Christian communities. Christian networks throughout Indonesia began to warn of plots to Islamize all of eastern Indonesia. Islamic groups reminded their supporters of long-standing efforts at Christianization, and warned that warriors from the 1940s Christian-controlled Republic of South Maluku were waiting for a chance to launch a separatist movement. Some factions of the armed forces that had continued to support Suharto after his downfall from the presidency gave material aid to Muslims.

Here the tensions leading to violence were material: conflict over jobs between poor Muslims and poor Christians, and conflicts over political power between Muslim and Christian politicians. But each side was able to draw on the repertoires of defense and survival to mobilize their co-religionists. Christians were as able to do this as were Muslims; the fact that Muslims had a convenient word at hand did not in itself give them an edge. Slogans used by protagonists do not furnish adequate analytical frameworks.

How Are People Able to Kill?

Even if we explain the role of religion in furnishing a repertoire for mobilizing in struggle, we are left with the matter of how people become able to kill other people. Do religions make it easier for people to kill when they are moved to do so for other reasons?

The psychiatrist Robert Jay Lifton (Lifton 1986) has discussed the psychological mechanism of "doubling" in killers, a process whereby a person creates a second self, cut off from his or her everyday self (or former self) that in its very thinness and separation from the rest of the world makes it possible to commit violence. Violence may be for many ends, of course. A doctor may create a "medical self" that can commit the violence of slicing open a living body for a life-sustaining medical operation, a soldier may create a "military self" that can shoot an enemy soldier at close range, or a member of a militant religious group may create a heroic version of him or herself as devoted to and even willing to die for a cause.

It is with respect to these processes of "doubling" that the specific actions taken by certain movements become more understandable: that movements that seek to lead their members toward violence will insist that they cut off ties from their everyday or former lives, that they will provide a charismatic figure who will exemplify the heroic doubled self for recruits to emulate. For example, many Palestinians invoke the right to fight an occupier to justify attacks against Israelis in occupied portions of the West Bank and Gaza. In 1991, Hamas carried out its first attacks inside Israel. Shortly thereafter many of its leaders were deported, and in their exile they began to develop the strategy of using young men and women to carry out suicide attacks, a method requiring little training or equipment, but the willingness to die for a cause.

The profile of suicide bombers suggests that they are typically young people who have found no way to advance in life, who have few social ties, and who find acceptance in religion. Those people, usually men who spend large amounts of time in the local mosque, might be noticed by Hamas leaders who then recruit them. They promise that the recruit will be a hero in this life and enjoy the privileges of martyrdom in the next—and that his family will receive both honor and significant material support. Then they isolate him, have him write letters about his impending martyrdom, and prevent him from reestablishing contact with his family (Stern 2003).

Similar steps are taken by leaders of Christian cults. James Ellison, the leader of a Christian Identity movement in rural Arkansas called the Covenant, the Sword, and the Arm of the Lord, sought to convince male recruits that they were new men, with a distinctive mission. He had them dress in combat fatigues and told them that they were the white race's last hope against the "Zionist Occupied Government" of the United States (Stern 2003). Followers of the Christian Identity movements believe that they will live into the Endtimes, a period described in Revelations during which the Antichrist will rule the world. They take as their duty to fight the Antichrist; their combat will lead toward the Apocalypse and the return of Jesus Christ. Because many such groups believe themselves to be already in the Endtimes, they seek out the identity of the Antichrist, who is variously described as the "world government" of the United Nations, or of a secret conspiracy developed by the Illuminati, or Zionism.

The specific identity of the enemy is less compelling to members than is the sense of a sacred and world-preserving mission. The rhetoric of the mission and the vision proposed to them fits with the Protestant teachings they have grown up hearing and believing: "End of Times, I've heard of that for years as a child in the Baptist Church. Everyone is left to fend for themselves," said one former member of Ellison's group (Stern 2003, 22). Thus prepared doctrinally for what they hear, and given a new sense of unity and purpose, with little contact with mainstream society, they can be led toward conflict, and even death.

Religion in general has no consistent relationship to violence or war: for every terrorist killing in the name of a deity there are countless other co-religionists leading peaceful lives. Furthermore, if religious ideas can provide a basis for inducing people to follow leaders in battle—and such has been the case from the Crusades to the small-scale violence associated with sects and jihadist groups—so can a range of other ideas, from racial or ethnic purity, to defense of the nation, to pretensions to imperial domination of the world. Religion monopolizes neither peace and charity nor war and violence.

15

The Place of Religions in Modern Nations and States

T he modern world is a world of states and nations, but in many parts of this world, "nations" and "states" sit in uneasy coexistence. Some states, like Japan, claim to be composed of one people, to possess a single national identity incorporating all, or nearly all, of its citizens. But these claims usually are made despite important internal differences in identity—think of the many Japanese of Korean descent or the sizable Christian (and even Muslim) minorities in the country. In other states, from Sri Lanka to Turkey to Bosnia, large minorities are fighting to create their own separate nation–state. Some states, such as Indonesia or the United States, are defined by the coexistence of different religious and ethnic groups, but even in those countries groups are struggling over national identity.

Religious identity and religious differences often enter into these debates and conflicts. Most countries today include several significantly large religious communities, and this *religious pluralism* is increasing. Muslims are becoming increasingly numerous minorities in countries where they never before played public roles. In the United States they already outnumber Episcopalians and are expected to overtake Jews within the next decade. In France they form the second-largest religious group after Catholics. Protestant Christians are rapidly increasing in numbers in Japan and Brazil, as well as in other countries.

Religious pluralism poses sharp and often divisive questions for the public life of a country. What contribution should each religion make to public political and social life? Can a unifying national identity coexist with publicly celebrated religious differences? If so, can a country avoid preferring one religion to others? From where does one select elements of a shared, civic morality and a common legal framework? These questions concern matters of public policy; other questions are matters of empirical study. What steps, if any, do minority religious communities take to conform to national models of religion or culture? To what extent are such minorities able to win recognition as valid religions or cultures? What changes are made in religious doctrines, or practices, or in the boundaries maintained between their members and others?

Religions play several different kinds of public roles. Religion may become identified with the *nation,* even if it does not play a direct role in government. In the largely Catholic countries of continental Europe and Latin America, church institutions have played major roles in public life, at times claiming to serve as the guardian of the nation. These claims have engendered conflict with citizens seeking an independent definition of the nation. Hindu nationalism in India and Buddhist nationalisms in Sri Lanka and Thailand (as well as movements of Protestant Christian nationalism in the United States) have similarly sought to define the nation around adherence to the religion and around key figures in its history.

Religion may also contribute directly to *state-enforced law.* Israel is defined as a Jewish state, with the enforcement of Jewish law, and many states with Muslim populations enforce Islamic law. We may find state-backed religious courts even in countries where the nation is not defined in religious terms, as in Indonesia, Kenya, and South Africa.

Finally, if we switch perspectives and consider the situation of religious minorities, we find that they must find ways to coexist with what José Casanova (1994) calls "public religions," religious traditions that do not form explicit parts of nation or state, but which nonetheless color public life. Muslims consider themselves to be minorities in the United States and Europe because the dominant public culture is strongly shaped by a Christian (and to a much lesser extent, Jewish) heritage. Around the world, European colonialism often left residues of Christian missionization that local peoples had to either join or resist. But public religions also exist on a smaller scale and place pressure on minorities. Protestants living in Hopi and Mayan communities in North America have had their rights to participate in public community life curtailed. Even if their formal rights were protected by the larger legal structure, their roles in "civil society" have been diminished.

We conclude the chapter with a more detailed look at the U.S. experience, where the separation of religion and state institutions is particularly emphasized.

Religious Nationalisms

We have already seen the ways in which Japanese rulers and others have drawn on Buddhism and Shinto as elements in a state ideology. But it is only since the late nineteenth century that the most thoroughgoing effort has been made to equate a state religion of Shinto with the shared identity of the Japanese people as a nation. This equation continues to underlie the ideologies of new religions in Japan, which stress the biological, social, and religious uniqueness of the Japanese people and the continued enshrinement of war dead as national deities.

What we may call *religious nationalism* involves the construction of an idealized nation in religious terms and the construction of an idealized religion in national terms. The identification of religion and nation is not ancient or primordial; it is part of the recent history of modern nation–states. It involves active efforts by religious and political leaders to convince people that national identity is essentially that of a particular religion, against alternative conceptions of the nation as secular or multiconfessional (with several, equally legitimate religions).

Among such efforts are the invention of religious practices that encompass a national territory. Religious identities are shaped through ritual practices; national religious identities, the sense of oneself as part of a national religion, are shaped through practices that give the actor the sense of being part of a nation. Processions of icons from border to border, pilgrimages to different religious sites within the country, and public speeches that define the nation's territory as religious territory all contribute to a sense of being part of a religiously defined nation. Religious nationalisms also often project backward in time an image of the nation as a long-lived entity that always was intertwined with religion.

The examples of Poland and India illustrate ways in which religious nationalisms can be forged and maintained. In both cases, religious nationalism draws strength from a shared opposition to a perceived foreigner. Poland's identification of the Catholic Church with the nation is in part the product of a history of foreign rule; India's movements of Hindu nationalism feed off of hostility between Hindus and Muslims, even as they maintain and exacerbate that hostility.

Church and Nation in Poland

The Polish people have a long history of struggle against foreign conquerors. Prussia, Russia, and Austria each incorporated parts of the Polish-speaking lands, and in the 1870s German Chancellor Bismark threatened the cultural identity of Poles by pushing for Germanization of all German citizens. Poles also battled against Nazi invaders and a communist state. The cumulative effect of these struggles was to fuse all elements of Polish society together with the Catholic Church. The Church was the only institution capable of cutting across the divided Polish lands. As José Casanova (1994) argues, during the nineteenth century Polish writers developed an ideology of national identity that incorporated Catholic identity. In the twentieth century the Church never became identified with the state—unlike its counterpart in Franco's Spain. The Polish Church thus remained untainted by collaboration, and retained its identification with the nation as a whole.

This argument—that outside oppression supported the identification of church and nation—receives confirmation from the experience between the two world wars, when in the independent Polish state the Church did side with one political party and thereby alienated supporters of other parties. Chauvinism also appeared in the form of oppression of Jewish and Ukrainian minorities. In this experience surfaces the perennial problem with any religious nationalism, namely, its difficulty in adopting tolerant (much less welcoming) attitudes toward religious and ethnic minorities. The religious underpinnings of nationalism may make it more intolerant of people of different faiths, while the nationalist side of religion locates it within a particular territory and may make it more intolerant of people of other origins or countries.

Nazi and communist rule returned Poland to the early situation of a strong church–nation alliance. In part this was because the massacres of Jews and deportations of Ukrainians left Poland in the late 1940s a predominantly Polish and Catholic nation.

Also, because of the evident dependence of the communist state on the Soviet Union, there appeared to be no leader representing an independent Polish nation. Given the situation, the head of the Polish Church, Cardinal Wyszynski, could draw on a centuries-old tradition that designated the head of the Church as a temporary leader of the nation in the absence of a head of state. He, in effect, played that role during the years of communist rule.

Equally critical in forging religious nationalism, however, has been the fact that Polish Catholicism is highly public, and could not be forced into becoming a private religion of at-home worship. Even more than in many other Catholic societies, Polish Catholicism centers on large-scale public rituals, including pilgrimages, processions in celebration of the feast of Corpus Christi, and passion plays. These rituals involve the entire territory of Poland and all its Catholic inhabitants. Particularly effective were the Cardinal's series of celebrations involving the national image of Mary, Our Lady of Czestochowa, or the Black Madonna. This shrine, writes Casanova (1994, 98), "serves as the national shrine of Polish Catholicism and as the symbolic fortress of the nation against foreign invasions." After he was released from imprisonment by the communist state in 1956, Cardinal Wyszynski rededicated the nation to the Black Madonna at the 300th anniversary of King John Kazimierz's vows, thus projecting the church–nation union back three centuries. Throughout the 1960s and 1970s he engineered an annual procession of the Black Madonna image to every town in Poland, this impressive achievement keeping salient the linkages between national territory and religious territory.

The Church urged that Poles accept the state's right to rule (it was this agreement that led to the cardinal's release from prison in 1956). However, Cardinal Glemp, the head of the Polish Church since 1981, was also advocating the creation of a confessional Polish state and the repeal of constitutional separation of church and state. The Church had indeed allied itself with the nation, but it also had designs on state power. The dangers of church–state identification in the modern world are best exemplified by Spain, where civil wars in the nineteenth and twentieth centuries became religious wars, with one party backed by the Church. The last of these religious wars, the Spanish Civil War of 1936–1939, served as a proving ground for fascism.

Casanova (1994, 107–113) notes that the Polish Church may well remain on its current course of involvement in public affairs as a player in civil society, not in politics per se. He argues that the direct relationships between churches and political parties in the Europe of the mid–twentieth century (best illustrated by the power of Christian Democratic parties in several countries) is now evolving into a separation of civil society, in which religion plays a public role, and political society, where parties are no longer tied to specific churches and therefore are free to pursue solutions to political problems flexibly, free of church dogmatism. Many Poles agree that the number of pilgrims making their way to Czestochowa each year has declined recently, and that the role of the Church as a political guide has passed (Brzezinski 1994).

Hindu Nationalism in India

Looming over India since its creation in 1947 has been the problematic relationship of the two major religious communities, Hindu and Muslim, to the ideas of "nation" and "state." Although India was created as a secular republic, its birth was accompanied by that of Pakistan and also by massive and blood-stained migrations of Muslims to Pakistan. Today Muslims constitute 12 percent of India's population, and the vast majority in Pakistan and Bangladesh (Bangladesh itself having emerged out of a division within Pakistan). Conflicts between Hindus and Muslims in India today are bound up both with the history of partition, migration, and violence, and with the continuing tensions between India and Pakistan. To some Hindus, Muslims and a Muslim state play the same role of foreign threat that successive conquerors did in convincing Poles of the internal links between church and nation.

The 1980s and 1990s have seen mass conflicts between Hindus and Muslims in India. Are these conflicts religious? Consider the continuing conflict in the north India city of Ayodhya, Rama's birthplace (van der Veer 1994). Ayodhya is a holy tīrtha, a ford over the holy river Sarayu and a place for the pilgrim to "cross over" from the mundane world to make contact with Rama. Most of the city's temples are controlled by members of the Ramanandi order mentioned earlier.

However, some Hindus claim that the Ayodhya mosque, built in the sixteenth century, stands on the spot where Rama was born. This "Babar mosque" (after the Muslim Mogul ruler who built it) has become the focus of increasingly hostile Hindu–Muslim confrontations. Hindus launched attacks on the Babar mosque during the celebration of the Feast of Sacrifice in 1912 and again in 1934. The conflict intensified after the 1947 Partition and the flight of many Muslims to Pakistan. In 1949, a statue of Rama appeared in the mosque. Hindus and Muslims naturally interpreted this event in very different ways. For the Hindus, Rama had appeared in their midst, giving them a sign to liberate his birthplace from the Muslims. For the Muslims, their mosque had been defiled. Riots ensued, and the army was called out. The government closed the mosque, and it remained closed to both Muslims and Hindus until 1984, when national politics came to a head in the city.

By the mid-1980s there had emerged a strong Hindu nationalist party, the Bharatiya Janata Party or BJP, which garnered support from Hindu nationalist movements and in particular from the Vishva Hindu Parishad (VHP). The VHP was an attempt to create a united Hindu organization. Given the diversity in religious practice and beliefs we have examined—diversity by region, by caste, and by class—creating a unified Hinduism would be a daunting task. What Hindus plausibly shared, however, was a belief in certain sacred objects and symbols. One was the sacred river, the Ganges, and in 1983 the VHP organized a drive to symbolize Hindu unity based on shared water. Large trucks were sent throughout the country, each carrying enormous bronze pots with water from the Ganges. This water was given to villagers en route, and the pots were replenished with water from local sacred sources, symbolizing Hindu unity—and also giving the VHP a way to firm up its local support network. Just as the processions of the Black Madonna throughout Poland emphasized the claim to a religion–nation unity, the water trucks' journeys underscored claims that all Indian territory, not just Ayodhya, was sacred Hindu territory.

Hindu unity of course also means opposition to Muslims, and the VHP also called for mosques to be removed from several sacred spots, including Ayodhya. By 1989 the VHP had begun to mobilize support for building a new temple in Ayodhya. In November, just before Indian general elections, Hindus were urged to send or bring bricks for the temple, and bricks poured in—from Hindus in Europe and the United States as well as from throughout India. The VHP was eventually stopped from building the temple by the ruling Congress government, but the flames thus fanned led to massacres of Muslims and numerous Hindu deaths in north and eastern India.

One year later violence erupted again, this time brought on by the political party, the BJP. The BJP joined forces with the VHP in part to oppose the government's plan to reserve a greater number of jobs and positions for lower-caste people. (In its mass support and vote-getting, the BJP appeals most to urban, upper-caste people.) Despite police bans, some volunteers bent on rebuilding "Rama's temple" made it to Ayodhya, where many were killed. In December 1990, to further dramatize BJP support for the Hindu nationalist cause, the party leader L. K. Advani began a "chariot"-led procession to Ayodhya, perhaps because the Ramayana had been serialized on television a few years earlier (Mankekar 1999). Advani decked his party out as Rama's army. His chariot, drawn by an air-conditioned Toyota, was carved and gilded to recall Rama's chariot. He carried the bow of Rama, brandishing it to ward off his enemies. Supporters, marching along-side, were decked out in warrior garb and handed bows as well. We might note the parallel to the way that the Polish Cardinal timed his processions with the Black Madonna to emphasize the antiquity of church and nation in Poland.

The procession began from a place in Gujarat, in western India, widely associated with the tenth-century destruction by a Muslim ruler of some beautiful Hindu temples. This choice of starting point reinforced anti-Muslim sentiments. The procession moved across India before being halted in the eastern state of Bihar, where Advani was arrested—an arrest that then led to the collapse of the fragile coalition government. Mass strikes and riots followed; all trains and buses that passed anywhere near Ayodhya were canceled, but many people were killed.

A little over a year later the mosque was destroyed. In 1992, supporters of the BJP/VHP drive rushed to Ayodhya and demolished the temple. The riots that ensued led to over one thousand deaths, mostly of Muslims (van der Veer 1994).

Though religious sentiments were front and center during the campaigns and riots, we would err in thinking of these conflicts as the emergence of "primordial" or tradi-tional sentiments in opposition to the nation–state. The conflicts and riots developed out of a modern idea of a Hindu nation–state, itself with roots in colonial constructions of religious communities and postcolonial electioneering. In the nineteenth century the British created the idea of a "Hindu majority"—and a Muslim minority—through the census. They interpreted these categories as native Hindus versus foreign Muslims. This view has had an effect on later Indian notions, promoting the idea that one's primary loyalty as a Hindu is to the "Hindu community" or as a Muslim to the "Muslim community," rather than to local communities or leaders. And it was on these notions that Advani and other Hindu nationalist leaders drew to mobilize support for Rama and anger against Muslims. Although Hindu–Muslim tensions predate colonialism and independence, the kind of violent religious nationalism exhibited in this case (and in many other places) is to a great extent a modern creation.

And for most Hindus, as for most people anywhere, nationalist claims have little to do with the practical bases and emotional pulls of religious practice. "Ram is supposed to dwell in our hearts, not in a temple" said one north Indian villager (quoted in Fuller

1992, 261). "We don't need to learn about our dharma (duty) from politicians seeking votes."

The contrast between Poland and India shows that religious nationalisms may have quite different outcomes. In Poland's case the foreigner was the communist state, and the result of the church–nation alliance seems to have been to promote the creation of an independent state with a relatively well-developed civil society, the church now adopting a lesser role. The contrasting case of India shows how a movement that identifies the foreigner to be a fellow citizen can produce intolerance and violence. The difference is not a matter of religious doctrine—the violence in Catholic Spain and the ambiguous, at best, role of the churches in Nazi Germany belie any notion that one religion develops more socially positive forms of nationalism than another (as does the relative intolerance of the Polish Church during the inter–world war period). The difference seems to lie rather in the extent to which a civil society, in which open debate and deliberation may take place, is part of a particular religious nationalism.

Does the existence of a live civil society require that religion and state (as distinguished from religion and nation) be kept separate? Several other societies allow us to test this notion.

Religion and State Law

*M*ost religions, perhaps all religions, carry with them positive and negative commandments or rules. For many religious people, it is these commandments that distinguish between people like them and people who are fundamentally different. Religious commandments also can enhance the meaning people derive from everyday life, as in the case of dietary rules.

In many countries today, some religious communities have judicial bodies that enforce some of their own commandments. In the United States, although neither state nor federal laws may grant privileges to one religion over others, the Constitution protects the right to freely exercise religion. In some cases the U.S. Supreme Court has interpreted that right to grant special legal rights to some religious communities. The Amish, for example, enjoy exemption from some state laws. Many Native American communities have their own judicial bodies with special legal status. Other communities have their own tribunals, such as the Jewish Bet Din, that act as binding arbiters among adherents of the religion.

In some other countries, religious law is enforced by the state at the national level. In Israel, state-supported rabbinical courts enforce Jewish law, *halakah*. In many Muslim countries (as well as in Israel), Islamic courts have jurisdiction over family law matters, and their decisions are backed by state authority. In these countries, religious authority has become part of a modern state system, with courts, police, and other enforcement agents. Do these arrangements have consequences for people of other faiths who are citizens of these countries? Are there other consequences for social and political life?

Jewish law in Israel, and Islamic law in Indonesia show similarities in the processes of integrating religious law to a modern state system and to local cultures. In both cases, religious courts predate the independent state. Since their independence following World War II, both Israel and Indonesia have tried to create religious court systems that could coexist with a secular legal system. Both experiences continue to raise troubling questions for the citizens of these states about the role of religious law in the modern world. These questions concern how laws are to be interpreted and enforced. Can the religious community agree on a single way of interpreting the law? Or does the existence of a religious court inevitably divide the community? Should everyone who identifies himself or herself as an adherent of a particular religion automatically be subject to religious law, or should it be a matter of individual choice? What areas of social life should be governed by religious law and which by secular law?

Gender and Marriage in Israeli Jewish Law

Although in some respects Moses holds the place in Judaism that Muhammad does in Islam, in fact the lives of the two prophets play very different roles with respect to modern authority and law. Muhammad's life casts a very direct and very specific shadow over daily decisions made by jurists, who base their decisions on his statements and actions. Moses delivered the first five books of the Hebrew Bible to his people as the original Torah, but at that point his life made no additional contributions to Jewish scripture. The Torah has since had a life of its own, accruing layers upon layers of commentary. Indeed, the term *torah* today can refer to the first five books of the Hebrew Bible, or to the entire Bible, or to both the Bible as written Torah and the "oral Torah," further commandments handed to Moses and embodied today in biblical commentaries.

As we saw in Chapter 8, each commandment in the Torah requires elaboration to make it specific and exceptions to adapt it to changing conditions of life. For example, the commandment to do no work on the Sabbath has required jurists to specify which activities count as work and which do not. The consensus today has it that certain activities, such as carrying an infant or pushing a wheelchair, constitute work when in public but not when in private. Because most Jews consider these particular activities essential even on the Sabbath (when babies and older people also attend worship services), authorities have created nominally private spaces, called *eruv,* within which the activities may still be carried out without violating religious law.

For some Jews, then, understanding Torah and living a religious life requires the interpretive intervention of religious authorities. For certain matters, such as resolving disputes and performing marriages, Jews living in many parts of the world have long had recourse to religious courts. In the Ottoman Empire, Jews had rabbinical courts, empowered to decide matters of marriage and divorce as well as such ritual issues as "carrying on the Sabbath." The courts continued to hold this authority under the British Mandate (1917–1948) and in the post-1948 state of Israel. Israel has continued the Ottoman practice of providing a certain degree of legal autonomy and distinct religious courts to each religious community, including Jews and Muslims.

The place of Jewish law remains contested, however (Edelman 1994). Officially, Israel is a nonconfessional state, meaning that no religion enjoys exclusive state support.

The parliament, or Knesset, has final authority over all matters, including religious ones. The law regulating the rabbinical courts, passed in 1953, stipulates that marriage and divorce of Jews will be handled by the courts "in accordance with Jewish law." But who is to interpret Jewish law? Prior to the creation of the Israeli state, political leaders had already committed themselves to granting this authority to Orthodox rabbis, who controlled the courts. In 1947, the executive body preparing for statehood entered into an agreement with an Orthodox body, the Agudah movement, stipulating that the new state would respect the Sabbath, require observance of dietary laws (*kashrut*) in all state institutions, maintain the authority of the rabbinical courts over matters of personal status (especially marriage and divorce), and establish religious schools.

How the remainder of social life would be regulated was left open, and the issue continues to inflame passions on both sides. Many Orthodox Jews see Israel as too secular and try to change social life through direct intervention, some even blocking off streets to traffic during the Sabbath to ensure that Jews follow the law. These men and women see most secular Jews as threatening Israel's distinctive character as a Jewish society. Most of Israel's Jewish citizens indeed consider themselves nonreligious, and they want the freedom to dress as they wish and to drive and visit restaurants and theaters when they wish, including on the Sabbath. They see the Orthodox rabbis as threatening their freedoms. Most of them think that Israel should retain its Jewish character as long as individuals may choose not to observe certain religious rules. What should the character of public life then be? The issue remains subject to debate and, at times, public confrontations.

The same tension emerges over the law to be applied in courts. The Knesset has ruled that the rabbinical courts must decide certain matters, such as the age of marriage, in accord with the statutes passed by the Knesset. Civil courts recognize all marriages conducted outside of Israel if they are in accord with the laws of the land, even if they are not conducted in accord with Jewish law. The rabbinical courts have responded to these pressures by becoming less flexible in their interpretations of religious law, especially on matters of marriage and divorce. Israel has no institutions of civil marriage, and Jews may only be married by an Orthodox rabbi. Jews may not marry non-Jews, nor may they marry people not properly (according to Orthodox rabbis) divorced.

Two resulting problematical questions in Israel (and among Jews in the United States) are: Who is a Jew? and What is divorce? Orthodox authorities accept as Jews only those persons whose maternal lineage (ties through women, starting with one's mother) contains only Jews, or those persons who converted to Judaism under the guidance of an Orthodox rabbi. Thus, many U.S. converts are not recognized as Jews in Israel, and children of Jewish fathers whose mothers either converted or are non-Jews are similarly denied Jewish status for purposes of marriage. But the Israeli government itself recognizes as a Jew anyone sincerely and plausibly identifying himself or herself as a Jew.

This disparity in definition has led to anomalies, such as the treatment of the 35,000 Ethiopian Jews airlifted to Israel in 1984 and 1990. These men and women were granted Israeli citizenship as Jews under the 1950 Law of Return. But the rabbinical courts refused to marry them unless they underwent conversion (and, for the men, recircumcision) on grounds that in the past their ancestors may have married non-Jews. The Ethiopian issue was further complicated by accusations of racism. At one point it was revealed that the blood banks had thrown out all blood donated by the Ethiopians for fear it was tainted with HIV. Finally, the rabbinical courts created a special court to allow Ethiopian Jews to marry among themselves, but still refused to permit them to marry other Jews (Edelman 1994).

Divorce presents additional problems in the gendered nature of Jewish law. Israel recognizes no civil divorce. Jews can obtain a divorce only from the rabbinical court, and the court recognizes divorce only when the husband presents his wife with a document called a *get*. The document, written in a combination of Hebrew and Aramaic, proclaims the husband's act of "releasing" his wife from the marriage. The court must authorize the divorce but cannot deliver the get in the husband's name. (They can imprison a husband if he refuses to grant the divorce but he may still refuse to do so.) If both parties agree to the divorce, then no problem arises. But when the husband refuses to grant it, the wife is unable to remarry. In other countries, including the United States, the Orthodox wife is placed in an anomalous status: she may obtain a civil divorce and legally remarry—and some women do so—but then she is considered by the rabbis to have committed adultery (Breitowitz 1993; Meislin 1981).

Religious Minorities and Public Religions

*E*ven when religion does not become intertwined with nationalist projects or state legal institutions, in both colonial contexts and contemporary nation–states one particular religious tradition may dominate public life or is able to exert power over religious minorities. In colonial contexts, very often Christian missions and schools became the main avenues to power and participation in government. Some people responded to the colonial challenge by converting; others resisted, presenting their own customs and beliefs as of equal worth.

Recall the case of the Wana from Chapter 3. A small people at the margins of Indonesia, Wana religious practices have centered on shamanism: healing and divining through direct contact between shamans and spirits. But as citizens of the modern state of Indonesia, the Wana are pressured to "enter religion," which means to affiliate with one of the five recognized religions (Catholicism, Protestantism, Islam, Hinduism, and Buddhism). Partly to counter such pressure, partly to win recognition as people with a worthy culture, Wana have changed the way they talk about their beliefs to make them comparable with beliefs of Islam and Christianity. They speak of God and heaven—they also do so in a way that promises rewards for them and misery for the Muslims and Christians who administer their region and control trade.

Like the members of prophetic movements, including the millenarian movements and cargo cults discussed in the previous chapter, the Wana have borrowed from the religion of a dominant group and used these borrowed ideas to predict their own eventual supremacy. But (as with the Ghost Dance of the North American Plains), they also drew on their own traditions and continue their shamanic practices. This dance of conformity and resistance is one strategy for preserving cultural distinctiveness in a world dominated by others.

Kwaio Strategies for Recognition

In the case of the Kwaio, on the island of Malaita in the independent nation of the Solomon Islands, religion has been central to struggles for recognition and power (Keesing 1982, 1992).

The spirits of ancestors figure centrally in Kwaio religious practice. The uplands Kwaio people studied by Roger Keesing observe many taboos regarding eating, drinking, menstruation, urination, and the proper and improper places for men or women to go in the village or woods. Kwaio consider major infractions of these taboos to be offenses against the ancestors, which must be recompensed through a pig sacrifice. Ancestors are important to magic, curing, and successful childbirth.

The British brought colonial domination and missionaries in the early decades of the twentieth century, but Kwaio have continued to recognize the power of the ancestors. Some Kwaio have left the hills and converted to Christianity, thereby, in their eyes, neutralizing the power of the ancestors (Keesing 1982, 231). The important Christian missions have been sponsored by Seventh-Day Adventists and the nondenominational South Sea Evangelical Mission. Both groups recognize the power of ancestral spirits but interpret the spirits as agents of Satan in his war against God. They have urged Kwaio to reject the old taboos and adopt new ones against swearing, stealing, and working on the Sabbath. The Adventists also enforce biblical food taboos. Some Kwaio have converted to find help in Jesus against sickness and death in the highlands (some of which was caused by British colonial invaders). The Kwaio have become aware that converts have been able to violate taboos, such as that against menstruation in houses, without being struck down by the ancestors. They have attributed this success to the power of the Christian God (Keesing 1982, 233–235).

About two thousand Kwaio people have resisted conversion, however. Some converts turned against the missionaries on the grounds that the Europeans were converting them but not giving them the education that would truly empower them. Other "pagan" Kwaio simply wished to preserve the traditional system, with the satisfactions of living in a well-known physical landscape of their ancestors (Keesing 1982, 237). These Kwaio insist on their right to apply their own customary laws, which they call *kastomu*. Many Kwaio have been making lists of customs, genealogies, and taboos in order to preserve them in a form recognizable by the government. Many believe that doing so will prevent their lands from being taken away by others (many have lost lands to logging operations) and also will keep Christian evangelists from invading their territory (Keesing 1992).

Initial Kwaio resistance to Christianity in the 1960s focused on a Seventh-Day Adventist hospital built on the northern coast. Some Kwaio thought that the hospital had acquired the land illegitimately, and Kwaio men killed the first administrator. Because of the way the land was obtained and because of the way "unclean" (menstruating and birthing) women were mixed with men in the hospital, Kwaio considered the hospital to be polluted. But the hospital stayed, and a Christian community developed around it, with banking and mail facilities and a store.

The very idea that writing down customs would protect the Kwaio against the outside world derived from watching Christians. Because the written Bible plays a central role in Christian practices, the Kwaio assumed that they, too, needed a written book to have something of the power held by Christians. It was about this time, when the idea that "writing brings power" was gaining ascendancy, that the anthropologist Roger Keesing arrived in the Kwaio pagan areas. They saw his coming as the fulfillment of a prophecy, made earlier by one of their leaders, that an American would come to write down their customs. (The Americans were remembered as the people who had driven off the Japanese in 1943.)

But *kastomu* and *customs* mean very different things, though they overlap. For Keesing, *customs* included how Kwaio behaved in everyday social life, as well as the meanings of rituals and taboos. For the Kwaio, the neo-Melanesian term *kastomu* refers to relationships with the ancestors, in the forms of ancestral genealogies, lists of shrines and lands, and ancestrally enjoined taboos with their penalties. Customs were behavior and the rules that govern it; kastomu were relationships with ancestors and the rules that derive from them.

But these lists were also understood as local equivalents to *loa,* or law, that would correspond to Kwaio ideas of propriety better than did the British-derived laws used to fine and imprison them. In 1989 Keesing obtained written documents from the son of Fifi'i, the Kwaio leader who had been working on his own to codify custom. These documents begin with the claim that the project was authorized in 1945 by a Kwaio council of chiefs. Fifi'i clearly saw the documents as representing in written form an unwritten Kwaio Constitution, which would have legal standing "besides National Laws" (Keesing 1992, 197). Their content concerns taboos and fines.

The outside world has thrown up strong challenges to Kwaio autonomy. First there was Christian missionization. The market economy led to the primacy of money in determining status. And the state gives power to the courts to jail and fine people for offenses Kwaio consider minor. The Kwaio response has been "not in confrontation but in compartmentalization" (Keesing 1992, 199). Kwaio pagans have tried to preserve older ways of exchanging shell valuables in marriage by prohibiting people from purchasing these valuables with cash. They realized that the ability to buy valuables would quickly inflate their price and make it impossible for Kwaio who did not earn cash through labor to marry. They have drawn sharp lines between the polluted Christian areas and pagan settlements. They have demarcated plantation areas, where taboos can no longer be observed, from the domain of the ancestors, where taboos continue to be observed. By the 1990s each of the two communities had come to define itself against the other, and to some extent acknowledge the power of each other's gods.

The Kwaio thus developed a double-edged strategy as a cultural and religious minority in a colonial setting dominated by Christianity. First, they demanded that the British, and later the rulers of the independent Solomons, acknowledge their own ancient constitution, the legitimacy of their claims to authentic law and custom. Second, they drew religious boundaries to prevent encroachment by polluting and threatening powers.

But the Kwaio strategy only worked, to the extent that it did, because of the relative isolation of the settlements and the willingness and ability of some Kwaio to not enter into direct social relationships with the rest of the colony and the nation–state. Most other minorities do not have that option, either because they are already in direct, face-to-face relationships with others, or because they must or wish to participate fully in the institutions of the larger society.

Protestants in the Pueblos

The reverse relationship between Christianity and an indigenous religion emerges when a minority of members of small-scale societies converts to Christianity.

In some Pueblo societies of New Mexico, for example, tribal governments are also religious hierarchies; the societies are "theocracies" or religious states in this sense. Pueblo social life involves compulsory performance of a number of duties, including religious rituals. Some Pueblo members converted to Protestantism, and thereafter withdrew from those community activities that they considered to be religious rituals and thus in violation of their new religious principles. In response, the tribal governments denied them some benefits enjoyed by other tribal members, such as rights to housing, or the right to use a community threshing machine to thresh wheat. Members of the community also ostracized them, avoiding them socially.

The Pueblo case has figured prominently in recent debates about individual rights and community rights (Kymlicka 1995; Svensson 1979). Were the civil rights of the Pueblo Protestants violated? Or do these communities have the right to perpetuate their way of life by requiring members to participate in communal activities?

Catholics in China

Beginning in the 1950s, China's communist leaders tried to repress Catholic religious practice and beliefs by creating a state-run Catholic Patriotic Association and persecuting those Catholics who sought to continue worshiping on their own. In the 1980s, the state permitted some churches to reopen. But in the late 1990s, with President Jiang Zemin evincing concern over a decline in socialist enthusiasm, officials began to prevent Catholics from holding Christmas celebrations. In early 1996, paramilitary police and helicopter units descended on a tiny village in the northeastern province of Hebei and destroyed a Marian shrine to which more than 100,000 Chinese Catholics had made pilgrimages during the preceding year.

At the same time, the estimated numbers of Christians in China have shot up. Perhaps 8 to 10 million Chinese are Roman Catholics today (the official number is 4 million). The number of Protestants has grown from about 1 million in 1949 to about 20 million today. Richard Madsen attributes the surge to the moral vacuum left by the collapse of communism as a "quasi-religious ideology" (Tyler 1997).

Minority Religions in Europe: Toleration or Public Recognition?

*E*uropean states have maintained a general attitude of official toleration toward minority religions, due in some part to the historical memory of the disastrous religious wars of the seventeenth century, in which Catholics and Protestants fought and slaughtered one another over their religious differences. European toleration of differences within Christianity remains, in one form or another, the public religious tradition in England (which has its official Church of England) and in most of continental Europe.

French Secularism versus Headscarves in Schools

France, however, has made state secularism a part of its legal framework. Throughout the nineteenth century, Republican and Catholic factions struggled for control of the schools—and through them, control of the hearts and minds of French children. From that struggle came strong laws preventing the state from granting official recognition to any religion and laws guaranteeing public, secular education to all French children. The French legal doctrine of *laïcité*, perhaps best understood as keeping religion out of public affairs and keeping public officials from displaying their religion, has generally been understood to constrain the state and its employees, but not citizens in their private capacity (Bowen 2004).

French laïcité also has a broader sociopolitical meaning, however, which transcends this legal doctrine. Many French teachers and public officials, particularly on the political left, have inherited a tradition of strong anti-Catholic sentiment that sometimes also is an antireligious sentiment. For them, the French Republic depends on a public sphere that is free of religious messages. French citizens become complete political individuals by being socialized in public institutions, and they retain their citizenship qualities by continuing to interact in such institutions qua citizens—and not as Muslims, Protestants, or Scientologists. They recognize each other as equivalent citizens, indistinguishable on the dimension of their participation in French public life.

The norm of public laïcité leads some teachers and principals of secondary schools to expel girls who come to class wearing headscarves, or some employers in private industry to demand that employees not wear "clearly Islamic" dress. When Muslim schoolgirls began to wear headscarves to school in the late 1980s, some teachers and principals resented the girls' public display of difference, and a number of prominent French intellectuals publicly cried out that the Republic was endangered. Within a few years the highest administrative law body, the Conseil d'État, had arrived at what would be its consistent ruling that nothing in French law prevents schoolchildren from expressing their religious beliefs by wearing garments that imply a religious affiliation, as long as such garments are not "ostentatious" and the children in question neither "proselytize" nor disturb "public order." Indeed, the Conseil d'État ruled that they had the right to engage in religious self-expression in school, and that the law restricted the apparel and the conduct only of teachers and other state employees.

Teachers and principals have continued to expel or isolate children wearing headscarves and sometimes they have declared strikes to dramatize their position. One such incident occurred in 2002 to 2003, when the teachers in a high school near Lyon threatened to strike if one female student was not expelled. In Lyon and elsewhere, some teachers and principals claimed that the presence of the headscarves was divisive, that it brought broader social tensions, and even the war in Palestine, into the schools. The headscarf issue surfaced in the media again in April 2003, when Muslims attending the annual assembly sponsored by the large Muslim association Union des Organisations

Islamiques de France (UOIF) booed the call by the Minister of the Interior to enforce the law requiring women to bare their heads for their identity photos. Newspaper articles in April and May 2003 replayed the arguments first heard in the 1980s, according to which the headscarf was a sign of female submission and a direct attack on the principle of laïcité. In March 2004, after public hearings by two governmental commissions and a continued media campaign against the scarves, France passed a law preventing the wearing of any clothing or signs that clearly displayed the religious affiliation of a student in public school.

Ironically, some women consider wearing the headscarf to be part of breaking with immigrant culture, a way of distinguishing between an Islam learned in France and the insufficiently Islamic traditions of the "old country." As many French observers have noted, when young women choose to wear a head covering, misleadingly called *le voile* ("the veil"), it often signifies a moment of personal growth and transition—such as graduating from school, traveling to another country, beginning work, or making a break with the social norms of their family. Wearing a headscarf rarely is a mark of continuity in family dress but a mark of discovery and self-identification as an individual.

France is fast becoming an openly multicultural and multireligious country, but at this point has chosen to reaffirm its tradition of public laïcité in an effort to bring people together under the umbrella of French values and customs. It is too early to know whether this policy will have the desired effect.

The National Church in Britain

In the European context France is an unusual case. Most other members of the European Union make available some state funding for religious organizations. In some European countries, political parties have links to particular religious denominations.

Britain, for example, has an established church, the Anglican or Episcopal Church, in which all state weddings and funerals take place. Other churches and religious organizations are allowed, and some even receive state support, but they take second place to the Anglican Church.

Some Britons recently have urged that the Church be disestablished, deprived of its official status. Non-Anglicans, including many Muslims and Jews, argue that for all British citizens to enjoy full citizenship, they all must enjoy an equal capacity to shape the public culture. Such an equality implies that the public culture cannot favor one religion over another, as it currently does.

However, some Jewish and Muslim leaders have come out publicly in support of the continuing establishment of the Anglican Church (Modood 1994). They argue that when there is a national religion the followers of that religion feel comfortable about their place in the society and therefore exert less pressure on minority groups to convert or conform. They also argue that Anglicanism is less threatening than secularism to Muslims and Jews, because at least it supports other religions' continued existence. By contrast, secularism contains an anti-Islamic sentiment. These people cite the example of France, where strict secularism makes it more difficult for some people to accept the public religious self-identification by Muslims.

The Crucifix in Bavaria

German attitudes toward public religion are still further away from French secularism than are British ones. Recent controversy in Germany has concerned both the wearing of religious dress in schools and whether the state of Bavaria may make compulsory the display of the crucifix in schools (Caldwell 1996).

In France the normal state of affairs had been, at least in theory, the absence of any religious markers in the classroom, and the signs of religious difference, the Muslim headscarves, introduced into the classroom clashed with secular state officials' expectations. In Germany, and especially in Bavaria, the normal state of affairs was quite different. The state required that all primary school classrooms prominently display a large crucifix.

In 1995, however, the Federal Constitutional Court responded to a suit from a non-Christian ("anthroposophist") family and overturned the Bavarian regulation. The decision set off a storm of protest. The court ruling did not require the crucifixes to be removed, only that schools would not be obliged to hang them. But the furor was intense. Even Chancellor Helmut Kohl objected that the state had an obligation to pass Christian values on to children, and numerous commentators compared the federal court's decision to the Nazis' acts of exchanging crucifixes for swastikas. Some politicians called for disobedience of the court order.

To explain the reaction it helps to consider how these key religious symbols give public solidity to boundaries between "Us" and the "Other." In France, the Other is either Islamic fundamentalism or religion taking over the state. In Germany, it is the denial of Christian values under Nazi and communist rule. In the United States, it is persecution of religious dissenters by a state-backed church.

The place of religion in Germany traces back to the aftermath of religious wars in the seventeenth century. The German lands adopted the principle that a ruler could determine the religion of his subjects, a principle that tolerated princes, not subjects. It provided for shared practices and beliefs throughout the realm.

This principle continues to claim legitimacy. In 1918 Catholic Bavaria demanded protection against the potential persecution of Catholics in a Germany now two-thirds Protestant. In response, the framers of the Weimar Constitution granted to the German states the right to administer public education. They also gave all registered churches the status of public corporations, to be supported by taxes. These articles were adopted into the 1949 Basic Law, the West German Constitution. The Basic Law continues to be interpreted as the expression of German values that the state should take active steps to promote. The furor over the Bavarian cross decision was thus aimed at a court seen as violating its obligation to promote Christian values.

German attitudes toward religion continue to be shaped by the idea that states could choose between established forms of religion, which meant in practice the Roman Catholic or Lutheran Churches. This historical background has led some Germans to strongly oppose the presence of new religions, or sects such as Scientology. These Germans see Scientology's claims to religious status as a cover for attempts to extract wealth from converts and have led state governments to limit the development of local

Scientology branches. By the late 1990s the controversy had reached international proportions, with Scientologists taking out full-page ads in newspapers in the United States and elsewhere to protest German state suppression of religious freedom.

Religion, Nation, and State in the United States

The German Constitution and the general attitude toward public religion and the state in Germany stands in marked contrast to the dominant interpretation of the U.S. Bill of Rights as a set of specific restrictions on the powers of the state. But U.S. history on religion, nation, and state is more complex than the phrase "separation of church and state" might imply.

Running through the history of debates and laws in the United States about religion and public life are two contradictory but strong lines of argument. One stresses the constitutionally mandated separation of church and state and the dangers to freedom posed by government entanglement in religious affairs. The second stresses the historically dominant role played in U.S. public life by Christianity—or more narrowly Protestant Christianity, or more broadly a Judeo-Christian tradition.

The first argument stresses rights and laws and echoes something of the French attitude. The second argument stresses historical tradition and shared values and resembles the German approach. Each has its claims to an antique lineage: the first, to Christian suspicion of government as inevitably corrupting (a view held by Saint Augustine, for example); the second, to the tradition of civic republicanism, where the state ensures that the community follows a set of moral, including religious, norms (Taylor 1990). The European cases discussed above remind us of other possible approaches to ensuring religious toleration, such as offering state support to all religions. They also remind us that other, relatively tolerant societies do in fact have an established church, such as the Church of England.

The rights argument for separating religion and state is based on the first 16 words of the Bill of Rights, which reads: "Congress shall make no law respecting an establishment of religion, or prohibiting the free exercise thereof." Many heated debates in our recent history—by the courts, in legislatures, among ordinary citizens—turn on how these 16 words are to be interpreted. Does the first clause, the establishment clause, prohibit all federal or state aid to religious schools, or all public displays in government buildings of religious symbols? Or does it more narrowly prohibit only laws that give special privileges or powers to a particular church? Does the second, the free exercise clause, protect the rights of schools to set aside a moment for silent prayer? Or does this practice run afoul of the first clause? What rights do parents have to further their children's exercise of religion? To what extent may Christian Scientist parents legally withhold medical aid from their children on religious grounds? May religious communities withdraw their children from school before the legal minimum age? Certain of these issues, such as the right to withdraw children from school, involve finding the right balance between the Constitution and the legislative power of the states. Other issues, such as silent prayer in the schools, may be seen as requiring a weighing of the two clauses against each other.

Religion in the Early Centuries

The emphasis on limiting the powers of government over religion was motivated by the colonists' experience of religious persecution (Berman 1990). This persecution occurred not only in Europe, but also in the colonies. The same religious groups that fled persecution abroad soon practiced it in their new homes. Authorities in New York and Massachusetts expelled Lutherans and Quakers along with Catholics and Jews. Even the relatively tolerant colony established by William Penn forbade deists to live in the colony and kept Jews from holding office.

The main purpose of the establishment clause was thus to prevent that kind of intolerance from developing at the federal level. The strongest advocates of the clause, James Madison and Thomas Jefferson, were fresh from their struggle to disestablish the Anglican Church in their home state of Virginia. Few other churches had universal pretensions; most were organized along *congregational* lines, meaning they were governed by the local congregation for the local congregation, and did not aim to become a universal church. Indeed, most residents of the colonies were Puritans, whose religious leaders were far more concerned with reserving church membership for the saved than they were with expanding their rolles.

The framers of the Constitution went further, preventing the federal government from supporting all Christian churches equally through taxation. As James Madison argued in 1785: "Who does not see that the same authority which can establish Christianity, in exclusion of all other Religions, may establish with the same ease any particular set of Christians, in exclusion of all other Sects?" (quoted in Frankel 1994, 27). This sentiment lay behind Thomas Jefferson's famous phrase that there should be "a wall of separation between church and state" (Berman 1990, 40).

There was, however, no single state and no single church in the United States, then as now. Rather, there were many different governments and many different ways in which people pursued religious beliefs. The Constitution only affected the powers of the federal government, and prevented it only from passing laws that would infringe upon the free exercise of religion or that would establish a church. It did not forbid officials from acting on their religious beliefs in passing other laws, nor did it keep them from effectively making one set of religions dominant in public discourse.

Nor did the Constitution say that religion was a matter for individuals to decide. As the legal historian Harold Berman argues (1990), for Americans of the 1780s and 1790s, free exercise of religion meant the freedom of religious communities to regulate family and social life, not the freedom of the individual to do as he or she pleased. Such was clearly true for the majority of American Puritans, for whom religious membership was seen as a binding social covenant, but true as well for denominations we now think of as highly individualistic, such as the Unitarians. One Salem Unitarian church even records that in the seventeenth century it flogged and sold into slavery some Quakers who refused to contribute to a new church building! In the late seventeenth and early eighteenth centuries, states aided parochial schools and all public schooling was explicitly intended to further Christianity. Well into the twentieth century, marriage was considered to be religious, and divorce law was derived from English ecclesiastical law (Berman 1990). The authority of the community, embodied in its church, was taken for granted by most citizens of the early Republic, and it is this set of experiences that those arguing for maintaining public religious tradition cite.

Balancing Rights and Tradition in a Pluralistic Nation

In the two centuries since independence the United States has changed from a nation dominated by Protestant, and particularly Puritan, Christians to a nation of diverse major religions, including Catholicism, Judaism, and Islam, and of many citizens not affiliated to a major religion. From a nation where most people thought of religion in terms of community norms as well as private faith, the United States has become a nation where most people think of religion in terms of individual beliefs alone.

In 1800, nearly everyone in the United States belonged to a Protestant denomination; Catholics, Jews, and other faiths taken together amounted to perhaps 2 percent of the population (Hunter 1990). Then came the enormous migrations of European Catholics at midcentury and again at the turn of the twentieth century, along with migrations of Jews and Asians of various religions. By the 1990s, Catholics constituted about 25 percent of the population, and Jews and Mormons each about 2 percent. Protestants of various denominations made up about 56 percent of U.S. residents. And within each of these large categories are more religious-based diversities than before. Whereas once the major divisions among Catholics were their countries of origin (especially among Irish, Italians, and Germans), today the major divisions concern the stands taken on doctrinal issues and on the authority of the pope. The severe cleavages today among fundamentalists, evangelicals, and others within the many Protestant denominations as well as between these denominations is paralleled in the nineteenth century only by the hostility exhibited by most Protestants against Mormons and Adventists. Nor was there an explicit "secular humanism" such as is professed by many today.

The relation between governments and religions has changed as well, but arguments for rights and those for tradition continue to have their strong supporters. Only in the 1940s did the Supreme Court explicitly hold that the Fourteenth Amendment prevented states from enacting laws establishing religion or preventing free exercise. In a 1947 case, *Everson v. Board of Education of Ewing Township*, the Court emphasized Jefferson's "wall of separation between church and state," and stated that states as well as the United States could not favor one religion over another. (Ironically, this broad doctrine was declared in a case in which the Court upheld a state law that gave state aid for buses used to take children to parochial schools.) The Court distinguished between aid to children and aid to schools, approving the former. In subsequent decisions the Court has upheld laws aimed at granting children equal opportunity, for example, the right for a deaf child to have a sign language interpreter in a parochial school when that right is already granted to public school students. But the Court struck down as illegitimately "advancing religion" state permission for a Hasidic Jewish group to form a public school district that included only their own adherents (Frankel 1994, 96–107).

Despite these decisions, to some degree law and public discourse in the United States continue to give special status to Christian religions. Christian prayers in the White House and Congress are a reminder of the tendency to mix Christian symbols into public life. In 1997, the second inauguration of President Clinton began with a prayer by the evangelical Christian minister Billy Graham.

Public prayer continues to be fought over in the courts. The current law of the land is that school-sponsored prayers violate the establishment clause. But this apparent consensus is tenuous, based as it is on a series of close decisions. For example, in the 1992 case *Lee v. Weisman,* the Supreme Court decided five to four that prayer delivered by a rabbi at a public school graduation was unconstitutional. The majority opinion stressed that any school-sponsored prayer, whether in the classroom or at an assembly, engendered social pressure on those not subscribing to the majority faith. But the dissent argued that graduation prayers were a tradition, the idea of coercive social pressure was fabricated, and that Americans have always thanked God for their blessings.

Some recent decisions have emphasized the argument from historical traditions. A 1984 case, *Lynch v. Donnelly,* upheld the right of a city to display a nativity scene, and in 1983, in *Marsh v. Chambers,* the Supreme Court upheld the right of the Nebraska legislature to pay a chaplain to open sessions with public prayer.

Although today a majority Court opinion would probably not state that "this is a Christian nation," as one did in 1892; nonetheless, judges and politicians from time to time continue to refer to the United States as a Christian nation or Judeo-Christian nation. Moreover, apparently neutral laws, such as laws mandating a "moment of silence" in schools, may be seen as discriminating in practice by stigmatizing students who do not adopt prayerful attitudes or who find the dominant model of "silent prayer" to be in fact a Christian model. Muslims, for example, carry out obligatory worship or ritual prayer (salat) at specific times of the day and in doing so stand, bow, and prostrate themselves—none of which actions can be performed during the "moment of silence." The Supreme Court recognizes this problem in general; in the *Yoder* case (406 U.S. 220) discussed below, the majority stated: "A regulation neutral on its face, in its application nonetheless offends the constitutional requirement for governmental neutrality if it unduly burdens the free exercise of religion."

One contested area concerns whether only beliefs, or beliefs and practices, are protected by the free exercise clause. In 1879, in a decision (*Reynolds v. U.S.*) that upheld a law against the Mormon practice of polygamy, the Court held that religious practices were not themselves protected: while laws "cannot interfere with mere religious belief and opinions, they may with practices" (98 U.S. 166).

But in 1972, in the landmark case *Wisconsin v. Yoder,* the Supreme Court ruled that a state had to prove a compelling interest before it could constitutionally compel a community to obey a state law that conflicted with its religious practices. In that case, an Amish parent had been sued by the State of Wisconsin for violating a law requiring school attendance until age 16. The parent had removed his child from school after finishing eighth grade and claimed that continuing in school would unduly subject the child to the influence of the secular world and would thereby endanger her salvation. The Court found that the state did not show the required compelling interest in this case. Spending the years after eighth grade at home, learning the skills that would serve children best on the farm, was not obviously inferior to continuing on in school. Compelling school attendance would infringe on the Amish religious way of life, so the Court ruled that the law violated the free exercise clause.

Justice Douglas dissented in *Yoder*, noting that the Court did not know the wishes of the children, and that many children do leave the Amish community and are disadvantaged if they do not have the years of high school education required by the state.

Under debate in these cases is not only how best to interpret the Constitution but also what weight to give the perception of an inherited religious tradition. As the country has become more religiously diverse, can the lengthening string of relatively well-represented religions be merged into a generic monotheism? The change from "Christian nation" to "Judeo-Christian tradition" leans in that direction; will it become "Judeo-Christian-Islamic"? The end point in this direction is Indonesia's state ideology of "belief in one God" and sanctioning of five religions as putatively monotheistic (Islam, Catholicism, Protestantism, Hinduism, and Buddhist).

An alternative direction is a public discourse around moral values, such as family. This direction poses several problems: that it allows the reemergence, albeit in a new guise, of confessionally specific values. This reemergence is evidenced in recent debates about same-sex marriage, where the argument that marriage is religious in origin is intended to mean Christian, allowing the quotation of biblical passages against homosexuality. In these instances phrases such as "family values" serve as general categories to be filled by those specific religious views that have the most sustained voices in public debates.

On any one street in most U.S. towns and cities live people who attend a variety of churches, temples, or other places of worship, or do not attend any such places at all. In principle, neither one's legal entitlements as a citizen nor one's standing as an American are affected by religious beliefs or practices. And yet, it is Christmas, not Hanukah or Ramadan, that receives public notice in lights and exhibits, in the pattern of public holidays and school vacations, in speeches and newspapers. And vast, nondenominational U.S. Christian organizations (such as the multimedia empire Focus on the Family) distribute Christian videos, books, newspaper columns, and radio programs throughout the world. Christianity continues to play a strong, if contested role in public life, even as courts and legislators maintain the "wall of separation" between religion and the legal activities of the state.

The study of religion as practice helps us understand the different forms that public religion can take. At issue in current controversies in France, Germany, the United States, as well as Indonesia, India, and Poland, is not the correctness of religious doctrine, or the beliefs of individual citizens, but the range of *public practices* that are appropriate. What messages are conveyed by exhibiting a cross or menorah in a state-supported building? Does wearing a headscarf send a challenge to dominant ideas of citizenship? Is setting aside a moment for silent prayer in a school an instance of religious freedom, or is it an implied endorsement of those religions that include such kinds of prayer?

These questions, and the controversies around them, turn on how different people interpret the practices of others, from wearing clothes to making speeches. Understanding the issues involved requires us to know something about the complex religious and cultural meanings attached to the objects and actions in question, about the histories of legal and social debate on religion's public place, and about the interests and values of the people engaged in these debates. We have only begun to pursue this quest for understanding.

References

Abou El Fadl, Khaled (2001). *Speaking in God's name: Islamic law, authority and women.* Oxford: Oneworld.

Ahmed, Leila (1992). *Women and gender in Islam: Historical roots of a modern debate.* New Haven: Yale University Press.

Ainsworth, Mary D. S. (1967). *Infancy in Uganda: Infant care and the growth of love.* Baltimore: Johns Hopkins University Press.

Alexander, Jeffrey C. (1982). *The antimonies of classical thought: Marx and Durkheim.* Los Angeles: University of California Press.

Ammerman, Nancy Tatom (1987). *Bible believers: Fundamentalists in the modern world.* New Brunswick, N.J.: Rutgers University Press.

Anderson, Nels (1942). *Desert saints: The Mormon frontier in Utah.* Chicago: University of Chicago Press.

Apter, Andrew (1993). Atinga revisited: Yoruba witchcraft and the cocoa economy, 1950–1951. In Jean Comaroff and John Comaroff (Eds.), *Modernity and its malcontents* (pp. 111–128). Chicago: University of Chicago Press.

Ariès, Philippe (1974). *Western attitudes toward death: From the Middle Ages to the present.* Baltimore: Johns Hopkins University Press.

Atkinson, Jane Monnig (1983). Religions in dialogue: The construction of an Indonesian minority religion. *American Ethnologist, 10,* 684–696.

Atkinson, Jane Monnig (1987). The effectiveness of shamans in an Indonesian ritual. *American Anthropologist, 89,* 342–355.

Atkinson, Jane Monnig (1989). *The art and politics of Wana shamanship.* Los Angeles: University of California Press.

Auslander, Mark (1993). "Open the wombs!": The symbolic politics of modern Ngoni witchfinding. In Jean Comaroff and John Comaroff (Eds.), *Modernity and its malcontents* (pp. 167–192). Chicago: University of Chicago Press.

Babb, Lawrence A. (1983). Destiny and responsibility: Karma in popular Hinduism. In Charles F. Keyes and E. Valentine Daniel (Eds.), *Karma: An anthropological inquiry* (pp. 163–181). Los Angeles: University of California Press.

Babb, Lawrence A. (1986). *Redemptive encounters: Three modern styles in the Hindu tradition.* Los Angeles: University of California Press.

Barker, John (1993). We are Eklesia: Conversion in Uiaku, Papua New Guinea. In Robert W. Hefner (Ed.). *Conversion to Christianity: Historical and anthropological perspectives on a great transformation* (pp. 199–230). Berkeley: University of California Press.

Barth, Fredrik (1987). *Cosmologies in the making: A generative approach to cultural variation in inner New Guinea.* Cambridge: Cambridge University Press.

Bastian, Misty L. (1993). "Bloodhounds who have no friends": Witchcraft and locality in the Nigerian popular press. In Jean Comaroff and John Comaroff (Eds.), *Modernity and its malcontents* (pp. 129–166). Chicago: University of Chicago Press.

Bateson, Gregory (1958). *Naven* (2nd ed.). Stanford: Stanford University Press.

Bauman, Richard (1983). *Let your words be few: Symbolism of speaking and silence among seventeenth-century Quakers.* Cambridge: Cambridge University Press.

Bax, Mart (1991). Marian apparitions in Medjugorje: Rivaling religious regimes and state-formation in Yugoslavia. In Eric R. Wolf (Ed.), *Religious regimes and state-formation* (pp. 29–53). Albany: State University of New York Press.

Bell, Diane (1981). "Women's business is hard work: Central Australian aboriginal women's love rituals." *Signs, 7*(2): 314–337.

Berkey, Jonathan Porter (2003). *The formation of Islam: Religion and Society in the Near East, 600–1800.* Cambridge: Cambridge University Press.

Berman, Harold J. (1990). Religious freedom and the challenge of the modern state. In James Davison Hunter and Os Guiness (Eds.), *Articles of faith, articles of peace* (pp. 40–53). Washington, D.C.: The Brookings Institution.

Bloch, Maurice (1982). Death, women and power. In Maurice Bloch and Jonathan Parry (Eds.), *Death and the regeneration of life* (pp. 211–230). Cambridge: Cambridge University Press.

Bloch, Maurice, and Jonathan Parry (1982). Introduction: Death and the regeneration of life. In Maurice Bloch and Jonathan Parry (Eds.), *Death and the regeneration of life* (pp. 1–44). Cambridge: Cambridge University Press.

Boddy, Janice (1989). *Wombs and alien spirits: Women, men, and the Zár cult in Northern Sudan.* Madison: University of Wisconsin Press.

Bohlen, Celestine (1995). Crying Madonna, blood and many, many tears. *New York Times,* April 8, 1995, A4.

Bokser, Baruch M. (1984). *The origins of the Seder.* Los Angeles: University of California Press.

Boon, James A. (1990). *Affinities and extremes.* Chicago: University of Chicago Press.

Bossy, John (1983). The mass as a social institution, 1200–1700. *Past and Present, 100,* 29–61.

Bourdieu, Pierre (1972). *Esquissue d'une théorie de la pratique, précédé de trois études d'ethnologie kabyle.* Geneva: Droz.

Bourdieu, Pierre (1990). *The logic of practice.* (Orig. French 1980) (Richard Nice, Trans.) Stanford: Stanford University Press.

Bourdieu, Pierre (1998). *Practical reason: On the theory of action.* (Orig. French 1994.)

Bowen, John R. (1991). *Sumatran politics and poetics: Gayo history, 1900–1989.* New Haven, Conn.: Yale University Press.

Bowen, John R. (1993). *Muslims through discourse: Religion and ritual in Gayo society.* Princeton, N.J.: Princeton University Press.

Bowen, John R. (2004). "Does French Islam Have Borders? Dilemmas of Domesticity in a Global Religious Field." *American Anthropologist, 106*(1): 43–55.

Bowlby, John (1980). *Loss: Sadness and depression.* New York: Basic Books.

Boyer, Pascal (2000). Functional origins of religious concepts: Ontological and strategic selection in evolved minds. *Journal of the Royal Anthropological Institute, 6*(2): 195–214.

Boyer, Pascal (2000). Cultural inheritance tracks and cognitive predispositions: The example of religious concepts. In H. Whitehouse (Ed.), *Mind, evolution, and cultural transmission* (pp. 57–89). Oxford: Berg Publishers.

Boyer, Pascal (2001). *Religion Explained.* New York: Basic Books.

Boyer, Paul, and Stephen Nissenbaum (1974). *Salem possessed: The social origins of witchcraft.* Cambridge, Mass.: Harvard University Press.

Brasher, Brenda E. (2001). *Give me that online religion.* San Francisco: Jossey-Bass.

Breitowitz, Irving A. (1993). *Between civil and religious law: The plight of the Agunah in American society.* Westport, Conn.: Greenwood Press.

Brison, Karen J. (1992). *Just talk: Gossip, meetings, and power in a Papua New Guinea village.* Los Angeles: University of California Press.

Brown, Diana DeG. (1986). *Umbanda: Religion and politics in urban Brazil.* Ann Arbor, Mich.: UMI Research Press.

Brown, Karen McCarthy (1987). Alourdes: A case study of moral leadership in Haitian vodou. In John Stratton Hawley (Ed.), *Saints and virtues* (pp. 144–167). Los Angeles: University of California Press.

Brown, Michael F. (1997). *The channeling zone: American spirituality in an anxious age.* Cambridge: Harvard University Press.

Brown, Michael F. (2000). The New Age and related forms of contemporary spirituality. In Raymond Scupin (Ed.), *Religion and culture: An anthropological focus* (pp. 421–432). Upper Saddle River, N.J.: Prentice Hall.

Brown, Peter (1987). The saint as exemplar in late antiquity. In John Stratton Hawley (Ed.), *Saints and virtues* (pp. 3–14). Los Angeles: University of California Press.

Brzezinski, Matthew (1994). Pilgrimage to Poland's holiest shrine losing its political role. *New York Times,* August 30, 1994, A12.

Bunzel, Ruth Leah (1992). *Zuni ceremonialism.* Albuquerque: University of New Mexico Press. (Original work published 1932)

Burns, John F. (1997). Gandhi's ashes rest, but not his message. *New York Times,* January 31, 1997, A1, A8.

Burns, J. Patout (1994). The atmosphere of election: Augustinianism as common sense. *Journal of Early Christian Studies, 2*(3), 325–339.

Burridge, Kenelm (1969). *New heaven, new earth: A study of millenarian activities.* New York: Schocken Books.

Bynum, Caroline Walker (1987). *Holy feast and holy fast: The religious significance of food to medieval women.* Los Angeles: University of California Press.

Caldwell, Peter C. (1996). The crucifix and German constitutional culture. *Cultural Anthropology, 11*(2), 259–273.

Campbell, Joseph (1949). *The hero with a thousand faces.* New York: Pantheon Books.

Cannon, Walter B. (1942). "Voodoo" death. *American Anthropologist, 54,* 169–181.

Casanova, José (1994). *Public religions in the modern world.* Chicago: University of Chicago Press.

Chodorow, Nancy (1974). Family structure and feminine personality. In Michelle Z. Rosaldo and Louise Lamphere (Eds.), *Women, culture and society.* Stanford: Stanford University Press.

Christian, William A., Jr. (1984). Religious apparitions and the cold war in southern Europe. In Eric R. Wolf (Ed.), *Religion, power and protest in local communities: The northern shore of the Mediterranean* (pp. 239–266). Berlin: Mouton.

Christian, William A., Jr. (1989). *Person and god in a Spanish valley* (rev. ed.). Princeton, N.J.: Princeton University Press. (Original work published 1972)

Clark, Francis (1967). *Eucharistic sacrifice and the reformation.* Oxford: Basil Blackwell.

Cohn, Norman (1970). *The pursuit of the millennium* (rev. ed.). Oxford: Oxford University Press.

Collier, Jane F., and Michelle Zimbalist Rosaldo (1981). Politics and gender in simple societies. In Sherry B. Ortner and Harriet Whitehead (Eds.), *Sexual meanings* (pp. 275–329). Cambridge: Cambridge University Press.

Comaroff, Jean (1985). *Body of power, spirit of resistance.* Chicago: University of Chicago Press.

Comaroff, Jean, and John Comaroff (1986). "Christianity and colonialism in South Africa." *American Ethnologist, 13*(1): 1–22.

Comaroff, Jean, and John Comaroff (1991). *Of Revelation and revolution: Christianity, colonialism, and consciousness in South Africa.* Chicago: University of Chicago Press.

Comaroff, Jean, and John Comaroff (1997). *Of Revelation and revolution: The dialectics of modernity on a South African frontier.* Chicago: University of Chicago Press.

Combs-Schilling, M. E. (1989). *Sacred performances: Islam, sexuality, and sacrifice.* New York: Columbia University Press.

Conkey, Margaret W., and Sarah H. Williams (1991). Original narratives: The political economy of gender in archeology. In Micaela di Leonardo (Ed.), *Gender at the crossroads of knowledge: Feminist anthropology in the postmodern era* (pp. 102–139). Berkeley: University of California Press.

Covington, Dennis (1995). *Salvation on sand mountain: Snake handling and redemption in Southern Appalachia.* Reading, Mass.: Addison-Wesley.

Cragg, Kenneth (1980). *Islam from within: Anthology of a religion.* Belmont, Calif.: Wadsworth.

Danforth, Loring M. (1982). *The death rituals of rural Greece.* Princeton, N.J.: Princeton University Press.

Daniel, Sheryl B. (1983). The tool box approach of the Tamil to the issues of moral responsibility and human destiny. In Charles F. Keyes and E. Valentine Daniel (Eds.), *Karma: An anthropological inquiry* (pp. 27–62). Los Angeles: University of California Press.

Davis, Natalie Zemon (1965). *Society and culture in early modern France.* Stanford: Stanford University Press.

Davis, Winston (1980). *Dojo: Magic and exorcism in modern Japan.* Stanford: Stanford University Press.

Delaney, Carol (1998). *Abraham on trial: The social legacy of biblical myth.* Princeton, N.J.: Princeton University Press.

Demos, John Putnam (1982). *Entertaining Satan: Witchcraft and the culture of early New England.* Oxford: Oxford University Press.

Doi, L. Takeo (1986). *Amae:* A key concept for understanding Japanese personality structure. In Takie Sugiyama Lebra and William P. Lebra (Eds.), *Japanese culture and behavior* (rev. ed., pp. 121–129). Honolulu: University of Hawaii Press. (Original work published 1962)

Douglas, Mary (1966). The abominations of Leviticus. In Mary Douglas (Ed.), *Purity and danger* (pp. 41–57). London: Routledge & Kegan Paul.

Durkheim, Émile (1995). *The elementary forms of the religious life* (Karen E. Fields, Trans.). New York: The Free Press. (Original work published 1912)

Durkheim, Émile, and Marcel Mauss (1963). *Primitive classification* (Rodney Needhamn, Trans.). Chicago: University of Chicago Press. (Original work published 1903)

Earhart, H. Byron (1982). *Japanese religion: Unity and diversity* (3rd ed.). Belmont, Calif.: Wadsworth.

Eck, Diana L. (1982). *Banaras: City of light.* Princeton, N.J.: Princeton University Press.

Edelman, Martin (1994). *Courts, politics, and culture in Israel.* Charlottesville: University Press of Virginia.

Edwards, David B. (2002). *Before Taliban: Genealogies of the Afghan jihad.* Berkeley: University of California Press.

Eickelman, Dale F. (1976). *Moroccan Islam: Tradition and society in a pilgrimage center.* Austin: University of Texas Press.

Eickelman, Dale F. (1985). *Knowledge and power in Morocco.* Princeton, N.J.: Princeton University Press.

Eickelman, Dale F. (1992). Mass higher education and the religious imagination in contemporary Arab societies. *American Ethnologist 19*(4): 643–655.

Eickelman, Dale F. (1999). Communication and control in the Middle East: Publication and its discontents. In Dale F. Eickelman and Jon Anderson (Eds.), *New media in the Muslim world: The emerging public sphere* (pp. 29–40). Bloomington: Indiana University Press.

Eisenstadt, S. N. (Ed.) (1986). *The origins and diversity of axial age civilizations.* Albany: State University of New York Press.

El Guindi, Fadwa (1999). *Veil: Modesty, privacy and resistance.* Oxford: Berg.

Eliade, Mircea (1954). *The myth of the eternal return.* Princeton, N.J.: Princeton University Press. (Original work published 1949)

Engels, Friedrich (1956). *The peasant war in Germany.* Moscow: Progress. (Original work published 1850)

Evans-Pritchard, E. E. (1937). *Witchcraft, oracles and magic among the Azande.* Oxford: Clarendon Press.

Evans-Pritchard, E. E. (1956). *Nuer religion.* Oxford: Clarendon Press.

Feeley-Harnik, Gillian (1981). *The Lord's table: Eucharist and passover in early Christianity.* Philadelphia: University of Pennsylvania Press.

Ferguson, R. Brian (1990). "Explaining the War." In J. Hass (Ed.), *The anthropology of war* (pp. 26–55). Cambridge: Cambridge University Press.

Fernea, Elizabeth W. (1982). *A veiled revolution* (film).

Firmage, Edwin B. (1991). Religion and the law: The Mormon experience in the nineteenth century. *Cardozo Law Review, 12*(3–4), 765–803.

Fischer, Michael, and Mehdi Abedi (1990). *Debating Muslims: Cultural dialogues in tradition and postmodernity.* Madison: University of Wisconsin Press.

Flynn, Thomas J., M.D., and Charles B. Fulton, Th.D. (2002). Letter to the editor. *Journal of the American Medical Association, 288*(20), 2541.

Forbes, H. D. (1997). *Ethnic conflict: Commerce, culture, and the contact hypothesis.* New Haven: Yale University Press.

Foster, Lawrence (1981). *Religion and sexuality: Three American communal experiments of the nineteenth century.* New York: Oxford University Press.

Fox, James J. (1975). On binary categories and primary symbols: Some Rotinese perspectives. In Roy Willis (Ed.), *The interpretation of symbolism* (ASA Studies no. 3) (pp. 99–132). London: Malaby Press.

Fox, Richard (1989). *Gandhian utopia: Experiments with culture.* Boston: Beacon Press.

Frankel, Marvin E. (1994). *Faith and freedom: Religious liberty in America.* New York: Hill and Wang.

Fraser, Caroline (1996). Mrs. Eddy builds her empire. *New York Times Book Review,* July 11, 1996, 53–59.

Frazer, James G. (1981). *The golden bough: The roots of religion and folklore.* New York: Avenel Books. (Original work published 1890)

French, Howard W. (1997). The ritual: Disfiguring, hurtful, wildly festive. *New York Times,* January 31, 1997, A4.

Freud, Sigmund (1930). *Civilization and its discontents.* London: Hogarth Press.

Freud, Sigmund (1989). *Totem and taboo.* New York: Norton.

Fuller, C. J. (1992). *The camphor flame: Popular Hinduism and society in India.* Princeton, N.J.: Princeton University Press.

Gargon, Edward A. (1997). Three things matter: Location, location, and feng shui. *New York Times,* January 27, 1997, A4.

Geertz, Clifford (1960). *The religion of Java.* Chicago: University of Chicago Press.

Geertz, Clifford (1966). *Person, time, and conduct in Bali: An essay in cultural analysis.* New Haven, Conn.: Yale

University, Southeast Asia Studies, Cultural Report Series No. 14.

Geertz, Clifford (1968). *Islam observed: Religious developments in Morocco and Indonesia.* New Haven, Conn.: Yale University Press.

Gerbrands, Adrian A. (1967). Art and artist in Asmat society. In Michael Rockefeller, *The Asmat of New Guinea.* A. Gerbrands (Ed.) (pp. 11–39). New York: Museum of Primitive Art.

Geschiere, Peter (1997). *The modernity of witchcraft: Politics and the occult in postcolonial Africa (Sorcellerie et politique en Afrique).* Charlottesville, Va.: University Press of Virginia.

Gill, Sam (1981). *Sacred words: A study of Navajo religion and prayer.* Westport, Conn.: Greenwood Press.

Gill, Sam (1987). *Native American religious action: A performative approach to religion.* Columbia: University of South Carolina Press.

Gluckman, Max (1963). Rituals of rebellion in South East Africa. In Max Gluckman (Ed.), *Order and rebellion in tribal Africa* (pp. 110–137). London: Cohen & West.

Gmelch, George (1978). Baseball magic. *Human Nature, 1*(8).

Gold, Ann Grodzins (1988). *Fruitful journeys: The ways of Rajasthani pilgrims.* Los Angeles: University of California Press.

Golomb, Louis (1993). The relativity of magical malevolence in urban Thailand. In C. W. Watson and Roy Ellen (Eds.), *Understanding witchcraft and sorcery in Southeast Asia* (pp. 127–145). Honolulu: University of Hawaii Press.

Gombrich, Richard, and Gananath Obeyesekere (1988). *Buddhism transformed: Religious change in Sri Lanka.* Princeton, N.J.: Princeton University Press.

Goodman, Felicitas D. (1988). *How about demons? Possession and exorcism in the modern world.* Bloomington: Indiana University Press.

Graham, William A. (1987). *Beyond the written word: Oral aspects of scripture in the history of religion.* Cambridge: Cambridge University Press.

Griaule, Marcel (1965). *Conversations with Ogotemmeli: An introduction to Dogon religious ideas.* London: Oxford University Press. (Original work published 1948)

Guillermoprieto, Alma (1990). *Samba.* New York: Knopf.

Gujar, Ram Bhoju, and Gold Ann Grodzins (1992). From the research assistant's point of view. *Anthropology and Humanism Quarterly 17*(3), 72–84.

Haberman, Clyde (1988). Shinto is thrust back onto the nationalist stage. *New York Times,* June 7, 1988, A4.

Hall, John R., Philip D. Schuyler, and Sylvaine Trinh (2000). *Apocalypse observed: Religious movements and violence in North America, Europe, and Japan.* London and New York: Routledge.

Hammoudi, Abdellah (1993). *The victim and its masks.* Chicago: University of Chicago Press. (Original work published 1988)

Hardacre, Helen (1989). *Shinto and the state, 1868–1988.* Princeton, N.J.: Princeton University Press.

Harding, Susan Friend (2000). *The Book of Jerry Falwell: Fundamentalist language and politics.* Princeton, N.J.: Princeton University Press.

Harris, Lis (1985). *Holy days.* New York: Collier Books.

Harris, Marvin (1974). Pig lovers and pig haters. In Marvin Harris, *Cows, pigs, wars and witches* (pp. 35–57). New York: Vintage Books.

Harris, W. S., M. Gowda, and J. W. Kolb, et al. (1999). A randomized, controlled trial of the effects of remote, intercessory prayer on outcomes in patients admitted to the coronary care unit. *Archives of Internal Medicine, 159,* 2273–2278.

Hefner, Robert W. (1993). World building and the rationality of conversion. In Robert W. Hefner (Ed.), *Conversion to Christianity: Historical and anthropological perspectives on a great transformation* (pp. 3–44). Berkeley: University of California Press.

Helm, J., J. C. Hays, E. Flint, H. G. Koenig, and D. G. Blazer (2000). Effects of private religious activity on mortality of elderly disabled and nondisabled adults. *Journal of Gerontology* (Medical Sciences), 55A, M400–M405.

Herdt, Gilbert H. (1981). *Guardians of the flutes: Idioms of masculinity.* New York: McGraw-Hill.

Herdt, Gilbert H. (1982). Fetish and fantasy in Sambia initiation. In Gilbert H. Herdt (Ed.), *Rituals of manhood: Male initiation in Papua New Guinea* (pp. 44–98). Los Angeles: University of California Press.

Hertz, Robert (1960). *Death and the right hand* (Rodney and Claudia Needham, Trans.). New York: The Free Press. (Original work published 1907)

Hill, Christopher (1961). *The century of revolution, 1603–1714.* New York: W. W. Norton.

Hiltebeitel, Alf (1985). On the handling of the meat, and related matters, in two south Indian buffalo sacrifices. *L'Uomo: Societa Tradizione Sviluppo, 9*(1/2), 171–199.

Hinton, Alexander Laban, ed. (2002). *Annihilating difference: The anthropology of genocide.* Berkeley: University of Califoria Press.

Hirsch, Susan F. (1994). Kadhi's courts as complex sites of resistance: The state, Islam, and gender in postcolonial Kenya. In Mindie Lazarus-Black and Susan F. Hirsch (Eds.), *Contested states: Law, hegemony and resistance* (pp. 207–230). New York: Routledge.

Hume, David (1993). *Dialogues concerning natural religion* and *The natural history of religion.* Oxford: Oxford University Press. (Original works published 1779 and 1757)

Humphrey, Caroline, and James Laidlaw (1994). *The archetypal actions of ritual.* Oxford: Oxford University Press.

Hunter, James Davison (1990). Religious freedom and the challenge of modern pluralism. In James Davison Hunter and Os Guiness (Eds.), *Articles of faith, articles of peace* (pp. 54–73). Washington, D.C.: The Brookings Institution.

Imperato, Pascal James (1978). *Dogon cliff dwellers: The art of Mali's mountain people.* New York: Kahan Gallery.

Introvigne, Massimo, and Jean-Francois Mayer (2002). Occult masters and the Temple of Doom: The fiery end of the Solar Temple. In D. G. Bromley and J. G. Melton (Eds.), *Cults, religion, and violence* (pp. 170–188). Cambridge: Cambridge University Press.

Jaeger, Werner (1961). *Early Christianity and Greek paideia.* Cambridge, Mass.: Harvard University Press.

James, William (1972). *Varieties of religious experience.* London: Fontana. (Original work published 1901–1902)

Johnson, Douglas (1994). *Nuer prophets.* Oxford: Oxford University Press.

Jung, Carl Gustav (1964). *Man and his symbols.* Garden City, N.Y.: Doubleday.

Kalb, Claudia (2003). Faith and healing. *Newsweek,* November 10, 2003, 44–56.

Kammerer, Cornelia Ann (1990). Customs and Christian conversion among Akha highlanders of Burma and Thailand. *American Ethnologist 17*(2), 277–291.

Kapferer, Bruce (1997). *The feast of the sorcerer: Practices of consciousness and power.* Chicago: University of Chicago Press.

Katz, Richard (1982). *Boiling energy: Community healing among the Kalahari Kung.* Cambridge, Mass.: Harvard University Press.

Keesing, Roger M. (1982). *Kwaio religion: The living and the dead in a Solomon Island society.* New York: Columbia University Press.

Keesing, Roger M. (1992). *Custom and confrontation: The Kwaio struggle for cultural autonomy.* Chicago: University of Chicago Press.

Kenyon, Susan M. (1995). *Zar* as modernization in contemporary Sudan. *Anthropological Quarterly 68*(2): 107–120.

Kepel, Gilles (2002). *Jihad: The trail of political Islam.* Cambridge, Mass.: Harvard University Press.

Kinzer, Stephen (2003). Interest surges in voodoo, and its Queen. *New York Times,* November 20, 2003, A18.

Kipp, Rita Smith, and Susan Rodgers (1987). Introduction: Indonesian religions in society. In Rita Smith Kipp and Susan Rodgers (Eds.), *Indonesian religions in transition* (pp. 1–31). Tucson: University of Arizona Press.

Kluckhohn, Clyde (1967). *Navaho witchcraft.* Boston: Beacon Press. (Original work published 1944)

Knauft, Bruce M. (1985). *Good company and violence: Sorcery and social action in a lowland New Guinea society.* Berkeley: University of California Press.

Koenig, Harold G. (2002). An 83-year-old woman with chronic illness and strong religious beliefs. *Journal of the American Medical Association, 288*(4), 487–493.

Koenig, H. G., et al. (1992). Religious coping and depression in elderly hospitalized medically ill men. *American Journal of Psychiatry, 149,* 1693–1700.

Koenig, H. G., et al. (1997). Attendance at religious services, interleukin-6, and other biological indicators of immune function in older adults. *International Journal of Psychiatry in Medicine, 27,* 233–250.

Kraybill, Donald B. (1989). *The riddle of Amish culture.* Baltimore: Johns Hopkins University Press.

Kuruwaip, Abraham (1974). The Asmat bis pole: Its background and meaning. *Irian, 3*(2), 32–78.

Kymlicka, Will (1995). *Multicultural citizenship.* Oxford: Oxford University Press.

La Barre, Weston (1964). The snake-handling cult of the American Southeast. In Ward H. Goodenough (Ed.), *Explorations in cultural anthropology* (pp. 309–333). New York: McGraw-Hill.

Laderman, Carol (1983). *Wives and midwives: Childbirth and nutrition in rural Malaysia.* Los Angeles: University of California Press.

Lafaye, Jacques (1976). *Quetzalcoatl and Guadalupe: The formation of Mexican national consciousness 1531–1813* (Benjamin Keen, Trans.). Chicago: University of Chicago Press.

La Fontaine, J. S. (1985). *Initiation.* Harmondsworth, UK: Penguin.

Leibovich, Lori (2000). The online religion with shopping, too. *New York Times,* April 6, 2000, D1, D10.

Leishman, Thomas Linton (1958). *Why I am a Christian Scientist.* New York: Thomas Nelson & Sons.

Leone, Mark (1979). *Roots of modern Mormonism.* Cambridge, Mass.: Harvard University Press.

Lévi-Strauss, Claude (1963a). *Totemism* (Rodney Needham, Trans.). Boston: Beacon Press. (Original work published 1962)

Lévi-Strauss, Claude (1963b). The effectiveness of symbols. In C. Lévi-Strauss, *Structural anthropology* (pp. 180–201). (Claire Jacobson and Brooke Grundfest Schoepf, Trans.). Garden City, N.Y.: Anchor Books. (Original work published 1949)

Lévi-Strauss, Claude (1976). The Story of Asdiwal. In C. Lévi-Strauss, *Structural anthropology* (vol. 2, pp. 146–197). (Monique Layton, Trans.). Chicago: University of Chicago Press. (Original work published 1958)

Lifton, Robert Jay (1986). *The Nazi doctors: Medical killing and the psychology of genocide.* New York: Basic Books.

Lukes, Steven (1973). *Émile Durkheim: His life and work.* Harmondsworth, UK: Penguin.

Lutkehaus, Nancy C. (1995). Gender metaphors: Female rituals as cultural models in Manam. In Nancy C. Lutkehaus and Paul B. Roscoe (Eds.), *Gender rituals: Female initiation in Melanesia* (pp. 183–204). New York: Routledge.

MacCormack, Carol, and Marilyn Strathern (1980). *Nature, culture, and gender.* Cambridge: Cambridge University Press.

Macleod, Arlene Elowe (1991). *Accommodating protest: Working women, the new veiling, and change in Cairo.* New York: Columbia University Press.

Makhlouf, Carla (1979). *Changing veils: Women and modernization in North Yemen.* Austin: University of Texas Press.

Malcolm X (1973). *The autobiography of Malcolm X.* Alex Haley (Ed.), New York: Ballantine Books. (Original work published 1964)

Malinowski, Bronislaw (1954). Magic, science, and religion. In B. Malinowski, *Magic, science, and religion and other essays* (pp. 17–92). Garden City, N.Y.: Anchor Books. (Original work published 1926)

Mankekar, Purnima (1999). *Screening culture, viewing politics: An ethnography of television, womanhood, and nation in post-colonial India.* Durham, N.C.: Duke University Press.

Marx, Karl, and Friedrich Engels (1965). *The German ideology.* London: Lawrence & Wishart. (Original work published 1846)

Mayer, Ann Elizabeth (1990). The *Shari'ah:* A methodology or a body of substantive rules? In Nicholas Heer (Ed.), *Islamic law and jurisprudence.* Seattle: University of Washington Press.

McNearney, Kelly (2002). Athletes believe rituals leading to winning games. *www.kusports.com/new/rowingstorypr/105011.*

McPherson, Robert S. (1992). *Sacred land, sacred view: Navajo perceptions of the four corners region.* Salt Lake City: Brigham Young University.

Meigs, Anna (1990). Multiple gender ideologies and statuses. In Peggy Reeves Sanday and Ruth Goodenough (Eds.), *Beyond the second sex.* Philadephia: University of Pennsylvania Press.

Meislin, Bernard J. (1981). Pursuit of the wife's right to a *"Get"* in United States and Canadian courts. *The Jewish Law Annual* (vol. 4). Kinderhook, N.Y.: E. J. Brill.

Metcalf, Peter (1982). *A Borneo journey into death.* Philadelphia: University of Pennsylvania Press.

Miller, Daniel, and Don Slater (2000). *The Internet: An ethnographic approach.* Oxford: Berg.

Miller, Perry (1956). *Errand into the wilderness.* Cambridge, Mass.: Harvard University Press.

Modood, Tariq (1994). Establishment, multiculturalism, and British citizenship. *Political Quarterly,* 65(1), 53–73.

Momen, Moojan (1985). *An introduction to Shi'i Islam.* New Haven, Conn.: Yale University Press.

Morris, Brian (1987). *Anthropological studies of religion.* Cambridge: Cambridge University Press.

Morrison, Michael (2003). Sports and the Number 13. *www.infoplease.com/spot/superstitions2.html.*

Moruzzi, Norma Claire (1994). A problem with headscarves: Contemporary complexities of political and social identity. *Political Theory,* 22(4), 653–672.

Murphy, Joseph S. (1994). *Working the spirit: Ceremonies of the African diaspora.* Boston: Beacon Press.

Nanda, Meera (2003). *Prophets facing backward: Postmodern critiques of science and Hindu nationalism in*

India. New Brunswick, N.J.: Rutgers University Press.

Nations, Marilyn, and Linda-Anne Rebhun (1988). Angels with wet wings can't fly: Maternal sentiments in Brazil and the image of neglect. *Culture, Medicine, and Psychiatry, 12,* 141–200.

Nemeroff, Carol, and Paul Rozin (1992). Sympathetic magical beliefs and kosher dietary practice: The interaction of rules and feelings. *Ethos, 20,* 96–115.

Newberg, Andrew B., Eugene G. D'Aquili, and Vince Rause (2001). *Why God won't go away: Brain science and the biology of belief.* New York: Ballantine Books.

Nolan, Mary Lee, and Sidney Nolan (1989). *Christian pilgrimage in modern Western Europe.* Chapel Hill: The University of North Carolina Press.

Norton, Mary Beth (2003). *In the Devil's share: The Salem Witchcraft Crisis of 1692.* New York: Alfred A. Knopf.

Nuckolls, Charles W. (1998). *Culture: A problem that cannot be solved.* Madison: University of Wisconsin Press.

Obeyesekere, Gananath (1981). *Medusa's hair: An essay on personal symbols and religious experience.* Chicago: University of Chicago Press.

Oe, Kenzaburo (1995). The day the Emperor spoke in human voice. *New York Times Magazine,* May 7, 1995, 103–105.

Ortner, Sherry B. (1996). *Making gender: The politics and erotics of culture.* Boston: Beacon Press.

Ortner, Sherry B., and Harriet Whitehead (1981). *Sexual meanings: The cultural construction of gender and sexuality.* Cambridge: Cambridge University Press.

Palgi, Phyllis, and Henry Abramovitch (1984). Death: A cross-cultural perspective. *Annual Review of Anthropology, 13,* 385–417.

Pargament, K. I., H. G. Koenig, N. Tarakeshwar, and J. Hahn (2001). Religious struggle as a predictor of mortality among medically ill elderly patients: A two-year longitudinal study. *Archives of Internal Medicine, 161,* 1881–1885.

Parsons, Elsie C. (1939). *Pueblo Indian religion* (2 vols.). Chicago: University of Chicago Press.

Passin, Herbert, and John W. Bennett (1943). Changing agricultural magic in southern Illinois: A systematic analysis of folk-urban transition. *Social Forces, 22*(1), 98–106.

Peacock, James L., and Ruel W., Jr. Tyson (1989). *Pilgrims of paradox: Calvinism and experience among the primitive Baptists of the Blue Ridge.* Washington, D.C.: Smithsonian Institution Press.

Peletz, Michael G. (1993). Knowledge, power and personal misfortune in a Malay context. In C. W. Watson and Roy Ellen (Eds.), *Understanding witchcraft and sorcery in Southeast Asia* (pp. 149–177). Honolulu: University of Hawaii Press.

Pernet, Henry (1992). *Ritual masks: Deceptions and revelations* (Laura Grillo, Trans.). Columbia: University of South Carolina Press. (Original work published 1988)

Peters, F. E. (1994). *Muhammad and the origins of Islam.* Albany: State University of New York Press.

Peters, Rudolph (1996). *The jihad in classical and modern times.* Princeton, N.J.: Markus Wiener.

Plath, David W. (1964). Where the family of God is the family: The role of the dead in Japanese households. *American Anthropologist, 66,* 300–317.

Pocock, David F. (1973). *Mind, body, and wealth: A study of belief and practice in an Indian village.* Oxford: Blackwell.

Pollack, Andrew (1996). This way to peace of mind: 750 miles and 88 stops. *New York Times,* March 20, 1996, A4.

Pollock, Sheldon (1993). Ramayana and political imagination in India. *Journal of Asian Studies* 52(2): 261–297.

Poole, John Fitz Porter (1982). The ritual forging of identity: Aspects of person and self in Bimin-Kuskusmin male initiation. In Gilbert H. Herdt (Ed.), *Rituals of manhood: Male initiation in Papua New Guinea* (pp. 99–154). Los Angeles: University of California Press.

Povinelli, Elizabeth A. (1993). *Labor's lot: The power, history, and culture of aboriginal action.* Chicago: University of Chicago Press.

Prell, Riv-Ellen (1989). *Prayer and community: The havurah in American Judaism.* Detroit: Wayne State University Press.

Qutb, Sayyid, and International Islamic Federation of Student Organizations (1978). *Milestones.* Beirut, Lebanon: Holy Koran Publishing House.

Radcliffe-Brown, A. R. (1965). Taboo. In Radcliffe-Brown (Ed.), *Structure and function in primitive society* (pp. 133–152). New York: The Free Press. (Original work published 1939)

Reader, Ian (2000). *Religious violence in contemporary Japan: The case of Aum Shinrikyo.* Honolulu: University of Hawaii Press.

Reader, Ian (1991). *Religion in contemporary Japan.* Honolulu: University of Hawaii Press.

Redfield, Robert (1956). *Peasant society and culture.* Chicago: University of Chicago Press.

Regan, Richard J. (1996). *Just war: Principles and cases.* Washington, D.C.: Catholic University Press of America.

Remnick, David (1992). Waiting for the apocalypse in Crown Heights. *The New Yorker,* December 21, pp. 52–57.

Richeport, Madeleine (1985). *Macumba, trance and spirit healing.* Film. New York: Filmmaker's Library.

Riding, Alan (1987). In Brazil, Evangelicals are on the rise. *New York Times,* October 25, 1987, A16.

Robinson, David (1985). *The Holy War of Umar Tal: The Western Sudan in the mid-nineteenth century.* Oxford: Clarendon.

Rogerson, J. W. (1980). Sacrifice in the Old Testament: Problems of method and approach. In M.F.C. Bourdillon and Meyer Fortes (Eds.), *Sacrifice* (pp. 45–59). London: Academic Press.

Rosaldo, Michelle Z. (1974). Woman, culture and society: A theoretical overview. In Michelle Z. Rosaldo and Louise Lamphere (Eds.), *Women, culture and society.* Stanford: Stanford University Press.

Rosaldo, Renato I. (1984). Grief and a headhunter's rage: On the cultural force of emotions. In Edward Bruner (Ed.), *Play, text, and story* (pp. 178–195). Washington, D.C.: American Ethnological Society.

Rosen, Lawrence (1989). *The anthropology of justice.* Cambridge: Cambridge University Press.

de Rosny, Eric (1997). *L'Afrique des guérisons.* Paris: Karthala.

de Rosny, Eric (1992). *L'Afrique des guérisons.* Paris: Karthala.

Rothstein, Edward (1996). Temple Emanu-El displays High Holidays Services on the Internet. *New York Times,* September 26, 1996, D4.

Rothkrug, Lionel (1980). Religious practice and collective perceptions: Hidden homologies in the Renaissance and Reformation. *Historical Reflections, 7*(1).

Roy, Oliver (1994). *The failure of political Islam.* Cambridge, Mass.: Harvard University Press.

Ruthven, Malisa (1984). *Islam in the world.* New York: Oxford University Press.

Sahlins, Marshall (1985). *Islands of history.* Chicago: University of Chicago Press.

Salomonsen, Jane (2002). *Enchanted feminism: The reclaiming witches of San Francisco.* London: Routledge.

Sanders, Todd (2000). Rains gone bad, women gone mad: Rethinking gender rituals of rebellion and patriarchy. *Journal of the Royal Anthropological Institute* (N.S.) 6: 469–486.

Sanger, David E. (1990). For a job well done, Japanese enshrine the chip. *New York Times,* December 11, 1990, A4.

Saunders, E. Dale (1964). *Buddhism in Japan.* Philadelphia: University of Pennsylvania Press.

Sayle, Murray (1996). Nerve gas and the four noble truths. *The New Yorker,* April 1, 1996.

Schauss, Hayyim (1938). *The Jewish festivals: History and observance.* New York: Schocken Books.

Scheper-Hughes, Nancy (1992). *Death without weeping: The violence of everyday life in Brazil.* Los Angeles: University of California Press.

Schimmel, Annemarie (1973). *Mystical dimensions of Islam.* Chapel Hill: University of North Carolina Press.

Shariati, Dr. Ali (1977). *Hajj.* (Somayyah and Yaser, Trans.). Bedford, Ohio: Free Islamic Literatures.

Sharma, Ursula (1980). *Women, work, and property in Northwest India.* London: Tavistock.

Sharp, Lesley A. (1993). *The Possessed and the dispossessed: Spirits, identity, and power in a Malagascar migrant town.* Berkeley: University of California Press.

Shipps, Jan (1985). *Mormonism: The story of a new religious tradition.* Urbana: University of Illinois Press.

Singer, Milton (1964). The social organization of Indian civilization. *Diogène, 45,* 84–119.

Smith, Robert J. (1974). *Ancestor worship in contemporary Japan.* Stanford: Stanford University Press.

Smith, Robert J. (1983). *Japanese society: Tradition, self, and the social order.* Cambridge: Cambridge University Press.

Smith, Wilfred Cantwell (1978). *The meaning and end of religion.* San Francisco: Harper & Row. (Original work published 1962)

Spencer, Jonathan (2000). *A Sinhala village in a time of trouble: Politics and change in rural Sri Lanka.* Oxford: Oxford University Press.

Starhawk (1979). *The spiral dance.* San Francisco: Harper & Row.

Starrett, Gregory (1998). *Putting Islam to work: Education, politics, and religious transformation in Egypt.* Berkeley: University of California Press.

Statler, Oliver (1984). *Japanese pilgrimage.* London: Pan Books.

Steinfels, Peter (1992). The vision that wasn't. Or was it? *New York Times,* September 2, 1992, A14.

Stern, Jessica (2003). *Terror in the name of God: Why religious militants kill.* New York: Ecco.

Stirrat, R. L. (1992). *Power and religiosity in post-colonial setting: Sinhala Catholics in contemporary Sri Lanka.* Cambridge: Cambridge University Press.

Sudarman, Dea (1984). *Asmat.* Jakarta: Penerbit Sinar Harapan.

Svensson, Frances (1979). Liberal democracy and group rights: The legacy of individualism and its impact on American Indian tribes. *Political Studies, 27,* 421–439.

Swain, Tony (1995). Australia. In Tony Swain and Garry Trompf, *The Religions of Oceania* (pp. 19–118). New York: Routledge.

Swallow, D. A. (1982). Ashes and powers: Myth, rite and miracle in an Indian god-man's cult. *Modern Asian Studies, 16*(1), 123–158.

Tabor, James D., and Eugene V. Gallagher (1995). *Why Waco?: Cults and the battle for religious freedom in America.* Los Angeles: University of California Press.

Tambiah, S. J. (1970). *Buddhism and spirit cults in northeast Thailand.* Cambridge: Cambridge University Press.

Tambiah, S. J. (1976). *World conqueror and world renouncer.* Cambridge, Mass.: Harvard University Press.

Tambiah, S. J. (1986). *Sri Lanka: Ethnic fratricide and the dismantling of democracy.* Chicago: University of Chicago Press.

Tambiah, S. J. (1987). The Buddhist arahant: Classical paradigm and modern Thai transformations. In John Stratton Hawley (Ed.), *Saints and Virtues* (pp. 111–126). Los Angeles: University of California Press.

Taylor, Charles (1990). Religion in a free society. In James Davison Hunter and Os Guiness (Eds.), *Articles of faith, articles of peace* (pp. 93–113). Washington, D.C.: The Brookings Institution.

Trillin, Calvin (1994). Drawing the line. *The New Yorker,* December 12, pp. 50–62.

Trompf, Garry (1995). Pacific Islands. In Tony Swain and Garry Trompf, *The religions of Oceania* (pp. 121–222). New York: Routledge.

Turner, Victor (1967). *The forest of symbols: Aspects of Ndembu ritual.* Ithaca: Cornell University Press.

Turner, Victor (1969). *The ritual process: Structure and anti-structure.* Ithaca: Cornell University Press.

Turner, Victor (1974). Pilgrimages as social processes. In *Dramas, fields, and metaphors* (pp. 166–230). Ithaca: Cornell University Press.

Tyler, Patrick E. (1997). Catholics in China: Back to the underground. *New York Times,* January 26, 1997, A1, A8.

Tylor, Edward Burnett (1970). *Primitive culture* (2 vols.). Gloucester, Mass.: Peter Smith. (Original work published 1871)

Urban, Greg (1991). *A discourse-centered approach to culture.* Austin: University of Texas Press.

van Gennep, Arnold (1960). *The rites of passage.* (Monika B. Vizedom and Gabrielle L. Caffee, Trans.). Chicago: University of Chicago Press. (Original work published 1908)

van der Veer, Peter (1994). *Religious nationalisms: Hindus and Muslims in India.* Los Angeles: University of California Press.

Volkman, Toby Alice (1985). *Feasts of honor: Ritual and change in the Toraja highlands.* Urbana: University of Illinois.

Wadley, Susan S., and Bruce W. Derr (1989). Eating sins in Karimpur. *Contributions to Indian Sociology, 23,* 131–148.

Walker, Sheila S. (1990). Everyday and esoteric reality in the Afro-Brazilian Candomblé. *History of Religions, 30,* 103–128.

Wallace, Anthony F. C. (1956). Revitalization movements. *American Anthropologist, 58,* 264–281.

Warner, Marina (1996). Blood and tears. *The New Yorker,* April 8, pp. 63–69.

Watson, James L. (1982). Of flesh and bones: The management of death pollution in Cantonese society. In Maurice Bloch and Jonathan Parry (Eds.), *Death and the regeneration of life* (pp. 155–186). Cambridge: Cambridge University Press.

Waugh, Earle H. (1977). Muharram rites: Community death and rebirth. In Frank E. Reynolds and Earle H. Waugh (Eds.), *Religious encounters with death* (pp. 200–213). University Park: Penn State University Press.

Webb, Malcolm C. (1965). The abolition of the taboo system in Hawaii. *Journal of the Polynesian Society, 74,* 21–39.

Weber, Max (1958). *The protestant ethic and the spirit of capitalism.* (Talcott Parsons, Trans.). New York: Charles Scribner's Sons. (Original work published 1904–1905)

Weber, Max (1978). *Economy and society* (2 vols.). Los Angeles: University of California Press. (Original work published 1956)

Weiner, Annette B. (1976). *Women of value, men of renown: New perspectives in Trobriand exchange.* Austin: University of Texas Press.

Weisman, Steven R. (1990). Akihito performs his solitary rite. *New York Times,* November 23, 1990, A7.

Weller, Robert P. (1987). *Unities and diversities in Chinese religion.* Seattle: University of Washington Press.

Westermarck, Edward Alexander (1968). *Ritual and belief in Morocco* (2 vols.). New Hyde Park, N.Y.: University Books. (Original work published 1926)

Whitehead, Harriet (1987). Fertility and exchange in New Guinea. In Jane Fishburne Collier and Sylvia Junko Yanagisako (Eds.), *Gender and kinship: Essays toward a unified analysis* (pp. 244–267). Stanford: Stanford University Press.

Wikan, Unni (1990). *Managing turbulent hearts: A Balinese formulation for living.* Chicago: University of Chicago Press.

Wilson, Bryan R. (1961). *Sects and society: A sociological study of three religious groups in Britain.* London: William Heinemann.

Witherspoon, Gary (1977). *Language and art in the Navajo universe.* Ann Arbor: University of Michigan Press.

Wolf, Arthur (1974). Gods, ghosts, and ancestors. In Arthur Wolf (Ed.), *Religion and ritual in Chinese society* (pp. 131–182). Stanford: Stanford University Press.

Wolf, Eric (1958). The virgin of Guadalupe: A Mexican national symbol. *Journal of American Folklore, 71,* 34–39.

Wolff, Alexander (2003). SI Flashback: That old black magic. *Sports Illustrated, 27,* August 2003.

Woodburn, James (1982). Social dimensions of death in four African hunting and gathering societies. In Maurice Bloch and Jonathan Parry (Eds.), *Death and the regeneration of life* (pp. 187–210). Cambridge: Cambridge University Press.

Worsley, Peter (1968). *The trumpet shall sound* (rev. ed.). New York: Schocken Books.

WuDunn, Sheryl (1996). In Japan, a ritual of mourning for abortions. *New York Times,* January 25, 1996, A1, A8.

Wuthnow, Robert (1988). *The restructuring of American religion: Society and faith since World War II.* Princeton, N.J.: Princeton University Press.

Wyman, Leland C. (1970). *Blessingway, with three versions of the myth recorded and translated from the Navajo by Father Berard Haile, O.F.M.* Tucson: University of Arizona Press.

Zegwaard, Rev. Gerrad A. (1959). Headhunting practices of the Asmat of Netherlands New Guinea. *American Anthropologist, 61,* 1020–1041.

Zimdars-Schwartz, Sandra L. (1991). *Encountering Mary: From La Salette to Medjugorje.* Princeton, N.J.: Princeton University Press.

Index